METAL
LICA
METALLA
MINERALIA
TURBINATA
CONCHILIA
MARIANA
LAPIDES
LAPIDES
LAPIDES
SUCCI
FRUCTUS
SEMINA
SULPHURA
SALIA
IMALIUM PARTES
CONCHILIATA
VARIA
LIGNA
CORTICES
HERBÆ
RADICES
EI
IANI
ORIA
TAVORUM
LSEVIRIANA
1655.

THE SORCERER'S BURDEN

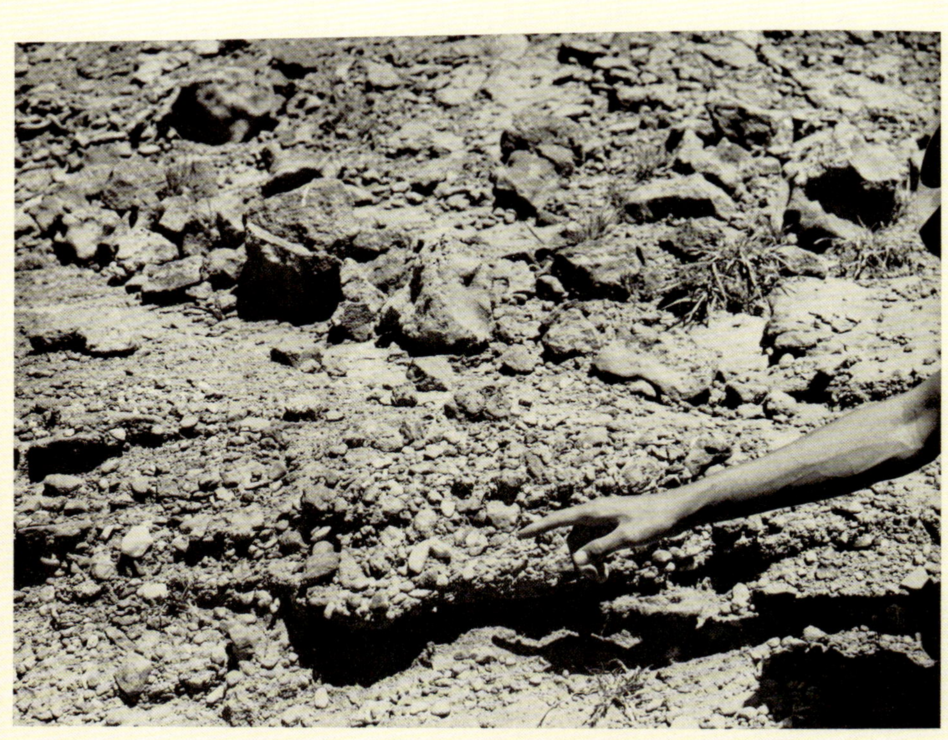

10. Close-up of gravel beds of Va

11. Bed

The Sorcerer's Burden

CONTEMPORARY ART
& THE ANTHROPOLOGICAL TURN

RADIUS BOOKS
THE CONTEMPORARY AUSTIN

THIS CATALOGUE offers a collection of ideas exploring the intersection of art and anthropology from a contemporary art perspective.

Interspersed throughout the book are photographs of influential historical anthropological book covers and pages that encourage loose associations with pioneers in the field, as well as provide conceptual and formal pauses in conversation with the rich content of this book's artists and authors.

A Midland Book MB-208

Mules & Men

Zora Neale Hurston

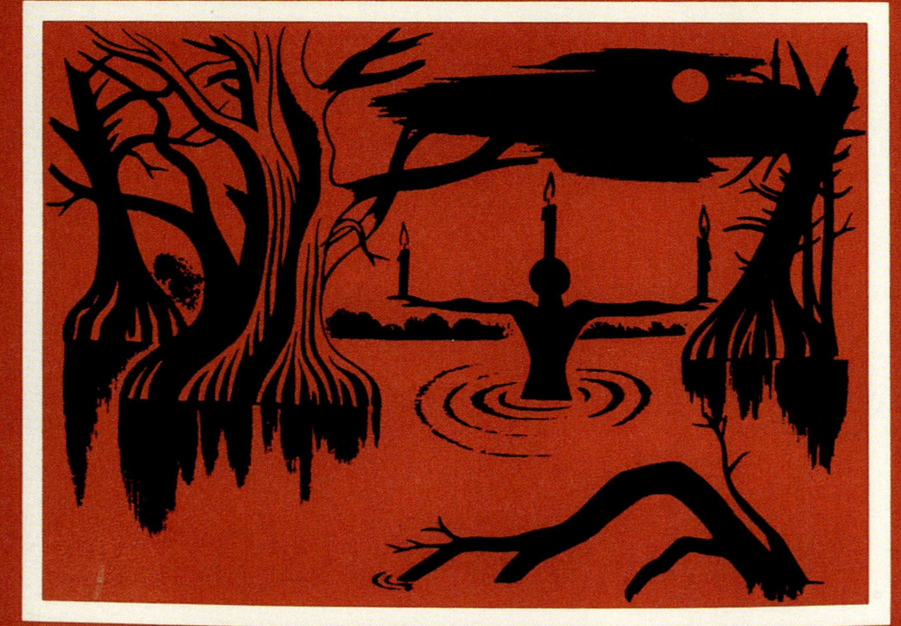

THE STONE BOWLS (d)
OBLONG & OVAL FORMS
INCHES
CENTIMETRES
1
2
3
4
5
6
7
8
9
10
11
12
13
14

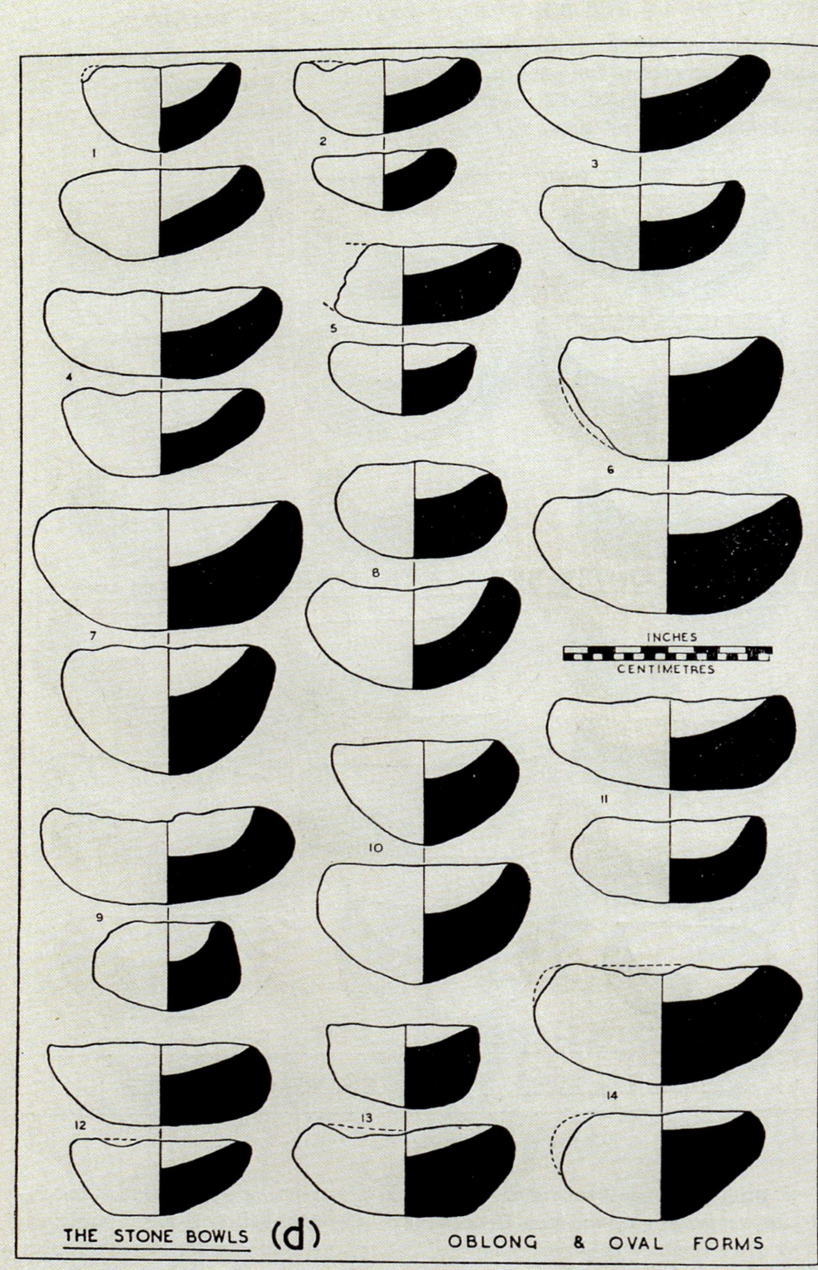

Fig. 7

Many of the bowls not otherwise burnt are extensively charred on the interior and must have been subjected to fire for a considerable time, since the carbonization when it is exposed in sections of broken bowls, frequently extends throughout the thickness of the bases.

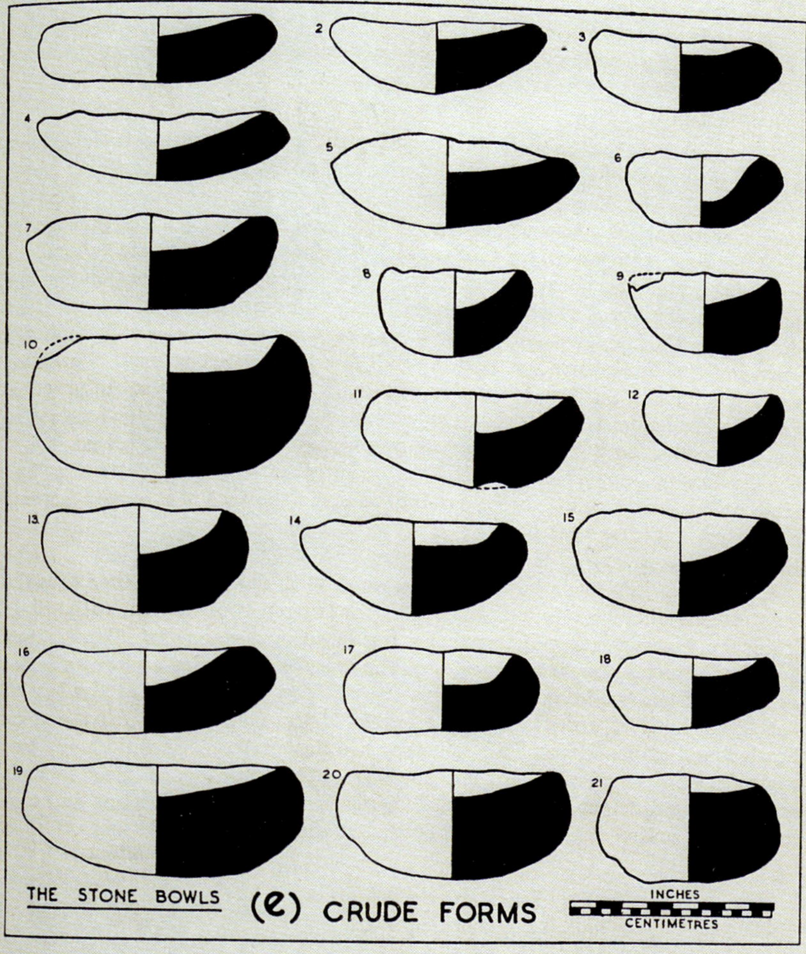

FIG. 8

The charring of the interior of many stone bowls is a feature which occurs not only at Njoro but also at many other sites in East Africa and indicates that although the bowls were sometimes unquestionably used as mortars, they were often used for some purpose connected with fire. No evidence bearing on this method of using the bowls has yet come to light, nor has it been possible to discover an explanation by means of modern parallels. However, it seems reasonable to assume that the bowls were probably used for one of the following

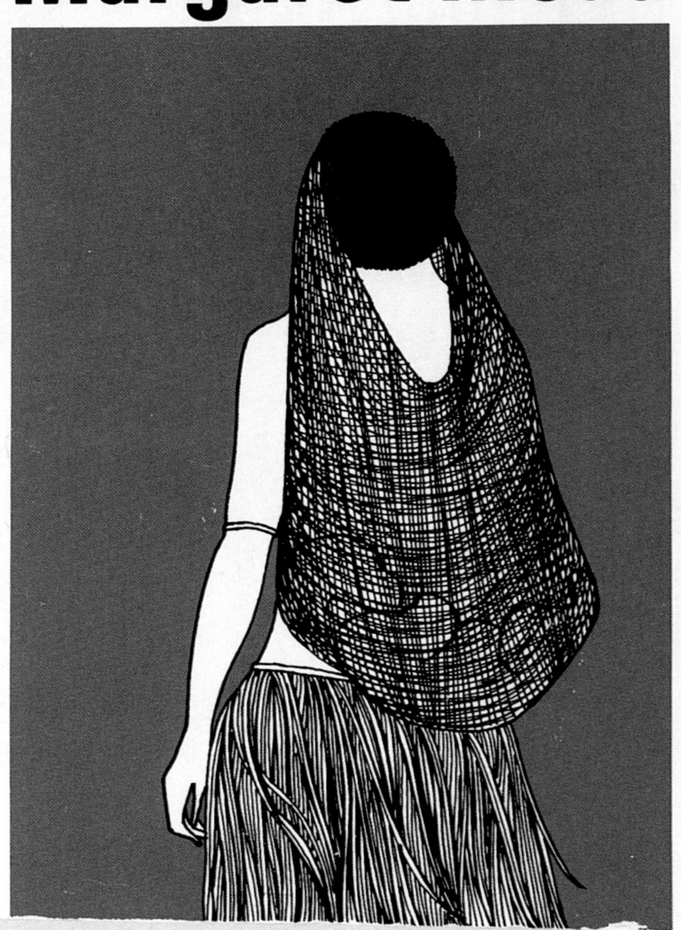
Sex and
Temperament
IN THREE PRIMITIVE SOCIETIES
Margaret Mead

This catalogue accompanies the exhibition:

The Sorcerer's Burden

CONTEMPORARY ART & THE ANTHROPOLOGICAL TURN

on view at The Contemporary Austin

Jones Center on Congress Avenue
Betty and Edward Marcus Sculpture Park at Laguna Gloria
September 14, 2019 – January 19, 2020

Organized by

Heather Pesanti
Chief Curator & Director of Curatorial Affairs
The Contemporary Austin

PLATE II

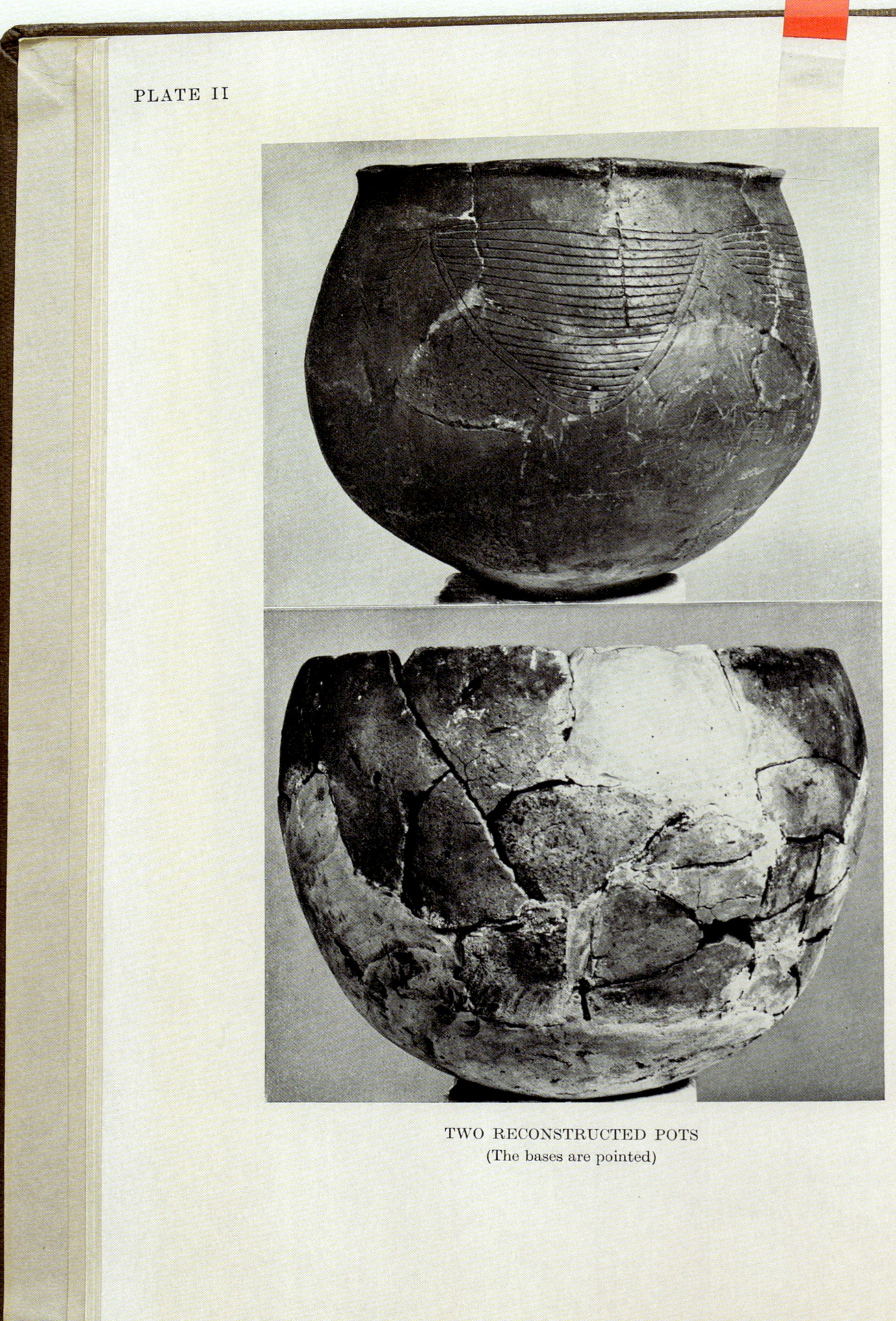

TWO RECONSTRUCTED POTS
(The bases are pointed)

EXHIBITION FUNDERS *as of May 2019*

MAJOR SUPPORT

The Andy Warhol Foundation for the Visual Arts
National Endowment for the Arts

ADDITIONAL SUPPORT

Horizon Bank
Cultural Arts Division of the City of Austin Economic Development Department
Linda L. Brown, MaddocksBrown Foundation
Texas Monthly
Cultural Services of the French Embassy

All exhibitions are generously funded by The Contemporary Austin's Exhibition Fund Supporters:

Janet and Wilson G. Allen, Suzanne Deal Booth, Michael Chesser, Kimberly and Timothy Dowling, Deborah Dupré and Richard Rothberg, Deborah Green and Clayton Aynesworth, Lindsey and Mark Hanna, Karen and Rick Hawkins, Jeanne and Michael Klein, Diane Land and Steve Adler, Kathleen Irvin Loughlin and Chris Loughlin, Susan and Richard Marcus, Chris Mattsson, Fredericka and David Middleton, Elysia and Jake Ragusa, Lora Reynolds and Quincy Lee, Jane Schweppe and Robert Johnson, Still Water Foundation, Gail and Rodney Susholtz, Teresa and Darrell Windham, Melba and Ted Whatley

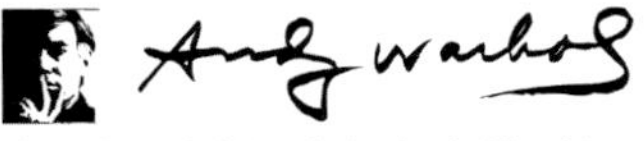

National Endowment for the Arts
arts.gov

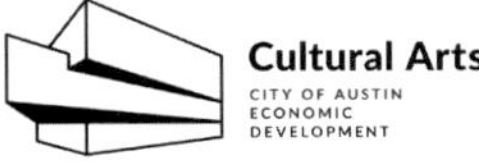

PRIMITIVE ART

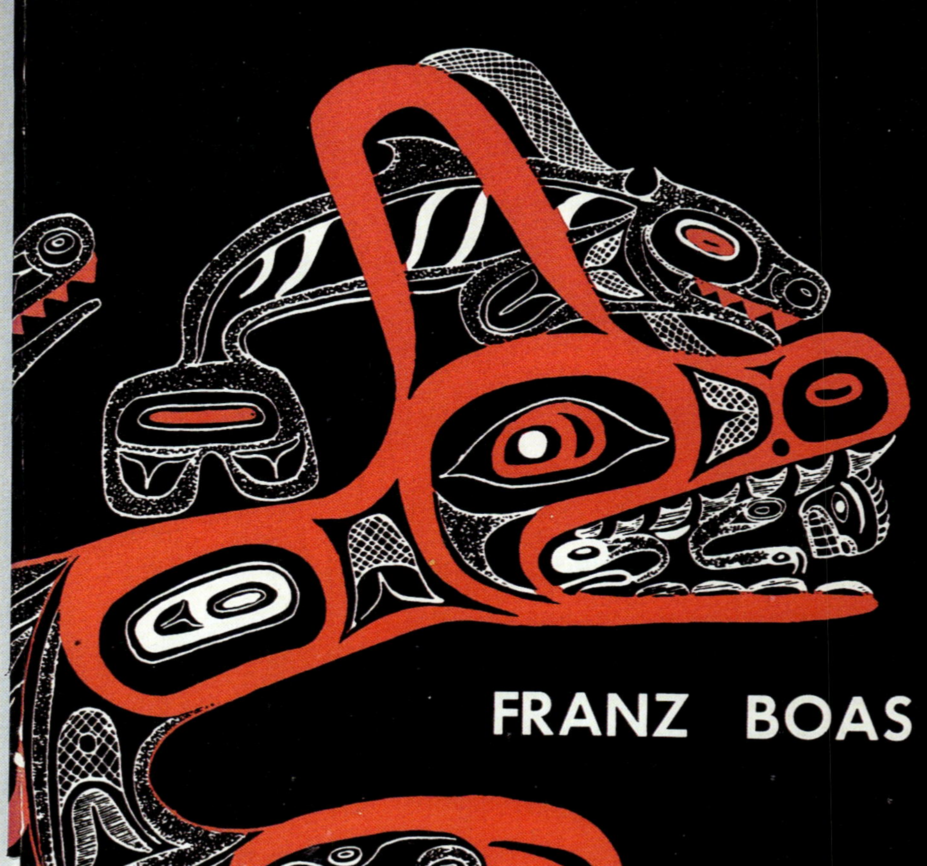

FRANZ BOAS

PETITE BIBLIOTHÈQUE PAYOT

MARCEL MAUSS

MANUEL D'ETHNOGRAPHIE

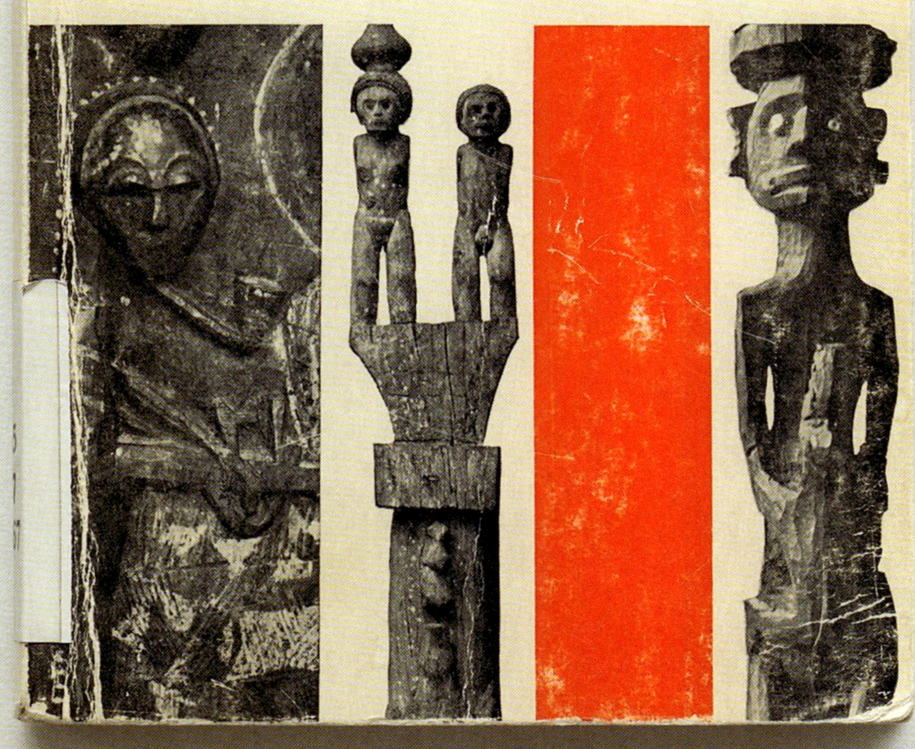

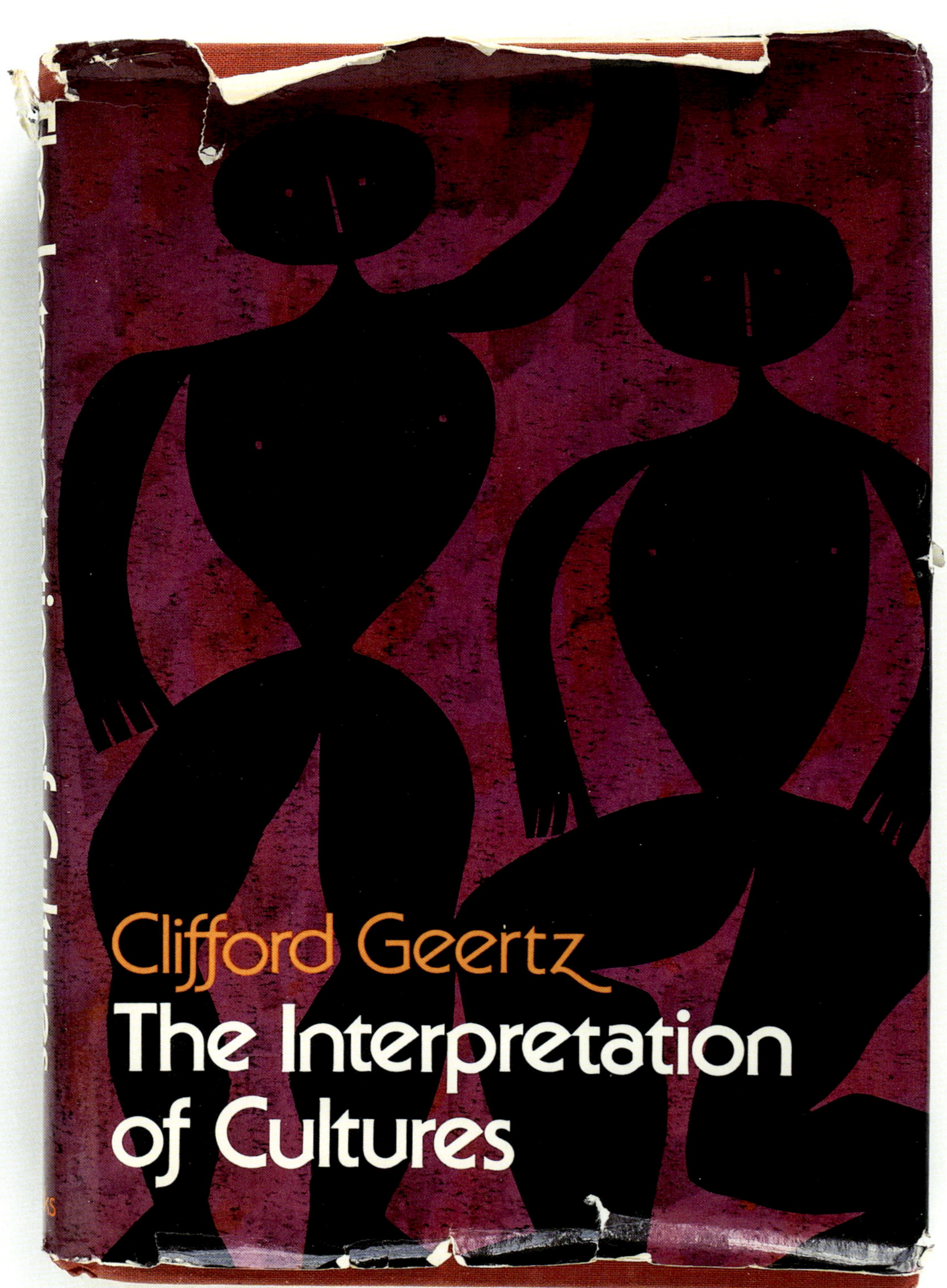
Clifford Geertz
The Interpretation
of Cultures

CONTENTS

TYPE A
TYPE E
TYPE B
TYPE C
TYPE F
TYPE G
TYPE D
CENTIMETRES
INCHES
NJORO RIVER CAVE
THE PESTLE-RUBBERS

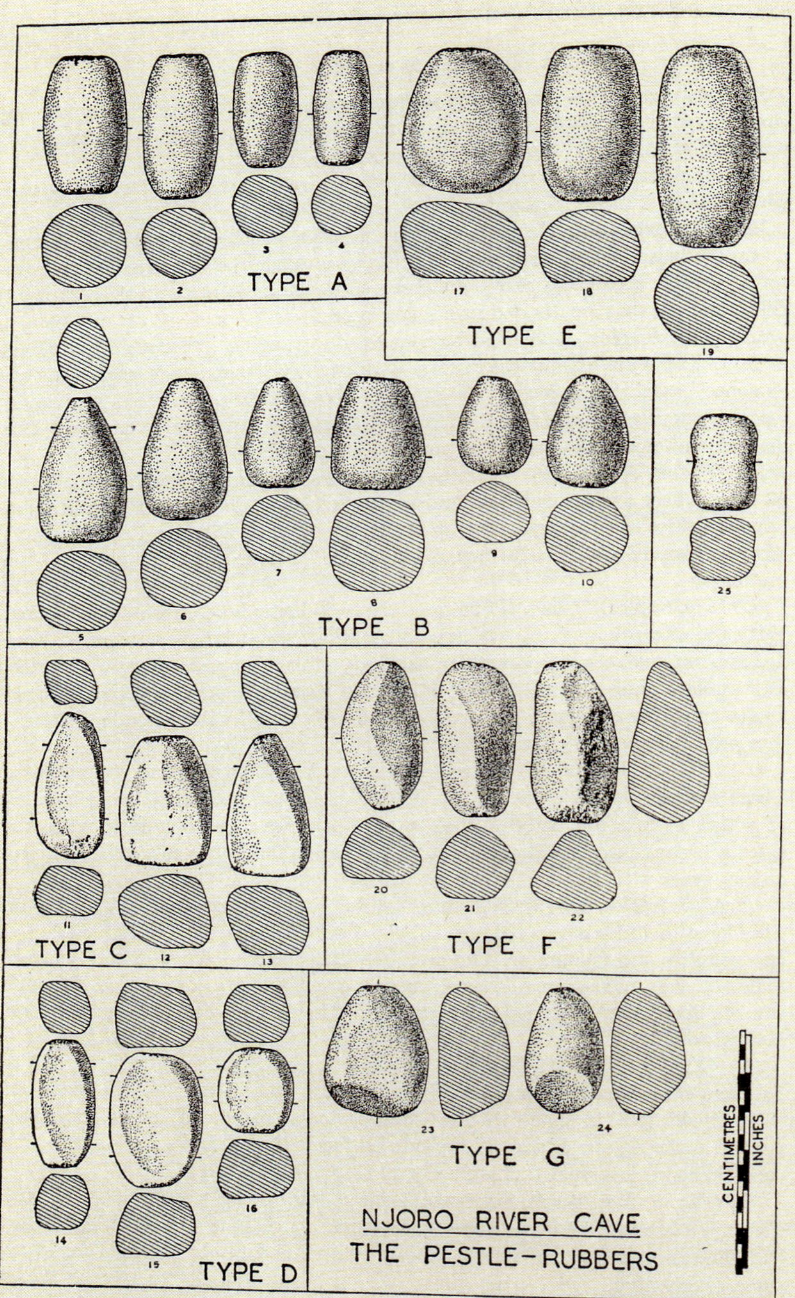

Fig. 9

Foreword & Acknowledgements

Louis Grachos

Ernest and Sarah Butler Executive Director & CEO, The Contemporary Austin

The Sorcerer's Burden: Contemporary Art and the Anthropological Turn, conceived by Heather Pesanti, Chief Curator & Director of Curatorial Affairs at The Contemporary Austin, offers a deep and exploratory study of the intersection between art and anthropology. Tracing these developments from modernism through the present day, Pesanti's thoughtful examination weaves historical and prescient moments, in which artists and scholars have grappled with this fascinating and at times contentious subject matter, together with the impact and consequences of their gestures in artistic, social, cultural, and political spheres.

Rooted in Pesanti's academic background in anthropology—a personal thread that runs throughout this project—both the catalogue and exhibition reveal the urgency and complexity of this theme universally. Through new commissions, existing work, and site-specific projects both inside and outside of the museum's two venues, Pesanti takes us on a journey through a diverse group of eleven artists working in a variety of media and practices: Ed Atkins, Nuotama Bodomo, Theo Eshetu, Cameron Jamie, Kapwani Kiwanga, Marie Lorenz, Nathan Mabry, Ruben Ochoa, Dario Robleto, Shimabuku, and Julia Wachtel. Along the way, Pesanti explores how cultural anthropology and ethnography remain a source of inspiration for contemporary artists—and how artists are using these ideas and methods for timely and critical investigations. It has been gratifying to see these artists' wide-ranging work brought together at The Contemporary Austin's two venues, the Jones Center on Congress Avenue and Laguna Gloria, where artists were invited to utilize both the natural setting of the sculpture park and the historic Driscoll Villa to produce and present work for this exhibition.

The Contemporary Austin is committed to supporting fresh scholarship and curatorial innovation, and Pesanti has made an important contribution through her clear and compelling vision for this exhibition. As a major publication and exhibition, *The Sorcerer's Burden* advances our organization's mission to engage audiences through ambitious exhibitions, vital scholarship, and enriching public programming. This catalogue offers not only significant original research on the topic of art and anthropology but original artist contributions; as such, it is both new scholarship and an artists' book, and I am particularly proud of its contents.

In addition to Pesanti's rich and insightful primary essay, this catalogue features a think piece by Robert Storr, artist, critic, and curator; an interview between Pesanti and David Odo, Director of Student Programs and Research Curator of University Collections Initiatives at the Harvard Art Museums, and Pesanti's former colleague in the University of Oxford's anthropology program; and an innovative letter by Julia V. Hendrickson, Associate Curator at the museum. Equally rich are the contributions by artists themselves: the museum invited each artist featured in the exhibition to submit "inspiration" for a section called *Farther Afield*, and gave the artists a wide berth for what this might look like. The range of images, texts, journals, and personal photos we received has made this publication incredibly unique.

This book also continues our rewarding partnership with the inimitable Radius Books, led by Publisher & Creative Director David Chickey, whose creative design and publishing vision have made this book what it is. We are honored and grateful that he selected this publication to be included among the exceptional list of Radius Books projects. Our thanks also to Radius Books' Megan Mulry, Editorial & Marketing, and Montana Currie, Design & Production, for their excellent work on and attention to this book.

The Contemporary Austin has a tight-knit team of individuals that make our publications happen. These include Heather Pesanti, Chief Curator & Director of Curatorial Affairs; Julia V. Hendrickson, Associate Curator; Julie Le, Administrative Assistant; Nicole Chism Griffin, Director of Communications; Phyllis Goodale, Editor; and Alexa Johnson, Communications Coordinator. Chelsea Weathers, who served as our freelance Publication Coordinator for this project, wrangled all parts adeptly to keep the book on track.

We are also honored by the support of agencies, foundations, and individuals without whom the expansive reach of this exhibition and book would not be possible. Having also supported our 2015 exhibition *Strange Pilgrims*, The Andy Warhol Foundation for the Visual Arts again stepped in to provide a generous grant for this exhibition and catalogue. Special thanks to Joel Wachs, President; Rachel Bers, Program Director; and James Bewley, Senior Program Officer, under whose leadership The Andy Warhol Foundation continues to have a profound impact on curators and museums worldwide. Likewise, the National Endowment for the Arts, a regular supporter of our museum, contributed an essential grant toward this project. I'm grateful to the Cultural Arts Division of the City of Austin Economic Development Department for their ongoing support of our programs, and to the Cultural Services of the French Embassy for supporting Pesanti's early curatorial research and travel for this exhibition. I would also like to extend my gratitude to our Corporate Sponsor, Horizon Bank; to Linda L. Brown,

MaddocksBrown Foundation; and to The Contemporary Austin's Exhibition Fund Supporters, whose multi-year support provides invaluable consistency to our programmatic endeavors. My appreciation also to *Texas Monthly*, Media Sponsor, for its generous and ongoing support of our exhibitions. I am especially grateful to our outstanding Board of Trustees, led by President Kathleen Irvin Loughlin, for its unconditional commitment to our museum and its keen vision toward our future.

At the museum, our talented team worked tirelessly to put this exhibition together. In the Exhibitions Department, this includes Heather Pesanti, Chief Curator & Director of Curatorial Affairs; Julia V. Hendrickson, Associate Curator; Steve Griffin, Director of Exhibitions Production; Erin Coupal, Registrar; Dave Culpepper, Preparator; Julie Le, Administrative Assistant; and Ted Carey, Assistant Preparator. Thank you to Margie Rine, Deputy Director & Chief Development Officer, whose fantastic leadership and fundraising efforts allowed this exhibition and publication to come to fruition, along with the exemplary work of Michelle Voss, Fund Development Manager. In response to the exhibition's theme and artists, Andrea Mellard, Director of Public Programs & Community Engagement, developed a valuable and timely set of public programs, while Matt Hoggle, Director of the Art School at Laguna Gloria, and James Tisdale, Ceramics Coordinator, collaborated with the curatorial team for Marie Lorenz's residency at the Art School and her outdoor ceramics commission on the grounds of our sculpture park. I am grateful to each and every member of The Contemporary Austin staff for their continued excellence and dedicated contributions to this exhibition. And to one we consider an honorary museum staff member, I'd like to thank our consultant Bill Haddad of Blue House Design, especially in regards to the work by Dario Robleto; his expertise allows us to foster new and experimental directions with artists in the realm of film, video, sound, and technology.

Of course, I must thank the eleven participating artists featured in this exhibition, without whose work, energy, and ideas this exhibition and catalogue would not be possible: Ed Atkins, Nuotama Bodomo, Theo Eshetu, Cameron Jamie, Kapwani Kiwanga, Marie Lorenz, Nathan Mabry, Ruben Ochoa, Dario Robleto, Shimabuku, and Julia Wachtel. They have each contributed innovative and thoughtful projects—some site-responsive, some experimental, others representative of recent work—all equally critical to the fabric of the exhibition and this book.

Finally, I'd like to thank Heather Pesanti for her creative vision, exceptional writing, and astute organization of this immensely important exhibition, one that advances the global scholarship around the intersecting fields of contemporary art practice and anthropology to revelatory, meaningful, and always thought-provoking ends.

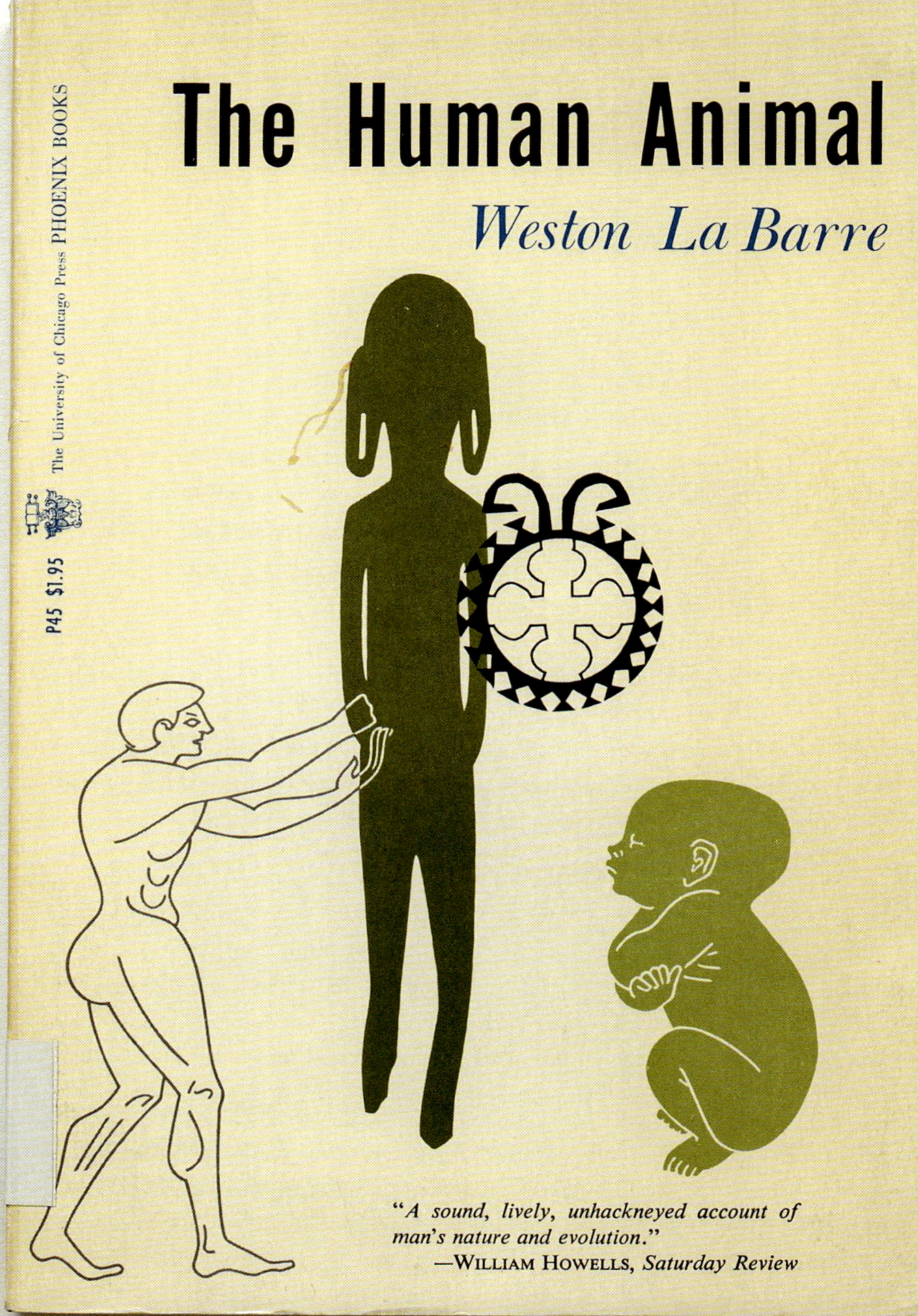
The Human Animal
Weston La Barre
"A sound, lively, unhackneyed account of man's nature and evolution."
—William Howells, Saturday Review
P45 $1.95
The University of Chicago Press PHOENIX BOOKS

ARGONAUTS OF THE WESTERN PACIFIC

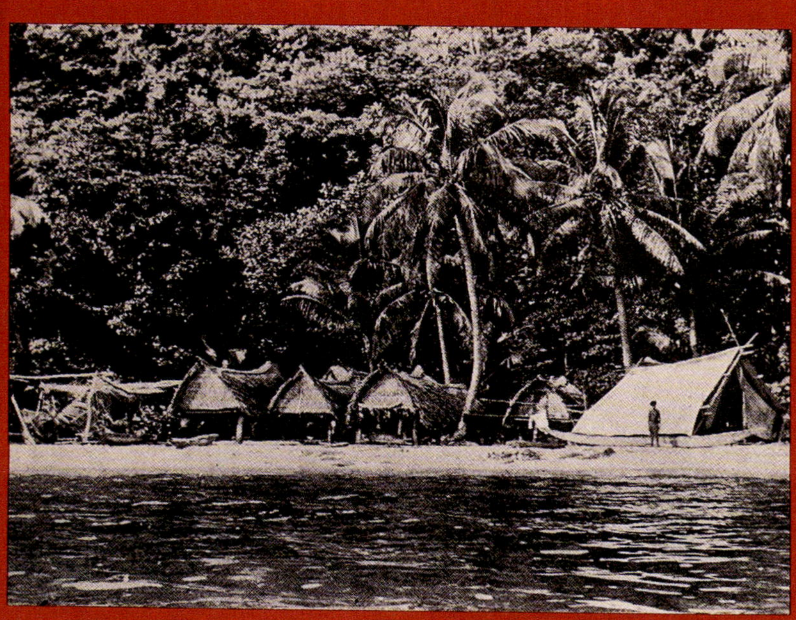

Bronislaw Malinowski

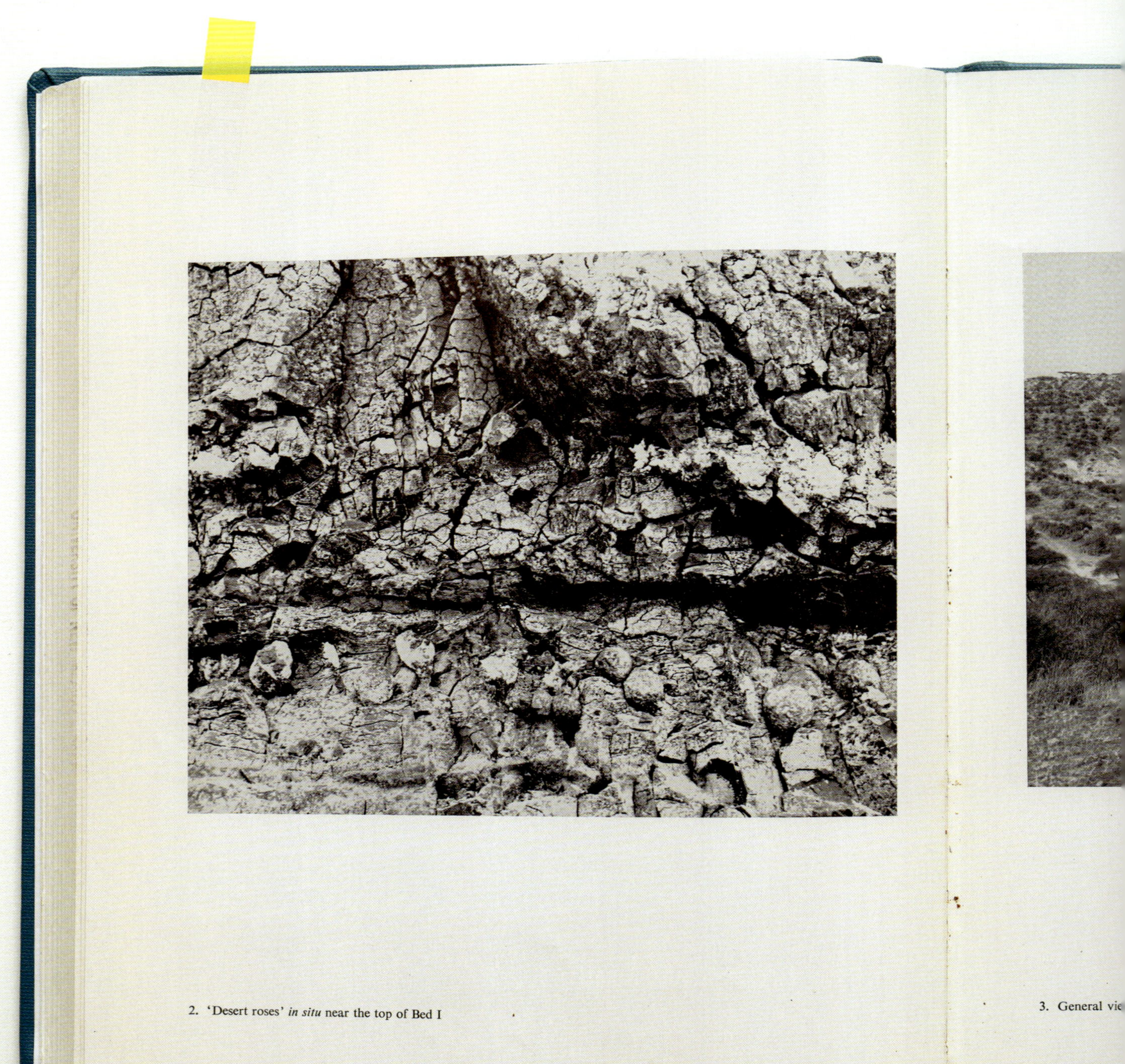

2. 'Desert roses' *in situ* near the top of Bed I

3. General vie

Being There

Heather Pesanti

Chief Curator & Director of Curatorial Affairs, The Contemporary Austin

So I will just muse on what everyone else has been musing on:
art and anthro, anthro and art, can we tell them together?
Can we tell them apart? [1]

—LUCY R. LIPPARD

PROLOGUE

Like many curators who found circuitous paths into the field, mine involved an interdisciplinary approach. From 1997 to 1998, I spent a year in England studying anthropology, completing a master's degree in Cultural Anthropology at the University of Oxford.[2] Prior to this, I was a painter and then an art historian, but had never formally engaged with the anthropological field. My pursuit of ethnology came about by happenstance: uncertain of what to do after college, I discovered an award that generously funded graduate study in the United Kingdom. While researching options overseas that would qualify, I came upon the Oxford degree, a program that seemed deeply connected to the art, material culture, and museum studies that had driven my undergraduate focus. Despite the potential difficulties of shifting fields, I applied to Oxford and to the award. As things go, the award went to someone else but I was

1. Lucy R. Lippard, "Farther Afield," in *Between Art and Anthropology: Contemporary Ethnographic Practice*, eds. Arnd Schneider and Christopher Wright (Oxford, UK: Berg Publishers, 2010; New York: Bloomsbury, 2014), 23. Citations refer to the Bloomsbury edition.

2. I received a Master of Studies (MSt) in Ethnology and Museum Ethnography, a division of Cultural Anthropology, from the University of Oxford, England, in 1998. The degree is now Visual, Material, and Museum Ethnology, a merger of two related programs. See https://www.anthro.ox.ac.uk/visual-material-and-museum-anthropology.

accepted into Oxford, and after some consideration, decided to take out a student loan, move to England, and attend. At the university, my two theses consisted of cross-disciplinary approaches: the first, a cultural study of the impact on the Basque community of the Guggenheim Museum in Bilbao when it opened in 1997; the second, a visual anthropological snapshot of British football from the perspective of an American, witnessing in situ matches of the Arsenal team with a fellow Oxford student, a Scottish physicist on my floor with season tickets. While more than two decades have passed since this interlude, the spirit of cultural anthropology's observational "nose and ears to the ground" methodologies, rooted in fieldwork and site- and cultural specificity, have remained central to my curatorial practice.

On the occasion of this exhibition at The Contemporary Austin, *The Sorcerer's Burden: Contemporary Art and the Anthropological Turn*, I went through my old files in storage, looking for evidence of this year of study. Pre-mainstream computers, I wrote my research and class notes in small wire-bound notepads that could be easily transported. I maintained a neat, meticulous handwriting style, hoping to be able to read the notes later. Since then, I've moved countless times, and the paper evidence of my year at Oxford seems to have vanished. In the context of an exhibition on the intersection of art and anthropology—with my intent to explore, in particular, the porous aspects of fact and fiction that result from their nexus—this disappearance seems fitting. Counter to this disappointment was a reunion with an Oxford colleague from those many years ago. Through my research, I came upon a public lecture by David Odo, one of my classmates in the anthropology program, on the subject of nineteenth-century Japanese souvenir photographs in the collection of Harvard's Peabody Museum of Archaeology and Ethnography, subsequently turned into a book.[3] Shortly thereafter, I traveled to Cambridge to interview him, and an edited version of that transcript is featured in this catalogue. The issues we discussed—I from the contemporary curatorial side, he from the anthropological museological one—traversed the various aesthetic, social, and political issues around the rich intersection between the two fields.

This complex, fascinating, and sometimes fraught relationship between contemporary art and anthropology shapes the subject of the catalogue and exhibition *The Sorcerer's Burden: Contemporary Art and the Anthropological Turn*. It would be hard to argue, at this juncture, that the disciplines are not inextricably intertwined. Timely discussions around identity, power structures, postcolonialism, and language theory have led to a renewed interest from both sides, perhaps warily peering across the street at each other, but no doubt looking to engage. Grounding this, an early and brief academic background in these overlapping fields has informed the lens through which I have

3. David Odo, *The Journey of "A Good Type": From Artistry to Ethnography in Early Japanese Photographs* (Cambridge, MA: Peabody Museum Press, 2015).

observed an increasing number of contemporary artists, curators, and exhibitions mining anthropology's methods and practices to varying degrees and effect. This book, while created on the occasion of this exhibition, stands on its own as a creative and poetic exploration of the topic. In addition to this essay and the conversation with David Odo, contributions include those by artist, critic, and curator Robert Storr, an influential force in my understanding of material culture and art from my years under his tutelage at The Institute of Fine Arts, New York University, and Julia V. Hendrickson, the museum's Associate Curator, who went down an imaginative rabbit hole with her letter of art historical critique. In addition, upon our invitation, all of the artists in the exhibition contributed original "artist inspiration" content for the *Farther Afield* section in this book: writings, memories, sketches, old photographs, or other reflections and influences prompted by this project, sometimes (although not necessarily) related to their work in the exhibition.

As an exhibition, *The Sorcerer's Burden* consists of eleven artists occupying both sites of The Contemporary Austin—the downtown Jones Center on Congress Avenue and the fourteen-acre Betty and Edward Marcus Sculpture Park at Laguna Gloria—with new commissions, site-specific iterations, and existing works. These contemporary artists, who directly or indirectly reference or interrogate the intersection of art and anthropology in their work, include **Ed Atkins** (born 1982 in Oxford, United Kingdom; lives and works in Copenhagen and Berlin), **Nuotama Bodomo** (born 1988 in Accra, Ghana), **Theo Eshetu** (born 1958 in London, United Kingdom; lives and works in Berlin), **Cameron Jamie** (born 1969 in Los Angeles, California; lives and works in Paris), **Kapwani Kiwanga** (born 1978 in Hamilton, Ontario, Canada; lives and works in Paris), **Marie Lorenz** (born 1973 in Twentynine Palms, California; lives and works in Brooklyn, New York, and Austin, Texas), **Nathan Mabry** (born 1978 in Durango, Colorado; lives and works in Los Angeles), **Ruben Ochoa** (born 1974 in Oceanside, California; lives and works in Los Angeles), **Dario Robleto** (born 1972 in San Antonio, Texas; lives and works in Houston), **Shimabuku** (born 1969 in Kobe, Japan; lives and works in Naha, Japan), and **Julia Wachtel** (born 1956 in New York City, New York; lives and works in Connecticut and Brooklyn, New York).

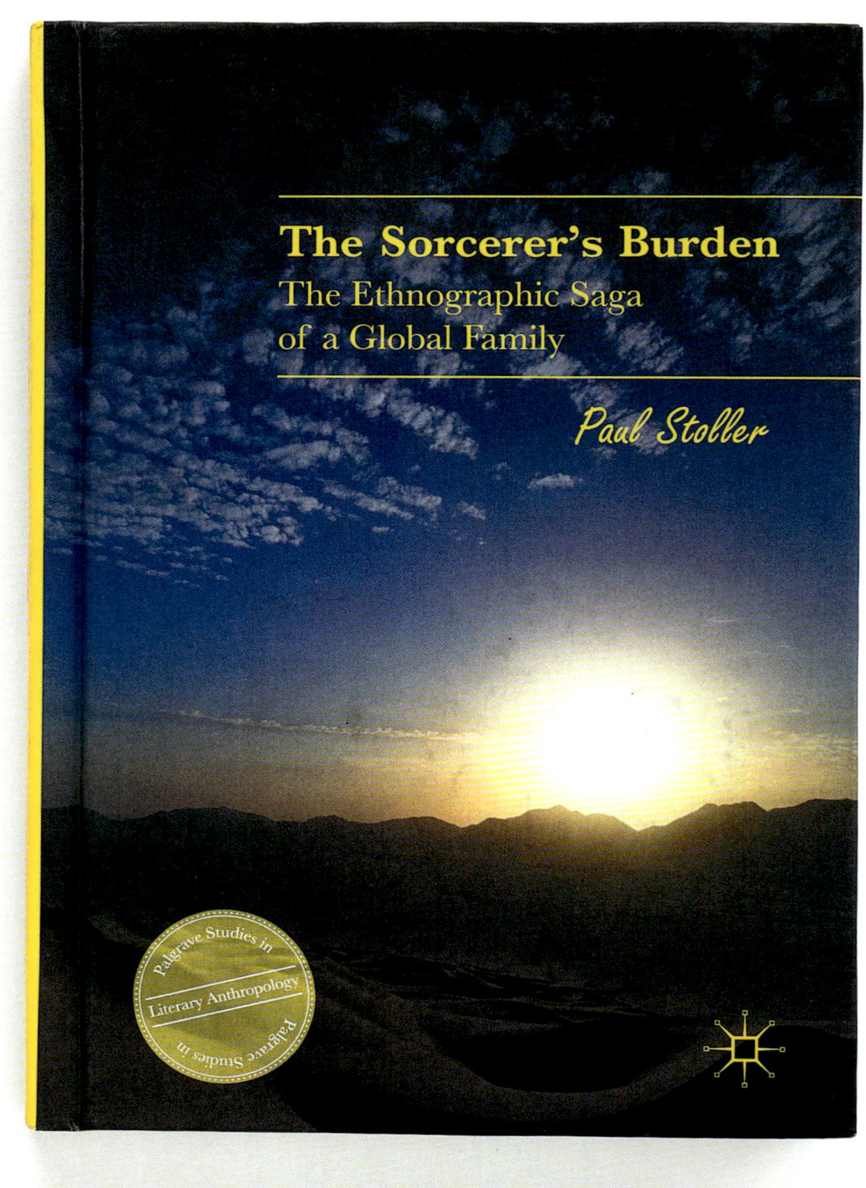

Fig. 1 Cover, Paul Stoller, *The Sorcerer's Burden: The Ethnographic Saga of a Global Family* (Switzerland: Palgrave Macmillan, 2016).

The exhibition sources its title from an ethnographic novel, *The Sorcerer's Burden: The Ethnographic Saga of a Global Family*, 2016, by the American cultural anthropologist Paul Stoller (who coincidentally received his PhD from The University of Texas at Austin in 1978). Initially based on a colleague of Stoller's, a "cosmopolitan African intellectual who had deep knowledge of literature and philosophy," as well as more than thirty years of Stoller's ethnographic research among the Songhay of the Niger River region, the work then reimagined the intellectual as a sorcerer from Niger (the fictional character of Omar Dia) who had run away from, and then returned to, his ancestral roots and cultural identity (see fig. 1).[4] Intertwining history and ethnography with poetic and fictive embellishment, the book occupies the territory of ethnographic fiction—in the spirit of French New Wave filmmaker Jean Rouch, who spent most of his life in Africa making films in collaboration with his subjects, birthing the genre of "ethnofiction"—offering a philosophical commentary on the complexity of "truth" in cultural knowledge, as well as on the challenges (the mutual *burden*, so to speak) faced by the intersection of Western with non-Western practices, interpretations, and experiences.[5] The allusion to magic and sorcery in the exhibition title likewise nods to the seminal early Western/non-Western hybrid art presentation, Jean-Hubert Martin's 1989 *Magiciens de la terre* in Paris—a phrase Martin used instead of "artist" and which, in the work of the artists featured at The Contemporary Austin, becomes a touchpoint for imaginative cultural critique (see fig. 2).[6] This exhibition's subtitle references Hal Foster's 1995 essay "The Artist as Ethnographer?"—his own title riffing on Walter Benjamin's use of the phrase "The Author as Producer" in 1934—in which he wrote of the problematic "turn to the ethnographic" in "quasi-anthropological" practices.[7] Since then, many curators, artists, and scholars have written salient texts on the subject, some of which ground this discussion. Two recent books edited by Arnd Schneider and Christopher Wright have been touchstones from an academic perspective for the possible overlaps between anthropology and art and their collaborative potentials for new strategies, and set the

4. Paul Stoller, "Author's Note," in *The Sorcerer's Burden: The Ethnographic Saga of a Global Family* (Switzerland: Palgrave Macmillan, 2016), 206.

5. Filmmaker and anthropologist Jean Rouch's 1955 film *Les Maîtres Fous* is considered the first film within the ethnofiction genre.

6. Translated as "Magicians of the earth," this iconic exhibition of global art from around the world intended to usurp the traditional format and content of the *Paris Biennial* at the Centre Pompidou and the Grande Halle de la Villette, Paris. See the exhibition catalogue for *Magiciens de la terre* (Paris: Éditions du Centre Pompidou, 1989).

7. Hal Foster, "The Artist as Ethnographer?" in *The Traffic in Culture: Refiguring Art and Anthropology*, eds. George E. Marcus and Fred R. Myers (Berkeley and Los Angeles: University of California Press, 1995), 305, 302. See also Walter Benjamin, "The Author as Producer," in *Understanding Brecht*, trans. Anna Bostock (New York: Verso Books, 1998). This text was originally delivered as a lecture at the Institute for the Study of Fascism, Paris, on April 27, 1934.

stage for conversations around their intersection.[8] And in Austin, anthropologists at The University of Texas, including Marina Peterson and Craig Campbell, both associate professors in the Department of Anthropology, have initiated important projects, student courses, and academic publications to this end.[9]

As fields of study, anthropology and art—themselves widely divergent across geographies and cultures—tend to have more in common than not. They are distant bedfellows, sharing an intellectual foundation based on curiosity about culture and difference, an impulse to collect and order, and a reflection of the human condition. Symbiotic concerns between the two fields with the Western modernist discussions of difference, homogenization, and heterogeneity have been central to the way that anthropologists and artists seek cultural value in their respective fields. Globalization, coupled with the rapid escalation of technology, has rendered culture and disciplines in close proximity to one another. In tandem, postmodern and postcolonial discourse has disrupted the easy conception of *otherness* central to cultural critique, and has resulted in reflexivity, introspection, and expanded dialogues across not only art and anthropology but the humanities and sciences more broadly. Over the past several decades, as artists strive to adapt, invent, and stay relevant, ethnographic methodologies and ambitions have become creative tools within the field of contemporary art.[10] In particular, notions of fieldwork—the practice developed by modern anthropology whereby research, notes, and immersion in a community are prioritized as methods for cultural interrogation—have led artists to anthropology as a perceived means of attaining "auras" of authenticity and objectivity. Likewise, the notion that greater veracity and objective truth can be achieved through firsthand, immersive observation—rather than abstract or distant theoretical or analytical posturing—has become commonplace. Conversely, for anthropologists today, fieldwork as a methodology has become perceived as irrevocably flawed, as its inference of truth has turned out to be fallible. As a science, anthropology has come to recognize the fictive aspects present in its scientific truths, as Schneider, Wright, and others have argued.[11] This direction within the field of anthropology has been labeled *sensory anthropology*, a fitting term to connote the acknowledgement that experiential factors reciprocally contribute to the determination of ideas and cultural memory.[12] Art, moving in the

8. See *Between Art and Anthropology*, along with *Contemporary Art and Anthropology* (Oxford, UK, and New York: Berg Publishers, 2006).

9. At the time of this writing, proposals for collaborative public programs between The University of Texas at Austin Department of Anthropology and this museum, on the occasion of this exhibition, are in development.

10. Foster, "The Artist as Ethnographer?," in *The Traffic in Culture*, 302–309.

11. *Between Art and Anthropology*, eds. Arnd Schneider and Christopher Wright.

12. Kris Rutten, An van. Dienderen, and Ronald Soetart, "Revisiting the ethnographic turn in contemporary art," *Critical Arts* 27, no. 5 (2013): 465.

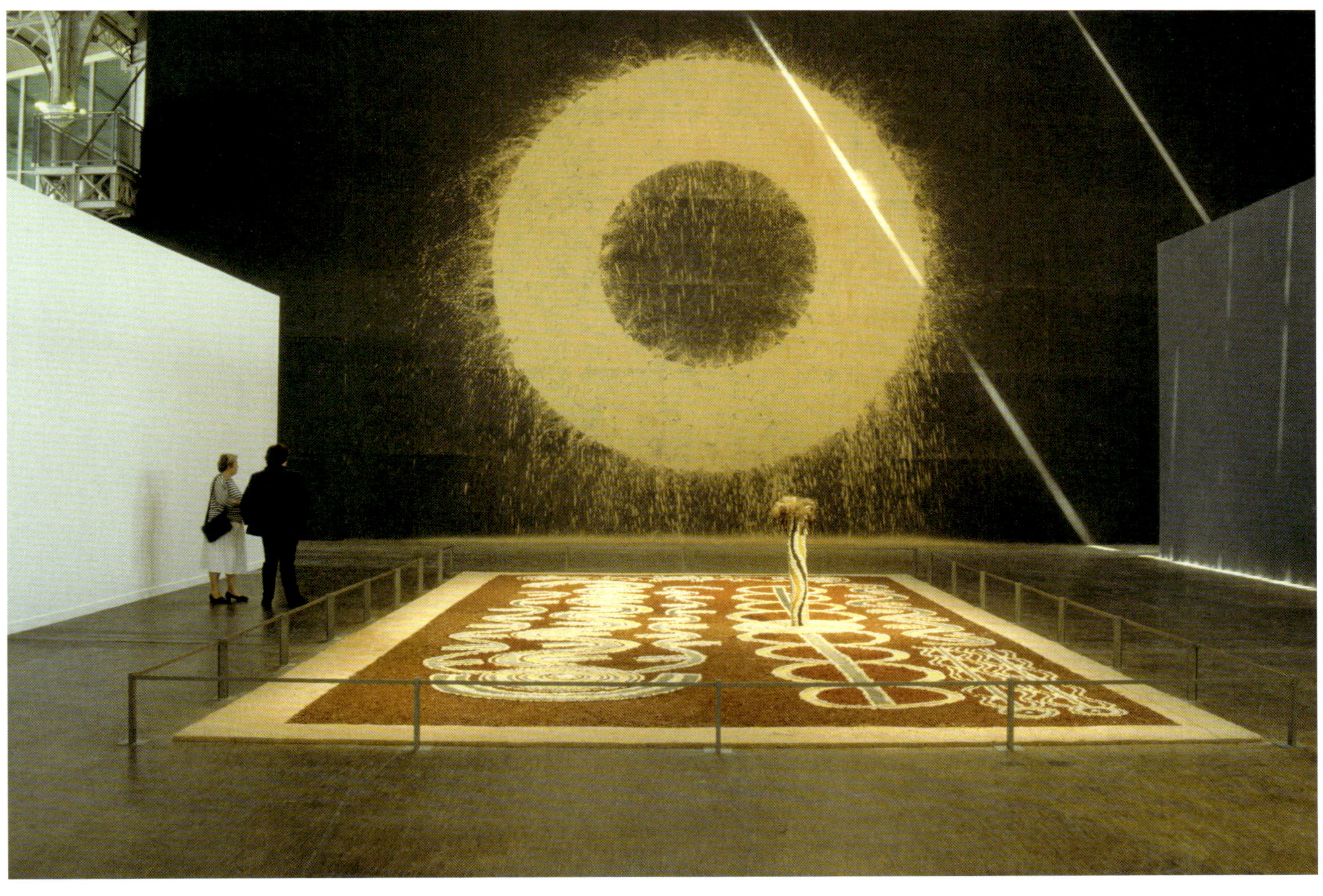

Fig. 2 *Wall*: Richard Long, *Red Earth Circle*, 1989. Clay from the river Avon. 39 feet 4 ½ inches x 65 feet 7 ⅜ inches. *Floor*: Paddy Japaljarri Sims, Paddy Japaljarri Stewart, Neville Japangardi Poulson, Francis Jupurrurla Kelly, Paddy Jupurrurla Nelson, Franck Bronson Jakamarra Nelson, Towser Jakamarra Walker, members of the Yuendumu Community, *Yam Dreaming*, 1989. Installation view, *Magiciens de la terre* [Magicians of the earth], in collaboration with Centre Pompidou, Grande Halle de la Villette, Paris, France, 1989.

other direction, has found ways to pull hard truths into fictive premises. Having always been beholden to aesthetics and thereby sensory experience as meaning, contemporary art has increasingly adopted fieldwork methodology and visual anthropological methods in a quest for the veracity of firsthand observation, social engagement with community, and authenticity of intent. "Being There," this essay's title, invokes anthropologist Bronisław Malinowski's doctrine of fieldwork, a discourse that recognized the value of showing up and doing the work, now widespread in contemporary curating and academia.

This evolution corresponds to art's reengagement with and interest in anthropology and ethnographic fieldwork methods over the course of the twentieth century, coupled with new formats and elevated interest in context, subjectivity, and site-specificity. As the twentieth century progressed, a number of artistic movements increasingly distanced themselves from individual authorship and exclusively formalist concerns while seeking to gain renewed relevance through engagement with communities and social structures. This anthropological turn can be attributed to a number of reasons: a perceived aura of authenticity, the ability to use anthropology's methods without rules, a desire to break out of the white cube gallery space, and an interest in social practice, among others. Walter Benjamin's influential 1936 essay "The Work of Art in the Age of Mechanical Reproduction" debunked the long-standing modernist artist-as-genius model in articulating the loss of a work of art's "aura" through reproduction of the work itself, opening avenues to a new definition of art and dissolving the importance of singular authorship.[13] This paved the way for Pop, Warhol, and the infinite iterations of appropriative art. In the 1960s and 1970s, Land art—earth as archaeological and anthropological site—and Beuysian "social sculpture" represented a continuation of ethnographic concerns within the field of art.[14] This was followed by the rise of participatory, socially engaged, and relational art in the 1990s and 2000s that centered around context, human engagement via the audience, and specific communities as part of the work's meaning, ranging globally from Allora & Calzadilla, Paweł Althamer, José Bedia, Christian Boltanski, Sophie Calle, Jeremy Deller, Mark Dion, Cao Fei, Thomas Hirschhorn, Wolfgang Laib, Postcommodity, and Sofía Táboas to local projects such as the installation *Lost Money*, 2009, by Danish artists SUPERFLEX, in the outdoor sculpture collection of The Contemporary Austin, and the various socially engaged activities by Texas-based artist and Project Row Houses co-founder Rick Lowe.

13. Walter Benjamin, "The Work of Art in the Age of Mechanical Reproduction," in *Illuminations*, trans. Harry Zohn, ed. Hannah Arendt (New York: Schocken Books, 1968). The first version of Benjamin's essay was originally published in Paris, 1936.

14. The term *social sculpture* was first coined by the German artist Joseph Beuys to suggest that art-as-life could transform society.

Of equal importance to the production of art has been exhibition making, a vehicle to identify, reflect, and propel the shifts and turns in art of our times. In particular, large-scale contemporary art exhibitions in the past several decades have increasingly engaged with the world of ethnographic objects and anthropological methodologies. Modeled after the World's Fairs, the *Venice Biennale* in Italy and the *Carnegie International* in Pittsburgh, founded in 1895 and 1896 respectively, were the first two and only biennials for nearly half a century, created as important platforms to represent international art practices. As surveys, they also represented the dominant colonialist ethos of their time: white and male, with few to no examples of women, people of color, or representation outside of Europe or North America for the first half century. It wasn't until the second half of the twentieth century, with biennials including *documenta* in Kassel, Germany, the *São Paulo Biennale*, and the *Skulptur Projekte Münster*, that exhibitions slowly began to adopt in earnest the expansive, more inclusive international survey model. By the 1990s, the biennial circuit had exploded, consisting of hundreds of exhibitions around the world, many of them non-Western, including in Busan and Gwangju (both in South Korea), Dakar (Senegal), and Shanghai (China). Exhibitions began to make efforts to work with diverse advisory committees. Since the 1990s, the *Carnegie International* has engaged a changing advisory committee of international curators from around the world. Taking this further, the exhibition *Balance 1990: views, visions, influences*, a contemporary art survey at the Queensland Art Gallery in South Brisbane, Australia, in 1990, engaged an Indigenous Murri advisory team, leading to a groundbreaking combination of Indigenous and non-Indigenous works. The 2002 *documenta11*, organized by the late Okwui Enwezor, a native of Nigeria and the first non-European curator of the exhibition, presented a complex interface of global "platforms" that argued for a dialectical, intertwined relationship across global art and culture. More recently, Carolyn Christov-Bakargiev expanded the anthropocentric focus and exploration of material culture from a global perspective in her remarkable and massive *dOCUMENTA (13)* in 2012, while Adam Szymczyk's 2017 edition of *documenta 14* not only included an exhaustive amount of ethnographic-inspired works conceivable as art only through their placement in an art exhibition, but bifurcated the project across two countries, Germany and Greece. Massimiliano Gioni's 55th *Venice Biennale*, in 2013, titled *The Encyclopedic Palace*, took direct inspiration from the history of the Wunderkammer, or Renaissance cabinets of curiosities, and placed both non-Western and historical ethnographic objects in conversation with contemporary artists and new commissions (see fig. 3). Conferences and symposia have similarly reflected this turn, as in the 2003 Tate Modern conference "Fieldworks: Dialogues between Art and Anthropology," which brought together anthropologists and artists for cross-disciplinary discussions, or the 2012 conference "The Artist as Ethnographer," presented by the curatorial platform le peuple qui manque in partnership with the Musée du Quai Branly – Jacques Chirac and Centre Pompidou in

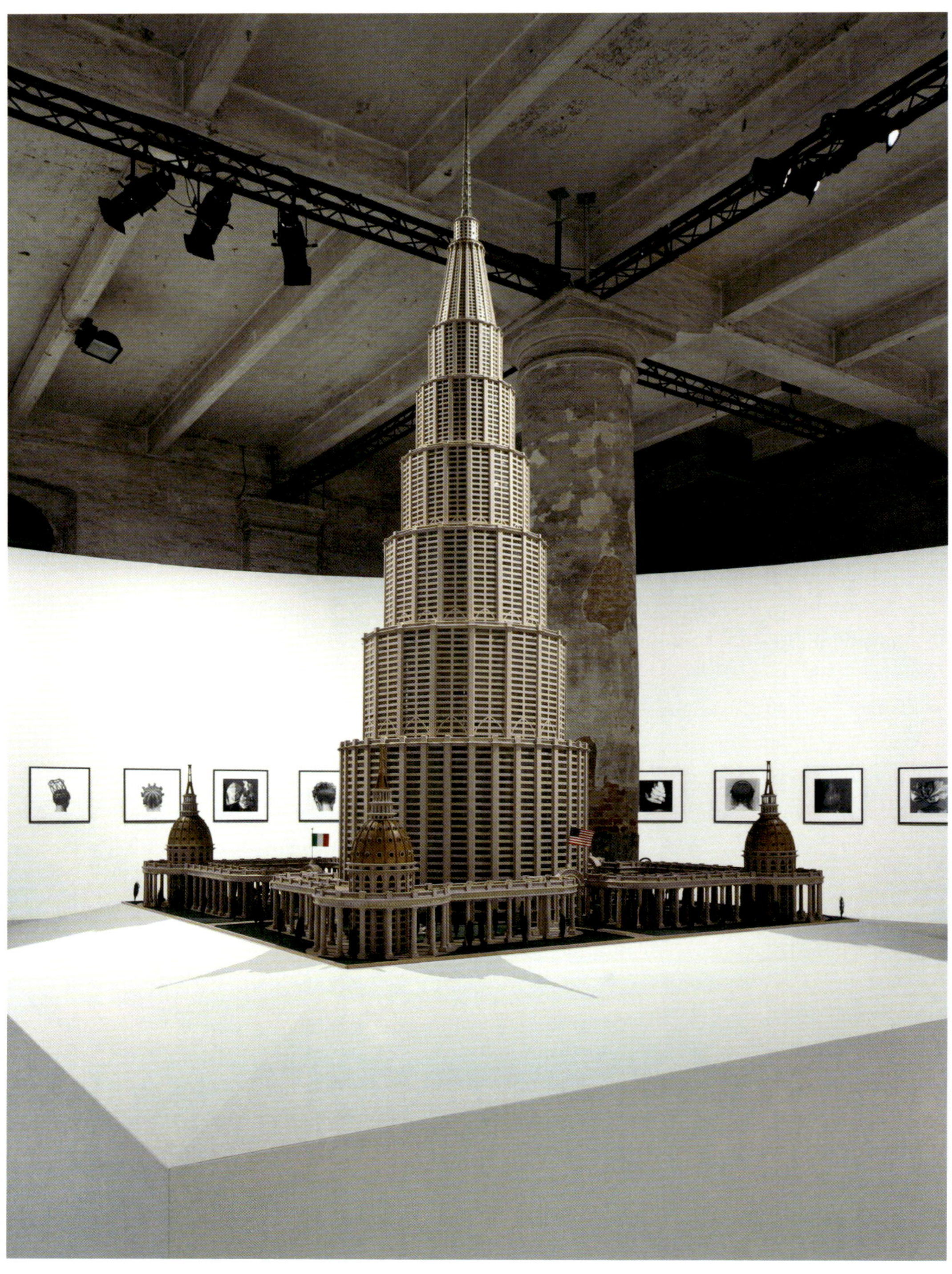

Fig. 3 Marino Auriti, *The Encyclopedic Palace of the World*, 1950–1959. Wood, plastic, glass, metal, combs, and components for modeling. Installation view, *The Enyclopedic Palace*, 55th *Venice Biennale*, Venice, Italy, 2013.

Paris.[15] These are but a few examples of significant exhibition developments that have influenced the field, and the topic of this exhibition.

In addition to both object and exhibition making, the language and discourse originating in the anthropological field have become increasingly mainstream. *Ethnology* and *ethnography* are terms used today not only by artists but within wide-ranging humanities and pop culture discussions, with expanded definitions. Also frequently used interchangeably with the term *cultural anthropology*, *ethnology* is a broad academic categorization to connote the analytical comparison of cultures, with *ethnography* tying onto this as the fieldwork method used in the ethnological process, namely case studies of research, notes, and observation, a "written representation of culture."[16] Art writers, with varying results—who could forget Sarah Thornton's *Seven Days in the Art World* and the author's claims to serious ethnographic concerns while embedded in the salacious high tiers of the capitalist art market—have often used these terms to categorize their insider views of the art world.[17] Similarly, *museum ethnography* connotes the study of material and visual culture as displayed in museums, including analysis of the objects themselves and the related issues of institutional power structures, techniques of display, curation, collecting, conservation, and restitution. The most frequent tie-in to contemporary art in museum ethnography might be *visual anthropology*, a subfield within cultural anthropology focusing on visual documentation of cultures, namely through film and photography—for this reason, a natural partner to the visual and fine arts. Generally speaking, art's appropriation of anthropology and its associated terms have led to not only their popularization, but their generalized classifications.

With this in mind, the eleven artists in *The Sorcerer's Burden* represent a small fraction of those addressing the themes and issues discussed here. As with any curatorial project, a wide range of artists could have been selected, but the ones here reflect those artists whose work I have encountered in recent years through travels, exhibition viewings, studio visits, political discussions, and other influences, and that have made a lasting impact on my psyche and thinking. Each artist's work contributes not only as an independent idea, but as a vital thread in this exhibition's argument, woven together within the fabric of both the exhibition and the city of Austin. *The Sorcerer's Burden* sidesteps the proliferation of works by artists presenting earnest and didactic ethnographic observations, namely those adopting the archetypal anthropologist fieldwork and documentary product in a straightforward manner but contextualizing it within an art world setting. Such formats—

15. Rutten, van. Dienderen, and Soetart, "Revisiting the ethnographic turn in contemporary art."

16. See, for example, *Writing Culture: The Poetics and Politics of Ethnography*, eds. James Clifford and George E. Marcus (Berkeley and Los Angeles: University of California Press, 1986; 25th Anniversary Edition, 2010).

17. Sarah Thornton, *Seven Days in the Art World* (New York: W. W. Norton & Company, 2008).

for example, artists without anthropological training traveling to non-Western countries and creating documentaries on particular ceremonies, rituals, tribes, or other aspects of a culture, and presenting them as factual documentaries within art exhibitions—have their place within the art world, but are not the focus of this exhibition. Nor does this exhibition revolve around the "greatest hits," those artists who are irrevocably identified with the anthropological turn through well-established careers. Instead, those included here favor the exploratory and experimental, rather than established or time-tested, utilizing open-ended approaches to build upon elements found in anthropological methodologies and practices toward hybrid and subversive ends. Many of the individuals with work in this exhibition are transnational and global, interested in cross-pollination and reinterpretation of identity and culture. Others are using particular media in new ways to generate social and philosophical critiques that bridge both fields. Eschewing literalism or heavy-handed politicism (a format that seems exhaustive today), their works are alternately imaginative, humorous, satirical, dark, melancholy, playful, enchanting, and mischievous. Representing a wide range of media including painting, sculpture, photography, film, video, sound, and performance, the contemporary artworks in *The Sorcerer's Burden* share a commonality not only in their allusions to elements of anthropology, but in their exploration of the intersection between fact and fiction, and the questionable proposal that any field, media, or genre might propose to convey "truth"—a subject at the core of this exhibition's intent. All of the works aim to engage with a current and timely chapter in this discourse.

CURIOSITY

On a recent trip to the McDonald Observatory near Fort Davis, West Texas, I learned of the forthcoming Giant Magellan Telescope (GMT), a project currently under construction at the southern end of the Atacama Desert in the Chilean Andes that will result in one of the largest telescopes in the world.[18] At the observatory, we visited the massive Harlan J. Smith telescope completed in 1968, a machine that, while incredibly futuristic to a layperson, has been far surpassed by technological developments in the astronomical field. The quest to build exponentially larger telescopes with greater resolution is propelled by the fact that, despite centuries of study, humans know very little about the infinite universe beyond our solar system. With the GMT, this Ferrari of telescopes, astronomers believe science will come closer to collecting and understanding information about the origin of life, how stars and the earthlike planets that orbit them are born, what makes

18. *Giant Magellan Telescope Science Book 2018* (Pasadena, CA: GMTO Corporation, 2018). The McDonald Observatory is a research unit of The University of Texas at Austin's Department of Astronomy; the administrative offices are housed at the Austin campus.

up dark matter, black holes, and dark energy, the age of galaxies, the expansion and contraction of our universe—and, perhaps most of all, whether or not we are alone in the universe, the ultimate search for truth. The capabilities of these telescopes are nearly impossible to grasp, tapping into the core of the engine of not only science but also art and anthropology: the quest to understand the purpose and phenomena of human existence.

Telescopes emerged during a broader Renaissance period of cultural bloom that sought to collect and analyze knowledge of the world. Ancient Egyptian and Mesopotamian sundials and obelisks, solar and astronomical observatories in South America, India, and China, and Islamic astrolabes and quadrants predated astronomical chapters that led to this Western glass invention for making the far seem near. While an early forefather of modern scientific instruments and an output of the Scientific Revolution, the telescopic concept was a product of the refined artistic glassmaking skills of Venetians in the thirteenth and fourteenth centuries—speaking to the intersection of science with the humanities—which eventually led to the first telescope in the Netherlands, followed by Galileo's discoveries as among the first to point a telescope skyward.[19] As countless more stars became visible through these instruments, the universe revealed itself to be an infinite field no longer simply limited to what could be seen by the naked human eye; from this bloomed not only Western astronomical science, but cosmology, astrology, and plain-old stargazing, fields not grounded in fact but subjective human experience.

This Western cultural quest for knowledge and experience also included the sixteenth-century European cabinet of curiosities, or Wunderkammer—collections of the royal, wealthy, and ruling elite and the precursor, by several centuries, to the modernist art museum—which came into existence at roughly the same time. As Western society's systematic accumulation and display of objects subjectively considered to be culturally valuable or "wondrous," these vessels held a motley arrangement of rare and unusual objects representing different cultures—with a colonialist penchant for the exotic—that were part scientific fact, part fiction. Chimera, serpents, multiheaded animals, skulls with unicorn horns (affixed with horns of other animals), skeletons, carved stones, exotic flora and fauna, and antiquated scientific tools could all be found behind curio cabinet doors. Meant to inspire and amaze, these cabinets began in private, domestic spaces but over time expanded to entire rooms in the public sphere, eventually becoming what we know today as natural history and ethnographic museums. They were also the products of colonialism: European and, later, American explorers mining other cultures for exotic memorabilia, procuring or stealing objects, often with ritual, religious, or ceremonial gravitas, and bringing the objects back to be exhibited for Western audiences.

19. "The Telescope," The Galileo Project, last modified 1995, http://galileo.rice.edu/sci/instruments/telescope.html.

The most well-known of these wonder cabinets was Museum Wormianum (see fig. 4), assembled by the seventeenth-century Danish physician Ole Worm, which not only included the magical and macabre categories discussed above but categories illustrating outdated evolutionary hierarchies of human race. Contemporary art museums such as The Menil Collection in Houston, the Barnes Foundation in Philadelphia, The Museum of Jurassic Technology in Culver City, California, and the Musée du Quai Branly in Paris have collections and/or permanent exhibitions whose inspiration lies in the Wunderkammer's beginnings. As a corollary, museums across the globe are being challenged to face their complicated histories, as objects in collections are being examined for restitution to their originating cultures.

The Pitt Rivers Museum, the ethnographic museum where I studied at Oxford, is among the most renowned examples in the world modeled after the Wunderkammer.[20] Embedded in the DNA of ethnographic museums from this era (the museum was founded in 1884) are both the beneficial impulse to recover and reference material culture in order to reveal information about human societies—an essential component for teaching about people and difference across generations—and the colonialist impulse of seizing objects and removing them from their native homes, often subjugating or terrorizing the populations in the process.. During my time there, some galleries of the Pitt Rivers Museum maintained the original organization of hierarchy and evolution as originally denoted by General Augustus Henry Lane-Fox Pitt Rivers, an English officer in the British Army, ethnologist, and archaeologist, whose collection of several hundred thousand ethnographic objects (as a collecting institution, now over two million) formed the beginnings of the museum. In most ethnographic and archaeological museums today, the displays are arranged according to geographical or cultural areas, but at the Pitt Rivers, several displays remain in clustered, crowded groups according to type, and within these groups, by evolution: for example, musical instruments, weapons, or masks displayed in groups to show how the same problems have been solved at different times by different peoples. This Darwinian organizational structure was used as an instrumental teaching tool, but one that could be viewed as somewhat controversial, as this type of structuring narrative has fallen out of favor given the ways in which it has been criticized as providing foundations for racist evolutionary theories. Then and now, the Pitt Rivers has made systemic efforts to approach these problems with rigor, critiquing its own program, engaging with Indigenous cultures and artists to reassess displays and objects, and putting forth progressive, nonhierarchical, integrated, and thematic organizational structures to offset this historical program.

20. "History of the Museum," Pitt Rivers Museum, University of Oxford, https://www.prm.ox.ac.uk/history-museum.

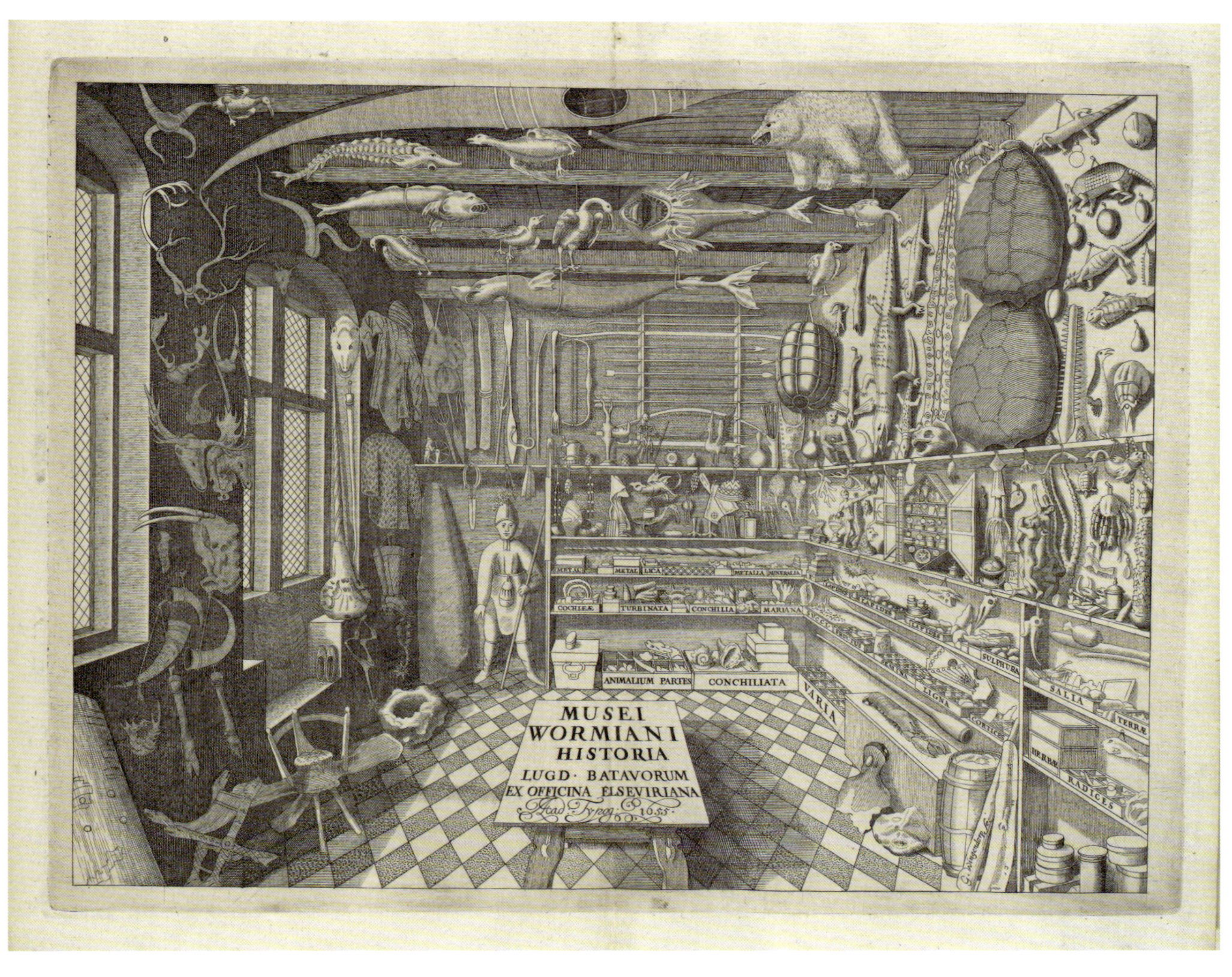

Fig. 4 Ole Worm, *Musei Wormiani Historia*, in *Museum Wormianum, seu, Historia rerum rariorum : tam naturalium, quam artificialium, tam domesticarum, quam exoticarum, quae Hafniae Danorum in aedibus authoris servantur*, 1655. Woodcut on paper.

The Wunderkammer's foundation of imagination and play, the intersection of science, anthropology, and art, and institutional critique leading to possibilities for rewriting the exclusionary narratives told by colonialist histories have inspired a number of contemporary artists. The Belgian conceptualist Marcel Broodthaers created installations of mock museums replete with faux money, ephemera, art objects, and fictional attributions to famous artists as a means of critiquing museums as arbiters of cultural currency, while American Surrealist pioneer Joseph Cornell's delicate shadow boxes might be seen as curios in miniature. More recently, the artist Fred Wilson excavated colonialist histories of collecting and display though installations such as *Mining the Museum*, 1992–1993, an intervention at the Maryland Historical Society in Baltimore in which the artist interspersed slave stocks and shackles among the museum's existing silver vessels and nineteenth-century armchairs.[21] For Wilson, his ability to exist both outside of and within the troubling histories of these ethnographic collections was essential to his revelatory exhibition; he noted that his visceral discomfort upon entering the museum led to his piecing together of the objects' references to slave histories and his subsequent nondidactic but blistering interventions.[22] Mark Dion has created elaborate museological installations out of contemporary curiosities, while Damien Hirst evoked the Wunderkammer through his ironic cabinets of pharmaceutical drugs. Houston-based artist Trenton Doyle Hancock has composed multimedia presentations around ethnographic and religious histories featuring wild characters and elaborate narratives and sets. In 2011, filmmaker Tacita Dean made *Manhattan Mouse Museum*, a film documenting the artist Claes Oldenburg as he meanders through his studio touching and cleaning the small objects on his bookshelves. And in 2013, Chicana artist Amalia Mesa-Bains curated the holdings of a major museum, the collection of the Fowler Museum at UCLA, in *New World Wunderkammer*, re-envisioning the narrative around African, Indigenous American, and colonial *mestizaje* objects and histories.

Likewise the work of artist **Dario Robleto** (born 1972 in San Antonio, Texas; lives and works in Houston), a creative polymath, hovers between worlds: the old curios cabinet of collecting and the future astronomical world of the cosmos. Robleto embodies the crossover and intersectionality of this exhibition through existential propositions that span the fields of science, engineering, technology, music, and pop culture with an aim to uncovering the unknown and overlooked histories. For example, *American Seabed*, 2014, appears at a glance to be a classic naturalist's butterfly collection, the

21. Haidy Geismar, "The Art of Anthropology: Questioning Contemporary Art in Ethnographic Display," in *The International Handbooks of Museum Studies: Museum Theory*, eds. Kylie Message and Andrea Witcomb (New York: Wiley-Blackwell, 2015), 183.

22. Kerr Houston, "How Mining the Museum Changed the Art World," *BmoreArt*, May 2, 2017, http://www.bmoreart.com/2017/05/how-mining-the-museum-changed-the-art-world.html.

colorful bodies positioned in an organized fashion under glass (see fig. 5). Upon closer inspection, the assemblage reveals itself to be conceptual, layered, and wry: the bases upon which the butterflies are arranged are fossilized prehistoric whale ear bones, and their antennae are composed of manipulated audiotape recordings of Bob Dylan's iconic 1965 song "Desolation Row," itself an existential weaving of both fictive and historical references. Anchoring moments within popular culture become fossilized relics on display in tandem with the natural world. Robleto proposes new ideas about which elements from cultural history should be collected and classified, and in what manner.

Propelled by his own galactic quest, one project by the artist revolves around the heart, a decades-long labor of love. Inspired by first hearing, at the tender age of seven, a brief snippet of the Golden Record—a gold-plated copper phonograph record propelled into space on the *Voyager* shuttles in 1977 as NASA's plea to other life-forms by way of a recorded time capsule, consisting of various examples in audio form of the human condition (the sound of a kiss, greetings in fifty-five languages, a heartbeat) as well as a selection of images—over time Robleto has conceived of numerous projects exploring the untapped possibilities of the heartbeat.[23] The story of Ann Druyan particularly captivates Robleto: as creative director of the NASA project, Druyan recorded the electrical energy of her brain and heart (EEG and EKG) during a period when she and the astronomer Carl Sagan had secretly fallen in love, and the idea that this ephemeral moment was projected into the universe for other life-forms to encounter has special resonance for Robleto. Although we know that the heart as an organ does not produce the emotion of love in the human body, the fact that the pace, tenor, strength, and other irregularities of the heartbeat reflect our emotions has allowed for this loose and lasting association. Quintessential of his work, Robleto also highlights the overlooked accomplishments of this female protagonist, Druyan—often referred to historically as "Carl Sagan's wife" despite her accomplishments as a director of the NASA project—as she sneaks a testimony of her clandestine love onto the vessel. While the official narratives around Druyan's story focused on the scientific brain waves, as Robleto articulated,

> *What my project hopes to reveal is that it was the interaction between both brain and heart that should be remembered, and how the narrative that focuses only on the brain loses sight of a much more complicated human history of just where we locate our selves and personal identity in our bodies. The question I formulated to drive this work—'What does one gift to the only woman whose heart and mind have left the solar system?'—is partly answered by my deep historical dive to trace where these divisions between heart and brain started to appear and why.*[24]

23. Dario Robleto, in conversation with author, August 6, 2018. See also the "The Golden Record," *Voyager*, Jet Propulsion Laboratory, California Institute of Technology, NASA, https://voyager.jpl.nasa.gov/golden-record.

24. Robleto, in email correspondence with author, February 4, 2019.

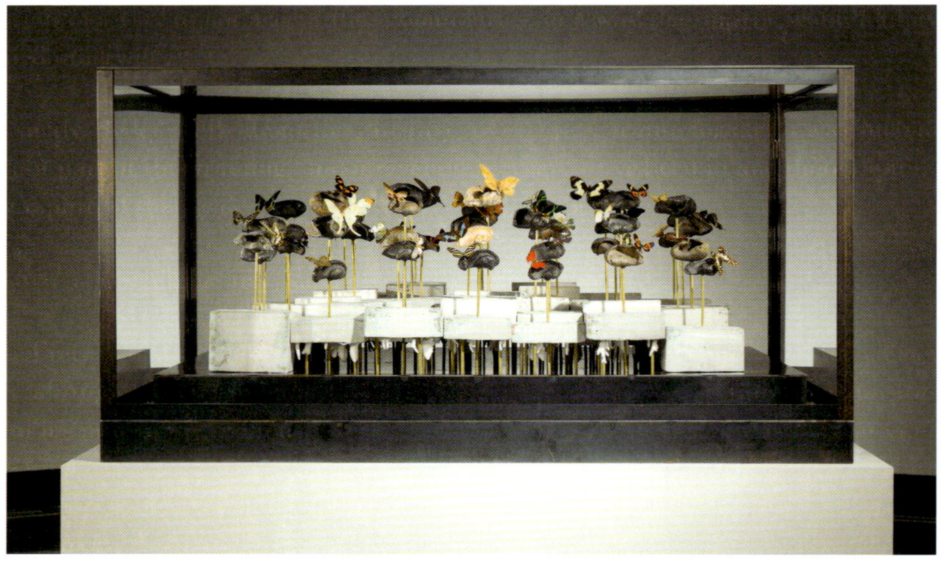

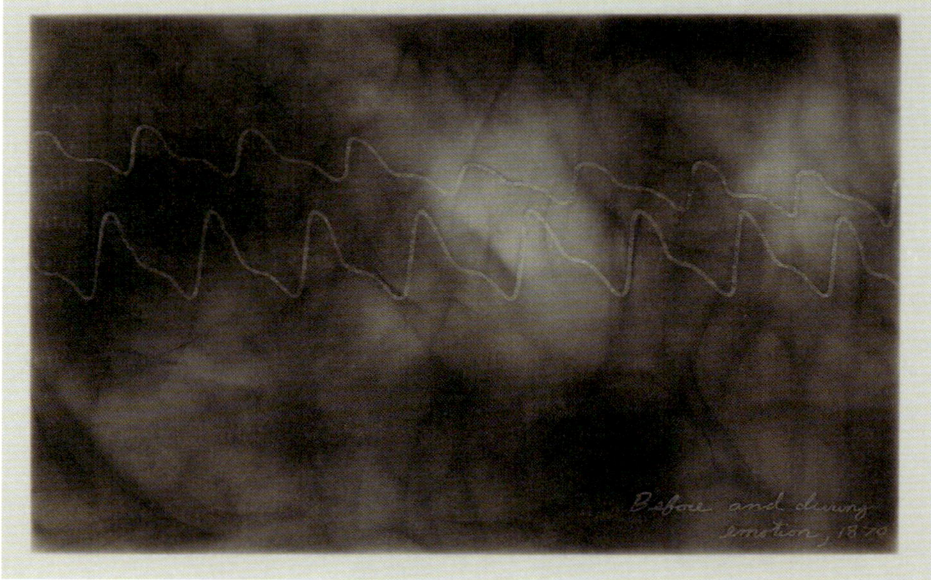

Fig. 5 Dario Robleto, *American Seabed*, 2014. Fossilized prehistoric whale ear bones salvaged from the sea (1 to 10 million years), various butterflies, butterfly antennae made from stretched and pulled audiotape recordings of Bob Dylan's "Desolation Row," concrete, ocean water, pigments, coral, brass, steel, and Plexiglas. 37 x 68 x 55 inches.

Fig. 6 Dario Robleto, *The First Time, the Heart (A Portrait of Life 1854–1913): Before and during emotion, 1870*, 2017–2018. From set of fifty photolithographs on Rising Drawing Bristol with transparent base ink and hand-flamed and sooted paper; image brushed with lithotine and lifted from soot, fused in a mild solution of shellac and denatured alcohol. Housed in portfolio box created by Bella Forte Designs; bound in Canapetta black Italian cloth with screen-printed text and image; eight-page essay booklet digitally printed on Classic Text natural white paper with saddle-stitch binding. Published by Island Press at Washington University, St. Louis, Missouri. Edition of 6. Each, 11 ½ x 14 ¼ inches, with four varying print window sizes.

Most recently Robleto has been collaborating with sound historian Patrick Feaster within the blossoming field of sound archaeology to expand the next chapter of this ongoing project, researching nineteenth-century heartbeats and brain waves—previously only in existence as rudimentary markings in smoke ash on paper, made by primitive recording equipment (variations on the sphygmograph and cardiograph)—and bringing their sound to life (see fig. 6). For this exhibition, Robleto worked with The Contemporary Austin to create *The Boundary of Life Is Quietly Crossed*, 2019, a sound and moving image experience of several heartbeats and brain waves, transformed into an immersive audio and visual room with the artist's first formal filmic work, allowing these forgotten living pulses to be resuscitated and their stories told for contemporary visitors. Robleto's ability to merge the historical lineages of art, ethnography, and science points to museological history come full circle. Modern and contemporary art museums have tended to distinguish themselves from ethnographic or natural history institutions. While in some sense simple pragmatics dictated this distinction—concise missions of exhibiting modern and contemporary art, for example—the underpinnings might connect to the underlying assumption of the superiority of "high" art objects over "low," the academy of art, and the tautological universe of the art world. In tandem, anthropological endeavors have held a well-known aversion to this aforementioned "high" culture, reflecting a discomfort with the exclusionary practices of elite members of a society, an animosity toward the aestheticization of ethnographic methods, and wariness of the creative, unproven, and avant-garde methodologies of the art world. As articulated by the anthropologist Alfred Gell in 1992, "anthropology is anti-art," in that the "aesthetic awe bordering on the religious" projected by art lovers onto the contents of art museums, while generating a rich cultural experience, is irrevocably ethnocentric because of its emotional and personal subjectivity, and therefore anathema to the objective intent of anthropology and its practitioners.[25] Art as anthropology's foil, and vice versa. Aware of such silo-ing, Robleto's practice charges through these boundaries, driven by curiosity, fostering collaboration, and fusing unlikely connections. The artist has pioneered residencies and teaching positions for himself at universities and institutions that bridge multiple departments and disciplines, to the surprise of some faculty, and has made deep inroads with organizations such as SETI, an institute that explores the origins of life in the universe, as well as neuroscience and engineering departments at institutions such as Northwestern and Harvard universities.[26] Beyond Robleto, today we see these borders being conclusively blurred again, particularly on the part of contemporary artists, coming full circle and reengaging with anthropology with varying results. Although the primary direction of appropriation comes from the field of art toward that of anthropology, both have at times sourced from the other, demonstrating a degree of admiration for the other's practices or methodologies. For example, ethnographers, particularly film and

25. Alfred Gell, "The Technology of Enchantment and the Enchantment of Technology," in *Anthropology, Art, and Aesthetics*, eds. Jeremy Coote and Anthony Shelton (Oxford, UK: Clarendon Press, 1992), 40.

26. Dario Robleto, in email correspondence with author, January 11, 2019.

video or visual anthropologists, are becoming less averse to avant-garde methods (found in art making) in their own fieldwork.[27] This complicated narrative, laden with admiration, appropriation, and skepticism from both sides, continues as a thread through the fields of art and anthropology, as contemporary artists continue to reference anthropological subjects and perform ethnographic practices.

FIELDWORK

Modern anthropology is distinguished by fieldwork, research, and notes, combined with the intent to immerse or embed in a particular community in order to observe another culture firsthand.[28] Immanuel Kant's 1798 treatise *Anthropology from a Pragmatic Point of View* branded anthropology a philosophical endeavor, while "armchair" anthropologists—including E. B. Tylor and James George Frazer in the nineteenth and early twentieth centuries—embodied the analytical practice of studying other cultures from a distance.[29] While theory and analysis remain critically important methodologies, the radical gesture of the next wave of anthropologists circa the early twentieth century—especially Franz Boas in the US, Bronisław Malinowski in England, and later Claude Lévi-Strauss in France—was to engage in situ, to go to places in person and identify the presence of human characteristics that are cultural and social, distinguishing the study of anthropology from science, nature, and biology, as well as to see value in the observation and documentation of subjects: a practice revolving around firsthand study and fieldwork. Early female anthropologists, while rare in the male-dominated field, included Zora Neale Hurston, who studied under Boas at Barnard College, graduating in 1928 as the first black student and among the first black female students in anthropology, and publishing the 1935 ethnographic work *Mules and Men*, among other seminal texts, her exploration of African American folklore in the South (see fig. 7).[30] Margaret Mead, Ruth Benedict, and Mary Leakey likewise contributed a feminist angle toward in-person engagement and ethnographic engagement of communities.

27. See, for example, discussion in Arnd Schneider and Christopher Wright, "The Challenge of Practice," in *Contemporary Art and Anthropology*, 2–5.

28. The discussion here will be concerned with cultural anthropology, as opposed to linguistic, scientific, or a number of other anthropological realms.

29. Immanuel Kant, *Anthropology from a Pragmatic Point of View*, trans. and ed. Robert B. Louden (Cambridge, UK: Cambridge University Press, 2006); originally delivered as lectures in anthropology courses Kant taught from 1772 to 1796, and subsequently published in 1798. E. B. Tylor began lecturing on the subject in 1883 at the Pitt Rivers Museum at the University of Oxford. A diploma in Anthropology was inaugurated at the university in 1905.

30. Zora Neale Hurston, *Mules and Men* (Philadelphia: J. B. Lippincott, Inc., 1935; repr., New York: HarperCollins Publishers, 2008).

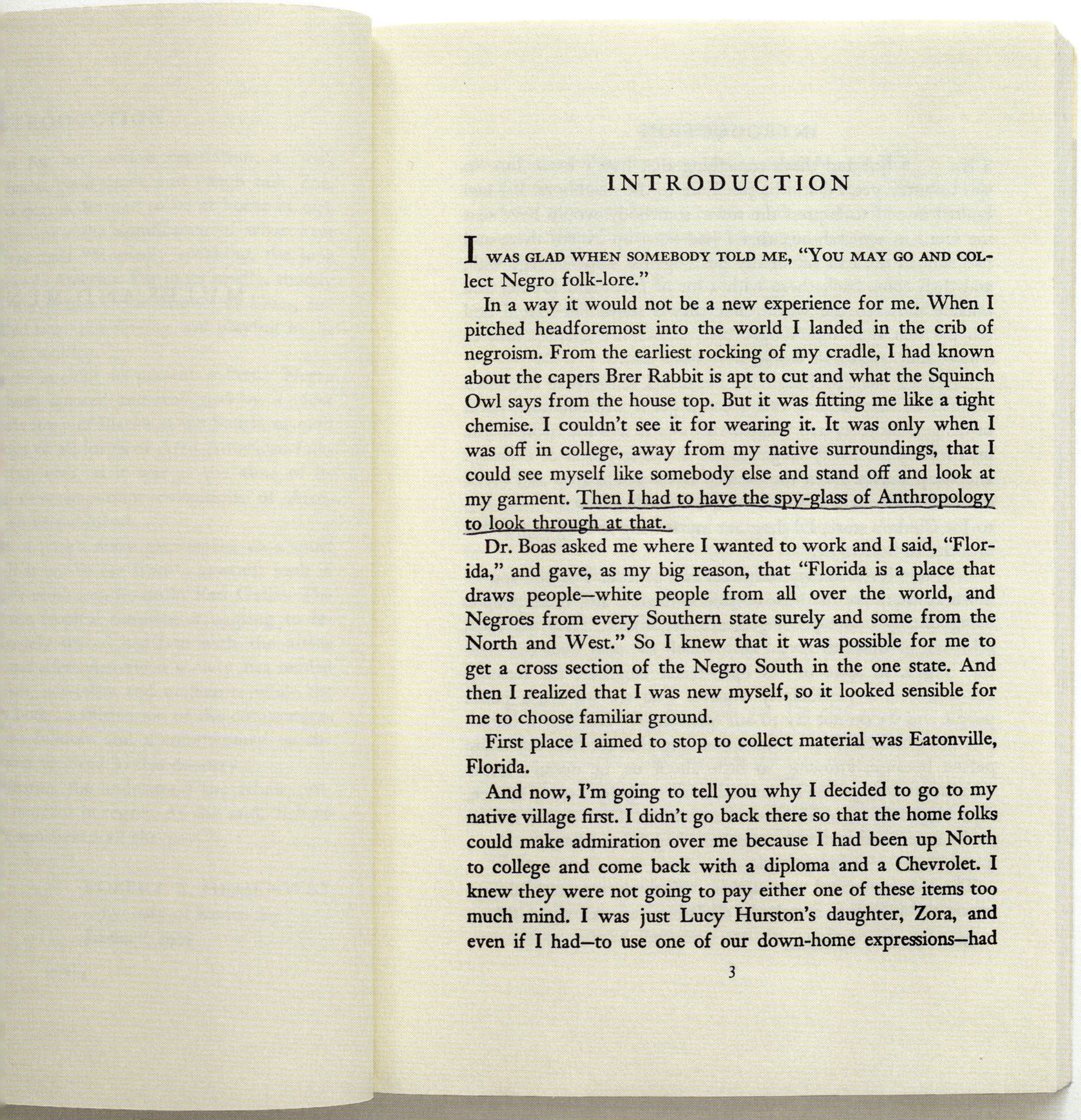

INTRODUCTION

I WAS GLAD WHEN SOMEBODY TOLD ME, "YOU MAY GO AND COLlect Negro folk-lore."

In a way it would not be a new experience for me. When I pitched headforemost into the world I landed in the crib of negroism. From the earliest rocking of my cradle, I had known about the capers Brer Rabbit is apt to cut and what the Squinch Owl says from the house top. But it was fitting me like a tight chemise. I couldn't see it for wearing it. It was only when I was off in college, away from my native surroundings, that I could see myself like somebody else and stand off and look at my garment. Then I had to have the spy-glass of Anthropology to look through at that.

Dr. Boas asked me where I wanted to work and I said, "Florida," and gave, as my big reason, that "Florida is a place that draws people—white people from all over the world, and Negroes from every Southern state surely and some from the North and West." So I knew that it was possible for me to get a cross section of the Negro South in the one state. And then I realized that I was new myself, so it looked sensible for me to choose familiar ground.

First place I aimed to stop to collect material was Eatonville, Florida.

And now, I'm going to tell you why I decided to go to my native village first. I didn't go back there so that the home folks could make admiration over me because I had been up North to college and come back with a diploma and a Chevrolet. I knew they were not going to pay either one of these items too much mind. I was just Lucy Hurston's daughter, Zora, and even if I had—to use one of our down-home expressions—had

3

Fig. 7 Interior, Zora Neale Hurston, *Mules and Men* (Bloomington, IN: Indiana University Press, 1978; first published 1935), 3.

While a select number of women and minorities were able to participate, from twenty-first-century hindsight, it is important to recognize traditional anthropology's overwhelmingly white, male, Western perspective, its colonialist tendency to classify race and rank humanity based on difference, and the lack of agency by the subjects themselves (also part of the colonialist impulse). In response, a later generation of anthropologists, circa the mid-twentieth century, began to turn camera and notes over to their subjects in a noble effort to update these methodologies and to cede control and gaze. The Malinowskian mise-en-scène was expanded in the mid-twentieth century by Clifford James Geertz, who popularized his predecessor's fieldwork mentality of "being there" and paved the way for incorporating how communities saw themselves, rather than simply presenting the anthropologist's perspective. While generative and essential to the progression of the field, this resulted in a different set of problems relating to the bias one may impart to project a desired image of oneself, a performative self-construction (perhaps a distant cousin to today's heavily scripted reality television stars, à la the Kardashians). Postmodern anthropology, or at least anthropology since the 1960s—paralleling the field of contemporary art—consists of an assemblage of techniques and modalities: collaborative research, multiple pedagogies, global diasporas, self-reflection, and differing ideologies. As an academic discipline, today anthropology's Sisyphean endeavor aims for the closest version of cultural "truth," with an awareness that an unbiased or factual projection is an impossibility and will always be beholden to the changing nature of time, culture, geography, and individuals. Where anthropologists have sought to increasingly engage their subjects and get off the proverbial sofa, art has had a related but divergent trajectory. Prior to postmodernism, so-called armchair art historians and traditional curatorship based on specialization within particular media were predominant. Since 1960, postmodern practices in contemporary art have overturned this definition, as many artists have moved away from the role of the hand in lieu of being directors, collaborators, instigators, or agents of concept or change—negating the importance of fabricating the works themselves or producing an object at all, as long as the idea is present. Likewise, curatorial practice has become a multi-platform assemblage of possibilities, some embracing the anthropological nose-and-ears-to-the-ground methodology, whereby ideas, themes, and artists are observed and collected through studied fieldwork of global exhibitions, studio visits, and geographic and cultural sensitivity to place.

My own curatorial methodology is a product of this anthropological turn. In each of the cities I've lived in during my curatorial career these past fifteen years, my process for developing ideas has been inspired by anthropological fieldwork: studio visits, research, observation, and notes based on my experience in that particular place. As a curatorial fellow at the Museum of Contemporary Art Chicago in 2005, having been given the opportunity to curate a small local exhibition at the museum (part of the *12x12* series of exhibitions of Chicago-based artists) and sensing an opportunity to embed in the community, I embarked on studio visits each weekend.[31] This resulted in more than sixty such visits in six months and several exhibitions at the museum for a number of the artists following these visits, including after my fellowship concluded. During my three-year position in Pittsburgh as part of the 2008 *Carnegie International* curatorial team at the Carnegie Museum of Art, I continued to engage community and fieldwork for exhibitions outside the museum. Through a friendship with John Fetterman, then the mayor of Braddock—a blighted, postindustrial steel town on the outskirts of Pittsburgh—I organized a large-scale local art exhibition in an old, empty schoolhouse across from Braddock's last remaining operating steel mill, inaugurating what is now an alternative arts space.[32] A year later, I organized a local group exhibition at the Mattress Factory, Pittsburgh's installation art museum founded by the late Barbara Luderowski, an uncommon partnership between a large institution (Carnegie) and its grassroots neighbor.[33] For my next position as Curator of the Albright-Knox Art Gallery in Buffalo, New York, inspired by the discovery that the now-late minimalist musician and video artist Tony Conrad was living and working in the city, I embarked on a four-year journey into the Buffalo arts community, including over fifty recorded interviews with individuals who were there in the 1970s, such as Conrad, Charles Clough, Nancy Dwyer, Robert Longo, Gerald O'Grady, Cindy Sherman, and Steina and Woody Vasulka, among many others. This foray resulted in *Wish You Were Here: The Buffalo Avant-garde in the 1970s*, an exhibition highlighting the dynamic experimental arts scene forged by Hallwalls Contemporary Arts Center, Artpark, the University at Buffalo (departments of Media Study, Music, and Poetry), CEPA (Center for Exploratory and Perceptual Art) Gallery, and the Albright-Knox Art Gallery during that time.[34] And here in Austin, influenced not only by the global art world's turn to performative and immersive art en masse but by the experimental nature of the city of Austin's vibrant film, video, and festival scene, I developed the immersive, experiential exhibition *Strange Pilgrims* in 2015.[35]

31. This was the Marjorie Susman Curatorial Fellowship, Museum of Contemporary Art Chicago.

32. *Out of This Furnace*, exhibition and event organized by Heather Pesanti, a collaboration with the Mayor's Office of Braddock and Carnegie Museum of Art for *Life on Mars*, the 2008 Carnegie International, held at Unsmoke Systems, Braddock, PA, July 19, 2008, http://ci08.cmoa.org/CI08/outofthisfurnace/images/out_of_this_furnace_flyer.pdf.

33. *Gestures 10: Illustrations of Catastrophe and Remote Times*, exhibition organized by Heather Pesanti, held at the Mattress Factory, Pittsburgh, PA, January 18 – June 15, 2008, https://www.mattress.org/archive/index.php/detail/occurrences/223.

34. See Heather Pesanti, *Wish You Were Here: The Buffalo Avant-garde in the 1970s* (Buffalo, NY: Albright-Knox Art Gallery, 2012). Exhibition catalogue.

35. See Heather Pesanti, *Strange Pilgrims* (Austin: The University of Texas Press and The Contemporary Austin, 2015). Exhibition catalogue.

To varying degrees, these curatorial premises came from my observation of and in situ research into a particular geographical site and interviews with members of a particular community. This idea that a place and its inhabitants can articulate important themes and concepts has roots in the tenets of ethnographic fieldwork.

The work of artist **Cameron Jamie** (born 1969 in Los Angeles, California; lives and works in Paris) occupies the territory of loose ethnographic fieldwork within a contemporary art framework, as Jamie explores the punk underbelly of ritual and myth in Western popular and vernacular culture firsthand through films, photographs, sculpture, and performance. Often using amateur, handheld footage techniques and grainy Super 8 and 35 mm film, Jamie's process brings performative action and rites of passage in subcultural communities—what Gilles Deleuze and Félix Guattari termed (later appropriated by the artist Mike Kelley) "minor" histories—to the forefront of his subject matter, including suburban backyard wrestling in Southern California and ritualized dancing involving dry-humping furniture.[36] Jamie's dark, messy explorations centered on hidden rites of passage, as well as his interest in and inroads into punk and noise music, root him in the Los Angeles era of 1990s *Helter Skelter* artists, apropos of Kelley, Paul McCarthy, Liz Larner, Raymond Pettibon, and others.[37] But while Jamie doesn't claim to be an ethnographer (although Ralph Rugoff labeled him a "backyard anthropologist," a moniker that stuck for some time), his films demonstrate an artist who approaches his subjects with empathy and a sincere gesture toward uncovering both the substance and spirit of these happenings.[38] In illuminating rituals that are both menacing and unfamiliar, Jamie employs a revisionist historical gaze, one focused on the antisocial edges, serving as foil to the ubiquitous streamlined violence of Hollywood movies, video games, and war culture. And the fact that Jamie is taking his camera into the midst of these rituals, with consent from the enactors, begs the question of how much his presence has influenced these rituals: are they performing for him, more or less violent or dramatic? The amateur lens is a postmodern artistic tool, but never an objective one, both providing a counterpoint to the professionalism of traditional academic art history and training and serving as a distancing mechanism from academic anthropology.

36. Gilles Deleuze and Félix Guattari, *Kafka: Toward a Minor Literature*, trans. Dana Polan (Minneapolis: University of Minnesota Press, 1986); first published as *Kafka: pour une littérature mineure* (Paris: Les éditions de Minuit, 1975). See also Mike Kelley, *Minor Histories: Statements, Conversations, Proposals*, ed. John C. Welchman (Cambridge, MA: The MIT Press, 2004).

37. See *Helter Skelter: L.A. Art in the 1990s*, ed. Catherine Gudis (Los Angeles: The Museum of Contemporary Art, Los Angeles, 1992). Published in conjunction with an exhibition of the same title, organized by Paul Schimmel and presented at MOCA Los Angeles, January 26 – April 26, 1992.

38. Ralph Rugoff, "Backyard Anthropology," in *Cameron Jamie*, ed. Günther Holler-Schuster (Ostfildern-Ruit, Germany: Hatje Cantz Verlag, 2006). As an anecdotal aside, while in high school Jamie regularly went dumpster diving with an older friend from the area, Matt Groening, who later went on to *The Simpsons* fame. See also Craig Hubert, "When Ritual Performances Slip Dangerously into the Real," *Hyperallergic*, May 19, 2017, https://hyperallergic.com/380357/when-ritual-performances-slip-dangerously-into-the-real.

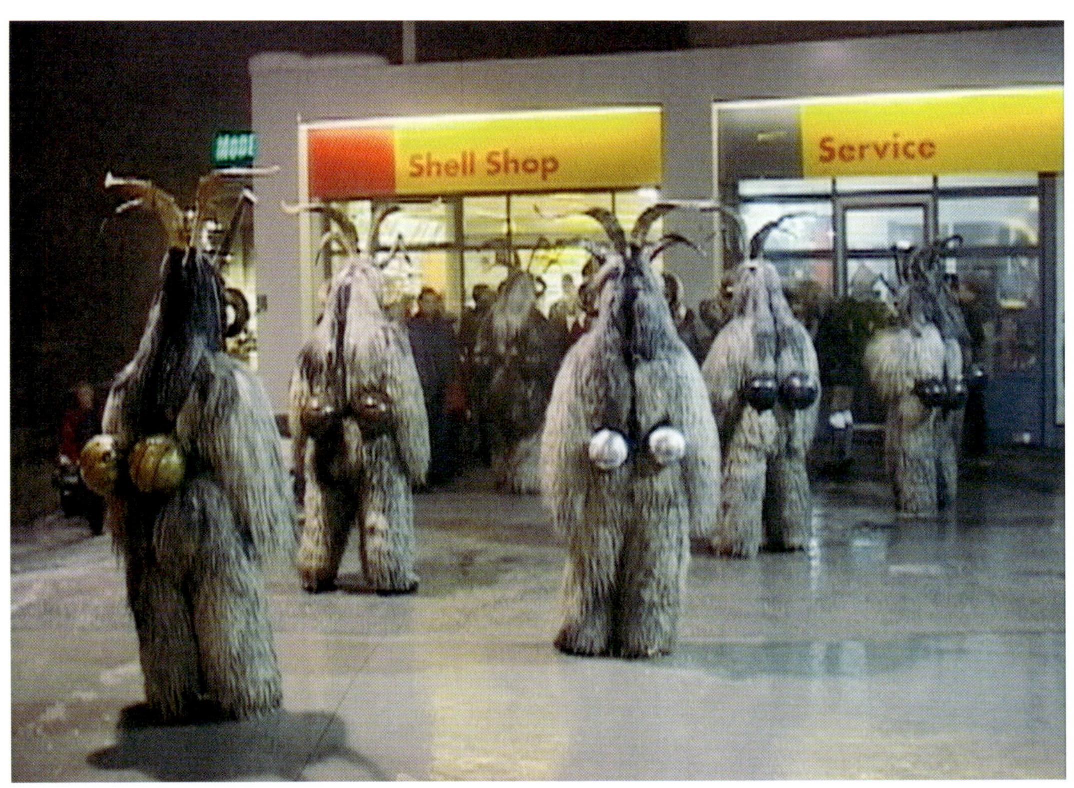

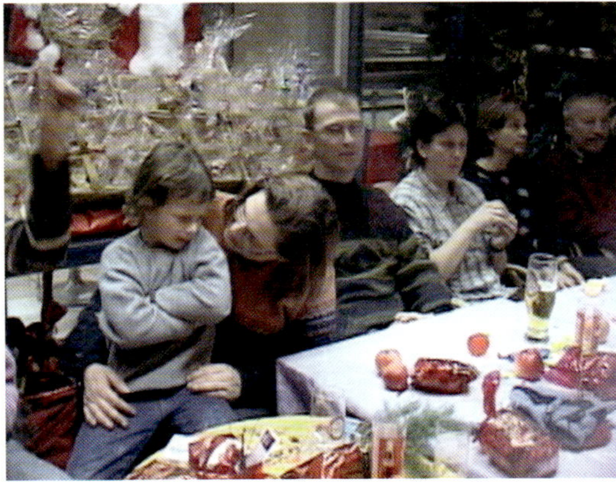

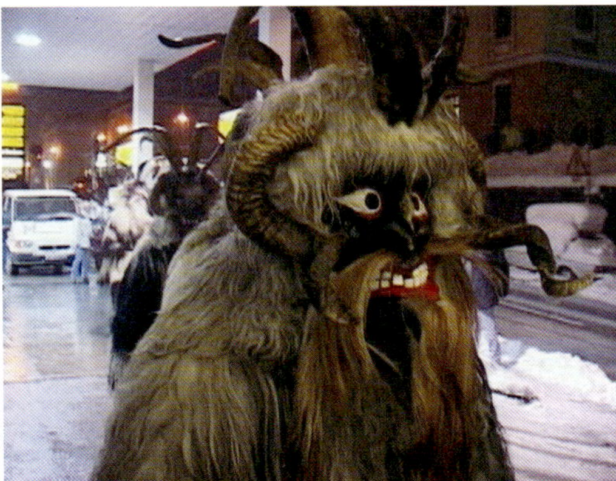

Fig. 8 Cameron Jamie, *Kranky Klaus* (stills), 2002–2003. Single-channel video. Soundtrack by the Melvins. Running time: 25:00.

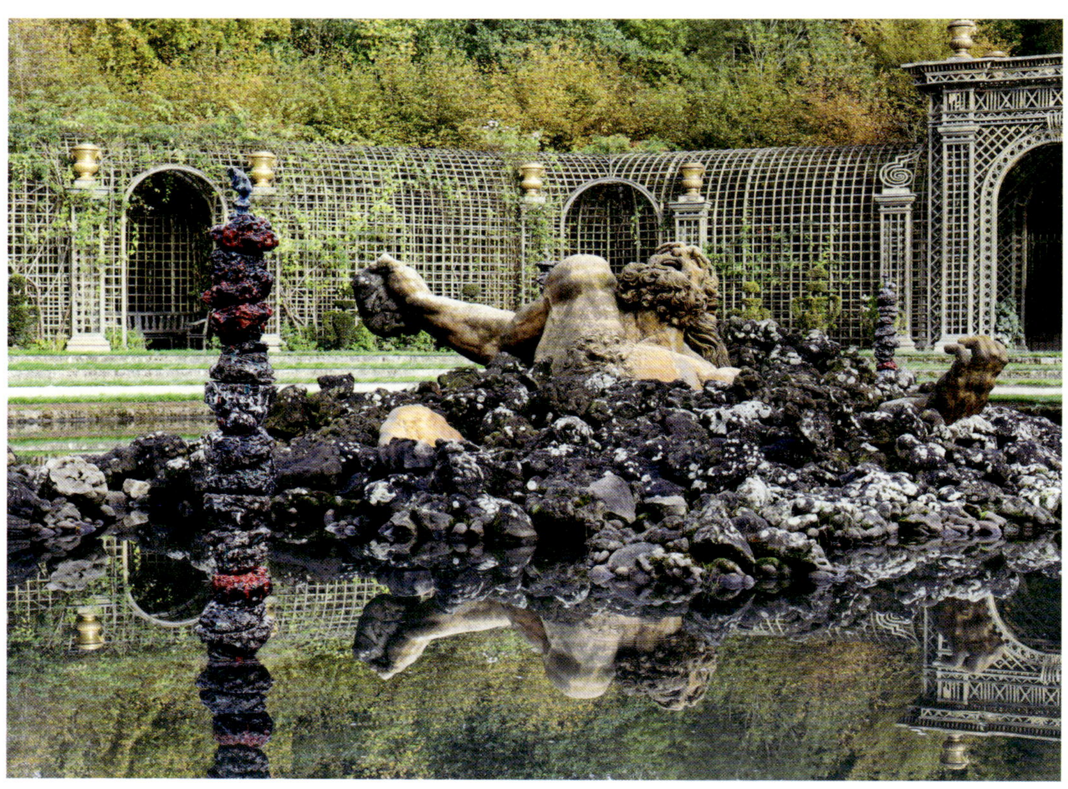

Fig. 9 Cameron Jamie, *Spine Station*, 2010. Nine sculptures: varnished stoneware and steel. Dimensions variable. Installation view, *Voyage d'Hiver*, in collaboration with the Palais de Tokyo, Jardins du Château de Versailles, France, 2017.

As proletarian ethnographer he joins artists such as Phil Collins, Jeremy Deller, and Cao Fei, among others, in sourcing real-world encounters sans anthropological credentials for subject matter. Perhaps free from the yokes of institutional framework, genre, or proscription, amateur artistic propositions can also, to paraphrase Edward Said, be the gateway to untethered avant-garde or radical discourse.[39]

Over the course of a decade, Jamie filmed and produced a series of documentaries recording various rituals and folklore of European and American subculture.[40] While his out-of-the-box thinking and somewhat fearless belief in his ability to embed have propelled him successfully into these subcultures, he is an outsider, not a participant or card-carrying member of these societies. His best-known film, *Kranky Klaus*, 2002–2003, follows the Krampus ritual in Austria, featuring men costumed as horned, furry beasts with wooden masks—Krampus demons—who run around terrorizing members of the local community during the Christmas season (see fig. 8). While the public seem both amused and resigned to the long-standing ritual, Jamie captures genuine moments of anxiety and fear in adults and children at the hands of the performative violence of the costumed Krampus beasts. The viewer also experiences misgivings at times while witnessing the scenes as the Krampus chase, knock over, wrestle, or even faux strangle onlookers, throw and break furniture, and bring children to tears. At their core, Jamie's films highlight this potent mix of violence, empathy, and shrewd humor, as seen when a Krampus approaches a crying teenage girl and says, "What's going on? You wanted to run away, and now here we are . . . There is no need to be afraid. You must behave yourself. It's OK to be a little bad, just like me."[41] Although dialogue, as here, is infrequent, sound is essential to Jamie's films. In *Kranky Klaus*, large sleigh bells worn by the Krampus around their waists compound the agitation, generating a cacophony of sound while the costumed figures wreak havoc. Along with these ambient components, the film is also scored with a jarring, mesmerizing soundtrack by the Melvins, a "sludge" or punk metal band formed in the 1980s.[42] Seen together, Jamie's films ask, what is the role of the artist/ethnographer when documenting questionable, unpredictable, or violent situations? Clearly the artist has forged trust with the communities he documents, evidenced by the fact that he is allowed to follow and witness their secretive activities and produce his immersive films. As further testament to his ability to embed, for *Kranky Klaus* Jamie had no advance preparation or outreach to this particular group; by his recollection, he met the group on the street and in

39. See, for example, Edward Said, *Representations of the Intellectual: The 1993 Reith Lectures* (New York: Random House, 1994).

40. The trilogy included *BB* (2000), *Kranky Klaus* (2002–2003), and *Spook House* (2003).

41. Excerpt from *Kranky Klaus*, 2002–2003. Dialogue is spoken in German, with English subtitles.

42. Jamie frequently uses metal, punk, and noise music bands to score his films, including the Melvins, Keiji Haino, and Sonic Youth.

the moment the revelers allowed him into their innermost circle.[43] In the spirit of Alfred Gell's warning about the freedom art maintains over ethnography, a subdued adoration comes through the lens, in the enjoyment and affection the camera seems to impart to its subjects.[44]

In the past several years, Jamie has made fewer films and more objects, in particular bulbous ceramics whose vertically inclined twisting forms and muddied rainbow of colors render them both beautifully grotesque and abstractly figurative. These forms suggest the process of fieldwork within landscape itself: an abstraction of the artist's experience of site. In October 2017, I traveled to Paris to see Jamie's work as part of the exhibition *Voyage d'hiver* (Winter's Journey) at the Château de Versailles, created in partnership with the Palais de Tokyo and marking the ten-year celebration of contemporary art presentations at Versailles.[45] The exhibition consisted of newly commissioned sculptures by seventeen artists placed throughout the garden of the palace. At sunset, I took the map to make the pilgrimage from one sculpture to another, navigating the labyrinthine gardens in the gathering dusk. Jamie's work, *Spine Station*, 2010, consisted of strange, serpentine ceramic totems in mottled blue, black, and red, emerging from the water in one of the palatial seventeenth-century fountains, this one featuring the baroque, half-submerged figure of Enceladus, the giant who challenged Jupiter (see fig. 9).[46] With its anti-monumental strangeness, eerie talismans bulging out of the water in an otherwise romanticized setting, Jamie's installation effectively disturbed certain narratives imparted by these mythical, imperialist gardens. The artist's work for *The Sorcerer's Burden*, *Mon Singe*, 2019—translated as My Monkey—offers a simian riff in this lineage: a bulbous, textured, semiabstract figure made from chunks of clay, pressed and molded by the artist's hand, and cast in bronze (see fig. 10).

43. Cameron Jamie, in conversation with author during Austin site visit, November 4, 2018.

44. Christopher Wright, "In the Thick of It: Notes on Observation and Context," in *Between Art and Anthropology*, 67–74.

45. This trip was funded in part through a grant from the Cultural Services of the French Embassy in Houston, Texas.

46. *Voyage d'hiver*, exhibition organized by Jean de Loisy, Rebecca Lamarche-Vadel, Yoann Gourmel, and Alfred Pacquement with the Palais de Tokyo, held at the Château de Versailles, Paris, October 22, 2017 – January 7, 2018.

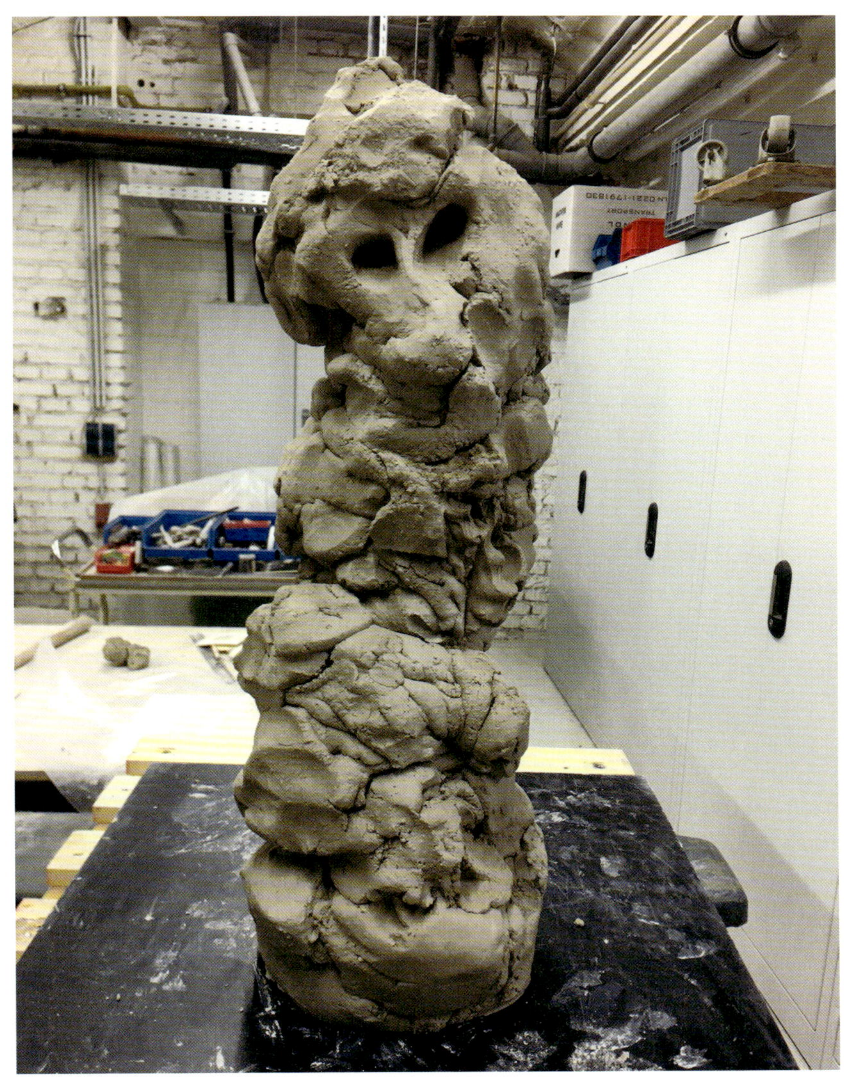

Fig. 10 *Mon Singe* clay figure in Cameron Jamie's art studio, Cologne, Germany, 2018.

"PRIMITIVISM"

As contemporary artistic practice engaged with fieldwork as well as ethnographic methods and subject matter, twentieth-century written art historical critique likewise began to address and interpret the burgeoning overlap. Seen from another angle, the writing culture may even have propelled the makers. Discussing the broader implications of this trend from an ethnographic standpoint, anthropologist George E. Marcus points to the rise of "Writing Culture critiques of the 1980s," in which, generally speaking, these examples from the art historical side are part of an interdisciplinary literary trend that engendered cross-pollination of writing, observation, research, and intellectual critique across the humanities.[47] By exposing the limitations of fieldwork, the anthropological field rendered it non-hermetic, opening the discipline to porousness, influence, and reciprocity across fields, including art and art history. An early example from Conceptual artist Joseph Kosuth, in 1975, noted that the "artist is a model of the anthropologist *engaged*," emphasizing the idea of activity and action and an anthropologized art in which the artist operates within an immersive sociocultural context with a responsibility for social impact.[48] At the same time, Kosuth accurately observed the challenges of being a "card-carrying member" of a society and objectively critiquing it.

By the 1990s, *October* magazine co-editor and theorist Hal Foster's essay "The Artist as Ethnographer?," a text on the anthropological turn in contemporary art, cornered the field as an important but now dated essay critical of these cross-disciplinary inroads, arguing that for centuries, artists' primary concerns and points of resistance revolved around class and capitalism; postmodernism shifted this interest into a tension around exoticism and colonialism, as well as a lean toward the interdisciplinary.[49] Foster saw little benefit in the overlap between art and anthropology, dubious of artistic endeavors he labeled as "*primitivist fantasy*."[50] Speaking to this shift, he wrote that "the site of artistic transformation is the site of political transformation, and, more . . . this site is always located *elsewhere*, in the field of the other: in the productivist model, with the social other, the exploited proletariat; in the quasi-anthropological model, with the cultural other, the oppressed postcolonial, subaltern, or subcultural."[51] The derogatory

47. George E. Marcus, "Affinities: Fieldwork in Anthropology Today and the Ethnographic in Artwork," in *Between Art and Anthropology*, 83.

48. Joseph Kosuth, "The Artist as Anthropologist," in *Art After Philosophy and After: Collected Writings 1966–1990*, ed. Gabriele Guercio (Cambridge, MA: The MIT Press, 1991); repr., *The Everyday: Documents of Contemporary Art*, ed. Stephen Johnstone (Cambridge, MA: The MIT Press, 2008), 182.

49. Foster, "The Artist as Ethnographer?," in *The Traffic in Culture*.

50. Ibid, 303. Emphasis in original.

51. Ibid, 302.

and self-serving implications were highlighted, and became a catchphrase. Foster suggests, and for some it is true, that by aligning themselves with the accoutrements of anthropology, an academic field associated with science, fact gathering, and firsthand observation, artists might in theory assume the mantle of a higher artistic calling that grants greater meaning or truth to their work, particularly within a social or political context. What the author doesn't account for are the artists recognizing the biases and challenges of fact-based fieldwork in individualized ethnographic endeavors and utilizing these contradictions to their creative advantage. Likewise, as globalism has increasingly democratized the art world and the Internet has fostered connectivity without travel, the idea that any culture is truly *other* is less and less viable. More recently, artist and critic Lucy R. Lippard has offered arguments to this end, amid tempered skepticism, in her essay "Farther Afield," inspired by her collection of writings from the late 1970s and early 1980s in *Overlay* exploring the intersection of art and prehistory, à la Land art. Lippard notes that artists "who adopt a surface critique of anthropology, composted with post-colonial verbiage, can get away with murder, sometimes for better, sometimes for worse. I attribute this to the fact that art is generally perceived as either above it all—out in the ether beyond the comprehension of ordinary people, or below it all—useless and frivolous. Anything goes."[52]

In modern and contemporary art, the ethnographic turn has equally been driven by the appropriation of the "other," based on observing, analyzing, and critiquing different cultures from the outside, an increasingly central preoccupation of artists since the turn of the twentieth century.[53] Art historians seem to agree that the road to "primitivism" in Western modernism was paved in the late 1880s and 1890s by Paul Gauguin, who left Europe to focus his life's work around the women of Tahiti.[54] Gauguin's paintings are not only inventive but gorgeous, demonstrating a radically experimental use of color and form for his time. Yet his lifestyle, like that of so many artists throughout history, leaves much to be desired: it's difficult to ignore in today's climate the terrible reality of his "noble savage" fetishizing of young Tahitian women in a French colony, sometimes prepubescent, three of whom he ultimately married and infected with syphilis. During Gauguin's time, the term *primitive* could connote any number of non-Western objects, including those from Egypt, Mesopotamia, or India. But as curator and scholar William Rubin (then head of the Painting and Sculpture Department at The Museum of Modern Art) wrote in 1984, it was circa the years 1905 to 1907 that a core group of artists, including André Derain, Henri

52. Lippard, "Farther Afield," in *Between Art and Anthropology*, 24.

53. Likewise, anthropologists, for decades resistant to the imaginative source of art methods as poisoning the factual intent of their field, have increasingly explored alternative or avant-garde methods in contemporary times.

54. See, for example, Kirk Varnedoe, "Gauguin," in *"Primitivism" in 20th Century Art: Affinity of the Tribal and the Modern*, ed. William Rubin (New York: The Museum of Modern Art, 1984). Exhibition catalogue.

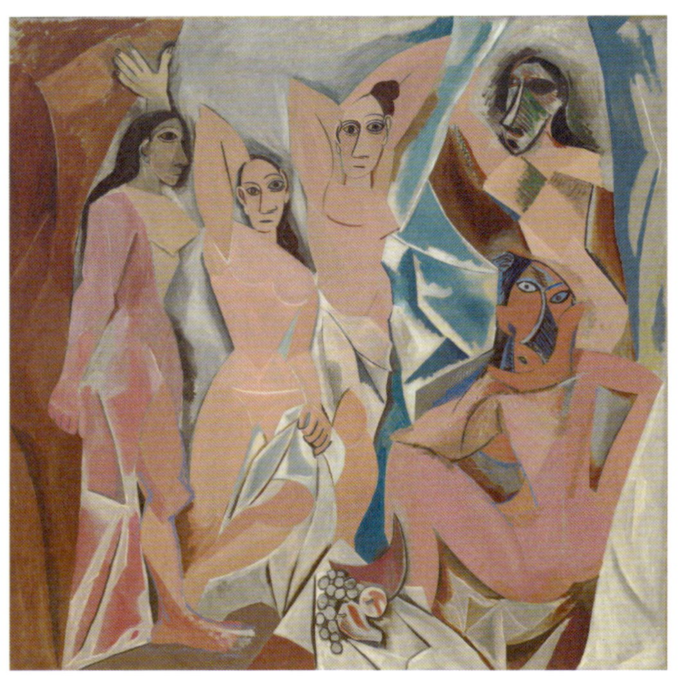

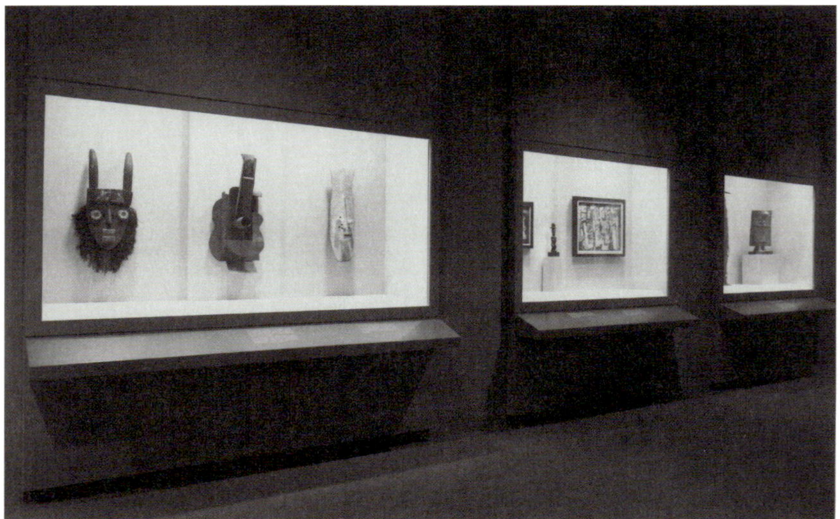

Fig. 11 Pablo Picasso, *Les Demoiselles d'Avignon*, June – July 1907, Paris. Oil on canvas, 8 feet x 7 feet 8 inches. Collection of The Museum of Modern Art, New York: Acquired through the Lillie P. Bliss Bequest.

Fig. 12 Installation view, *"Primitivism" in 20th Century Art: Affinity of the Tribal and the Modern*, The Museum of Modern Art, New York, 1984. *Far left*: Described in the exhibition catalogue as Grebo Mask, Côte d'Ivoire or Liberia, from the collection of Pablo Picasso, next to a work by Picasso titled *Guitar*, 1912.

Matisse, Pablo Picasso, and Maurice de Vlaminck, turned to African and Oceanic masks and reliquaries for subject matter. In the wake of the public exhibition of such objects via the Wunderkammer and the resulting ability to see private collections in public spheres, these artists co-opted the term *primitive* specifically to describe the hybridization of art, artifacts, and iconography with modern painting and sculpture.[55] Picasso's *Les Demoiselles d'Avignon*, 1907, was directly inspired by his visit earlier that year to the Musée d'Ethnographie du Trocadéro in Paris; the fractured, flattened, masklike faces of the five naked women, influenced by Iberian and African culture, were a radical departure in style and composition from previous European examples of painting (see fig. 11). Likewise, the field of anthropology underwent shifts in its analysis of visual representation; in his 1927 essay "Primitive Art," pioneering anthropologist Franz Boas wrote (referencing Nass River Indian artifacts): "We have thus recognized that the representations of animals . . . must not be considered as perspective views, but as representing complete animals more or less distorted and split."[56] This formal and compositional mandate emerges in Picasso's radical new painting style. Picasso's contemporary Derain likewise spent a period drawing and painting ethnographic sculptures, ultimately incorporating their influences into his Fauvist style. In addition to painting, hybrid works such as Picasso's *Guitar*, 1912—a wall-hanging construction made of cardboard and wire, later remade in sheet metal—marked a departure from the isolated categories of painting or sculpture, clearly referencing specific Grebo masks (see fig. 12).[57] This trend spurred European Surrealist interests in the subversive other, which heightened from the 1920s through the 1950s, influencing global trends in art as ethnographic notions of ritual, spirit possessions, and modes of representation took shape within artistic genres.

Such developments were influential for their considerations of form and composition, and pioneered the road to abstraction. The historic exhibition *"Primitivism" in 20th Century Art: Affinity of the Tribal and the Modern*, organized by William Rubin in collaboration with Kirk Varnedoe at The Museum of Modern Art in 1984, represented a shift, identifying the primitivist turn in modernism via Derain, Gauguin, Picasso, et al. by exhibiting approximately 150 modernist paintings and sculptures alongside some 200 "tribal" objects from Africa, Oceania, and North America that were either directly referenced in or shared affinities with the modern works. Also exhibited were masks and reliquaries from the personal collections of these artists, demonstrating their firsthand

55. William Rubin, "Modernist Primitivism: An Introduction," in *"Primitivism" in 20th Century Art: Affinity of the Tribal and the Modern*.

56. Franz Boas, "Primitive Art," in *The Anthropology of Art*, eds. Howard Morphy and Morgan Perkins (Oxford, UK: Blackwell Publishing, 2006), 44; originally published in 1927.

57. Arnd Schneider, "Appropriations," in *Contemporary Art and Anthropology*, 29.

interest in and engagement with the works.[58] The central figure of the exhibition was Picasso, not only through his artworks but also through his private collection and references to objects he would have seen at the Trocadéro when painting *Les Demoiselles d'Avignon*.

In response, criticism of the primitivist mode, and the MoMA exhibition, suggested that artists like Picasso were naively taken with the magic and exoticism of the other, appropriating these forms for their own use and heedless of obligations to native cultures. *"Primitivism"* curator Rubin's argument regarding the "magic" of these objects, an apt topic for *The Sorcerer's Burden*, proposed in part a nostalgic and potentially dangerous concept for the way in which these objects held sway over the artists.[59] The art critic Hilton Kramer, in a review of the exhibition that same year, pointed out that Picasso once said to his cohort André Malraux that the works he saw at the Trocadéro consisted of "magical objects . . . intercessors . . . against everything—against unknown, threatening spirits . . . . They were weapons—to keep people from being ruled by spirits, to help free themselves."[60] The idea that "primitive" cultures would hold "magical" sway over the viewer was intended as a genuine attempt at understanding the power of these unfamiliar objects; however, this line of thinking maintained the subtext of colonialization of the exotic, strange, and dangerously witchy other. While important in its premise and lauded by some, the exhibition received critical lashings that stuck. In particular, Thomas McEvilley's influential 1984 article "Doctor Lawyer Indian Chief" argued that the exhibition promoted Western egoism around "souvenirism" and colonialism.[61] In particular, by not including any labels or information about the non-Western works, namely artists, dates, or motifs, the curators and museum reinforced a problematic and superficial reading of primitivist art, led by the widespread misappropriation and misinterpretation of these objects.

The question remains as to whether or not such gestures and styles breach ethical concerns, as artists were not claiming to take on the cultural or ethical responsibility of anthropologists, nor were their agendas or intentions remotely the same. One can attest to the fact that, then and often the case now, there was little exchange (in the form of payment, dialogue, or feedback) from the artists toward the cultures from whence the

58. The Museum of Modern Art, "New Exhibition Opening September 27 at Museum of Modern Art Examines 'Primitivism' in 20th Century Art," news release no. 17, August 1984, https://www.moma.org/documents/moma_press-release_327377.pdf.

59. Ibid.

60. Hilton Kramer, "The 'Primitivism' Conundrum," *The New Criterion* 3, no. 4 (December 1984), https://www.newcriterion.com/issues/1984/12/the-primitivism-conundrum.

61. Thomas McEvilley, "Doctor Lawyer Indian Chief: '"Primitivism" in 20th Century Art' at The Museum of Modern Art in 1984," *Artforum* 23, no. 3 (November 1984): 54–61.

objects or imagery came. For the most part, these artistic movements decontextualized the African, Oceanic, and Caribbean objects from their origins, a notion that becomes highly complex from an anthropological perspective, as the objects are separated from their native intent, presented in ways insensitive to the originating culture, and thereby misused. But artists and art historians alike could argue that appropriation en masse has been central to the trajectory of twentieth and twenty-first-century art, complicating the issue. At the core of appropriation's premise is the notion that individual authorship is moot, the artist-as-genius model is irrevocably flawed, and no one person has invented an original idea. Nonetheless, even today, the art world is not without its challenges around art appropriation: the central argument tends to revolve around whether or not using another's existing artistic idea is stealing intellectual property, or artistic interpretation. One need only witness the lawsuit initiated in 2015 against the artist Richard Prince by fellow artist Donald Graham, after Prince used Graham's photograph (as posted on another user's Instagram account) without permission or alteration, to see that ethical complications remain.[62] But with anthropological appropriation, the issues have the potential to touch on deeper anxieties, in that images and objects represent the property and identity of a culture or community rather than an individual. Furthermore, often these things may have been considered sacred, and their appropriation, borrowing, or theft, depending on how one sees it, hits a particularly painful nerve in their decontextualization and removal from their originating source. Many artists take this as their subject matter. Among those included in the 1989 exhibition *Magiciens de la terre* at Centre Pompidou in Paris, the Cuban painter José Bedia, operating as artist, anthropologist, and religious practitioner (Bedia is of Palo Monte faith, an Afro-Cuban religion related to Santería, as well as an empath of Native American spirituality, which he studied in situ in the US, Mexico, and South America), references and critiques the colonialist history from which his mythical figures, altars, and sacramental images come, while transforming them into his own distinctive figurative style.[63] Like many of the Surrealists, such as André Breton, Bedia also collected traditional African art during his extensive travels over many decades throughout Africa, including in Botswana, Kenya, Tanzania, Egypt, South Africa, and Zambia.

Transcultural appropriation between the African diaspora and Western cultures provides fodder for the artist **Theo Eshetu** (born 1958 in London, United Kingdom; lives and works in Berlin). Eshetu's biography—he was born in London to a Dutch mother and

62. Eileen Kinsella, "Outraged Photographer Sues Gagosian Gallery and Richard Prince for Copyright Infringement," *artnet*, January 4, 2016, https://news.artnet.com/market/donald-graham-sues-gagosian-richard-prince-401498.

63. Lucy Steeds et al., *Making Art Global (Part 2): 'Magiciens de la Terre' 1989* (London: Afterall Books, 2013), and Julia P. Herzberg, "Ritual in Performance," in *NeoHooDoo: Art for a Forgotten Faith*, ed. Franklin Sirmans (New Haven, CT: Yale University Press, 2008), 58–59.

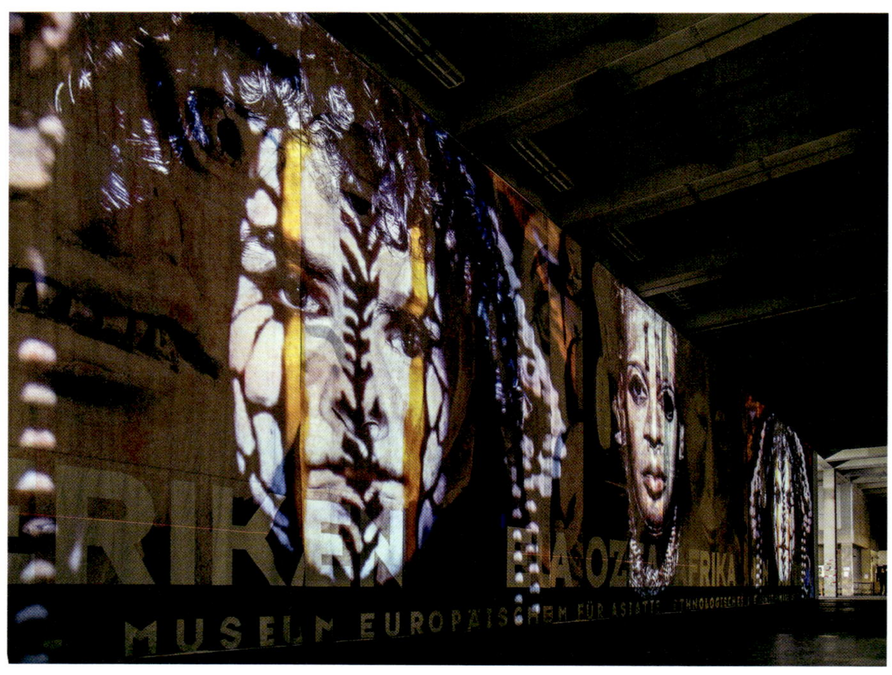

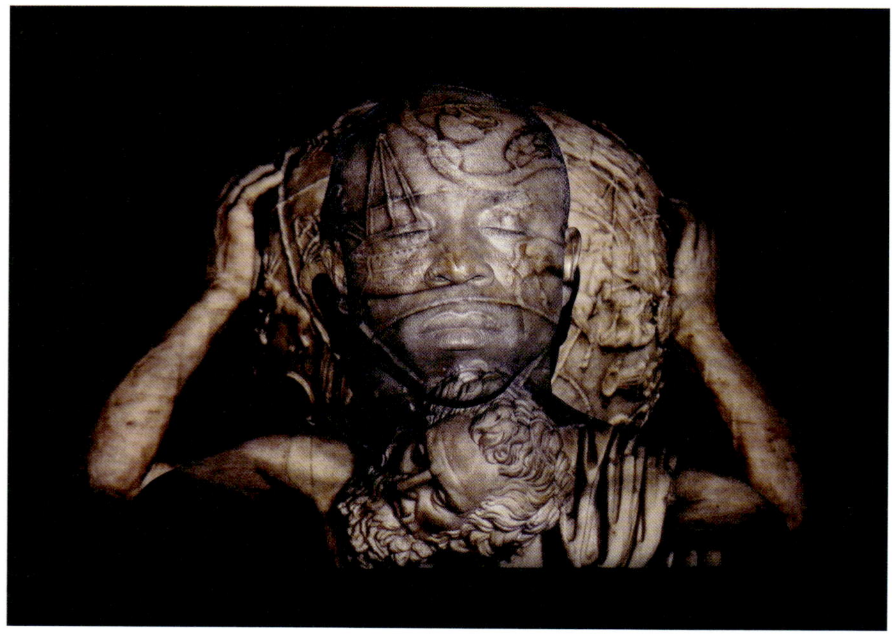

Fig. 13 Theo Eshetu, *Atlas Fractured*, 2017. Digital video projected on banner, color, sound. Running time: 35:00. Installation view, *documenta 14: Learning from Athens*, Neue Neue Galerie, Kassel, Germany, 2017.

Fig. 14 Theo Eshetu, *Atlas Fractured* (still), 2017.

Ethiopian father, raised in Addis Ababa, Dakar, and Belgrade, and has since resided in Rome, Istanbul, and now Berlin—might lend itself to an anthropological distance toward the critical observation of systems of cultural difference. Eshetu's films and multimedia installations generate cultural mash-ups that question the meaning of myths, religions, and rituals across various cultures and geographies, illuminating the complex webs that tie them together. While he is also a documentary filmmaker, several of Eshetu's best-known works reference ethnographic histories with contemporary elements, parlaying them into hybrid historical fictions. For *documenta 14*, in 2017, the artist presented a spectacular, large-scale video installation, *Atlas Fractured*, 2017, projected onto a wall at the entrance to the Neue Neue Galerie, Kassel, Germany (see figs. 13 & 14). The origins of the work trace back to spring 2014, when Eshetu was filming footage for his new video installation at the Ethnologisches Museum in Berlin (whose collections are scheduled to be transferred to a new home in the controversial Berlin Palace, or Stadtschloss, upon completion of its reconstruction by 2020).[64] As Eshetu filmed, he witnessed workers cutting and removing the large banner that decorated the front facade of the museum, consisting of five masks representing five regions, below which read: Afrika, Amerika, Ozeanien, Asien, and Europa.[65] Without prior agenda, the artist salvaged the pieces imagining that one day he might make use of them. Eshetu was later invited to participate in *documenta 14*, where he proposed to remount the banner and make a video to be projected on it. He then invited friends, models, and actors to his studio and filmed their faces alongside projections of statues and masks to make *Atlas Fractured*, with an immersive audio soundtrack of speeches scored to give the images depth and suggest meaning. The video, which was presented as a stand-alone work in the Athens portion of *documenta 14*, was later adapted for Eshetu's installation in Kassel as a projection onto the pieced-together, original banner of the Ethnologisches Museum.[66] The booming audio component, seemingly emanating from the large visages, imparts a jarring, nonvisual element that renders the work as much a sound piece as a visual one. Cameroonian curator and scholar Bonaventure Soh Bejeng Ndikung, referencing Eshetu's *Atlas Fractured* as visual illustration, writes that this represents "sonic as resistance," where "orality and sound are not only a means of sharing knowledge and archiving memories in or on a moving and vulnerable body: they provide the possibility of embedding that

64. The Berlin Palace was originally demolished in 1950 as a symbol of Germany's imperialist authority; its reconstruction has provoked an outcry around amnesia regarding the Ethnologisches Museum's colonialist history, heightened by its scheduled move to a fraught structure. Theo Eshetu, in conversation with author, December 3, 2018.

65. Monika Szewczyk, "Theo Eshetu," in *documenta 14: Daybook*, eds. Quinn Latimer and Adam Szymczyk (Munich: Prestel, 2017).

66. Theo Eshetu, in email correspondence with author, January 3, 2019.

knowledge and those memories within specific times and spaces."[67] Translated as an illusory, shape-shifting video painting, the slippery nature of these collaged images—their doubled features and blurred edges, alongside the visual confusion between the banner's static mask images and the moving, filmed faces—pokes holes in affirmed cultural history. By replacing perceived colonialist iconography with uncertain, changing images, the work metaphorically questions who decides the facial characteristics, or identity, representative of a particular culture.

Eshetu returns to these complicated threads with his new filmic commission, *Adieu Les Demoiselles*, 2019, premiering as part of *The Sorcerer's Burden* (see fig. 15). Centered around Picasso's *Les Demoiselles d'Avignon*, Eshetu's new work for The Contemporary Austin expands on the philosophy and technique of *Atlas Fractured*—projecting live filmed faces onto static images at a grand scale, but in this case, onto a re-created image of Picasso's iconic painting. For this work, Eshetu filmed several performers in various scenes and poses related to the five figures in *Les Demoiselles*: a group of individuals alternately nude and dressed in clothes in the painting's poses; abstracted silhouettes against backgrounds of color and imagery; a single individual executing all of the poses; close-ups of their faces with nuanced and personalized expressions; and so forth. He also interspersed the film with fragmented shots of works by Picasso and others (such as Matisse and Yves Klein), African sculptures, and other influences to both Eshetu and Picasso. Through this, Eshetu decomposes and then recomposes not only the painting, but Picasso and the "primitivist" intention. The visual anthropology of presenting moving portraits consisting, on one hand, of a famous iconographic image (Picasso's) with, on the other, living representations of specific cultures today (Eshetu's) provides a powerful, real-time transformation of cultural construct through identity and human features. More broadly, the gesture proposes alternatives to existing canonical histories, here of an exalted modernist art forefather, unearthing the fallibility of cultural tropes that are ripe for rewriting. As Eshetu said, with a touch of irony, "Within the story of my African heritage as an artist of the African diaspora, it's great that I can take from Picasso in the way that he has taken from African cultures in a productive way, and continue the conversation. I have after all always felt uncomfortable with the label of contemporary artist, believing that my practice is a continuation of the modernist tradition."[68]

67. Bonaventure Soh Bejeng Ndikung, "For They Shall Be Heard: On Sonic Trajectories and Resistance," *Frieze*, no. 199 (November–December 2018): 122.

68. Theo Eshetu, in conversation with author, December 12, 2018, and in email correspondence, January 11, 2019.

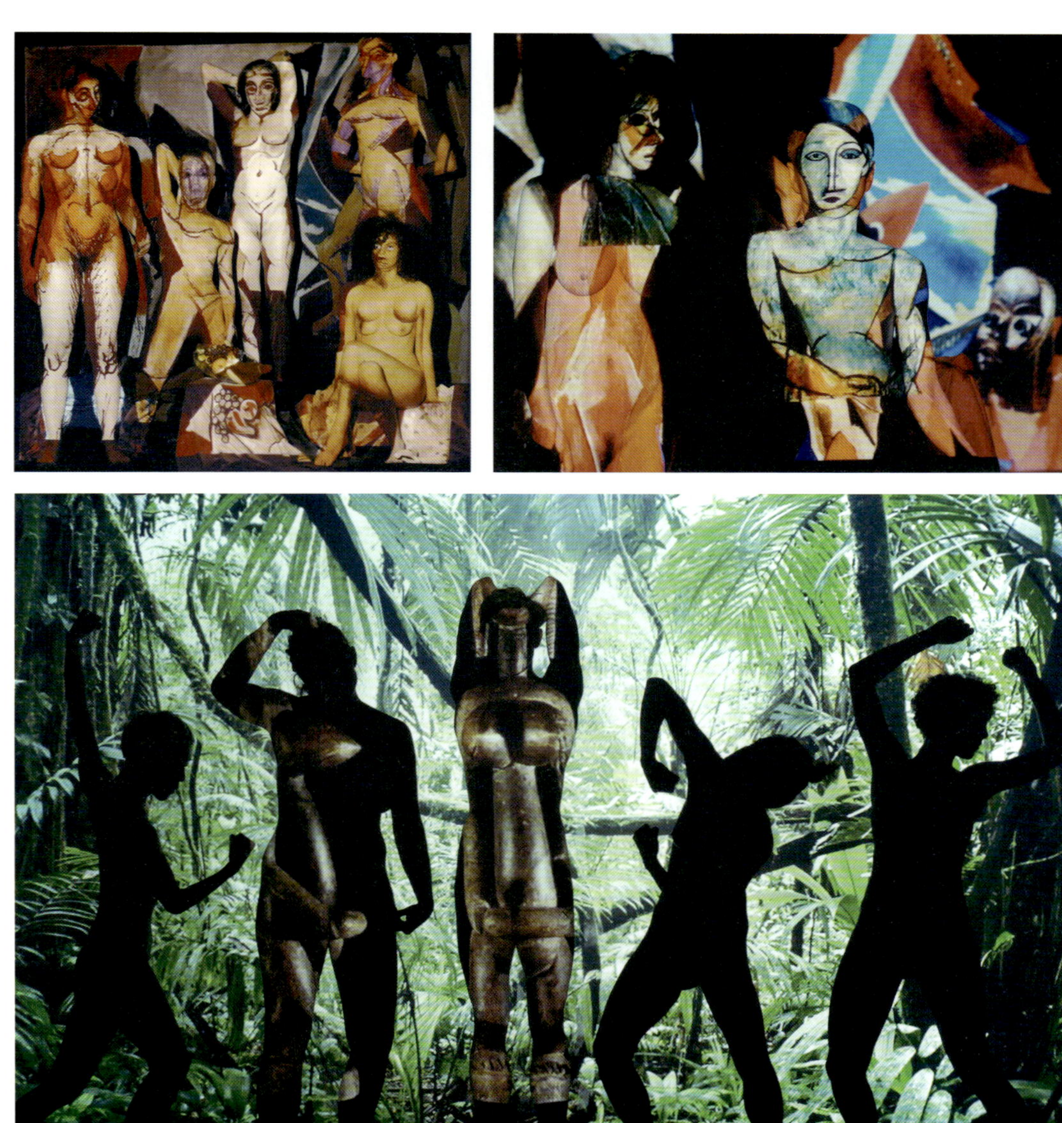

Fig. 15 Theo Eshetu, *Adieu Les Demoiselles* (stills), 2019. Single-channel HD video, color, sound. Running time: 8:45, looped. Commissioned by The Contemporary Austin.

ELSEWHERE

When critic Hal Foster wrote of the anthropological site in contemporary art as an exotic "*elsewhere*, in the field of the other," he astutely identified an emerging ethnographic impulse in contemporary art. Yet overwhelmingly concerned about such art's departure from formal and aesthetic concerns and limiting it to the framework and language of the colonialist impulse from which it came, Foster was unable to observe any significant or productive examples that might result.[69] In 1995, his thinking was also to some degree a reflection of the times: artists and scholars had not yet developed a holistic language around globalization and the resultant trends in the art world, nor a contemporary discourse responding to postcolonial cultural difference. *Elsewhere*, in Foster and others' conception, by definition connotes binary difference: an *us* and *them* mentality. Turning to anthropology, the foundation of ethnographic work is indeed based on the identification of difference, or alterity, across people and cultures, as well as the question of who gets to tell their stories. A few years prior to Foster—similarly responding to Walter Benjamin's theories—the Australian anthropologist Michael Taussig undertook a history of mimesis, or imitation, in relation to alterity, or cultural otherness, in his 1993 text *Mimesis and Alterity: A Particular History of the Senses*.[70] Taussig's anthropological fieldwork focused on South America and the Cuna Indians, and his nontraditional premise highlighted the ties to colonialism and racism inherent in much of Western interpretation of non-Western traditions, art, and practices, using specific examples of objects as seen through the intention of the Indigenous communities from which they came. Two radically different perspectives, Taussig's marked a way forward in the lineage of Franz Boas's cultural relativism (the Boasian theory that suspends judgment toward the difference in other cultures by understanding that they develop equally, and that difference is the result of conditions), utilizing fieldwork from within the communities he was writing about, while Foster's was rooted in the old-guard idea of armchair critique from a distance.

Over the course of the twentieth century in anthropology, the development of fieldwork, or immersing oneself in another culture to study it and then working from within—in the tradition of Boas and his student Hurston, who used the "spyglass of anthropology" to study the rural African American South, in particular northern and central Florida, where she spent her childhood—points to a paradigm shift toward a model not of elsewhere, but of proximity: both in the overlapping of cultures in a global world, as well as ethnography from within.[71] This speaks to a quintessential fieldwork-based conundrum, whereby one is unable, despite best efforts, to work around one's originating sociocultural spectacles. In

69. Foster, "The Artist as Ethnographer?," in *The Traffic in Culture*.

70. Michael Taussig, *Mimesis and Alterity: A Particular History of the Senses* (New York: Routledge, 1993).

71. Hurston, introduction to *Mules and Men*.

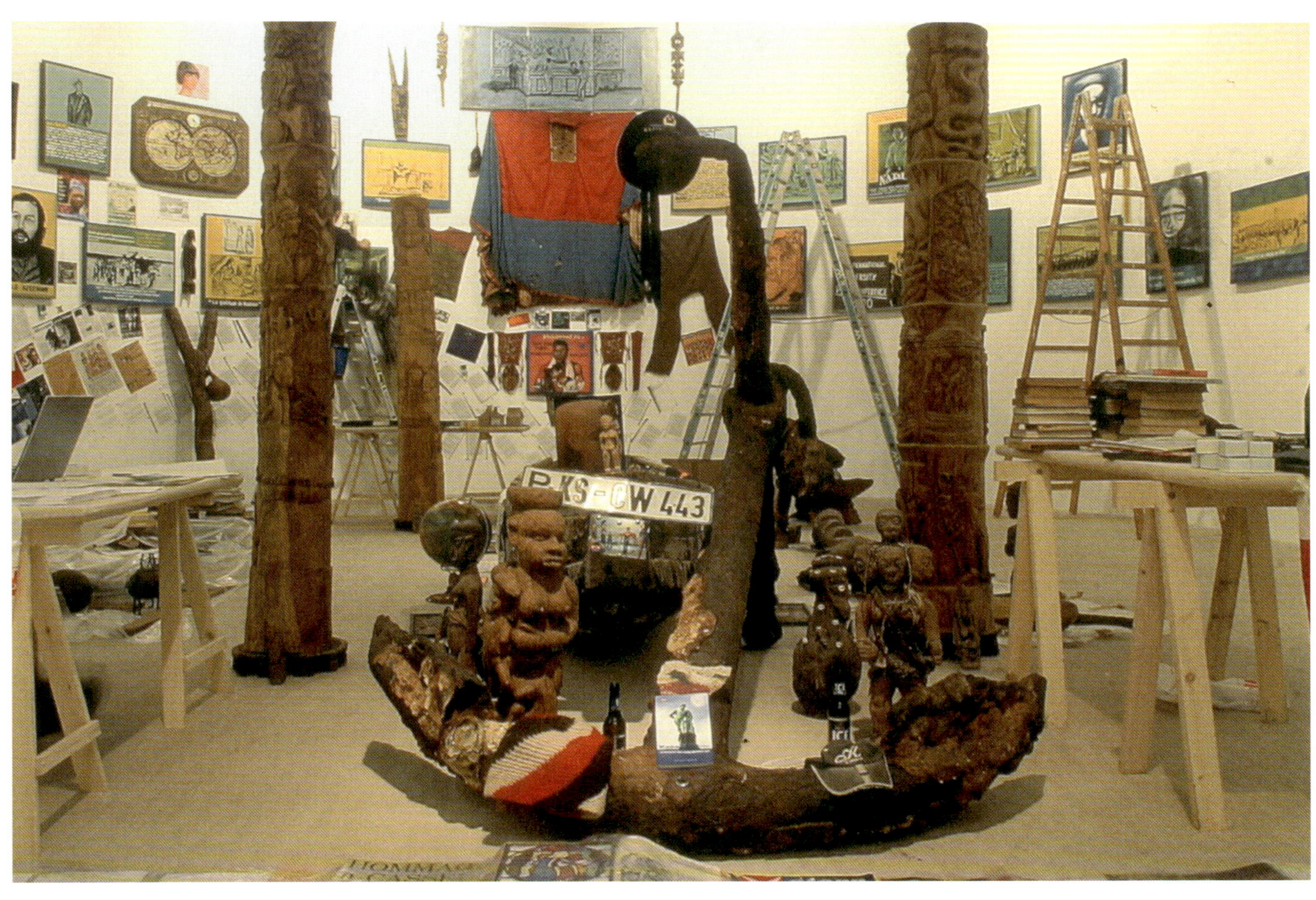

Fig. 16 Georges Adéagbo, *L'explorateur et les explorateurs devant l'histoire de l'exploration . . . ! Le théâtre du monde* [Explorer and explorers confronting the history of exploration . . . ! The theater of the world], 2002. Installation view, *documenta11*, Kassel, Germany, 2002.

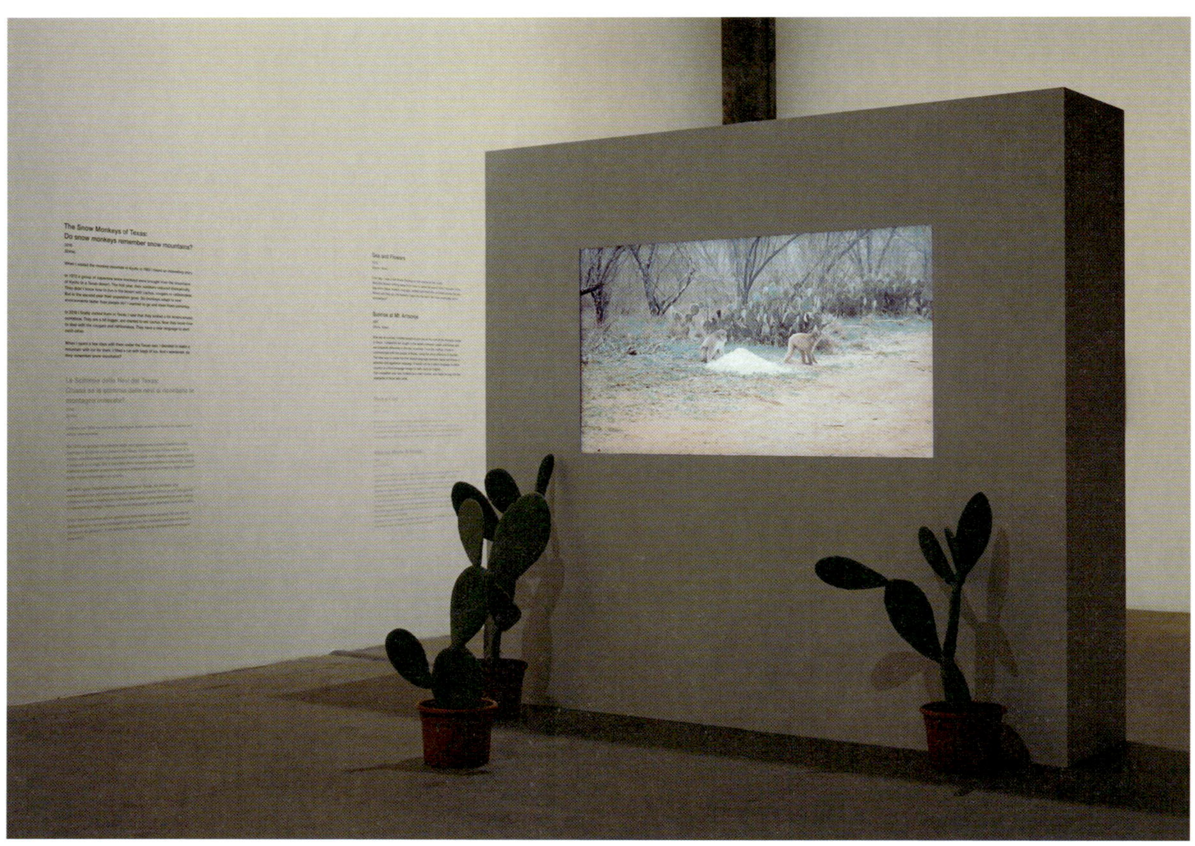

Fig. 17 Shimabuku, *The Snow Monkeys of Texas: Do snow monkeys remember snow mountains?*, 2016. Single-channel HD video projection, color, sound; vinyl wall text; and cacti. Edition of 3, 2 AP. Running time: 20:00, looped. Installation view, *Viva Arte Viva*, 57th *Venice Biennale*, Venice, Italy, 2017.

a later text, *The Magic of the State* (1997), Taussig used ethnofiction to accomplish these ends, positing his fieldwork in an unspecified "European Elsewhere," a place resembling South America (where he conducted actual fieldwork), and thereby destabilizing the specificity of his argument and allowing the reader to experience the novel as an imagined and universal possibility—in some sense, giving the reader a mechanism through which to place themselves within the narrative.[72] As author Darlene M. Juschka writes about Taussig's later ethnofictional narratives, here "stories and actualities are merged so that holding to a difference/binary between myth and history, ritual and episode, symbol and utensil are made impossible."[73] Some are beginning to address the colonialism within the academic field of anthropology itself, such as the Kenyan anthropologist Mwenda Ntarangwi, whose ethnographic text *Reversed Gaze* mines his own experience living in both Africa and the United States to self-reflexively interrogate the colonialist and racist history that has led to the field's us/them mentality.[74]

In recent years, this shift has been mirrored in contemporary art. The pivotal work of the late, Nigerian-born curator and scholar Okwui Enwezor represents an important example in regards to proximity curating, dissolving calcified us/them binaries, particularly as it relates to the anthropological turn in art within contemporary global society. He is widely recognized as the first African-born curator to organize major exhibitions that radically shifted the stage toward global platforms, including the 2002 *documenta11*, followed more than a decade later by his 2015 *Venice Biennale, All the World's Futures*. By turning his eye to, in his words, "the postcolonial constellation," Enwezor gave substantial turf to non-Western continents, in particular Africa (see fig. 16).[75] As he wrote in the *documenta* catalogue, "The postcolonial today is a world of proximities. It is a world of nearness, not elsewhere."[76] For the contemporary art world, a less uniform field of curators and artists expanding on subjects that relate to their own experience, heritage, or identity might begin to change and evolve the discussion, a corrective to the homogeneous history of the artistic canon in which far too few voices from within have been able to participate in the conversation. Enwezor's significant accomplishments are just one example, among many today, of the work of artists and exhibition makers

72. Michael Taussig, *The Magic of the State* (New York: Routledge, 1997).

73. Darlene M. Juschka, "The Writing of Ethnography: Magical Realism and Michael Taussig," *Journal for Cultural and Religious Theory* 5, no. 1 (December 2003): 96, http://www.jcrt.org/archives/05.1/juschka.pdf.

74. Mwenda Ntarangwi, *Reversed Gaze: An African Ethnography of American Anthropology* (Champaign: University of Illinois Press, 2010).

75. Okwui Enwezor, "The Postcolonial Constellation: Contemporary Art in a State of Permanent Transition," *Research in African Literature* 34, no. 4 (2003): 57–82.

76. Okwui Enwezor, "The Black Box," in *Documenta11_Platform 5: Exhibition Catalogue* (Ostfildern-Ruit, Germany: Hatje Cantz Publishers, 2002), 44.

who attempt global platforms, diversity, and within/without dialogues in their artistic and curatorial platforms.

An artist using personal experience and cultural identity as a nexus for his work, **Shimabuku** (born 1969 in Kobe, Japan; lives and works in Naha, Japan) generates simple, poetic gestures around nature, food, travel, and customs, imparting a sense of wonder to everyday interactions and behaviors. In *Tour of Europe with One Eyebrow Shaved*, 1991, for example, the artist shaved off one eyebrow and then traveled around Europe, using his strange appearance as catalyst for interaction and friendship with strangers. Another series of works consisted of the artist interacting with an octopus, known to be a highly intelligent mollusk, serving as both experience and metaphor.[77] For his project *The Snow Monkeys of Texas*, 2016, Shimabuku was inspired by a visit to the "monkey mountain" in Kyoto. The work is based on a historical event: in 1972, the entire population of a region's Japanese macaques (*Macaca fuscata*), also called "snow monkeys," was evicted from the suburbs of Kyoto after overpopulation and loss of its forest habitat through development. These monkeys were then relocated, of all places, to Dilley, Texas, south of San Antonio (the group currently resides in an animal sanctuary).[78] In the first year, most of the population died due to heat and lack of adaptation to their new ecological setting. But over time, and with assistance from the observatory—including a wild setting, water tanks, and food—the monkeys began to thrive (see fig. 17).[79] Shimabuku, in the text accompanying his work, poeticizes the story, omitting the assisted-living situation—the idea of their independent survival perhaps adding to the romance, and the artist having no ethnographic obligation to disclose such things—instead focusing on the monkeys' incredibly tenacious adaptation and repopulation. For his film *The Snow Monkeys of Texas: Do snow monkeys remember snow mountains?*, 2016, the artist traveled to Texas to visit the monkeys in their sanctuary, with the premise of seeing if they remembered snow after so many decades. The twenty-minute video features the monkeys seated on and climbing around a pile of crushed ice in the Texas desert, eating it with their hands, pushing it around, picking at it; Shimabuku's varying installation of the work also potentially consists of living cacti on the floor, a photograph of one of the monkeys with a mound of snow, and ice bags. He writes, in a text that accompanies the work's installation:

77. Gallery press release for Shimabuku exhibition, *Flying Me*, Kunsthalle Bern, Bern, Germany, 2014. "Shimabuku at Kunsthalle Bern," *Contemporary Art Daily*, June 13, 2014, http://www.contemporaryartdaily.com/2014/06/shimabuku-at-kunsthalle-bern.

78. In 1997, Richard M. Lewis, a professor at The University of Texas at Austin, wrote and directed a documentary for National Geographic about the monkeys. *The Snow Monkeys of Texas*, produced, written, and directed by Richard M. Lewis, cinematography by Harrison Witt (New York: National Geographic Television, 1997), 23 min, https://vimeo.com/67763441.

79. Ed Baker, "The Legendary Snow Monkeys of Texas," *The Austin Chronicle*, August 5, 2005, https://www.austinchronicle.com/news/2005-08-05/283057.

> *In 2016, I finally visited them in Texas. I saw that they looked a bit Americanized, somehow. They are a bit bigger, and started to eat cactus. Now they know how to deal with the cougars and rattlesnakes. They have a new language to alert each other.*
>
> *When I spent few days with them under the Texan sun, I decided to make a mountain with ice for them. I filled a car full of ice bags. And I wondered, do they remember snow mountains?*[80]

Shimabuku's fieldwork approach is gentle and curious, with a poignant message: could it be that the ice is simply refreshing, and any warm-blooded mammal would do the same in the Texas heat? Or were there traces of vestigial memory from the animals' long-ago relatives displaced from their home in Japan, unfamiliar but imprinted onto their DNA? The same philosophical questions underlie the study of genetics, scientific anthropology, and sociological proposals around the human condition. Harking back to anthropologist Jane Goodall's unmatched work in primate studies, the implicit understanding that these primates proximate humans in their genetic DNA takes us into emotional and existential terrain: they mirror our own struggles in both a tragic tale of exclusion and neglect, and a hopeful tale of survival. In this era of escalating climate change and destruction of the natural environment around the globe, the question becomes one of whether or not it's better to remove something from a culture in order to save it (as in zoos), or to create an ecology and correctives to problems within the originating culture so that the native inhabitants can survive there. Clearly the monkeys' original problems came about because of humans, as is almost always the case. What is to be done when the imprint of humans transforms or destroys an ecology so much that a species gets out of hand and becomes an unbearable nuisance? In researching the history of these macaques, I also discovered a brief period in 1996 when, after the animals had been removed from their federal status as a threatened species, the Texas Parks and Wildlife Department was slow to clarify the regulations around their protection, resulting in the perception of an "open season" of monkey hunting. This resulted in a degree of brutality toward these animals that ultimately led to their protection in the preserve.[81] And then there is the subject of immigration: as the monkeys were expats from their native home, the implications of their relocation to a foreign land reference this issue at the forefront of discussions today, especially in Texas, and the painful debates around who is welcome in a place.

80. Shimabuku, exhibition text for *Shimabuku: The Snow Monkeys of Texas*, Freedman Fitzpatrick, Los Angeles, 2016, http://freedmanfitzpatrick.com/exhibitions/shimabuku.

81. Baker, "The Legendary Snow Monkeys of Texas," *The Austin Chronicle*.

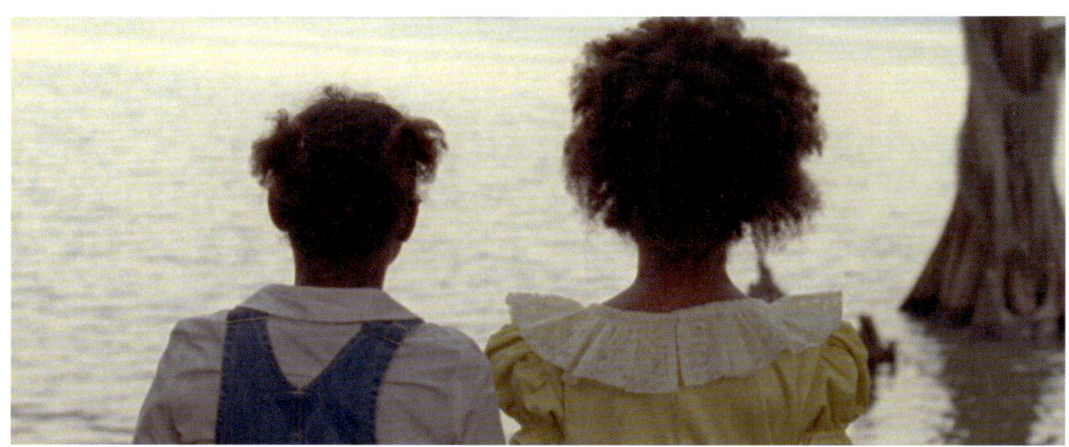

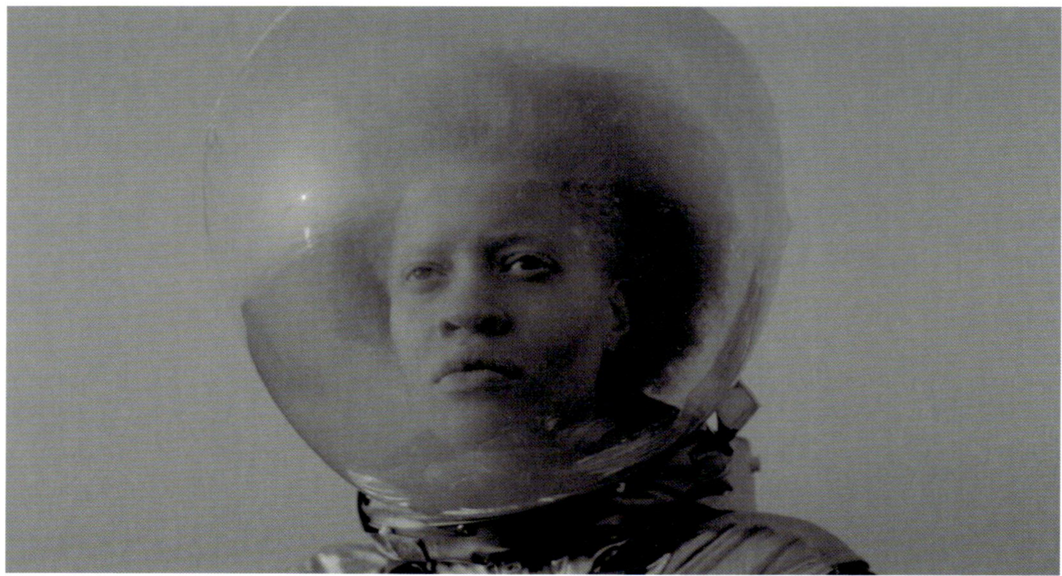

Fig. 18 Nuotama Bodomo. *Boneshaker* (still). 2013. Single-channel HD video, color, sound; converted from Super 16 mm. Running time: 13:00.

Fig. 19 Nuotama Bodomo. *Afronauts* (still). 2014. Single-channel HD video, black and white, sound. Running time: 14:00.

The filmmaker **Nuotama Bodomo** (born 1988 in Accra, Ghana) also grapples with problematic histories by using them as jumping-off points for exploratory narratives of the imagination—in this case, those that are self-authored and transformative—critiquing issues and events from the model of within. Having lived in Ghana, Norway, California, and Hong Kong before moving to New York to attend Columbia University, Bodomo evidences a transnational perspective of the African diaspora, a characteristic shared by several artists in this exhibition (including Theo Eshetu and Kapwani Kiwanga). A filmmaker whose work has bridged the commercial and art worlds, in one of her earliest works, *Boneshaker*, 2013, Bodomo presents a ritualistic story of a young girl—actress Quvenzhané Wallis from the 2012 Oscar-nominated film *Beasts of the Southern Wild*—a perceived problem child who opens the film with a piercing tantrum, and whose mother brings her to a Louisiana church hoping to banish the "evil spirits" who must be possessing her (see fig. 18). Another recent work, a kitschy, oddball short called *Everybody Dies!*, 2016, which premiered at the South by Southwest Festival in Austin as part of a larger group anthology called *Collective: Unconscious* inspired by dreams, features a darkly comedic game show in which a female grim reaper teaches black children that they are going to die. Mimicking the projections of 1970s CRT monitors, the program in the film cuts in and out and ends on a dourly slapstick note. With wildly different techniques—the former a cinematic, symphonic short; the latter a searing composition of kitsch and honesty camouflaged behind a morbidly playful premise—the artist engages with both conceptual and anthropological techniques in her films.

In between *Boneshaker* and *Everybody Dies!*, Bodomo made *Afronauts*, 2014, a short fictional film based on true events surrounding the Zambia National Academy of Science, Space Research and Philosophy's attempts to enter the space race at the height of the Cold War. The figure leading these efforts, Edward Festus Mukuka Nkoloso, who also coined the term "Afronaut," was an outspoken grade school science teacher who trained twelve Zambian astronauts in the style of a backyard amateur, with the well-publicized hopes of beating the US and the Soviet Union to the moon. Among these were Matha Mwamba, a teenager who planned to take her cats into space. Not surprisingly, the Zambian program never progressed, as by 1965, among other obstacles, the program suffered from lack of funds and attrition of its young astronauts-in-training.[82] Bodomo sets her film shortly before the actual *Apollo 11* mission witnessed Neil Armstrong and Buzz Aldrin landing on the moon on July 20, 1969. Not detracting from Armstrong and Aldrin's accomplishments or the incredible moment of the 1960s space race, Bodomo rather hitches a playful,

82. Among those who left, one astronaut joined a local dance troupe, while Mwamba became pregnant and dropped out. Namwali Serpell, "The Zambian 'Afronaut' Who Wanted to Join the Space Race," Culture Desk, *The New Yorker*, March 11, 2017, https://www.newyorker.com/culture/culture-desk/the-zambian-afronaut-who-wanted-to-join-the-space-race.

science fiction ride on the coattails of this historical event. Instead of white American men, *Afronauts* features Mwamba's character as an African albino female with ethereal white skin and a halo of blond hair (played by the striking actress Diandra Forrest), embarking on amateur astronaut training on a deserted African hillside (see fig. 19). And instead of multiple cats, the film's Mwamba cajoles a single, one-eyed feline to join her, perhaps emphasizing the existential disadvantages faced by the primary character in her mission. The protagonist is surrounded by chanting and drinking men who, a maternal figure assures Mwamba, do not believe in her. In the end, the ramshackle rocket holding Mwamba catapults into the sky, falling empty back to Earth; we read the faces of the crowd as they realize she is gone. The final scene shows her walking alone on the moon. Bodomo envisions a wonderfully subversive account: female over male; African over Western; black albino over white. This work, an ethnographic visual poem of proximity instead of *elsewhere*, suggests an alternate history: here, a young woman is launched into another realm, against the odds, imparting those left on Earth with a new perspective. Bodomo rewrites an influential childhood myth into a transformational narrative of possibilities.

TECHNOLOGY

Technology plays an important role in the field of anthropology for its contributions to the conditions that effect social change. A common use of the term *technology* today might suggest the proliferation of the Internet, advanced computers, smartphones, social media, virtual reality, artificial intelligence, and other ubiquitous digital interfaces. But the broad definition of technology, particularly for anthropologists, encompasses the tools and processes developed by a society to simplify daily tasks. Typically the revolutionary technology—that which inserts itself into a culture and creates radical social change—is embraced by some and resisted by others. For example, the rise of social media may be anathema to many today, and they may perhaps decline to participate in the technology on principle or because it feels unfamiliar or uncomfortable; yet history shows that denying technological change can often be futile and misdirected. As one such case, during my time at Oxford we studied the impact of technology on culture through the snowmobile in Finland in the 1970s. The concept that a snowmobile could radically change a society seems almost quaint today, but for the Skolt Lapp, a small population of reindeer herders innately connected to land, animals, and community, the members witnessed increasing social and economic stratification (between the haves and the have-nots), delocalization (for those now dependent on gas and other outside sources for their livelihood), and dispersal of social groups and collective collaboration previously engendered by the shared livelihood of reindeer herding.[83]

83. Pertti J. Pelto, *The Snowmobile Revolution: Technology and Social Change in the Arctic* (Menlo Park, CA: Cummings Publishing Company, 1973).

What is characteristic about the technology of our time, since the invention of the mass-produced computer, is the *digital*. Anthropologists Heather A. Horst and Daniel Miller define the digital as "all that which can be ultimately reduced to binary code but which produces a further proliferation of particularity and difference."[84] The digital has influenced and embedded itself into all disciplines and aspects of life, providing an exponentially rapid means of exchange that doesn't require in-person human interaction. While this doesn't decrease the importance of material culture, it democratizes access to information (in theory, contingent on unimpeded access to that information via digital platforms) and increasingly renders analog forms, such as celluloid film or paperback books, a specialization. Access to the digital has created some of our best advances (communication, mobility, medicine, and activism) and our most potent challenges (disinformation, hyper-connectivity, sensationalism, and overexposure).

Art has a complicated relationship with the digital. Early pioneers in the 1960s and 1970s, such as Tony Conrad, Bruce Nauman, Nam June Paik, and Steina and Woody Vasulka, made basic digital formats including television, video, and computer programming their primary medium, experimenting with the material, social, and cultural aspects of these formats on a profound cultural level. Not until the 1990s did contemporary artists begin to engage with the digital more frequently, seen via artists working in virtual formats, online projects, and what has regularly been termed "new media." But while a majority of artists working in film and photography use digital formats by default, those effectively tackling the digital on a sociocultural level, as their predecessors did with television and video, remain a minority. Critic Claire Bishop identifies this as the "structuring paradox" of contemporary art today, a "subterranean presence" whereby the bulk of artists have been "curiously unresponsive to the total upheaval in our labor and leisure inaugurated by the digital revolution."[85] She further suggests that analog practitioners, social practice, and the messy "unmonumentality" of sculpture of the past twenty years are likewise a subconscious resistance to the digital. In effect, artists are responding to the digital subconsciously en masse, but most are not effectively addressing it head-on.

Concurrently, in response to the proliferation of digital in everyday life that threatens analog media, artists such as Edgar Arceneaux, William Kentridge, and Sharon Lockhart have resisted digital formats while others, notably Tacita Dean through her championing of 16 mm film, have become activists in the matter, intent on preventing certain analog formats from becoming obsolete. Working in analog media when digital

84. Heather A. Horst and Daniel Miller, "The Digital and the Human: A Prospectus for Digital Anthropology," in *Digital Anthropology*, eds. Horst and Miller (Oxford, UK: Berg Publishers, 2012; New York: Bloomsbury, 2014), 3. Citations refer to the Bloomsbury edition.

85. Claire Bishop, "Digital Divide: Contemporary Art and New Media," *Artforum* 51, no.1 (September 2012), https://www.artforum.com/print/201207/digital-divide-contemporary-art-and-new-media-31944.

formats are readily available has validity: older formats maintain a hand-to-material sense of making, a particular richness in color and presence on screen, and the physical, tactile experience of the media and playback equipment, as well as the accompanying sound, generated by now antiquated EIKI projectors or slide carousels, for example. Structuralist filmmakers from the 1960s and 1970s, such as Hollis Frampton and Paul Sharits, brought film into three-dimensional space with rich and moving 16 mm filmic installations incorporating then radical techniques such as visual filmic collage, hand-painted celluloid, and sculptural components to allover installations. It's not a stretch to say that an elemental part of their work would be lost if rendered digitally. But for these artists, there was no alternative; by default, one argument goes, those using such formats today risk associations with rarity, craft, and nostalgia, a superficial reading that Hal Foster might have filed within his "quasi-" category (perhaps "quasi-Structuralist," in this case), one he associated with indulgence, fantasy, and the illusion of particular psychic and creative access.[86]

Seated squarely within the dialogue around contemporary angst—or avoidance, as it may be—provoked by the digital age, **Ed Atkins** (born 1982 in Oxford, United Kingdom; lives and works in Copenhagen and Berlin) works with high-definition video and technology to tease out issues from the subterranean to the surface level. Atkins often uses digital animation to create arresting, fragmented videos of abstracted archetypal figures representing the darker side of the human condition, including loneliness, angst, shame, hopelessness, and death. In *Warm, Warm, Warm Spring Mouths*, 2013, the animated protagonist narrates the video while submerged in greenish water, long hair floating out behind him, while in the related *Material Witness OR A Liquid Cop*, 2012, included in this exhibition, a shadowy, alternately silhouetted and masked figure—the narrator reading from a journal—ruminates on ritual, death, disparity, and materiality (see fig. 20). His protagonists are typically white males in pathetic, debased repose, sometimes floating heads without bodies, other times replete with tattoos and shaved heads, drinking beer. They seem to represent the existentials of doleful survival, while at the same time flipping the proverbial anarchist middle finger in fierce subversion: barfly British Beat poets of the future. Created from CGI technology as avatars, narrated by the artist and replicating his expressions, Atkins's figures have a slow-moving, awkward quality that seats them between human and android, or mannequin. Although digitally born from Atkins's DNA, these figures are not autobiographical to the artist but rather generalized ethnographic portraits of Western (male) culture, searing stereotypes of cultural tropes. In other works, such as *The Trick Brain*, 2012, Atkins doesn't use digital at all, but rather employs language and a camera that slowly pans over the

86. Foster, "The Artist as Ethnographer?," in *The Traffic in Culture*, 302–303.

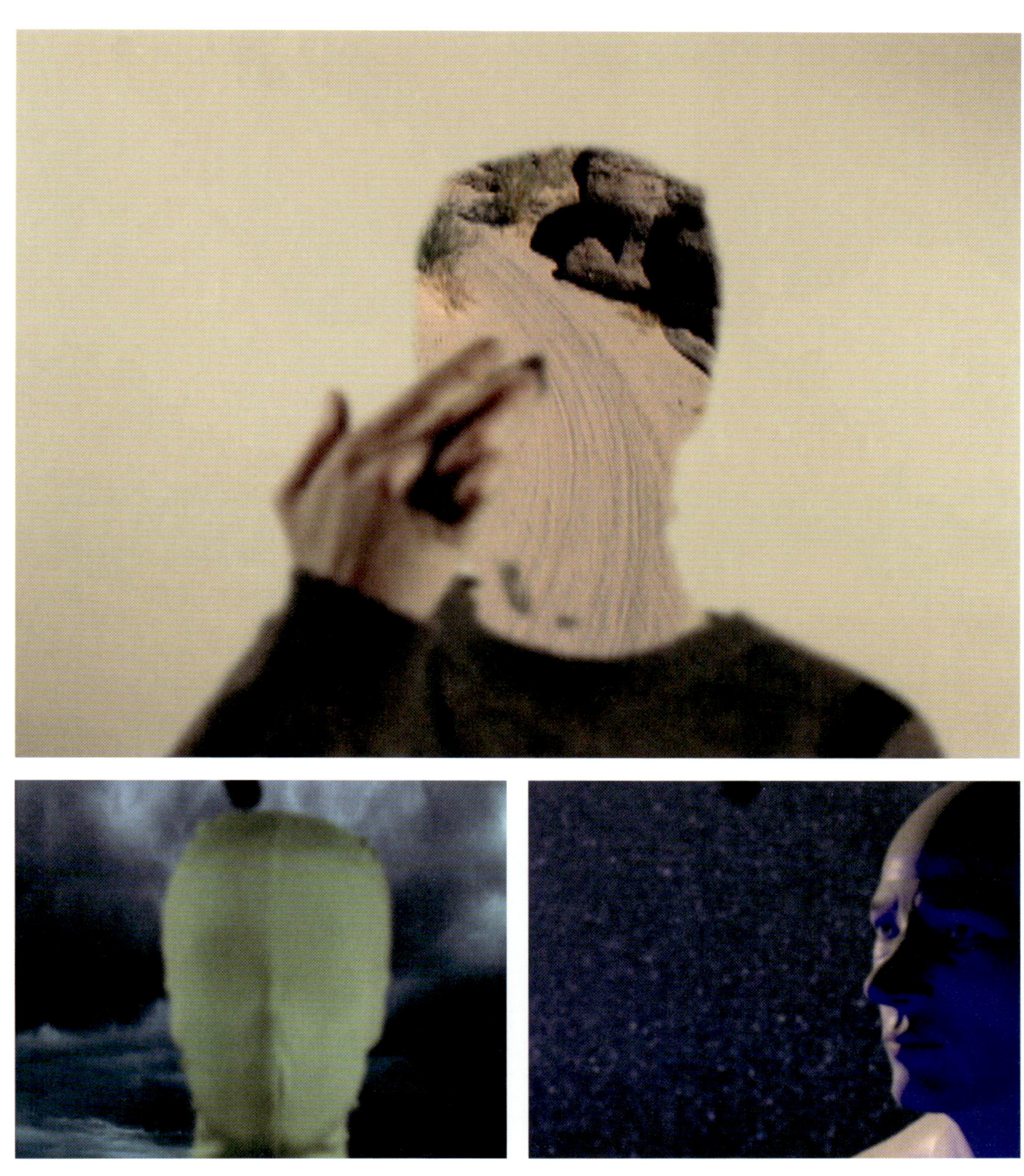

Fig. 20 Ed Atkins, *Material Witness OR A Liquid Cop* (stills), 2012. Single-channel HD video, color, stereo sound. Running time: 19:17, looped.

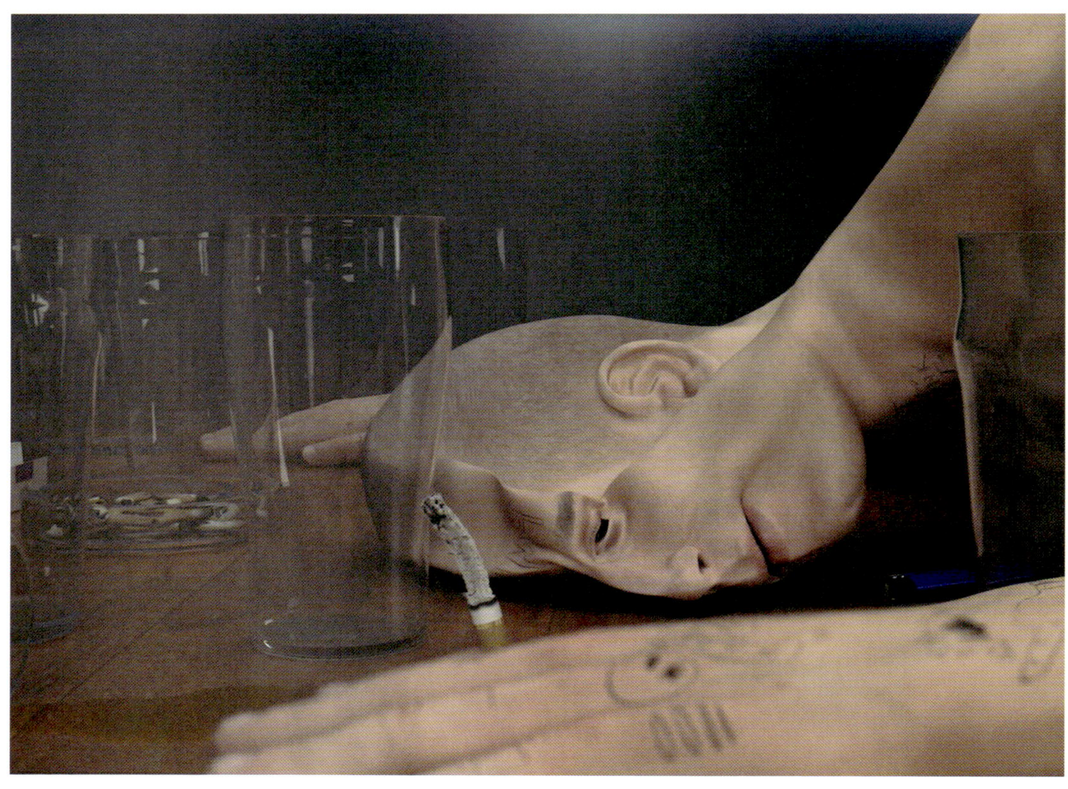

Fig. 21 Ed Atkins, *Ribbons* (still), 2014. Three-channel HD video, color, sound. Running time: 13:18.

historic apartment of Surrealist André Breton, filled with his collection of modern and primitive two- and three-dimensional art. Part nostalgia, part critique of collecting, the work includes Atkins's mesmerizing, stream-of-consciousness dictation around the narcissism of the capitalist acquisition impulse, with a tenor voice, piano, and drumbeats periodically providing the musical score.

In the lineage of experimental moving images, Atkins cites Hollis Frampton as one of his primary influences, and while Frampton and Atkins seem at first to occupy sharply divergent spheres (the former using material celluloid film and cameras; the latter, computer-generated digital animation as visual and audio collage), the two share deep affinities.[87] One could speculate about whether or not Frampton, were he working today and had current technologies available, might use digital avatars as Atkins does to pioneer new ground. After all, in the 1960s, using film as Frampton did—outside of the theater, sans narrative, via abstract frames of color, image, and text—*was* innovative and unprecedented. A dip into the oeuvre of Atkins reveals similar undercurrents of inventive filmic abstraction, seen in the artist's mastery of digital effects whereby his sense of slow visual abstraction, shutter-like movement, and asynchronous noise, although made possible by today's technology, mirror Frampton's inroads into the moving image via filmic abstraction and compositional minimalist sound.[88]

But where Frampton was uninterested in social or anthropological commentary in his work, Atkins's videos engage deeply with visual and linguistic ethnology. Revisiting Marcus's ethnographic discussion of the rise of 1980s Writing Culture, language is essential to Atkins's premise, both in spoken and text form. Words, phrases, and sentences flash across his videos, interspersed with representational figures and frames of monochrome color. As the artist has said, "Building up an animation, for me, is not that different to building up a sentence," and "Language is the way that I think."[89] The protagonist of *Ribbons*, 2014, a three-channel video animation whose narrative revolves around a punkish bloke smoking and drinking in a bar, begins in one channel with a hand holding the letters "WHERE ANIMALS EXPIRE." We then see the protagonist's face with a tattoo of "FML" (the millennial acronym for "Fuck My Life") drawn backwards on his forehead and the label "cymothoa exigua" beneath him, the

87. Ed Atkins, interview by Hans Ulrich Obrist, *KALEIDOSCOPE*, no. 13 (Winter 2011–2012), http://kaleidoscope.media/ed-atkins.

88. Furthermore, when observing Atkins's existential interpretation of death and his references to macabre and melancholy figures in his work—what the artist has referred to as "cadavers"—one can't help but consider Frampton's life story: the brilliant filmmaker worked for ten years on an epic work that he called his most important, the Magellan cycle, but left unfinished because of his untimely death at the age of forty-eight. A tragic story that resonates in its unfinished futility with the themes of Atkins's oeuvre.

89. Ed Atkins, "Something is Missing," interview by Marc-Christoph Wagner, Louisiana Channel, Louisiana Museum of Modern Art, October 2017, http://channel.louisiana.dk/video/ed-atkins-something-missing.

name for a "tongue-eating louse," a disgusting and fascinating parasitic isopod that attaches itself to a fish's tongue, devours it, and then replaces the organ while keeping the fish alive (see fig. 21).[90] This beginning sets the tone for *Ribbons*' adventurous assemblage of debased human satire, in which a Dada-esque collection of poems, monologues, and song lyrics contributes to the fragmented story line. Using computer-generated binary code to render abstraction in the twenty-first century makes sense, in that, as Claire Bishop noted, "The digital . . . is code, inherently alien to human perception. It is, at base, a linguistic model."[91] Perhaps this explains why Atkins so effectively captures and exploits its potential for critiquing the human condition.

SEEING

Images are a contested site of culture. Visual anthropology, a relatively recent subfield of cultural anthropology that emerged primarily in Britain in the 1990s, centers around the notion that visual worlds are subjective, culturally based, and reflect different ways of seeing. Anthropologists, such as Marcus Banks and Howard Morphy, argue a now widely held belief that vision and perception are, to some extent, "socially and/or culturally constructed."[92] This has had great impact on the complications surrounding both interpretation and fieldwork, particularly for non-Western perspectives, in that, as anthropologist Eric C. Thompson wrote in the *Asian Journal of Social Science*, "anthropologists have come to thoroughly recognise and embed within our theory and methods an understanding that our subjectivity and identity as researchers is deeply implicated in the research process. That is to say, who one is has important implications for the ways in which one conducts research, the information one uncovers, and the ways in which we interpret and write about what we learn."[93] The very nature of information collected is biased by the cultural identity of the gatherer. Returning to visual anthropology, the field typically revolves around film and photography as media for documentation and recording, with the goal of rendering communities, practices, and material culture not previously visible accessible for interpretation. A parallel field exists in art. Influential texts emerged in the 1970s, including John Berger's *Ways of Seeing*,

90. Matt Simon, "Absurd Creature of the Week: This Parasite Eats a Fish's Tongue—And Takes Its Place," *Wired Magazine*, November 22, 2013, https://www.wired.com/2013/11/absurd-creature-of-the-week-the-parasite-that-eats-and-replaces-a-fishs-tongue.

91. Claire Bishop, "Digital Divide: Contemporary Art and New Media," *Artforum* 51, no. 1.

92. Marcus Banks and Howard Morphy, "Introduction: Rethinking Visual Anthropology," in *Rethinking Visual Anthropology*, eds. Banks and Morphy (New Haven, CT, and London: Yale University Press, 1997), 22. Banks was also one of my professors at the University of Oxford.

93. Eric C. Thompson, "Anthropology in Southeast Asia: National Traditions and Transnational Practices," *Asian Journal of Social Science* 40, no. 5/6 (2012): 673.

1972 (first a television show and subsequently a book), and Susan Sontag's *On Photography*, 1977, that raised game-changing critical questions about subjectivity and symbolism in representational images.[94] The Pictures Generation, a catchy label coined by the critic and curator Douglas Crimp, characterized a Conceptual and Minimalist-influenced group of artists in the late 1970s and 1980s, including John Baldessari, Dara Birnbaum, Troy Brauntuch, Charles Clough, Robert Longo, Cindy Sherman, Michael Smith, and Julia Wachtel, among others, who appropriated recognizable imagery from mass culture into hybrid, self-reflexive forms.[95] By the 1990s and 2000s, art historians such as Hans Belting, James Elkins, W. J. T. Mitchell, and Griselda Pollock had further developed the field of visual culture and "picture theory" (to use Mitchell's phrase) in contemporary art historical discourse to envelop a wide range of phenomena, including not only moving images, photography, and digital media but philosophy, psychoanalysis, phenomenology, optics, spectatorship, and display.[96] Academia in art and art history underwent an equivalent evolution, with the rise in university degrees around visual culture, visual studies, and media studies.

Appropriation, and the question of authorship, is inherent to this trajectory. Where traditional Western notions of art typically held individual or unique creation as the gauge of an artist's merit, promoting the concept of the lone artist as genius, contemporary art has deflated at least part of that notion (perhaps not the artist as genius) through appropriation and intentional non-authorship. Returning to the idea of "primitivism," a core underpinning was the appropriation of formal shapes and imagery from anthropology's cultural *otherness*, paving the way for art's commandeering and absorption not only of past artistic genres and lived experience, but of other cultures, geographies, and artistic contemporaries. Western artists saw the unfamiliarity and exoticism found in the material culture of African and Oceanic cultures as a means to disrupt existing canons of art. While problematic, one could no longer deny the potential for appropriation to generate new paths forward. Contemporary anthropologist Arnd Schneider goes so far as to write that "notions of the primitive were responsible, along with the adoption of theories from psychoanalysis, for changes in our understanding of what art is and what it does; how it appeals to us, how it affects us, and what we

94. John Berger, *Ways of Seeing* (UK: BBC Two, January 1972); John Berger, *Ways of Seeing* (London: British Broadcasting Corporation and Penguin Books, 1972); and Susan Sontag, *On Photography* (New York: Farrar, Straus and Giroux, 1977). The first publications of Sontag's *On Photography* essays appeared in *The New York Review of Books* from 1973–1977.

95. Douglas Crimp, "Pictures," in *Pictures* (New York: Artists Space and Committee for the Visual Arts, Inc., 1977).

96. W. J. T. Mitchell, *Picture Theory: Essays on Verbal and Visual Representation* (Chicago: The University of Chicago Press, 1994). Also see synopsis in Ruth B. Phillips, "The Value of Disciplinary Difference: Reflections on Art History and Anthropology at the Beginning of the Twenty-First Century," in *Anthropologies of Art* (New Haven, CT: Yale University Press, 2005), 245.

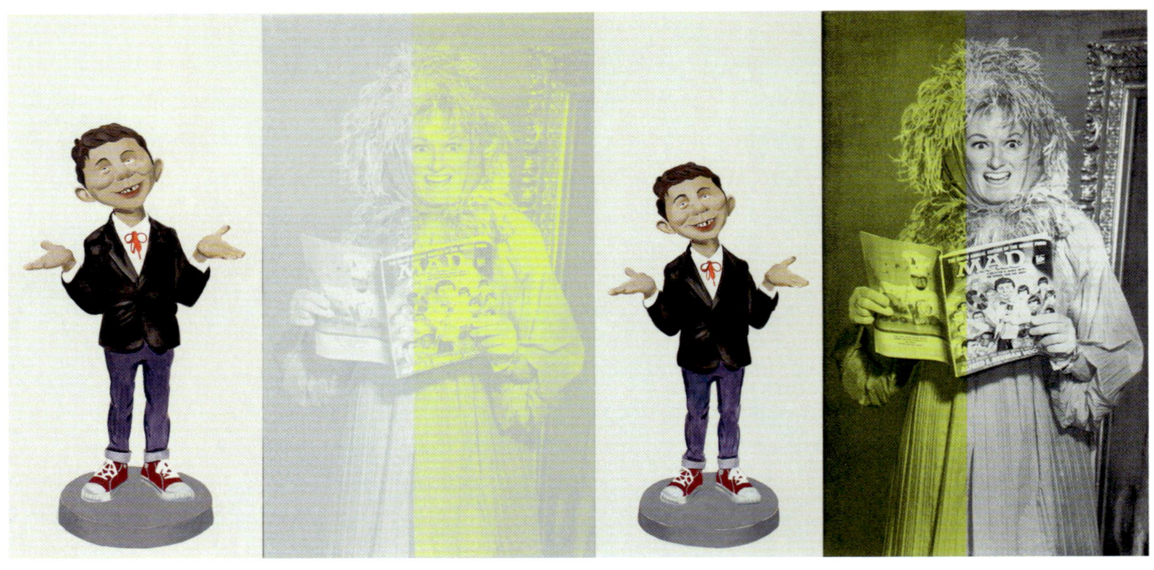

Fig. 22 Julia Wachtel, *Me*, 2014. Oil, acrylic ink, and Flashe on canvas. 60 x 124 inches.

expect from it."[97] Likewise, around the same time period in the early twentieth century, Duchamp's theft of everyday utilitarian objects rendered functionless and labeled as art paved the way for borrowing en masse and indiscriminately from the world around us. By the 1960s, with the onset of Conceptual and Pop art, appropriation became de rigueur; today it is typically the exception when appropriation in contemporary art is perceived as negative.[98] Minimalism similarly paved the way for non-authorship with its industrial methods. And the rise of social and relational art in the 1980s and 1990s turned the authorship over toward the audience and participants. But when seen from an anthropological perspective, sourcing from cultures not one's own becomes an act of cultural, rather than artistic, appropriation, raising questions around colonialism, subjugation, and power structures. Things become complicated as both meaning and ownership of images, symbols, and culture are disputed.

Considered an early member of the Pictures Generation, **Julia Wachtel** (born 1956 in New York City, New York; lives and works in Connecticut and Brooklyn, New York) extends this interrogation of visual culture and authorship through her trademark "mash-up" paintings: assemblages of images relating to art, commerce, politics, and entertainment. Her unique, post-Warholian style consists of single, double, or triptych canvases, alternately screen-printed or hand-painted, featuring combinations of cartoonish images from pop culture sourced by the artist from greeting cards, magazines, and, more recently, the Internet, and recombined into strange and dislocating caricatures. The artist has worked on a specific series for some forty years, with characters emerging and receding, and has focused on particular aspects of cultural topography, primarily in two veins: celebrity paintings and landscape/history paintings.[99] Some content mines kitschy and recognizable elements from advertising and entertainment—Minnie Mouse, Colonel Sanders, and *MAD* magazine's iconic mascot Alfred E. Neuman have all made appearances, elements that Wachtel has said are not necessarily cartoons but "anything that functions as a placeholder for the position of subjectivity" (see fig. 22).[100] Other references source from political imagery and celebrity cultural moments via journalistic or documentary photographs, the former including images of political protests and boys enacting machine gun target practice, and the latter including images of Cher, John Travolta, and Kim Kardashian and Kanye West. Critic Bob Nickas writes that when Wachtel's practice emerged in the 1980s, it existed under the (somewhat

97. Arnd Schneider, "Appropriations," in *Contemporary Art and Anthropology*, 33.

98. There are still some exceptions, for example, Donald Graham, the artist who sued Richard Prince and Gagosian Gallery, as previously mentioned.

99. Julia Wachtel, "Profile of the Artist Part I: Julia Wachtel in Conversation with Tara Plath," interview by Tara Plath, *The Seen: Chicago's International Online Journal of Contemporary & Modern Art*, July 8, 2014, http://theseenjournal.org/art-seen-national/profile-artist-pt-julia-wachtel.

100. Ibid.

dubious-sounding) banner of "Infotainment—Pop-inflected merging of information and entertainment," alongside artists such as Sarah Charlesworth, Jessica Diamond, Steven Parrino, et al.[101] This incongruity—combined with formal tactics of flipping pictures upside down; printing or hand-painting components, often in bright colors, evidencing the artist's hand; and repetition and seriality—serves to question the power of images, asking whether context begets meaning entirely or if an image's reading can stand on its own. By removing elements from their original context and repeating and recombining them into seeming non sequiturs, Wachtel destablilizes visual iconography and examines whether cultural value is inherent in images, or whether it is contextually and temporally contingent.

Wachtel's satirical style uses humor to dissolve the limited reading of images as cultural tropes. Typical of the best comedy, a dark subtext courses beneath the faux cheeriness of her imagery in the evidential psychological weight of the images she uses—perhaps in the line of Hans Belting's theories on the anthropology of images, or the way they manifest as mental images and lived experiences in our bodies—alluding to their potential for misinterpretation and recontextualization.[102] It's not the artist who tells us this, as the works are intentionally fragmented and devoid of narrative structure, but the act of looking at the intentionally confusing assemblage of images, as well as their anonymity and repetition. No more is this evident than in *Bad*, 2015, a canvas featuring a doubled image of actor Bryan Cranston's notorious suburban dad drug kingpin, Walter White, from the TV series *Breaking Bad*, clad in his yellow meth-making hazmat suit (see fig. 23). Adjacent to each White image crouches a doubled black and white line cartoon character, peering through a door's keyhole. A black geometric form impinges on White's face in each image, elongating and partially obscuring it in the first one—perhaps it is the encroaching black hole of abstraction or the keyhole through which the cartoon man peers at White, a voyeuristic act that exposes him. The fragmentation and layering of the image erode the boundaries between computer- (or machine-) generated and handmade, and, by extension, the porous edges between authenticity and truth.

Some of Wachtel's works directly critique the use of ethnographic iconography in this manner, such as *Spirit*, 2015 (see fig. 24). Here a reserved portrait of Hillary Rodham Clinton, wearing a ruffled shirt beneath a blazer and standing next to an American flag, is juxtaposed with a doubled, hand-painted image of an ancient Kostenki Venus figure. The implication is both obvious and obtuse. Without taking a moral high ground, the

101. Bob Nickas, "Julia Wachtel: No Representation Without Taxation, and the Pain of Modern Life," in *The Dept. of Corrections: Collected Writings 2007–2015* (New York: Karma, 2015), 69.

102. Hans Belting, *An Anthropology of Images: Picture, Medium, Body*, trans. Thomas Dunlap (Princeton, NJ: Princeton University Press, 2011); first published as *Bild-Anthropologie: Entwürfe für eine Bildwissenschaft* (Munich: Wilhelm Fink Verlag, 2001).

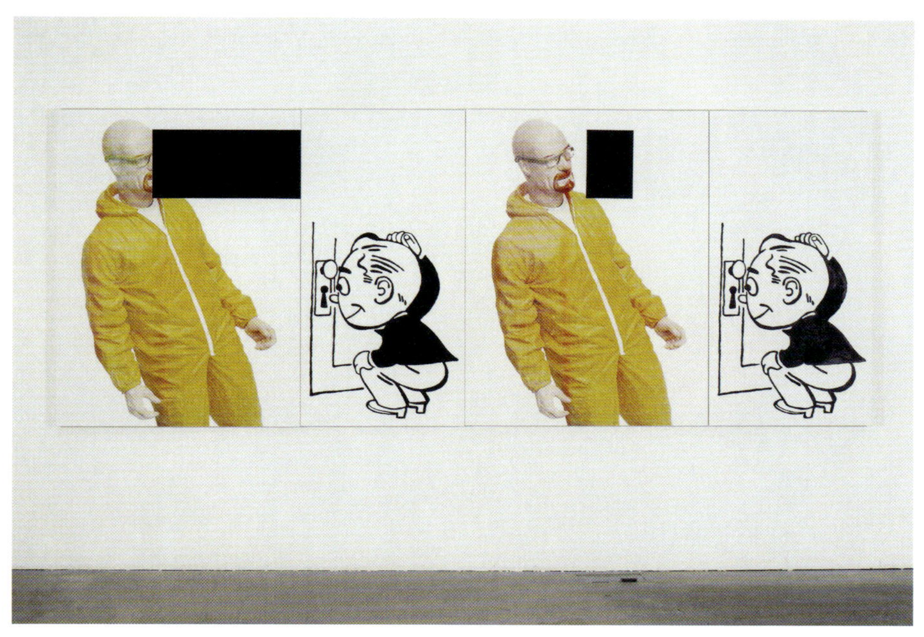

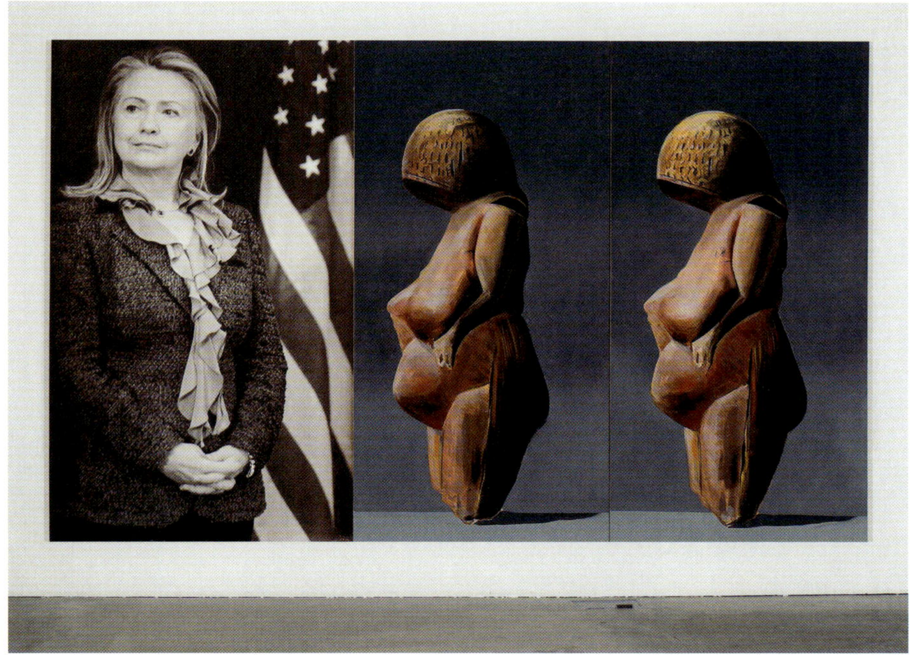

Fig. 23 Julia Wachtel, *Bad*, 2015. Oil, acrylic ink, and Flashe on canvas. 60 x 150 inches.

Fig. 24 Julia Wachtel, *Spirit*, 2015. Oil and acrylic ink on canvas. 60 x 92 inches.

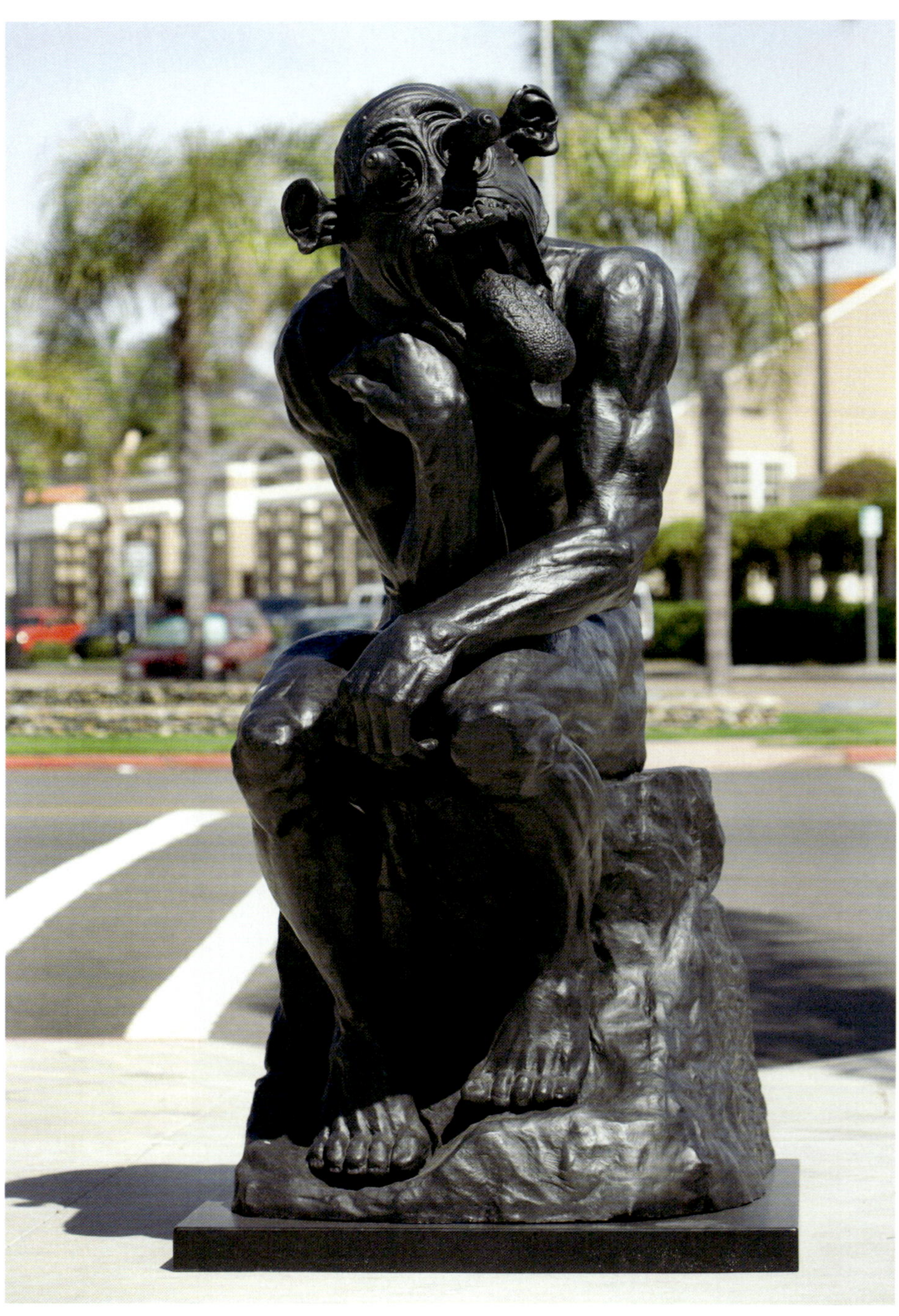

Fig. 25 Nathan Mabry. *Process Art (Dead Men Don't Make Sculpture)*, 2008. Bronze. 87 x 58 x 41 inches.

work offers a flat comparison between the two figures, putting forth the possibility that both have been misinterpreted; that they have nothing in common, or everything. Wachtel questions the idea that these ancient figures embody "naïve" connotations of authenticity, stating, "I feel that this view of them as pure, unsophisticated and unsocialized is a complete misreading, and is an interpretation filled with racist and materialist overtones."[103] While the artist does not explicitly reference the ethics of appropriating non-Western ethnographic objects, her viewpoint clearly articulates the misinformed generalizations and assumptions within Western culture and contemporary art from outside the anthropological field, which often lead to the appropriation of these objects and iconography carte blanche.

The borrowing of cultural artifacts and the problematic readings that might ensue take sculptural form in the work of **Nathan Mabry** (born 1978 in Durango, Colorado; lives and works in Los Angeles). Like Wachtel, Mabry puts forth a conceptual pastiche of time periods and influences, ranging from anthropology and archaeology to Dadaism, Surrealism, and Minimalism. Formally, Mabry critiques neoclassical figuration, sometimes through direct appropriation. In *Process Art (Dead Men Don't Make Sculpture)*, 2008, the first in a series of *Process* sculptures that feature iconic sculptures wearing grotesque masks, Mabry covered and then cast a copy of Auguste Rodin's *The Thinker* with a mask of an exploding face—eyes and tongue popping out of a protruding visage—in bronze (see fig. 25). To make the sculpture, Mabry described how he sourced a non-authorized replica of *The Thinker* (probably by a contemporary artist or company), purchased it, and, once it arrived in his studio, began covering it in various Halloween masks.[104] The juxtaposition of a macabre pop culture disguise covering a highly recognizable classical sculpture is startling and unexpected, the quintessential merging of "high" and "low," dismantling Rodin's original premise. But the incongruous assemblage ends up being wildly successful on a formal level—the pained, bulging face reflecting the absurdity of contemporary culture and slyly offering a new rendition of a twenty-first-century classical masterpiece.

Mabry pairs disparate geographic and cultural iconography of both Western and non-Western origins for formal and conceptual purposes, but uses both sets of iconography sans cultural context. In his *T/O/T/E/M* series, replicas, hand-crafted by Mabry, of ancient "anonymous" pre-Columbian ceramic vessels—here, Peruvian Moche stirrup spout vessels, which are ubiquitous as examples of early ceramics in encyclopedic museums

103. Julia Wachtel, interview by Bob Nickas, "Anxious Objects: Parrino, Stahl, Wachtel," *Flash Art*, no. 132 (February/March 1987). Reproduced in Bob Nickas, *Julia Wachtel*, eds. Martin Clark and Steinar Sekkingstad (Chicago: Museum of Contemporary Art Chicago, 1991; Bergen, Norway: Bergen Kunsthall, 2014). Exhibition catalogue.

104. Nathan Mabry, interview by Jed Morse, *Sightings: Nathan Mabry* (exhibition brochure), Nasher Sculpture Center, Dallas, 2013, np.

across the world—sit atop spare boxes that the artist has said are inspired by those of the Minimalist sculptor Donald Judd, offering a contrast between non-Western handmade and Western machine-fabricated iconography (see fig. 26).[105] A similar juxtaposition occurs in Mabry's wall-mounted sculptures, such as *u.n.t.i.t.l.e.d. (Crouching Figure – Blue)*, 2012 (see fig. 27). For the pre-Columbian forms, the methods of appropriation by Mabry are layered: the artist sources from personal photos and books, then re-creates these forms by hand through coil building, emphasizing detail and volume.[106] From the vantage of Mabry's objects, there's some irony in the fact that Judd's forms (or at least, those of Western Minimalism) have become entrenched in the Western canon with specific attribution and authorship, despite being machine-fabricated geometric shapes, while there's an assumed anonymity to the pre-Columbian vessels that allows for mass appropriation and sentimentalized inference of meaning. That said, the attribution of individual artists to work was not necessarily part of early non-Western practices, and it would be difficult to discern individual authorship or trace the origins of the work, particularly for a Western artist not versed in the anthropological field from which the object comes.

This points to the ethical issues that develop in the mining of anthropology from within the art world, as Mabry himself elaborates: "Through the handmade ceramic object and manufactured base there is dialogue of unexpected symbiosis, where neither object operates in its original context . . . . The *T/O/T/E/M* series further explores my interest in the combination of 'authorized' Minimal objects and 'anonymous' anthropological objects, as well as the formal combination of hard edge geometry and soft organic forms."[107] The double-sided visual conundrum confounds the suspect nature of both considering ethnographic non-Western objects as generic and idolizing a single Western sculptor, and raises a loaded proposition concerning the ethics of taking cultural iconography and objects for one's art from outside the culture—specifically, as in Mabry's case (white, Western, male), from the dominant culture that has historically subjugated the other. The answer is murky, especially as Mabry seems highly aware of the sensitive nature of his premise; perhaps another gesture to consider is that he places the Peruvian-inspired objects on top of the Judd-like boxes, suggesting a reversal of the colonialist trope. And while Mabry appropriates Rodin and Judd in the same democratic, nonhierarchical gesture as he does the ethnographic objects, for the latter, the edge of the colonizing culture taking from non-Western cultures might pour lemon into the timeworn wound. But as it was for the edgy Los Angeles generation before him, à la Mike Kelley, Liz Larner,

105. Nathan Mabry, in email correspondence with author, November 13, 2018.

106. Ibid.

107. Ibid.

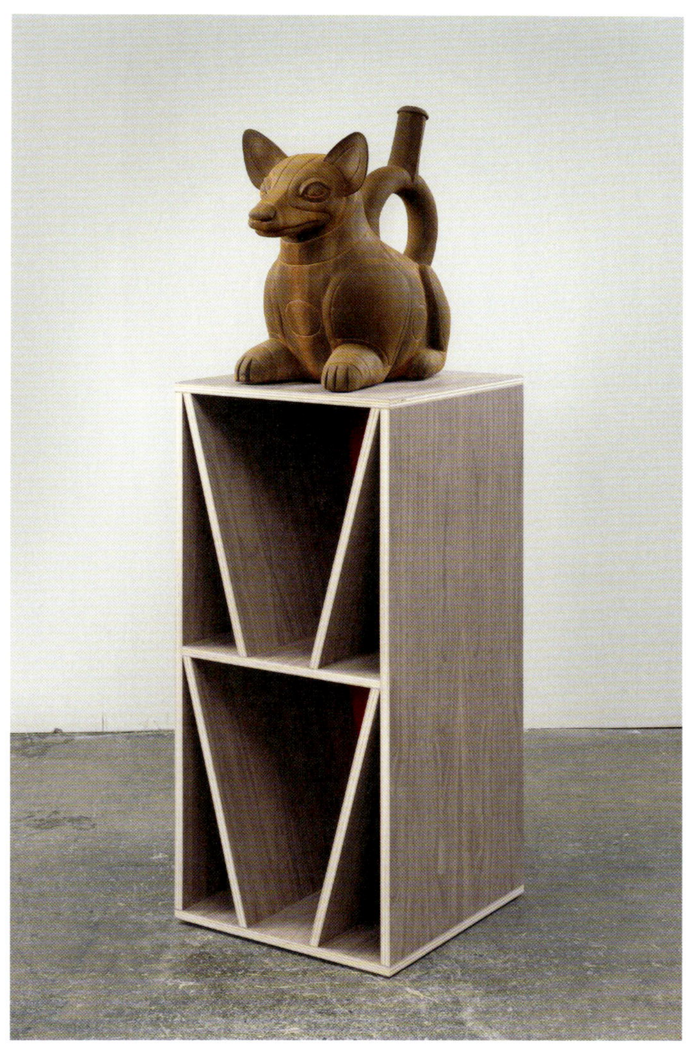

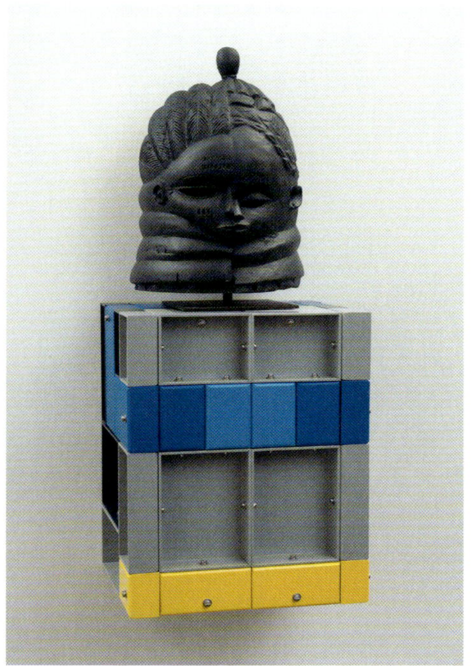

Fig. 26 Nathan Mabry, *T/O/T/E/M (. . . dog eat dog . . .)*, 2014. Terra-cotta, patina, walnut plywood, and Plexiglas. 63 x 18 x 18 inches.

Fig. 27 Nathan Mabry, *u.n.t.i.t.l.e.d. (Crouching Figure – Blue)*, 2012. Bronze, aluminum, paint, and stainless steel. 28 x 12 x 11 inches. Edition of 1, 1 AP.

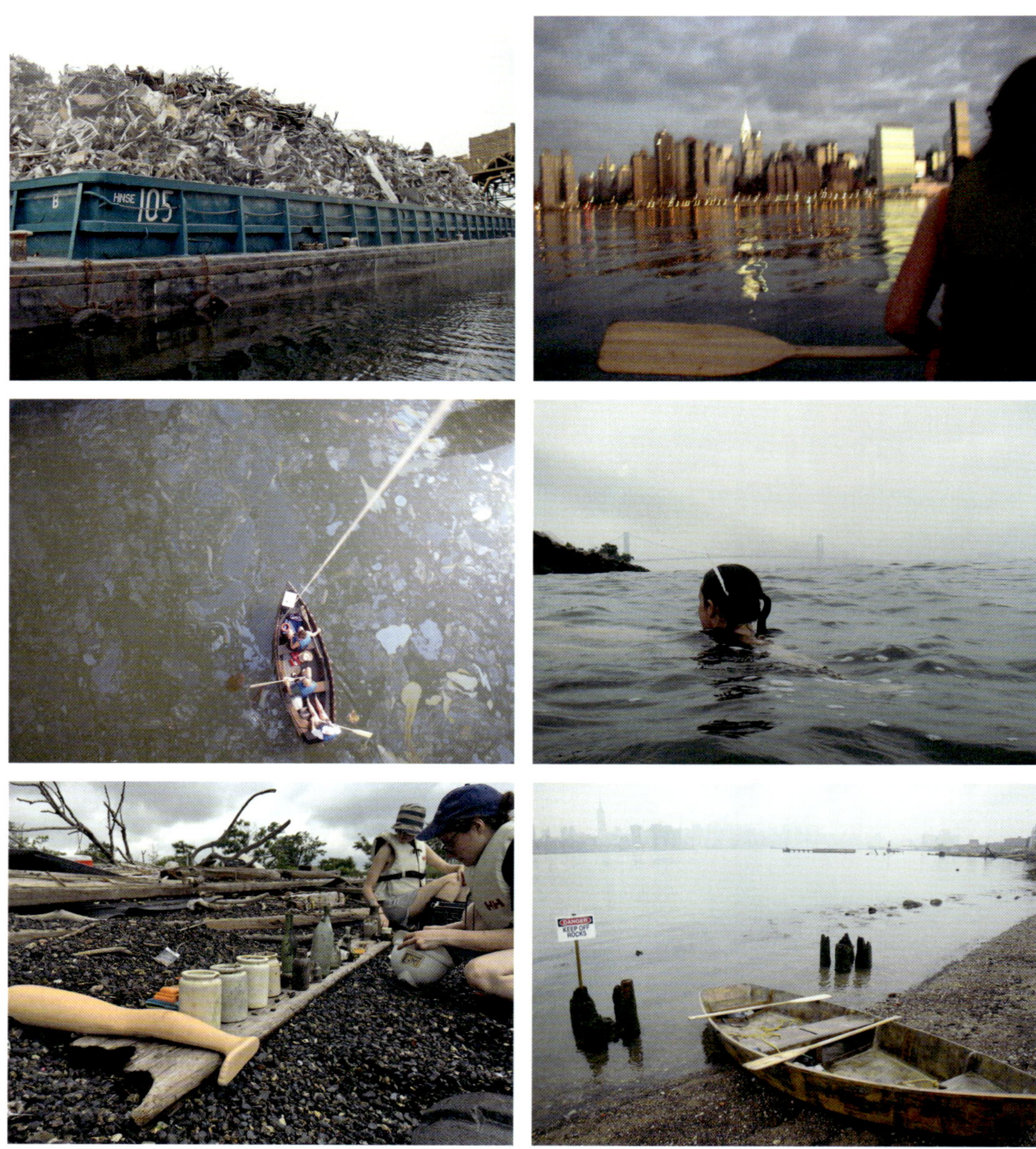

Fig. 28 Marie Lorenz, *Tide and Current Taxi*, 2005 – ongoing. Participatory boat excursions with the artist; boats designed and built by the artist.

Clockwise from top left:

Gowanus Canal, New York, with Anne Daems and Josiah McElheny, 2006
East River, New York, with Melissa Brown, Brian Dunn, Erinn Fierst, and Birgit Rathsman, 2007
Hoffman Island, New York, with Rachel Mason, 2009
East River, New York, with Yutaka Sho, 2010
Arthur Kill Waterway, New Jersey and New York, with Babbie Dunnington and Essye Klempner, 2017
Gowanus Canal, New York, with Iben Carlsen and Kristian Johansson, 2013

Paul McCarthy (Mabry's former professor at UCLA), Nancy Rubins, et al., this is part of the work's intent: adventurous, irreverent, and profane, neither didactic nor impartial, but perhaps walking the line of cultural ethics and generating discourse along the way.

EXCAVATION

With her emphasis on discarded objects in urban waterways—what art historian Norman Bryson referred to as "rhopography," or the focus on overlooked things—**Marie Lorenz** (born 1973 in Twentynine Palms, California; lives and works in Brooklyn, New York, and Austin, Texas) bridges the worlds of contemporary art, anthropology, and archaeology, the latter a field related to anthropology in its study of people through material culture, but focused on historical objects of past nonextant cultures.[108] Lorenz's current practice (pun intended) involves exploring the rivers and passageways in cities firsthand, recording and recontextualizing the resulting found detritus and experiences. While the cultures who discard plastic bottles and other refuse along the waterways are ostensibly still alive (us), Lorenz suggests worlds past in the loose interpretations that appear in her work. For her project *Tide and Current Taxi*, 2005 – ongoing, begun in New York Harbor, Lorenz takes guests in a canoe (including beautiful wooden examples she built herself) or rowboat on an undetermined adventure (see fig. 28).[109] This format evolved from boating excursions Lorenz would take on her own, sometimes for weeks at a time. In spring 2018, Lorenz organized one of her tide taxi adventures in Austin, and invited me along as a passenger. The point of this particular excursion was to witness the evening migration of the Mexican free-tailed bats, a phenomenon whereby at sunset from March through early November, these winged creatures come pouring out from under the Congress Avenue Bridge in a torrent at dusk to go find their insect dinner. We set out onto the Colorado River and approached the bridge, home to approximately 1.5 million of these diminutive mammals. There, we were surrounded by a cotillion of boats—canoes, kayaks, small motor boats, and a swan pedal boat—and above us, throngs of tourists lining the bridge peering down. Soon enough, the bats came swarming out, wings feverishly flapping, in a moving black cloud like a tidal wave pouring out from beneath the bridge. Soon after, we rowed up to the flashy neon sign of Joe's Crab Shack, a place where nobody aspires to eat but one always wonders about, climbed up the bank to the surprise of the other customers, ate what seemed like an inordinate amount of mediocre crab, and boated away. The experience was exciting, unpredictable, and memorable, a voyage of discovering the little-seen parts of Austin from the unfamiliar vantage of the water's underbelly.

108. Norman Bryson, *Looking at the Overlooked: Four Essays on Still Life Painting* (London: Reaktion Books, 1990).

109. Marie Lorenz, *Tide and Current Taxi*, 2005 – ongoing, http://www.tideandcurrenttaxi.org.

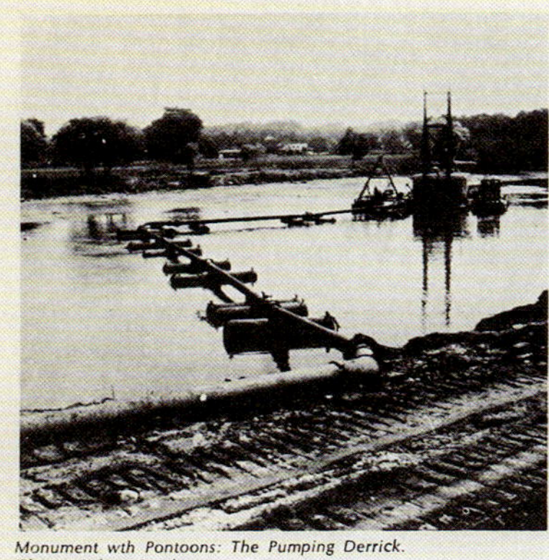

Monument with Pontoons: The Pumping Derrick. (Photo: Robert Smithson)

The Great Pipes Monument. (Photo: Robert Smithson)

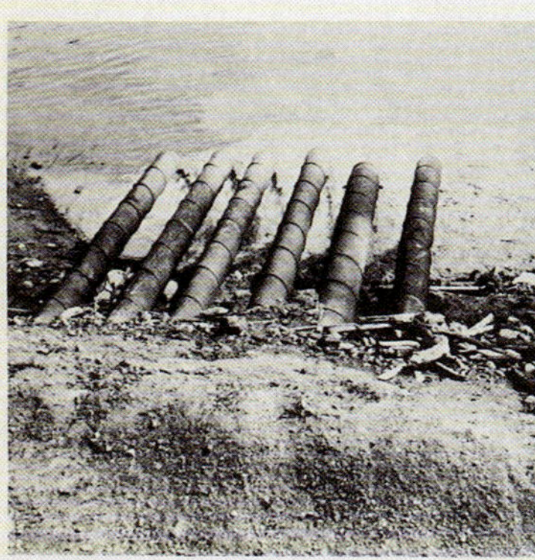

The Fountain Monument—Bird's-Eye View. (Photo: Robert Smithson)

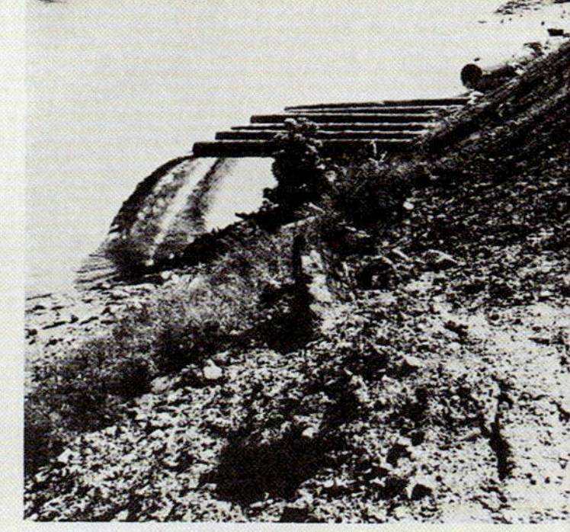

The Fountain Monument: Side View. (Photo Robert Smithson)

debris rattling in the water that passed through the great pipe.

Nearby, on the river bank, was an artificial crater that contained a pale limpid pond of water, and from the side of the crater protruded six large pipes that gushed the water of the pond into the river. This constituted a monumental fountain that suggested six horizontal smokestacks that seemed to be flooding the river with liquid smoke. The great pipe was in some enigmatic way connected with the infernal fountain. It was as though the pipe was secretly sodomizing some hidden technological orifice, and causing a monstrous sexual organ (the fountain) to have an orgasm. A psychoanalyst might say that the landscape displayed "homosexual tendencies," but I will not draw such a crass anthropomorphic conclusion. I will merely say, "It was there."

Across the river in Rutherford one could hear the faint voice of a P. A. system and the weak cheers of a crowd at a football game. Actually, the landscape was no landscape, but "a particular kind of heliotypy" (Nabokov), a kind of self-destroying postcard world of failed immortality and oppressive grandeur. I had been wandering in a moving picture that I couldn't quite picture, but just as I became perplexed, I saw a green sign that explained everything:

YOUR HIGHWAY TAXES 21
AT WORK

Federal Highway Trust Funds 2,867,000	U.S. Dept. of Commerce Bureau of Public Roads State Highway Funds 2,867,000

New Jersey State Highway Dept.

That zero panorama seemed to contain *ruins in reverse*, that is — all the new construction that would eventually be built. This is the opposite of the "romantic ruin" because the buildings don't *fall* into ruin *after* they are built but rather *rise* into ruin *before* they are built. This anti-romantic *mise-en-scene* suggests the discredited idea of *time* and many other "out of date" things. But the suburbs exist without a rational past and without the "big events" of history. Oh, maybe there are a few statues, a legend, and a couple of curios, but no past — just what passes for a future. A Utopia minus a bottom, a place where the machines are idle, and the sun has turned to glass, and a place where the Passaic Concrete Plant (253 River Drive) does a good business in STONE, BITUMINOUS, SAND, and CEMENT. Passaic seems full of "holes" compared to New York City, which seems tightly packed and solid, and those holes in a sense are the monumental vacancies that define, without trying, the memory-traces of an abandoned set of futures. Such futures are found in grade B Utopian films, and then imitated by the suburbanite. The windows of City Motors auto sales proclaim the existence of Utopia through 1968 WIDE TRACK PONTIACS — Executive, Bonneville, Tempest, Grand Prix, Firebirds, GTO, Catalina, and LeMans — that visual

50

51

Fig. 29 Robert Smithson, "The Monuments of Passaic," *Artforum*, December 1967.

When Robert Smithson wrote in 1967 about his wanderings in the blighted landscape of Passaic, New Jersey—a graying, postindustrial topography of steel beams, bridges, wooden planks, and ramshackle constructions—he referred to these structures as "ruins in reverse," buildings that "*rise* into ruin before they are built" (see fig. 29).[110] Smithson's challenge to Turner-esque Romanticism through the identification of such territory for creative exploration resonates with contemporary archaeological excavations of dystopic landscapes, as in the work of Lorenz. On her walkabout at our sculpture park at The Contemporary Austin – Laguna Gloria, the artist identified an overlooked location along the edge of Lake Austin (the name for a section of the Colorado River between two central dams): an old but sometimes-used concrete boat launch at the end of a pathway, where Lorenz has installed a site-specific work, *Trap and Weir*, 2019, a collection of cast ceramic vessels and steel forms, evoking ancient Mesopotamian octopus traps and conventional steel lobster traps, seemingly abandoned in the fresh waters of Austin. As Lorenz notes, "I've always loved looking at piles of fishing traps; they have this contingent or incidental beauty. I guess fishing traps have to blend in with their environment so they take on natural qualities, but you wonder, is this broken garbage or an extremely well designed tool? I want my sculpture to have a hidden purpose, and for your imagination to wander over the object and put it to use."[111] The installation offers a strange and off-kilter assemblage that might lead one to wonder whether recent rains brought marine crustaceans to these freshwater bodies. Complementing this, Lorenz will reconstitute her water adventures with *Graybelt Field Trips*, 2019, a series of sojourns with Austin residents departing from Laguna Gloria and traveling along the Colorado River.

Archaeology's interest in the ancient and near past materializes a complex proposal for contemporary art: one that excavates undiscovered, forgotten, or overlooked corners while grappling with nostalgia and the fetishization of old things. As anthropology's ancient sibling and a field that developed without the crutch of language, archaeology analyzes material culture of the past to gain information about humankind, and can reach further back in time than its anthropological relative (which evolved around written ethnographic accounts).[112] But as with cultural anthropology, the projection of patterns, explanations, and interpretations as to cause and effect, and similarity and difference, onto archaeological remains is filtered through subjective ethnological processes: namely, individuals and their cultural lenses. With postmodernism's destabilization of narrative and classification, issues of ethnocentrism, postcolonialism, technology, and other biases recur, rendering

110. Robert Smithson, "A Tour of the Monuments of Passaic, New Jersey," in *The Writings of Robert Smithson*, ed. Nancy Holt (New York: New York University Press, 1979), 54. Originally published in *Artforum* as "The Monuments of Passaic," 1967.

111. Marie Lorenz, in email correspondence with author, February 9, 2019.

112. Society for American Archaeology, http://www.saa.org.

archaeology similarly porous to interpretation and fiction. As Michel Foucault wrote in his 1969 text *The Archaeology of Knowledge*, "when the researches of psychoanalysis, linguistics, and ethnology have decentered the subject in relation to the laws of his desire, the forms of his language, the rules of his action, or the games of his mythical or fabulous discourse, when it became clear that man himself, questioned as to what he was, could not account for his sexuality and his unconscious, the systematic forms of his language, or the regularities of his fictions, the theme of a continuity of history has been reactivated once again."[113] In the quest to uncover knowledge through material culture, these regular fictions become part of the narrative. Or in the words of a proletarian source, Hollywood's crooked-nosed archaeologist Dr. Indiana Jones, "Archaeology is the search for fact . . . not truth. If it's truth you're looking for, Dr. Tyree's philosophy class is right down the hall."[114]

The cultural implications of archaeological evidence similarly occupy the practice of artist **Ruben Ochoa** (born 1974 in Oceanside, California; lives and works in Los Angeles). Ochoa uses the vernacular materials of landscape and urban construction—rubble, rust, concrete, metal rebar, chain-link fences, and plain old California dirt—as quiet critiques of class and culture. A large part of his practice consists of sculpture, material forms mining Land art's conceptual premise of using the earth as material, but imbued with social and geographical implications toward community. Slabs of hollow concrete and dirt, as in *Once Extracted*, 2006–2009, a concrete rectangle (that turns out to be hollow, a facade) toppled into a pile of soil within a narrow indoor gallery space, become illusionistic mechanisms for formal and social concerns. *Flock in Space*, 2013, whose title riffs on Constantin Brancusi's iconic 1928 sculpture *Bird in Space*, consists of concrete footings and bent steel fence posts—recalling those that might be used to create border walls to prevent illegal immigration. Sited in a field outside the Trinity River Audubon Center in Dallas, Texas, a nature preserve on what was previously an illegal dump site, the upside-down and twisted fence posts take on the appearance of birds in flight or the kinetic tendrils of a jellyfish in motion.[115] For *The Sorcerer's Burden*, Ochoa's concrete pillar, *A bit of detritus*, 2011, marks Laguna Gloria's grounds with an anti-monumental totem, a continuation of the artist's interest in the refuse of urban construction placed in an outdoor natural landscape (see fig. 30).

113. Michel Foucault, *The Archaeology of Knowledge*, trans. A. M. Sheridan Smith (UK: Tavistock Publications, 1972; repr., London: Routledge, 1989); first published as *L'Archéologie du savoir* (Paris Éditions Gallimard, 1969).

114. Steven Spielberg, dir. *Indiana Jones and the Last Crusade* (Hollywood, CA: Paramount Pictures, 1989).

115. Ruben Ochoa, *Flock in Space*, 2013. Concrete and steel. Dimensions variable. Commissioned by the Nasher Sculpture Center for *Nasher XChange* and installed at the Trinity River Audubon Center, Dallas, October 19, 2013 – February 16, 2014.

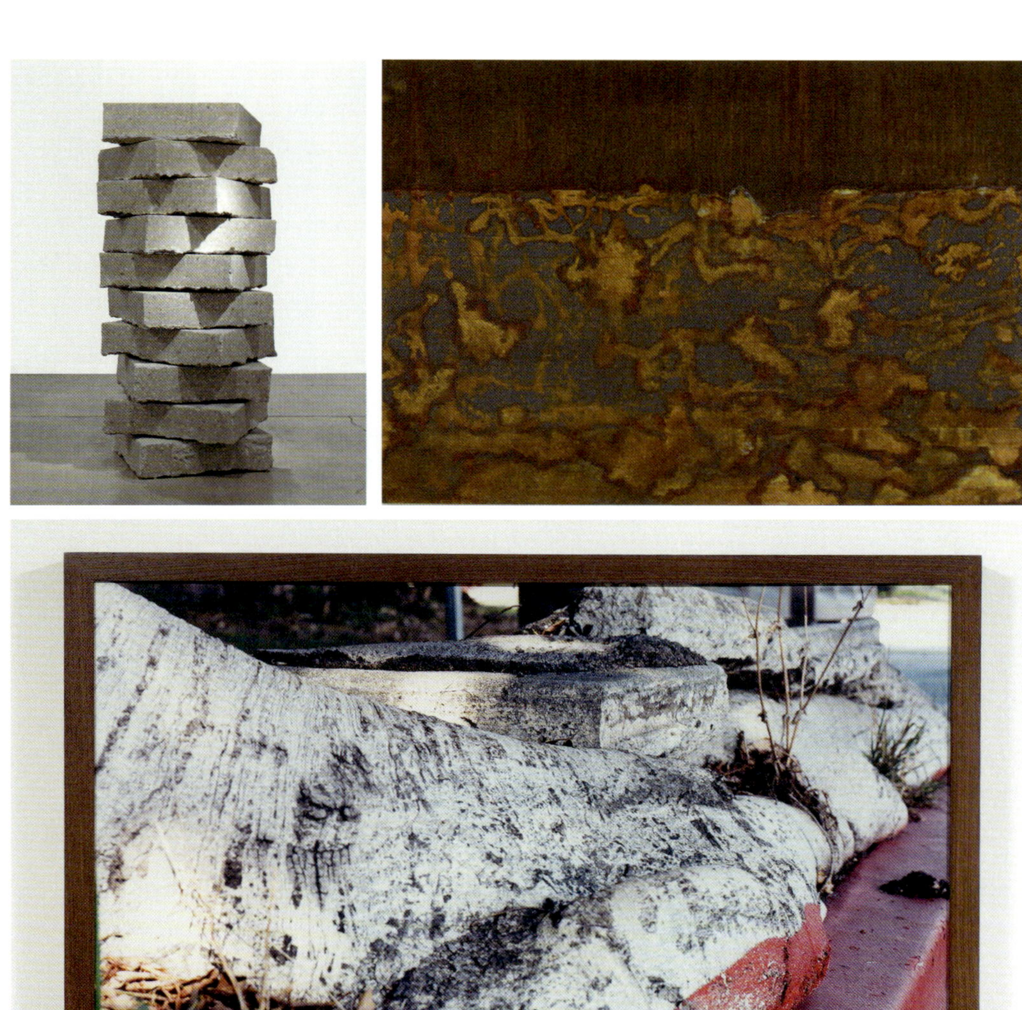

Fig. 30 Ruben Ochoa, *A bit of detritus*, 2011. Concrete, metal, and dirt. 80 x 32 x 32 inches.

Fig. 31 Ruben Ochoa, *Glyphs in the nite*, 2016. Rust on linen over panel. 90 x 126 inches.

Fig. 32 Ruben Ochoa, *Kissed in the 90011*, 2007. Chromogenic print in custom wenge frame. 43 x 53 ⅛ inches. Edition of 3, 2 AP.

Family history and personal experience also weave into Ochoa's practice, tying materials of the earth to his subjective memory. In our first conversation, Ochoa recounted a story from his childhood in Los Angeles, remembering that the roots of a massive ficus tree along the highway near his home had destroyed the sidewalk, creating an uneven and perilous passageway for the artist and his siblings. Ochoa recounted that in upscale neighborhoods, the trees were pruned and the sidewalks restored, while near his home and in other lower economic areas, they were left to run wild, creating inconsistent pathways and walking hazards. As the artist wrote:

> *When my parents bought their home, the city and developers planted a couple of ficus trees in front of the home. These were the familiar ficus trees that line most of the 1970s tract homes in Southern California.*
>
> *The first one was struck by lightning. The second remained, taking root, and eventually outgrowing its allotted space. The nature of these non-native trees is that their roots are always growing and searching for water. Over time this search for water began to uproot the sidewalk.*
>
> *I recall my father contacting the city for months to have the tree removed, but with no luck. My dad decided to take matters into his own hands and one weekend he invited over his construction buddies. Dressed in their official construction outfits, they laid out street cones, and my dad chopped down the ficus tree.*
>
> *I was too young to understand the significance of my dad's public intervention back then. All I could remember was how cool it was to have not only a sidewalk to ride bikes and skates, but now we had twice the width of a concrete sidewalk pad to ride about.*
>
> *It wasn't till I reflected on it years later that I realized it was my first encounter of an act of subversion and self-empowerment.*[116]

Ochoa pays homage to this in his series of detail photographs of the roots of ficus trees protruding through Los Angeles sidewalks, chromogenic prints in custom frames made from another specialized wood, wenge, a dark-toned, difficult-to-work-with material from the now endangered *Millettia laurentii* tree found in parts of Tanzania, Mozambique, Zimbabwe, and South Africa.[117] A series of these ficus tree photographs—along with Ochoa's recent rust paintings, such as *Season of Darkness*, 2015, *Tripping the Light Fantastick*, 2015, and *Glyphs in the nite*, 2016—are featured

116. Ruben Ochoa, in email correspondence with author, December 17, 2018.

117. Another name for the wood is African rosewood. See Gene Wengert, "Wenge highly favored, but endangered," *Woodworking Network*, June 17, 2013, https://www.woodworkingnetwork.com/wood/wood-month/wenge-highly-favored-endangered.

in *The Sorcerer's Burden* (see fig. 31). As natural elements intersecting with urban topography, ficus trees represent the constant struggle of municipal management to maintain flat sidewalks throughout the city, and serve as testimony to what scholar Elly Van Eeghem refers to as "urban cracks," defined as "transitory zones falling between the conventional boundaries of urban planning and often labelled as wastelands."[118] The roots almost look like the gentle curvatures of elephant feet, beautiful and large, wanting our sympathy, and similar in their mottled gray-scale tone to the irregular concrete. Blocks of concrete jut irregularly at odd angles, exposing dirt and grass beneath. In one photograph in the series, *Kissed in the 90011*, 2007, the haphazard treatment by the city becomes evident in the iridescent fuchsia spray paint intended to demarcate a curb zone that has spilled messily onto the tree roots themselves (see fig. 32). The images are installed low, eight inches from the ground, suggesting the sidewalks they depict and putting the trees' bodies in proximity to the viewer's body. The images uncover beauty in neglected areas while testifying to the struggles between man and nature and the disparity in geographies revealed through the overlooked details of urban construction.

MAGIC

In Argentinean author and magical realist Jorge Luis Borges's short fiction "The Library of Babel," four walls of bookshelves, each lining an indefinite number of hexagonal galleries within a singular library, house all the information needed for human survival. Although most of the books contain pure gibberish, somewhere in their midst exists every manuscript ever written and all its possible permutations, including the mythological lure of the "Crimson Hexagon," or books that were "omnipotent, illustrated, and magical."[119] The promise of total and universal knowledge creates a spiraling cacophony for Borges's fictive custodians and philosophers, with conflicted and opposing reactions around the assessment, categorization, elimination, and even destruction of various aspects of the library's contents in order to better understand them. The story concludes with a revelation: rather than a singular truth or knowledge to be found within the library's holdings, Borges instead writes of a periodic information gathering delineated by subsequent generations, who interpret the disorder of the library and the information within its books in perpetuity. Here the beauty of magical realism lies in its ability to juxtapose time, space, and reality in a complex continuum, where past, present, and future can coexist and overlap simultaneously, and the resulting paradoxes reveal information about our current lives.

118. Elly Van Eeghem, "Urban cracks: sites of meaning for critical artistic practice," *Critical Arts* 27, no. 5 (October 2013): 587.

119. Jorge Luis Borges, "The Library of Babel," in *Collected Fictions*, trans. Andrew Hurley (New York: Penguin Books, 1998), 116. First published in 1944 as part of Borges's collection *The Garden of Forking Paths*.

Although rare to find such a perfect bard as Borges, storytelling, and the overlapping of past, present, and future temporal spaces, drives both ethnography and exhibition making. In the attempt to highlight narratives and events around people, objects, or themes, within the systemic fields of both art and anthropology one must assess key questions of power and subjectivity: Who gets to tell the story, and why? How does one determine what is incorporated and what is left out, or the process of inclusion and omission? What role do fact and fiction play in the retelling of stories, and how does this impart knowledge? In a 2016 lecture, Paul Stoller, author of the ethnofiction *The Sorcerer's Burden: The Ethnographic Saga of a Global Family* and the inspiration for this exhibition's title, quoting American author Tim O'Brien, noted, "Stories are for those late hours of the night when you can't remember how you got from where you were to where you are. Stories are for an eternity, when memory is erased, when there is nothing to remember except the story."[120] Stoller was speaking to the imaginative narrative capabilities of ethnofictive filmmaker Jean Rouch, whereby the quality and importance of ethnographic film or text devolves from its ability to connect past to future. The idea that through storytelling, a field that leans toward the fictional, one might tell greater truths than through objective historical accounts is worth considering. While storytelling admits to imaginative falsities for the sake of pleasure, poetry, and entertainment, intellectual, philosophical, and existential concepts can be conveyed with equivalent veracity. Likewise, "objective" accounts, when taken at face value, risk the omission of partisanship and subjectivity inherent in their premises, while parading as hard truths.

Within both Western anthropological and art historical veins, magic aligns with storytelling as a means of detaching from perceived, non-negotiable categorizations (in Western culture) such as linear time and scientific facts, allowing for imaginative reinterpretations that lend insight into lived realities. In non-Western cultures, magic can hold religious and spiritual power in regards to belief, ritual, healing, and death. Contemporary North American and European cultures tend to regard magic as secular fetishism, or the idolization of objects' powers without the religious component, as well as a means to describe wishful thinking, unexplained occurrences, or the theme of a Halloween costume. But the word also alludes to dark histories around men and women persecuted as witches in Salem, Massachusetts, and elsewhere in colonial North America and Europe during the fifteenth to eighteenth centuries (examples from antiquity and other periods also exist)—a terrible interlude not unlike the acts of colonialism discussed throughout this exhibition. The difference between Western and non-Western conceptions of magic can become complicated in exhibition

120. Tim O'Brien, *The Things They Carried*, 1990; quoted by Paul Stoller, "The Burden of Writing the Sorcerer's Burden: Ethnography, Fiction and the Future of Anthropological Expression" (lecture, Granada Centre for Visual Anthropology, The University of Manchester, April 19, 2016), https://vimeo.com/164230194.

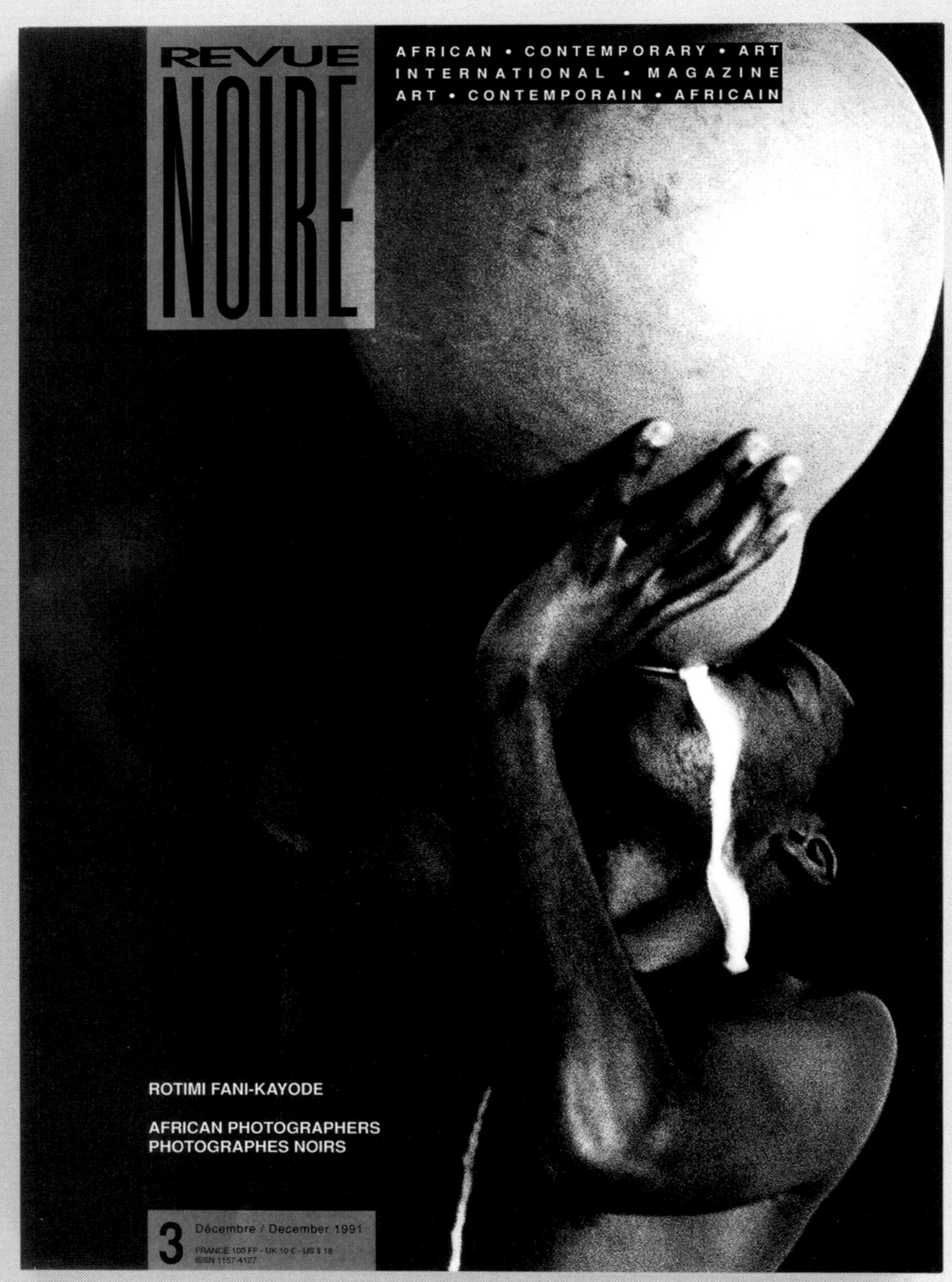

Fig. 33 Cover, *Revue Noire* No. 3, December 1991, featuring photograph by Rotimi Fani-Kayodé, *Milk Drinker* (detail), 1983.

making, and a recent history of exhibition making evidences the thread of "magic" and its various disputed meanings, using them as a linchpin for discussions around the intersection of art and anthropology.

The early twentieth-century debate around primitivism and Picasso's attraction to the "magic" of tribal objects began the contested discussion for art world modernism, while decades later, the 1984 MoMA exhibition *"Primitivism" in 20th Century Art: Affinity of the Tribal and the Modern* reiterated and further mythologized the "magic" of these non-Western objects.[121] The primitivist movement represents an innovative but problematic gesture that potentially opened the door for widespread appropriation, misappropriation, and (mis)interpretation in subsequent generations. The 1989 exhibition *Magiciens de la terre*, curated by Jean-Hubert Martin at the Centre Pompidou and the Grande Halle de la Villette in Paris, attempted to challenge the Picasso/MoMA model by replacing the label "artist" with "magician," ostensibly suggesting individual authorship for each artist included in the show.[122] With over one hundred artists evenly split between the West and the rest of the world, the exhibition aimed to counter the hegemony of the MoMA exhibition and the concept of primitivism by promoting a transnational, democratic sensibility among the artists and their work. But equally fraught was the gesture of appropriating magic's non-Western meaning and transferring its intent to one of European, artist-as-genius individualization. While the exhibition made progress in terms of perspective on contemporary global practices, in particular non-Western ones, it nonetheless promoted neocolonialist impulses, including the decontextualization of the ethnographic objects and the use of Westernized aesthetic rationales to pair artists with others—a problem that Martin himself acknowledged in his curatorial writings.[123]

This resulted in several counter-initiatives. One stands out: *Revue Noire* (Black Review), an art space and magazine founded in Paris in 1991 by Simon Njami, Loup Pivin, Pascal Martin Saint Léon, and Bruno Tilliette (see fig. 33). Emerging shortly after *Magiciens* and in direct response, the magazine (which ran for a decade, until 2001) proposed conversations around and critiques of African artists and contemporary practices from *within*, engaging non-Western perspectives and leaving aside ethnographic interpretations for social, political, and art historical ones. As Njami said, "The founders of *Revue Noire* were above all interested in contemporary practices. Therefore, our aim was to show that it was not that different in Africa and that people should stop looking at

121. The Museum of Modern Art, "New Exhibition Opening September 27 at Museum of Modern Art Examines 'Primitivism' in 20th Century Art," news release no. 17, August 1984.

122. Steeds et al., *Making Art Global (Part 2)*.

123. Jean-Hubert Martin, "The Death of Art – Long Live Art," 1986; repr. in *Making Art Global (Part 2)*, 218.

African production with an ethnographic eye."[124] African art on its own terms, without the European gaze.

Deeply invested in the ethnographic practice of archival research and the lineage of African history, folklore, and magic as avenues for storytelling, the artist **Kapwani Kiwanga** (born 1978 in Hamilton, Ontario, Canada; lives and works in Paris) operates within this contested space, often turning to museological display and historical archives for source material. Born in Canada, based in Paris, and of partial Tanzanian heritage (on her father's side), Kiwanga originally studied anthropology and comparative religion at McGill University in Montreal before moving to Paris to attend the École Nationale Supérieure des Beaux-Arts de Paris, a cross-disciplinary and cultural pollination that informs her critiques around historical narratives and power structures. For much of her work, Kiwanga conducts extensive archival research into African histories, gravitating toward recorded factual "truths" in historical memory and cultural identity, which she then recontextualizes, alters, or transforms to reveal and critique their subjectivity as well as to raise questions around authorship. In this fusion of fact and fiction, her work has affinities to Afrofuturism, a historical movement that emerged in the 1990s blending visual art with film, literature, music, folklore, and science fiction to create utopian (or dystopian) narratives around black identity. In *Afrogalatica*, 2011 – ongoing, Kiwanga invented an anthropologist who has come back from the future to tell the story of the Afronauts and African space initiatives in the 1950s—similarly explored by Nuotama Bodomo in her 2014 film *Afronauts*. Such projects propose concepts of alternative utopias with imaginative fictions woven into historical truths. In her 2014 exhibition at the Jeu de Paume in Paris, *Maji Maji*, Kiwanga took magic as her subject matter through a revisiting of a historical event: the Maji Maji Rebellion from 1905 to 1907, an African uprising in Tanganyika (now Tanzania) against oppressive German colonial rule. With a culture steeped in the belief of supernatural forces, the war was initiated by the shaman and prophet Kinjikitile Ngwale, also called Bokero, who inspired the rebellion by promoting the belief that sacred water, or maji, would protect the insurgents from German bullets (a failed premise).[125] Kiwanga's conception for the exhibition focused on abstracted ideas of untold narratives, a "subjective archive" highlighting absence and presence.[126] Continuing her exploration of the magical alongside the traumatic past, for *The Sorcerer's Burden*, Kiwanga's new project, *Glow*, 2019,

124. Simon Njami, interview by Paula Kupfer, *Aperture*, September 12, 2002, https://aperture.org/blog/qa-simon-njami.

125. Alys Beverton, "Maji Maji Uprising (1905–1907)," *BlackPast*, June 21, 2009, https://blackpast.org/gah/maji-maji-uprising-1905-1907.

126. Nataša Petrešin-Bachelez, curatorial statement for the exhibition *Kapwani Kiwanga: Maji Maji*, Jeu de Paume, Paris, 2014, http://www.jeudepaume.org/index.php?page=article&idArt=2067.

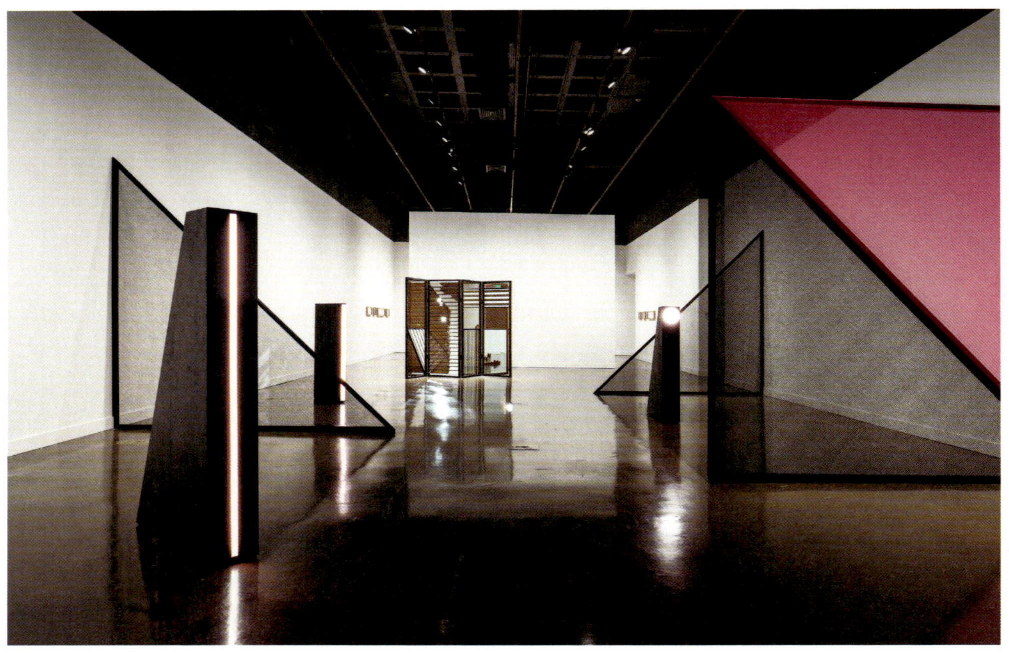

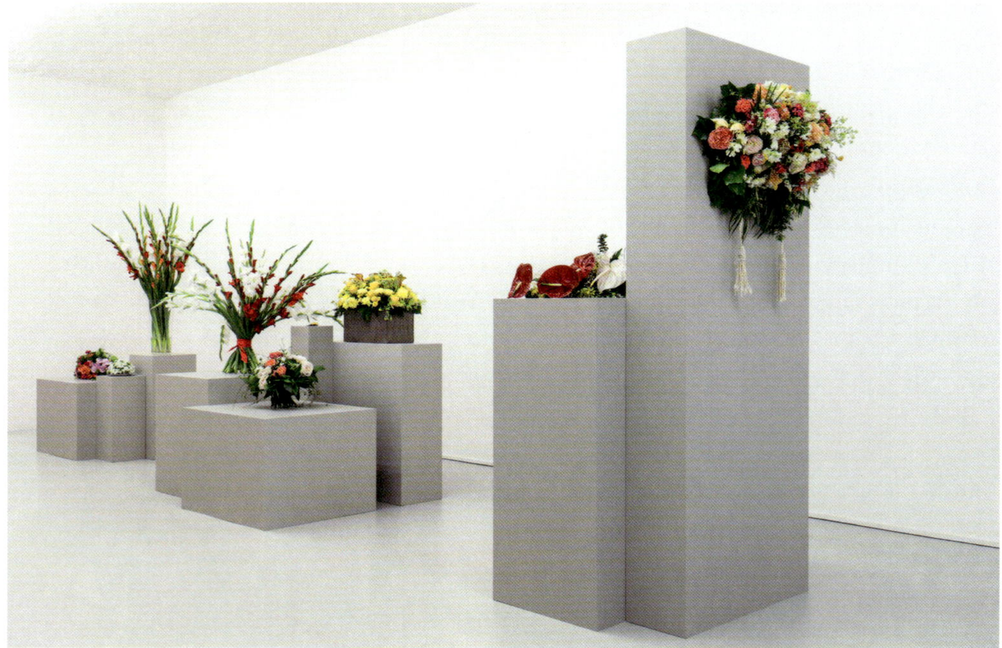

Fig. 34 Installation view, *Kapwani Kiwanga: Safe Passage*, MIT List Visual Arts Center, Cambridge, Massachusetts, 2019.

Fig. 35 Kapwani Kiwanga, *Flowers for Africa*, 2013 – ongoing. Floral arrangements. Installation view, *Flowers are Documents – Arrangement I & II*, ar/ge kunst, Bolzano, Italy, 2017.

touches on the experiences of enslaved people of color living in North America. Obscured in low-lit galleries, the installation consists of four human-scaled, darkly painted abstract sculptures with interior, glowing light components within each three-dimensional form, referencing eighteenth-century surveillance measures known as "lantern laws," which were enacted to deter public assembly and required all unaccompanied slaves to carry a lantern or lit candle after dark to ensure their visibility (see fig. 34).[127]

As the artist has stated, seemingly impenetrable and fixed aspects of both history and lived experience "can be deconstructed and circumnavigated," through either the critiquing and retelling, or conversely the fetishization, of objects and events.[128] Both are apparent in her ongoing series *Flowers for Africa*, an example of which has been produced for this exhibition. For this project, Kiwanga initiates the re-creation of floral arrangements present in defining moments of independence in African countries, found by the artist in photographs and grainy moving image footage in various research archives (see fig. 35). From a bouquet handed to a dignitary to a boutonniere on the lapel of a politician, Kiwanga pushes these celebratory occasions to the forefront by bringing a subtle but symbolic element back to life (literally), and death again. For example, *Flowers for Africa: Tunisia*, 2014, a single red flower—dependent on the florist's choice in each instance—commemorates the moment when the leader of the Neo Destour Party, Habib Bourguiba, returned from Paris to Tunis, Tunisia, to celebrate his nation's independence in March 1956.[129] For each installation, the artist offers a written protocol, with details and interpretation left to the museum and/or particular florist. The flowers are presented on a simple pedestal, exposed, without water—left to wilt and die over the course of the exhibition. Here Kiwanga interrogates the myths or fallacies around historical events, identifying the perceived, and misleading, magic of *things*—what cultural "Thing Theory" theorist Bill Brown phrases as objects' "force as a sensuous presence or as a metaphysical presence, the magic by which objects become values, fetishes, idols, and totems."[130] The reconstitution of these bouquets, resuscitated from the past like talismans, followed by their fragile organic decline over time in the exhibition space, suggests a metaphor for the blind spots manifested by history's neglected moments, of minority or subjugated groups—perhaps also a fable that flowers, like stories, if not tended will die.

127. Kapwani Kiwanga, in Skype conversation with author, October 16, 2018.

128. Kapwani Kiwanga, interview presented by Harbourfront Centre in conjunction with the exhibition *Kapwani Kiwanga: A wall is just a wall* at The Power Plant, Toronto, Ontario, February 2017, https://www.youtube.com/watch?v=Pj9JfbZp2yc.

129. Kathleen Ritter, curatorial statement for the exhibition *Kapwani Kiwanga: Flowers for Africa*, Or Gallery, Vancouver, British Columbia, 2017, http://www.orgallery.org/Flowers-for-Africa.

130. Bill Brown, "Thing Theory," in *Things*, ed. Bill Brown (Chicago: The University of Chicago Press, 2004), 5.

While contemporary art exhibitions that directly or indirectly address the intersection of art and anthropology have been numerous in recent decades, *The Sorcerer's Burden* has particular resonance today in the context of contemporary museological and political currents. Museums that include ethnographic objects (including anthropological and encyclopedic art institutions) are facing unprecedented challenges to ownership in light of the distress of colonial theft. And while this global tide change of attitudes toward the ownership of non-Western objects is recent, the concept of returning looted art is not. Provenance research, or the inquiries that determine a work of art's ownership from inception to the present day, became a rigorous and essential component of modern art museums post–World War II. For decades, collecting institutions have followed strict procedures in regards to artwork dated pre-1950, both for existing objects in the collection and for those being proposed for acquisition, as a means to prevent the possibility of housing Nazi-looted art. Labeled "degenerate art" by Hilter's Third Reich, countless priceless works of art and collections in their entirety, primarily belonging to state-owned museums and Jewish families, were either stolen or dispersed during World War II. In recent times, there have been continuous examples—often contentious, emotional, and mired in long legal battles—of challenges to artworks in major museums whose provenance was found to trace to theft during this era; many of these works have been returned to the families of the original Jewish owners. Such contests often lead to sales of the artwork by the current families and well-deserved financial compensation, as well as the unfortunate re-dispersal of the work into private collections not accessible to the public.

Likewise, restitution and repatriation, referring to the return of something to its original owner, have been a topic of discussion in academic and museum anthropological circles for decades. My colleagues at Oxford and I studied several cases during my time there—including the return of an Indigenous American object meant for a burial ground and never intended to be preserved in a museum—often using particular items in the Pitt Rivers and other British ethnographic museum collections as examples. Over the past few decades, the British Museum has offered to loan objects to originating countries who request them, but has historically set the bar with an immutable stance against restitution, resisting the possible permanent return of its myriad colonial treasures, such as the Parthenon Marbles, Egyptian Rosetta Stone, and hundreds of Benin bronzes. Recently, however, the potential widespread restitution of non-Western objects in museum collections around the world has become a topic at the forefront of public discussions, alluding to a shift in the status quo. In early 2018, French president Emmanuel Macron commissioned a report by two independent scholars—French art historian Bénédicte Savoy and Senegalese academic Felwine Sarr—around the possible restitution of France's objects of sub-Saharan African heritage back to their original colonies. This would apply to all objects acquired pre-1960, some two-thirds of France's ninety thousand African pieces.[131] The report came to the dramatic conclusion that *all* objects taken without consent during the colonial period, as inventoried by France, should be returned if the countries of origin elect for this action after a series of bilateral commissions. The report also took important steps to refer to artifacts acquired in improper manners as "theft, looting, despoilment, trickery, and forced consent," in support of the use of the term "restitution," thus altering the colonialist language into one that acknowledges the aggression toward and subjugation of its victims in the acquisition of these objects.[132] In response, Macron announced that the Musée du Quai Branly, an iconic (and contested) ethnographic museum in Paris, would immediately return twenty-six objects looted by French colonialist forces in 1892 to Benin, their country of origin.[133]

As to be expected, the conversation remains complex. One might also humor a degree of skepticism around such a benevolent mandate, wondering what, if any, other political intentions might also be driving the agenda. At the time of this writing, no other museums have rushed to return objects, and Macron has assigned a task force and called for a conference to discuss the matter. Scholars, museum directors, curators, and others have made public calls for regulation of and guidelines for colonial-era objects in museums, while others have strongly protested the recommendations.[134] But while the intention behind returning all objects might be necessary as a corrective to a system heavily weighted in the colonialist direction, the situation is more nuanced than undergoing such an action immediately would suggest, especially as histories and provenance require research and many questions arise. Would this result in the emptying en masse of European museums housing these objects? How far back in time does this apply? What about non-Western colonies that themselves looted things; will they be held accountable? What if returning the objects to their homes will cause their unintentional decay and destruction, either due to lack of proper conditions or a dangerous political climate? Certainly, returning immediately at least the most obvious and worst

131. Vincent Noce, "'Give Africa Its Art Back,' Macron's Report Says," Cultural Policy, *The Art Newspaper*, November 20, 2018, https://www.theartnewspaper.com/news/give-africa-its-art-back-macron-s-report-says.

132. Kate Brown, "In a Groundbreaking Report, Experts Advise French President Macron to Begin the 'Restitution' of Looted African Art," Art World, *Artnet*, November 20, 2018, https://news.artnet.com/art-world/french-restitution-policy-macron-1399429.

133. Farah Nayeri, "Return of African Artifacts Sets a Tricky Precedent for Europe's Museums," Art & Design, *New York Times*, November 27, 2018, https://www.nytimes.com/2018/11/27/arts/design/macron-report-restitution-precedent.html.

134. "Scholars Urge Germany to Create a National Institute Addressing Colonial-Era Objects," Artforum.com, posted December 14, 2018, https://www.artforum.com/news/-77992.

offending objects to their rightful owners and countries would begin to break down the walls between countries and allow for further discussion. Recently, the Museum of Black Civilizations opened in Dakar, Senegal; among its objects was a prized nineteenth-century sword on loan from France that, after Macron's report, could fall within the parameters of being illegitimately acquired, and thus could be argued to remain in Senegal permanently. As a Senegalese artist said in a *New York Times* article about the new institution, the museum "is a significant turning point for us as a continent to be able to know about ourselves through our very own teachings and rewrite our own history through these objects."[135] These and other questions tap the central nervous system of this exhibition's premise—that the burden of the appropriation of cultural property in relation to material culture and identity is complex, nuanced, and personal. All of the artists in this exhibition address these issues around culture, identity, race, and colonialism in direct and indirect ways in their work.

On the broader stage, the works in this exhibition point to current discussions around issues of nationalism, immigration, gender, diversity, and the environment. What could be more colonialist than the global resurgence in nationalist and white supremacist movements, as seen in Trumpism in the US, Russia, China, Brazil, and Poland? Although academia categorizes ours as a "post-" era—postmodern, poststructuralist, postcolonial—in many ways, we are not significantly post- nor past these originating scenarios. The unprecedented political groundswell of responses in the form of the #MeToo, Black Lives Matter, Women's March, Decolonize This Place, and other grassroots movements testifies to the continuation of our culture wars. The protests have been long overdue for their inroads into raising awareness and engendering a gradual cultural shift toward acknowledging victims, women, minorities, and others whose voices have historically been suppressed. For those caught in the middle, a more general sense that our country has lost the ability to listen to those of differing opinions has led to cultural and political fatigue. Within this context, both the fields of contemporary art and anthropology are struggling with their own homogeneous histories, through self-reflexive and self-critical attempts to diversify and expand perspectives, leading to the next chapter, one that will be more transnational, cross-disciplinary, and polyvalent. The conflicting sides suggest an era of potential decolonization, even as isolationism and nationalism, inflamed by the threatened loss of centuries of power, are also on the rise. Yet driven by increasing diversity in our cultures, secularism, grassroots resistance, and growing internationalism and diversity within institutions, the grip of European and American hegemony on cultural canons might gradually begin to loosen. As Harvard Art Museums colleague

135. Farah Nayeri and Dionne Searcey, "A Welcome Home for Art in Senegal," Arts Section, *New York Times*, January 16, 2019.

David Odo points out in the interview in this book, more diversity at the table and more listening by the dominant culture are pathways to improvement. But, as Odo and many others question, will this be enough?

In a recent issue of *Frieze* magazine dedicated entirely to the issue of "decolonizing culture," the artist Naeem Mohaiemen wrote: "Expecting the Global South to always 'bring' its narratives into the proscenium places all the *burden* on one side: for us to know equally our stories and yours – a project of twice the work. What is needed is much more joyous entanglement between the two, not only in listening to these stories, but also in their making: not as duty, but as pleasure—the way things could be."[136] Returning to the evolution of biennial exhibitions as temperature takers for the art world's climate, celebration as political resistance took shape in the most recent *Carnegie International*, the 57th Edition in 2018, organized by Ingrid Schaffner with an advisory committee of international curators. The exhibition's premise and hashtag (a tactic to capture young audiences) promoted #MuseumJoy, a phrase Schaffner coined to refer to the happiness inspired by the shared experience of looking at art. As I was surrounded by art world colleagues at the October 2018 opening—typically a jaded crowd—the concept was at first difficult to digest in its apparent blanket optimism. But after consideration, while at times "joy" could be accessed in the projects included and at times not, as an overarching theme it became somehow quietly relevant to our times. And so we return to *The Sorcerer's Burden*, and the myriad subversive and poetic ways that the works included approach the intersection of art and anthropology, questions around cultural identity, and the possibilities for alternative futures in a decolonized space. Within this environment, where play, imagination, and mischief temper the painful gravitas of past and present trauma, these many forms of storytelling around objects, memory, and people, enacted through the eyes of the artists and works in this exhibition, have the potential to communicate vital insights about the human condition in today's complicated world.

136. Naeem Mohaiemen, "Same Old Stories: The meaning of 'hegemony,'" *Frieze*, no. 199 (November–December 2018): 20. Emphasis added.

DISCLOSING THE PAST

AN AUTOBIOGRAPHY

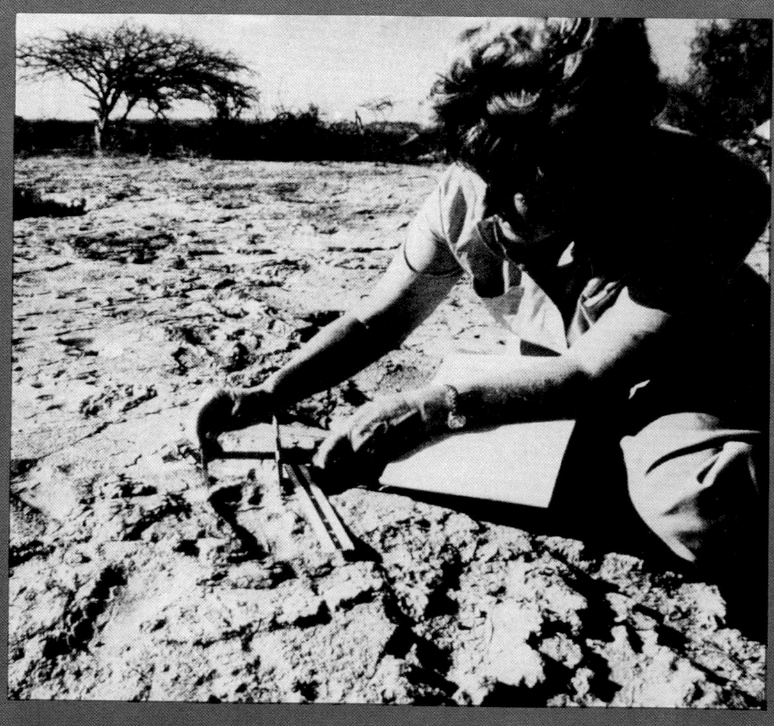

MARY LEAKEY

Claude
Lévi-Strauss

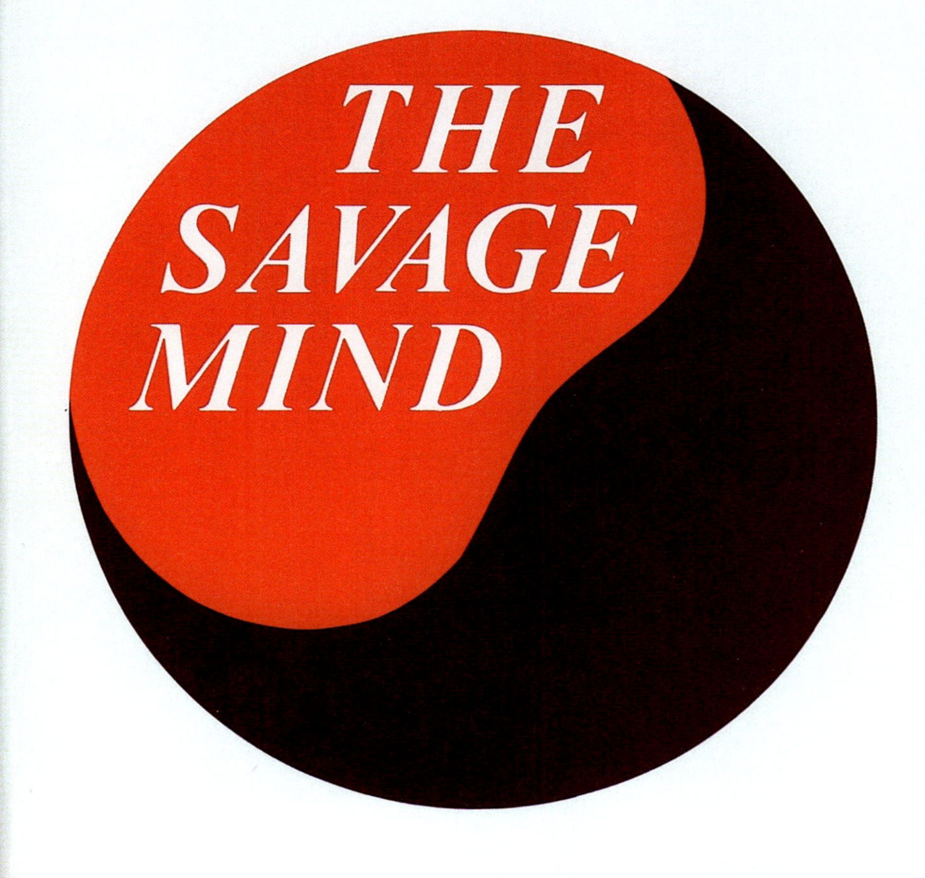

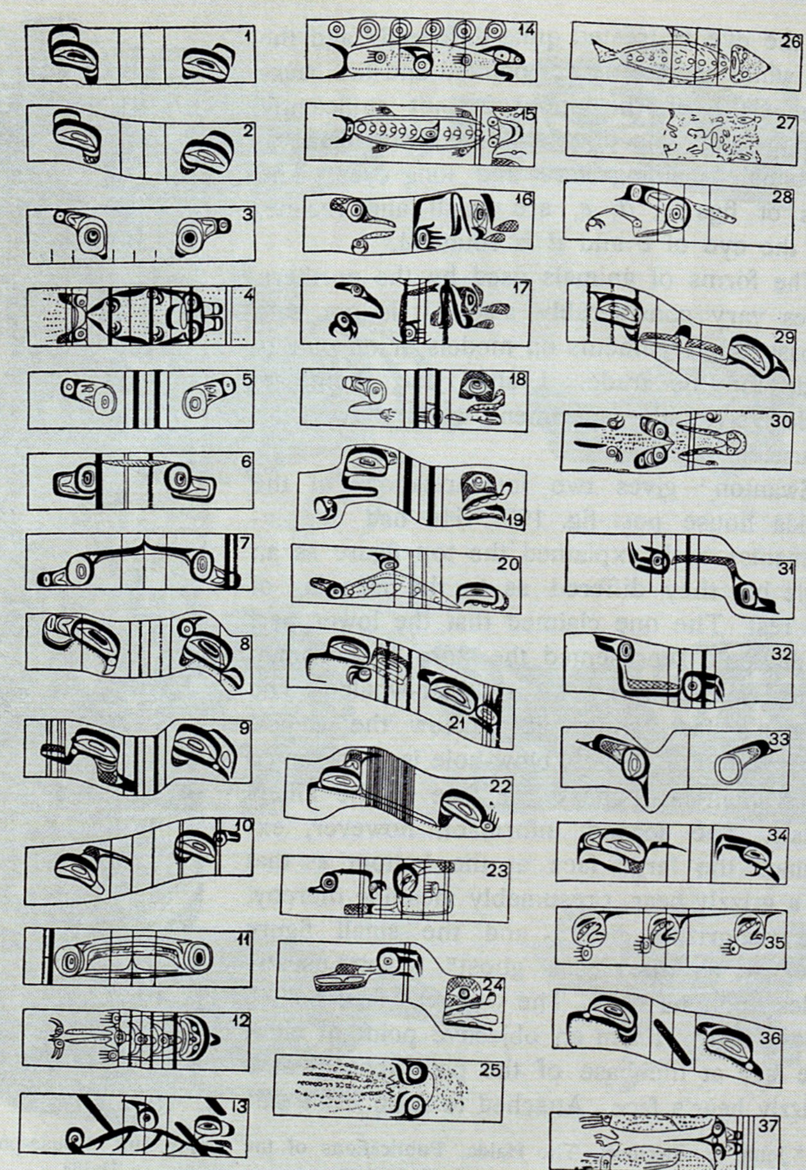

Fig. 200. Designs from a set of gambling sticks.

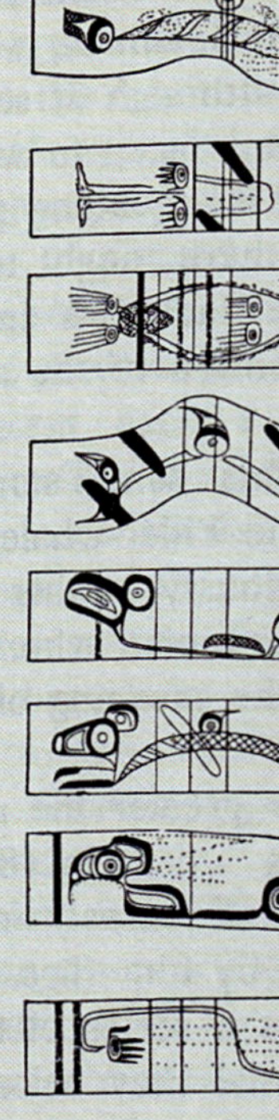

Fig. 20

Between an Aesthetic Hunch and a Hard Science

Robert Storr

In 1946 the Anglo-American writer W. H. Auden delivered a Phi Beta Kappa address to the graduating class of Harvard University in verse. Titled "Under Which Lyre: A Reactionary Tract for the Times," Auden's poetic fulmination against the emerging positivist pieties of the postwar world consisted of one dry zinger after another aimed directly at the mind-set of the multitiered hierarchy of that august institution. And, time after time, his words struck right between the eyes of his capped and gowned hosts. The two stanzas of this longish lyric diatribe that follow give a fair sense of the acuity of Auden's barbed wit, and I have chosen to end on one rebuke in particular that bears on the context of this exhibition.

> Thou shalt not do as the dean pleases,
> Thou shalt not write thy doctor's thesis
>   On education,
> Thou shalt not worship projects nor
> Shalt thou or thine bow down before
>   Administration.
>
> Thou shalt not answer questionnaires
> Or quizzes upon World-Affairs,
>   Nor with compliance
> Take any test. Thou shalt not sit
> With statisticians nor commit
>   A social science.

Infatuation with the social sciences was a wholly understandable characteristic of societies digging themselves out of the rubble of the late global catastrophe insofar as they seemed to offer a way through or around the ignorance and prejudice that had precipitated it. Yet it was Auden himself who was among the first to state clearly in his premonition of that disaster, "September 1, 1939," that it was the "clever hopes . . . / Of a low dishonest decade" that had brought disaster upon Europe and the wider world. Moreover, by "clever hopes" he meant ideological idealism inspired by the scientific methods of the Enlightenment in the broadest possible sense, from liberalism to socialism to communism. All in all, Auden's disabused skepticism before and after the war echoed a far deeper pessimism that was to express itself in myriad ways and multiple registers in the Existentialism of Jean-Paul Sartre and Albert Camus, and in Samuel Beckett and Eugène Ionesco's Theater of the Absurd as well as in Antonin Artaud's Theater of Cruelty. There were many more manifestations during the postwar era and after, though Auden himself had aversions to most and rarely ventured outside the confines of his own genteel and increasingly anti-avant-garde sensibility.

In 1959, just over a dozen years after Auden set forth his urbanely peevish Ten Commandments, the English polymath—novelist, essayist, and chemist—C. P. Snow picked up the gauntlet his erstwhile literary compatriot had thrown down in a pair of radio lectures penned for the BBC. The first was called "The Two Cultures," meaning the Humanities and the Sciences. That rubric neatly framed his entire polemic and, by virtue of the economy of his summation, almost instantly became the talk of transatlantic educated elites. In it Snow was thinking mostly of the so-called "hard sciences" rather than the comparatively "soft" social sciences, but back then many if not most of adepts at the latter were at pains to demonstrate that they were no less certain of the truth of their assertions than practitioners of the former, and so went to great length to prove the rigor of their methodologies. Understandably given his dual vocation, Snow was more prepared than Auden to acknowledge and explore the points at which those seemingly antithetical discourses met; indeed he was eager to do so, citing the origins of the Wunderkammer and the invention of the telescope as incidences of the convergence of aesthetic insight and inquiry where the aesthetic led the way.

Art historically, we might also recognize the role that "book learning" in exacting intellectual disciplines played in the formation of Renaissance artists and in codifying the concept of the Renaissance Man. Intensive study of mathematics, anatomy, and the natural sciences generally were as basic a part of the training of artists in the original

Italian, and subsequently the French and other continental academies, as history, literature, rhetoric (the art of persuasion), and traditional studio techniques. Such knowledge not only served aesthetic ends but raised the status of the painter or sculptor from that of an artisan to that of a cultivated modern gentleman.

Paradoxically, just when Snow was making the case that the gap between the "two cultures" could and urgently should be closed, in the visual arts, at least, a profound suspicion of rational systems, if not an active anti-intellectualism, spread. Again, as was the case after World War I with the rise of Expressionism, Dada, and Surrealism, among a host of improvisatory tendencies, Reason was in the dock for crimes against humanity. As noted, the alienation triggered by the Holocaust, the Bomb, and so much else argued for intuitive if not actively disruptive practices rather than logically consistent ones. That many of the most important artists of the 1940s and 1960s were insatiable autodidacts did little to diminish the stigma of knowing too much, such that the seminal sculptor David Smith, a remarkably thoughtful, verbally gifted, and historically well-informed abstract sculptor, felt compelled to write an essay opposing the concept of the artist as a "well-rounded" person. Eventually, however, college graduates began to outnumber those with more traditional studio educations under the tutelage of their elders. A Columbia University graduate, Allan Kaprow, the inventor and promoter of Happenings and Environments, was the frankest and most articulate defender of this new breed of comprehensively educated men and women, whom he advised to become men (and women) of the world in a 1964 essay titled "The Artist as a Man of the World," and shun the lure of insular old-school though little-schooled Bohemia, fixated as it was on its alienation from the rest of society and more than half in love with failure.

Thus, from the end of the 1960s onward, art has, in the main, witnessed a steady flow of young talents inclined to test their mental and technical skills on propositions resulting from the more or less close study of other disciplines ranging from geometry and set theory to linguistics, sociology, and anthropology. This last opens up some of the most radical perspectives because it implicitly redefines art. Rather than being the creation of an inspired genius working alone, from this vantage point art is often better understood as a social or cultural activity into which flows a collective consciousness prompted by collective aspirations or needs.

This shift frightens many who feel that their personal freedom and subjectivity is threatened by joining any club that would have them. And, of course, it has prompted a tsunami of specious theoretical writing by academics in other fields moonlighting as art critics who have been granted or granted themselves the license of playing fast and loose with key concepts borrowed from their own area of specialization or those of adjacent areas, without heeding the rules of genuine scholarship or philosophical rigor that would apply if they were speaking to peers of equal professional standing about matters of common interest, much less those of art history. And then, disregarding the old adage that a little knowledge is a dangerous thing, there are art historians and critics who, having wearied of conventional "art talk," run to their local academic bookstores and bone up in areas they've never before researched and proceed to recklessly deploy glosses of what they've learned as a means of lending their criteria an added weight of authority. In either case, discussing, much less arguing over, questions of art with such "experts" can be like playing three-card monte on the sidewalk.

My concern is not with the observer/commentator who overestimates or oversells their breadth of knowledge. On that score all I can say is *caveat lector*, or quoting the streetwise Nelson Algren, Simone de Beauvoir's Chicago-based Existentialist diamond in the rough and lover: "Never play cards with a man called Doc." No, my concern is with how ideas filter into the alchemy of artistic creation.

For a useful model we do best to look further back in history to the days of the seventeenth-century English metaphysical poets, who premised their avowedly artificial literary constructs on philosophical analogies or extended metaphors they termed "conceits," for which the proof of the pudding was in the eating, not in endless casuistry. Or else we might turn to the pre-revolutionary French salons of the eighteenth century, whose hostesses (women ruled the intellectual world of this important period through the power of invitation) would announce that the evening was to be devoted to discussion of a *lieu commun* or commonplace, then step back and watch the competition knowing that the full statement of their guests' opinions—be it Voltaire or Diderot—would appear in print, while they, the conveners and sometime contributors to the dialogue, wrote extensively about what had been said in longhand correspondence published later on.

Better yet let us call them the curators of fertile conversations, much as Heather Pesanti is the curator of this symposium of works of art, all of which speak in the shared parlance of anthropology more or less loosely defined. In such settings winning arguments is irrelevant as well as inconceivable, and in this particular period of American history everyone should understand the dangers of trying to "trump" an unverified assertion with another still less verifiable one. Correspondingly, let us agree to step back from feigning a greater grasp than we actually have of subjects that have simply sparked our imaginations and served us as well as artists as the predicates for reverie and reflection, the better to savor those flights of fancy and the delights of speculation unburdened by the strictures of academic discourse and rules of evidence. Instead, let us trust in the power and authority of suggestion and explore realities both outside and inside of us for as far and wide as the mind's eye can see.

Brooklyn 2019

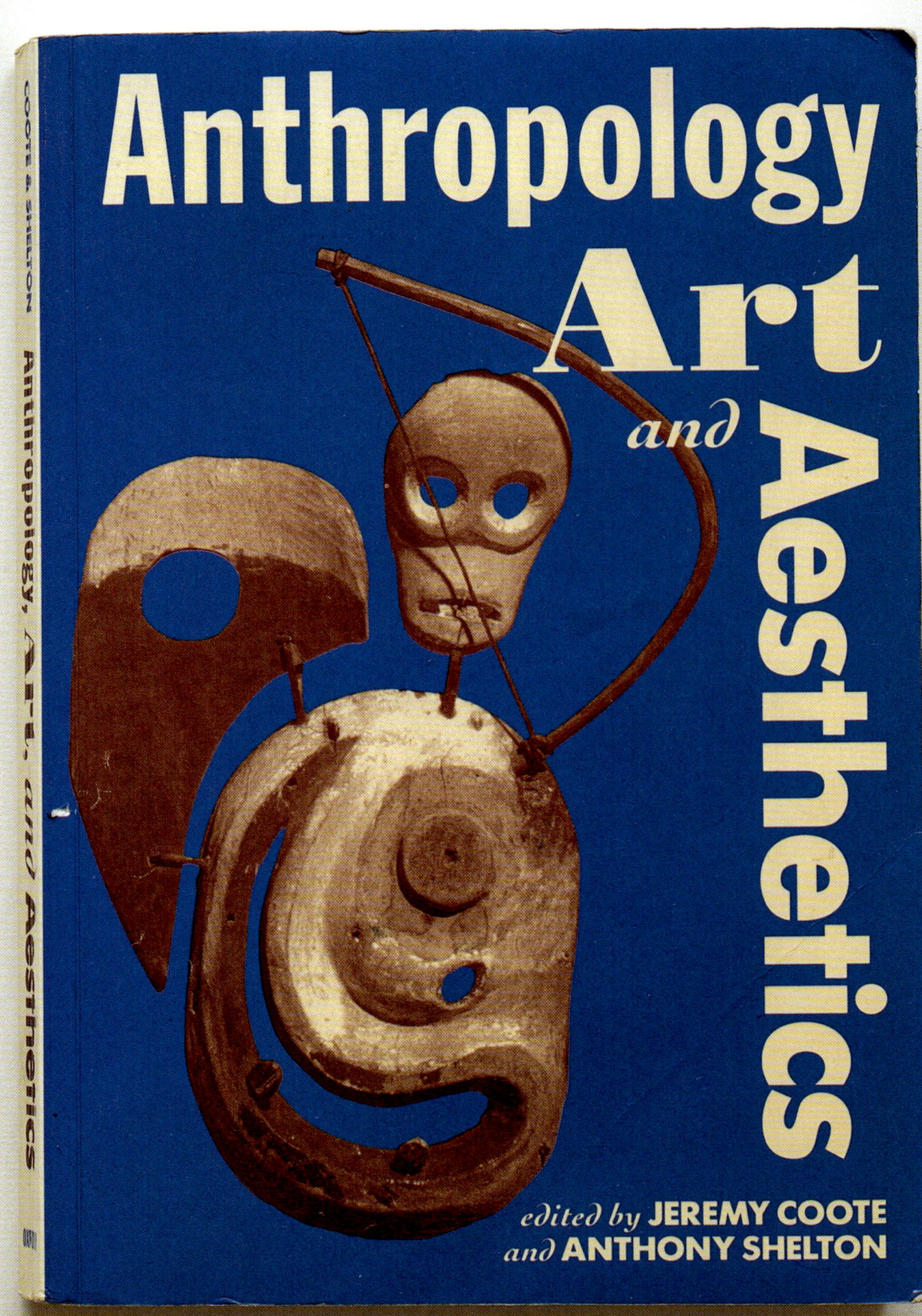
Anthropology
Art
and
Aesthetics
edited by JEREMY COOTE
and ANTHONY SHELTON
COOTE & SHELTON
Anthropology, Art, and Aesthetics

On the Ethics of Art and Anthropology: A Conversation

David Odo & Heather Pesanti

Following is an edited and condensed transcript of a conversation between Heather Pesanti and David Odo, which took place on January 14, 2019, at the Harvard Art Museums in Cambridge, Massachusetts. Pesanti and Odo attended the University of Oxford's Ethnology and Museum Ethnography graduate program in England together from 1997 to 1998, and studied with Jeremy Coote, Curator and Former Head of Collections at the Pitt Rivers Museum, and Marcus Banks, Professor of Visual Anthropology in the School of Anthropology & Museum Ethnography, among others.

Heather Pesanti: I'm here with David Odo and it is Monday, January 14, 2019. Maybe you can introduce yourself.

David Odo: Sure. I'm David Odo, Director of Student Programs and Research Curator for University Collections Initiatives at the Harvard Art Museums.

HP: Can you talk about what that means?

DO: Let me start with the teaching side of my job. As Director of Student Programs, I oversee a few programs, one being the Undergraduate Student Guide program, where I work with students from across campus from different disciplines to think about the art collections for their own intellectual development but also in a public humanities way. We train the students to conduct primary research on art objects using our collections, archives, and human resources, through discussions with the curators, faculty, conservators, security attendants, artists, and other members of the museum community, to try to understand different approaches to art and to translate these kinds of complex ideas into a public conversation. I also oversee our graduate student teachers, primarily master's students from the Harvard Graduate School of Education, who teach high school visits from the Cambridge Rindge and Latin School, the sole public high school in the city of Cambridge, located a block away. We work with them to expose the students to the world of the art museum, integrating it into their learning and lives and identities as Cantabrigians.

Then there is the Research Curator part of my job. This involves thinking about Harvard-owned collections outside of the art museum, including library collections, scientific instruments, and of course, as an anthropologist, the Peabody Museum of Archaeology and Ethnology. I'm not an exhibitions curator, so I think more about how research across collections, especially the intersections between our collections and other collections, might help push our teaching and research.

HP: Can you briefly talk about the collections at the Harvard Art Museums, which are quite fantastic?

DO: The Harvard Art Museums is actually comprised of three museums under one roof, with a really astounding, fabulous collection, ranging from ancient to contemporary art, from many art traditions around the world, including ancient Chinese bronzes and jades, Italian early Renaissance, German Expressionism, works on paper, and an increasingly diverse contemporary collection. I think we are the fifth or sixth largest collection by volume of art museums in the United States, somewhere in the neighborhood of 250,000 objects—quite a comprehensive collection.

We also have a world-renowned conservation department, the Straus Center for Conservation and Technical Studies, so this furthers the ideas around studying materiality—which of course for me as a visual and material anthropologist is extremely exciting. The Peabody Museum, as I mentioned, is out of this world, with strong holdings in Native American, Maya, Inca, as well as Pacific Island material. My particular interest is their collection of photographs, an archive of about half a million objects. It's absolutely, by volume, astonishing, but also really important for the history of anthropology, particularly American anthropology. That's where I came across the Japanese souvenir photographs that I have written about [*The Journey of "A Good Type": From Artistry to Ethnography in Early Japanese Photographs*, published by Peabody Museum Press in 2015].

HP: Let's talk about those, because I discovered your Japanese photographic project last year through my own research for this exhibition, *The Sorcerer's Burden*. You and I had studied cultural anthropology as graduate students at Oxford University in 1997 and 1998, but we hadn't talked for, I don't know, decades.

DO: A number of years. [*Laughs*]

HP: Right, a number of years. And in my research for this exhibition, I came upon a lecture that you gave on these Japanese photographs and it seemed relevant to this topic of the intersection of contemporary art and anthropology that this exhibition explores. Can you talk about that?

DO: I think it dates back to 2004–2005, when I came to Harvard initially to do a postdoctoral fellowship at the Reischauer Institute of Japanese Studies. Toward the

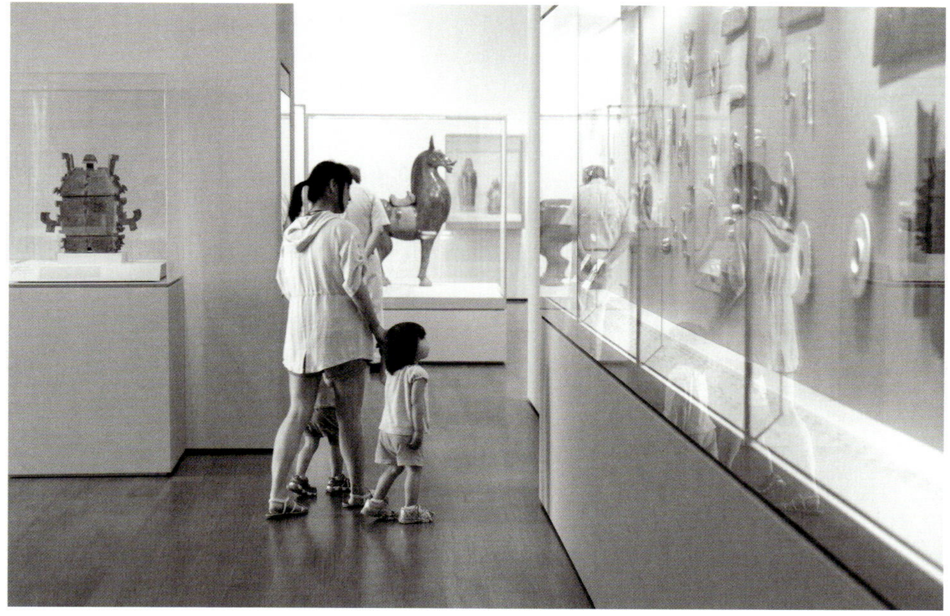

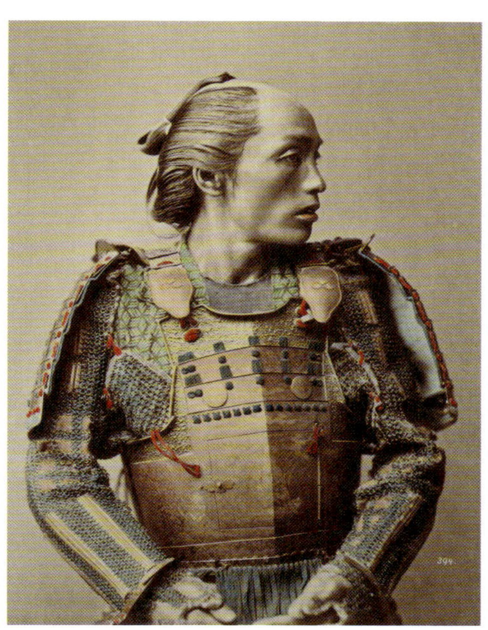

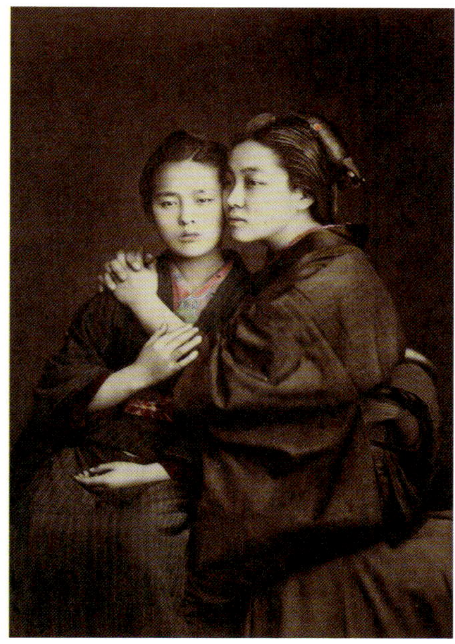

Top Ancient Chinese bronzes, ceramics, and jades at the Harvard Art Museums, Cambridge, Massachusetts, 2017.

Left Raimund von Stillfried, Japanese samurai in colorful armor, 1870s. Hand-tinted albumen print. 9 ¾ x 7 ⅜ inches. Collection of the Peabody Museum of Archaeology and Ethnology, Harvard University. Gift of Miss Mary B. Lothrop.

Right Raimund von Stillfried, Two women, 1870s. Hand-tinted albumen print. 9 ¼ x 7 ⅝ inches. Collection of the Peabody Museum of Archaeology and Ethnology, Harvard University. Gift of Miss Mary B. Lothrop.

end of that year, the then director of the Peabody Museum, Rubie Watson, invited me to come take a look at their collection of Japanese souvenir photographs. These were circa 1860s, 1870s, and later photographs made by European photographers—so early Western photographers working in Japan mainly for the export market—for foreign visitors to Japan and sold in Europe and the United States. And to be honest, I wouldn't say I was skeptical but I was working on another project at the time and, you know, I thought, "Well, I'll get to it at some point."

When I finally made it over there, I was absolutely blown away by this collection, which the museum actually informally refers to as "Japanese art prints," which should have been my first clue. They're just stunningly beautiful. Many are exquisitely hand painted. The core collection is hand-tinted albumen prints in absolutely pristine condition and I wondered, "What are these doing in an anthropology collection? Why aren't they at the Harvard Art Museums? They absolutely look like works of art." Through that kind of initial shock, I created this project that resulted in an exhibition for the Peabody as well as a book about my research. Particularly through the medium of photography, I saw how malleable these definitions are, how plastic meaning is when it comes to the question of what is anthropology, and what is art. That was very exciting to me. I was particularly interested in the context of Japan and this kind of photography because within anthropology, we don't necessarily think of this early kind of photography as working in concert with photographs of, for example, colonized peoples. "The other," right? It was really often a different realm politically, let's say. And so when I saw the connections between the way this commercial or souvenir photography of Japan worked, feeling that it was more adjacent to art photography than anthropology photography, it made me question those categories. Looking at it in relationship to other kinds of commercial photography that nevertheless were directly related to colonial photography was when it came alive for me as a subject.

HP: From the contemporary art side, do you think this is connected to the fact that photography was the last medium to be allowed into the contemporary art lexicon? It wasn't until the 1930s and 1940s that museums began to consider photographs as art and acquire them into their collections as such, and even now some of the great art institutions still have contemporary art departments separate from photography ones. But maybe you could also talk about who was taking the photographs and why, and whether this also played into why they were not considered art objects.

DO: That's such a great area to think about and, likewise, in anthropology museums as well still today I would say there is a problem with photography. The Peabody Museum, you know, in spite of having this incredible archive, one of the things is, it is considered an archive . . .

HP: Not a collection.

DO: Not a collection in the same way as other objects. In fact I think some of the most productive tensions we had while I was working on the book and the show were around this notion of the object status of the photograph. It took me right back to our graduate education actually. The museum and I basically had to come to an understanding that we needed to think about these photographs as objects, not merely as illustrations or by-products of fieldwork. They could be considered data, for sure, but the definitions of what constitutes art, however contested in terms of photography itself, are broad enough to encompass a lot of the work that is actually held in that anthropology archive, including the Japanese photographs.

HP: And so who took these photographs and painted them?

DO: The primary photographer I worked on was Raimund von Stillfried, an entrepreneurial Austrian baron and quite a character. He worked all over the world, following, in a sense, the colonial trail. He was also a classically trained painter, so there's an early art connection there, and to technology as well (in photography). Although painted photographs were produced all over the world, mainly using oil-based pigments, Japanese photographs were primarily made with watercolors—natural pigments—so the look is much softer. And the colorists in Japan were mainly from the ukiyo-e woodblock print industry. So there was this big pool of highly skilled artisans who could be brought into the photo industry.

This was a kind of mass production, so I think this challenges the status of photography as an art form. They're multiples as well as commercial products; one wonders, "Are they really art?" And so by the same token, are they really anthropology? My argument is absolutely yes, but the tensions between this notion of art or not, anthropology or not, are interesting.

Even the study of photography within anthropology is a later phenomenon, versus other kinds of objects.

HP: Yes, yes. More like visual anthropology . . .

DO: Absolutely.

HP: So that is a good transition into Oxford. We met at Oxford in 1997, as two of five graduate students in the Anthropology Department's Master of Studies in Ethnology and Museum Ethnography program, in which you continued for a Doctor of Philosophy.

I would love to hear about how you found your way there because for my part, I was not an anthropologist previously.

DO: Right.

HP: We both came to anthropology through a somewhat nontraditional path. For my part, I was a painter and then an art historian, but in my thinking I always leaned toward material culture. I remember I discovered the program at Oxford through the material culture affinities it had to art history. At Oxford I continued the cross-disciplinary approach when I wrote one of my long papers on the Guggenheim Museum in Bilbao (as it had just opened the year we went to school), as an anthropological study of a contemporary art museum within the Basque community. So I'd love to hear about how you ended up in our program.

DO: Well, as an undergraduate, I was at Columbia University and majored in East Asian Studies, but I worked with an anthropologist, Ted Bestor, to write my thesis. So I had some background in anthropology, but after graduating I went to Japan for a year to study the language, and then went back to Hawaii, where I worked as a contract archaeologist. Eventually, I landed in television for over seven years, where I did everything from advertising sales to voiceovers for commercials, and eventually produced corporate videos and documentaries. My grandmother used to watch (and hear) me on television, so I was aware of the relationship of our programs to the community. It was pre-anthropological in a sense. [*Laughs*] And it was ethnic television, broadcast in twenty-one different languages with our prime-time language being Japanese—and that's how I got involved in it, through my language background. To me, it makes sense that eventually I went into anthropology and gravitated to the Oxford program, because of this ability to combine the visual with anthropological sensibilities. But we, we got very lucky I would say—

HP: [*Laughs*] Yes. Let's talk about what it was like at Oxford. I feel like they were exceptionally open to cross-disciplinary, multicultural perspectives, from ancient to contemporary, for the time. I remember being the only person interested in contemporary art in the program.

DO: I think so.

HP: In terms of the cross-disciplinary nature of the program, the British system of tutorials—basically, weekly short, sketchy papers for various departments—made a big impact on me.

DO: Well, your papers were sketchy. Mine were fabulous. [*Laughs*]

HP: [*Laughs*] But you could do a paper with an engineering department, or science professor, etcetera.

DO: Very different from the American system.

HP: Right.

DO: I remember my first paper, I wrote on Pierre Bourdieu and I hadn't written an academic paper in, what, eight years? Previously, I was used to writing research papers, and I thought, "How can I do this in one week?" And basically, I stayed up all night and I just couldn't do it. I got to my tutorial and the professor said, "Look, this is not a research paper, this is meant to be free-flowing, a quick synthesis of the reading and thinking you've been doing." It's a very different way to learn. I finally got the hang of it and found it absolutely liberating—it encouraged experimentation.

HP: From a different perspective.

DO: And having to explain yourself really quickly was incredibly disciplining and liberating at the same time.

HP: Absolutely. Coming from the art-making side, I thought of those tutorials in the way that an artist sketches while she's working on the bigger painting, like loosening up your brain muscles and stretching them out.

DO: I think that's a great analogy and it's something I never had as an undergraduate, that feeling of freedom to experiment without being graded. I think the two systems, the Oxford system and the US system, really complemented each other, and were formative to my current scholarship.

HP: And maybe laid the groundwork, from the perspective of academic validation, that the enmeshed, porous, and—to use your word—plastic boundaries between these fields are quite constructed and not real.

DO: Absolutely.

HP: They're real in the sense that the silo-ing—

DO: They exist. [*Laughs*] But there's no reason that they have to be this way. I haven't really thought about it until this conversation but this idea that the training we had, that environment, at the right stage of our careers and our development, has given us permission in a way to not accept those boundaries, in a way that maybe wouldn't have happened otherwise.

HP: Exactly. So let's talk about the Pitt Rivers Museum because for me, it was such an important part of this training, and a revelation. I had never been in an ethnographic museum quite of that scale.

DO: There are no others like it.

HP: As I recall, it started out with a couple hundred thousand objects from the collection of General Augustus Henry Lane-Fox Pitt Rivers, and through a continuous acquisition program it's now in the millions, I think. What struck me at the time was the Darwinian organization of objects in the museum that they maintained as a teaching tool, in spite of politically correct pressures to perhaps reorganize and erase old and potentially incendiary ways of thinking and categorization.

DO: Yes, I think it had already begun when we were students, way back in the dark ages. In that sense it wasn't the dark ages, right? I was very impressed by how, even in the nineties, they were working with contemporary artists and in particular Indigenous artists from different parts of the world represented in the collections to explore postcolonial, contemporary ideas about nineteenth-century and early twentieth-century collecting and exhibition practices. It's a very self-critical institution, and they did a good job of interrogating colonial histories there. Their answer has not been to remove most of the objects from view.

From when we were graduate students until this very moment, the Pitt Rivers Museum has engaged with contemporary artists and others to respond to colonial histories through the collection, via installations, public programs, and other avenues. They engage with members of Indigenous communities as living people, not relics, but rather as active participants invited to interrogate the collection and the history of the museum. I think anthropology museums should be doing this more in order to think critically about their collections.

HP: The process of how museums collect, both past and present, seems important to this discussion. Thinking back to the earliest relative of today's ethnographic museums, the Wunderkammer, is interesting not only in the way those archaic collections evolved but for the fact that they were not tied to telling the facts. And in relation to this exhibition, where anthropology is always endeavoring to update its practices, methodologies, and systems in order to be more, quote unquote, "objective and factual"—art has never tried to be that way and yet somehow when they intersect there is kind of equal parts

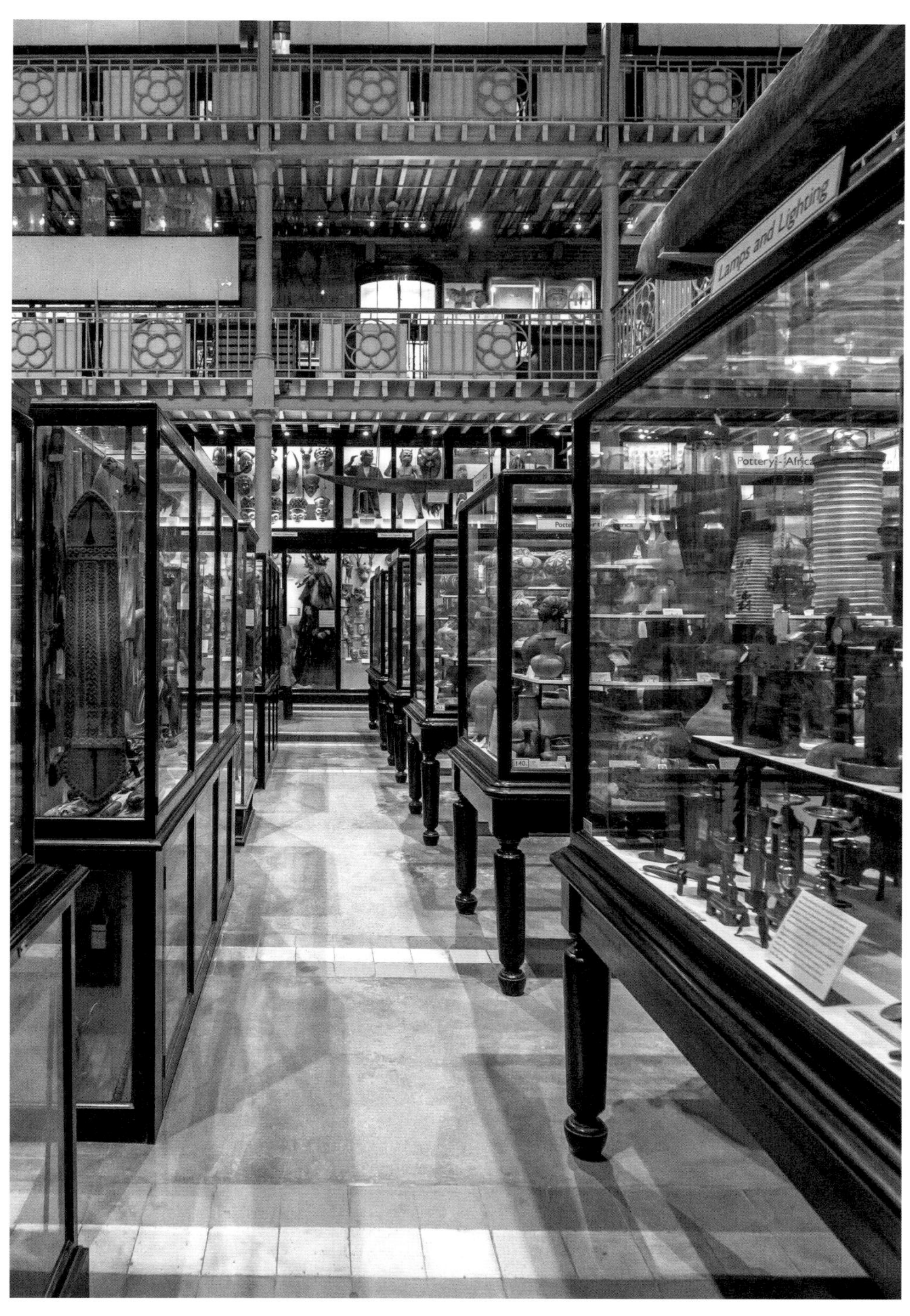

Installation view, Pitt Rivers Museum, University of Oxford, Oxford, United Kingdom, 2017.

of both. I find that to be such an interesting connection to these "cabinets of curiosities," where their values were in line with, "I'm going to put a horn on a turtle and call it a unicorn tortoise."

DO: [*Laughs*]

HP: [*Laughs*] That type of thing. Maybe from here we can address some of the deeper issues around the intersection of contemporary art and anthropology as they relate to ethics.

DO: Sure. I think a good place to start is, as you just mentioned, with this idea of objectivity or factuality. Something that I think anthropology shares, at least in spirit, with art and artists is a consideration of the objects and the people who make them. Part of contemporary anthropology is this notion that objectivity and facts are contested. There's no one objective truth or one way of doing things. That ethos is baked into our methodology, and really aligns us with a kind of artistic point of view. So in the broad picture, as an anthropologist I personally feel very much a kind of kinship [*laughs*]—if I can say that—with artists even more than with other academics. I love working with artists because of these kinds of different ways of looking at the world.

HP: One thing that stood out to me, in both the academic and museological realms of art and anthropology, is the way these fields are endeavoring to break apart the calcified narratives, whatever they are at whatever point in time. And one of the main ways to do that is to bring in artists because they either think out of the box or they might be from within that culture—both of which offer valuable and important perspectives that may not have been considered before.

DO: Right.

HP: This relates to being an artist, art historian, or anthropologist from within. You mentioned your background and fluency in Japanese culture and language, and your roots in Hawaii. How does that influence your critique of that culture, having connections to it, versus being from outside? And how does that relate to the notion of authorship, or anonymity, as so many ethnographic objects have come to be in Western settings?

DO: Growing up as a faculty brat—my father was a professor and one of the pioneers in ethnic studies—combined with my upbringing in Southern California and in Hawaii, in multiracial, multiethnic communities, I felt that multiple identities were normal. My so-called minority identity was layered and based on home, larger family communities, and society at large. But when you belong to a smaller community within a largely white community and you're not white, as in my case, it creates a sense of being both inside and outside. Rather than a negative thing, I've always seen it as, "Wow, I can understand multiple worlds." That has informed what I wanted to study and how I've approached living in different countries and different cultures. I see it as a very natural way of being in the world. Maybe I'm a natural-born anthropologist, which is of course against the idea of anthropology [*laughs*]—

HP: [*Laughs*]

DO: —but that inside-outside perspective, it's obviously not the only perspective to have, but I think does lead in some ways to breaking down these boundaries between disciplines.

HP: I want to address this in terms of the social and political applications because in the contemporary art world, who has the right to talk about what seems to be at play. Recent examples—Dana Schutz's painting *Open Casket*, 2016, depicting the abstracted, mutilated face of Emmett Till at the Whitney Museum of American Art, or Sam Durant's outdoor sculpture *Scaffold*, 2012, which in part referenced the site of execution of Dakota men, installed at the Walker Art Center, come to mind—have become touchpoints for these discussions, in the most extreme examples calling for the destruction of artworks. In the case of the Schutz painting, it was not removed or destroyed, but the Durant work was returned to the Dakota community in Minnesota and ultimately buried in the ground. But to my mind, these two examples also bring up very different issues.

DO: I think the larger shared issue is about rights over ideas or output in a sense, and part of the problem is that everything is case by case. I think what it points to at a very basic level is that the art world is extremely homogeneous. There are so many different points of view and ideas but when you're talking about diversity and inclusion issues, by now some people are, in some ways, fed up, they don't want to talk about it, but it's a huge problem with the art world, with museums, with academia, and a lot of fields of life, frankly. Who's sitting at the table?

HP: It's striking a deeper issue.

DO: Right. These are symptoms. I'm not saying that the content of a given problem is not a problem. But I am saying that the tensions that are surfacing now are ways that, for example, communities of color and others can make their voices heard too, you know? And that without actually dealing with the underlying issues of power, it's, it's almost boring. I mean, haven't we been talking about this forever? And I think we need to be more courageous in addressing those sorts of things.

But it's surfacing in a particular way now, with movements such as Black Lives Matter and #MeToo, for example. You can't just look at the particular moment or point of tension, as that's distracting from the underlying, much deeper, much more problematic, systematic issues that are at play.

HP: Right.

DO: And this ties back to the concept of negative appropriation, not a sharing of ideas—it's not sharing if you're only taking, and then who is profiting, literally? Who can make a living from their art and who can't? It's not a simple male/female, white/nonwhite binary . . . it's a huge problem.

HP: Let's talk about appropriation. With Andy Warhol, Richard Prince, Sherrie Levine, Pop art, Conceptual art, et al., circa the 1960s, 1970s, and 1980s, appropriation in contemporary art became ubiquitous, with the gesture of authorship no longer the sole definer of what makes a work of art. In the context of this exhibition, I would be curious to hear your take on when appropriation crosses over into stealing cultural identity, relating to objects of immense gravitas that were perhaps, let's say, ceremonial or family-based.

DO: Absolutely. You gave great examples, and from Duchamp to Warhol, if you're taking a urinal, or a Campbell's Soup can, you're not harming anyone. From a commercial point of view, Campbell's might disagree. But you're appropriating from the powerful. I think there's an important distinction to be made there versus, for example, the controversy around fashion brands appropriating traditional aesthetic motifs and profiting. I use the word *profit* both in terms of commercial and intellectual property, in regards to ideas of rights and knowledge.

HP: I'm understanding what you're saying is, from the colonizer to the subjugated is the direction that is the most inflammatory.

DO: Right, the most problematic.

In regards to the idea of artistic ethics, and whom you are taking things from, appropriation does not have to be an exclusively negative concept. But if you are crossing into areas of knowledge, appropriating things where you're basically then lauded as this amazing artist, and selling your works and not sharing, it might be something else. As a Westerner or a white person or whatever category you want to use, it's not just that you shouldn't be doing that but rather *if* you're going to do that, what are the conditions that make it ethical? That to me is the larger point; namely, how did you earn the right to do this?

I understand that some have a rather elevated view of their own work, a journalistic sense that they are shedding light on something that deserves to be known.

HP: The misguided notion of "I've discovered this." [*Laughs*]

DO: Right, "I've discovered something." But I don't buy that in most cases. I'm not saying never, because artists do have such an important role to play in exposing both things of great joy and beauty but also terrible problems, interesting things in the world that they've noticed, and their art is maybe one of the few ways in which the public might encounter these exciting things. But what are you actually doing? This relates to anthropological fieldwork.

For example, early on in fieldwork for my doctoral dissertation, I remember one of the individuals I was working with in a Japanese island community said, "Scholars come from the outside all the time and they take and take and take, and what do they ever give back to us?" And he was giving very generously of his time and knowledge to me. So as an anthropologist you have to say, "Well, what can I give back? Do you want my paper?" And he said yes. One can give a presentation to the community, one gives what one can. For this particular person, that was good enough, he wasn't expecting to be paid with money. Often it isn't about a financial arrangement. In our system now, we are so hung up on things like copyright, which, fair enough, that's our society, but there are other things that are sometimes more important, such as this idea of recognition and giving credit.

HP: Going back to the early twentieth century, how do you see this in relationship to the appropriative impulses of "primitivists" like Picasso and Matisse and Derain, etcetera, which eventually led to Cubism and ultimately abstraction, and scholarship discussing the artists' kind of preoccupation with "primitive" objects in a kind of magic sense and breaking apart their own tropes, versus the perspective you're offering here, which is to say I don't believe they were giving back in any sense—

DO: [*Laughs*] Absolutely not.

HP: —and the Surrealists like André Breton, who collected large amounts of African and pre-Columbian objects, which became touchstones for their creative manifestos.

DO: It's taken me decades to reassess, for my own visual pleasure, Gauguin's work or Picasso's work or—

HP: —and Gauguin being someone who lived within the community he was painting.

DO: Absolutely. And, um, infecting—

HP: Infect, literally.

DO: —literally infecting girls and women there. Art historians and museums have not necessarily done a very good job of revealing the colonial structures that have enabled so-called individual genius. You would not have had any of this without colonialism. And that is the inconvenient truth of these art movements. So the question always becomes, "Are we supposed to remove Picasso and the others?" In our moment, with sexual harassment and sexual abuse at the forefront, it's up for discussion. Do we leave everything in place or not? How many of us have an answer to any of these things? Few people might argue with the importance of Picasso, it's incredibly breathtaking work, but we also know he wasn't the nicest person in the world to the women in his life. The misogyny was unbelievable. All these things are part and parcel. This is the kind of appropriation that we talk about in a negative sense from a twenty-first-century point of view. It's also unquestionable that the art is incredible.

It's a terrible conflict and it's a problem. But to me the answer isn't necessarily to remove all Picassos from the wall.

HP: I guess that would be the question. What is the gradation of response?

DO: The response is political and ongoing and we'll change our minds over time and we'll go back and forth. But at the very least, it needs to be part of our interpretation.

HP: I think that's a great answer. Because maybe the solution has to do with the articulation around it.

DO: That's right.

HP: In the case of Picasso, I agree with you, it doesn't make sense to remove the work of this important creative figure from the narrative. Instead, it seems appropriate steps could be to expand and enhance the narrative around his work, both including other aspects of his own history as we're discussing, as well as including other figures omitted by the colonial structure.

DO: Right. What we lose by thinking of Picasso as the greatest singular genius who ever lived and there will never be anyone like him—which, by the way, is just absolute bullshit, right?

HP: Except for Kanye West. [*Laughs*]

DO: [*Laughs*] Oh my God, wow.

HP: Who has said he is the Picasso of the music world.

DO: Absolutely. Who could disagree with that?

HP: Nobody. [*Laughs*]

DO: My goodness. But by doing that, who are we blocking from rising up, from surfacing—in our consciousness, right? If Picasso is taking up all the space on this elevation in your exhibition, who's not being allowed in? And I think that's the better answer than artificially suppressing something.

I mean, there are things that, you know, I think are really legitimately taken off the wall for all sorts of reasons.

HP: Certain Confederate monuments being one example . . .

DO: Right. But I think who we're letting into our contemporary view, into exhibitions in this moment, says so much also about our views of history, too. In that the more we can be honest about our values now and move away from this idea of objectivity—because in museum spaces, it's naive in 2019 for any museum curator or museum director to think that these are objective spaces.

HP: Well, from an anthropological sense it will never be objective, right?

DO: No.

HP: Anthropology is good at saying that; "I'm striving to be objective but aware that it will never be."

DO: It will never be and it's much more effective and honest to be clear about what your values are. And I think there is something valuable in articulating one's mission, being clear about what you believe in. Not just doing the kind of PR version of, you know, diversity, inclusion, and belonging things, but if you actually believe in these principles, it's going to change your curatorial practice in massive ways, right? This is true for all aspects of anthropology and life in general, but what I mean is in terms of thinking about historical art objects too, created, collected under certain conditions, all that.

By changing our own contemporary practices, I think these historical objects and issues can be contextualized in a way that we will have an easier time deciding what to do with them. Look, how did Gauguin even make those incredible works of art? Well, by spreading VD, by being bourgeois . . . how else could he have even traveled to Tahiti? He was part of a colonial power. All these things were very tied to class and power and it's also true in our contemporary moment. Who is able to succeed—financially, even—in a society without health care, who can be an artist, you know? Now there are lots of people who manage to do it. There's a lot of resilience and a lot of talent but—

HP: Same for the curatorial world, by the way. It's a historically bourgeois profession, but to some degree that's changing; many of us took out loans and paid for our own education and it can be a struggle.

DO: It's a huge struggle, there's no question about it, but I think even if you look at the backgrounds of curators, you know, they are not ninety percent from working-class families. Let's face it.

HP: Good point.

DO: The ability to hang on in those many, many, lean years with student loans and all that, for ultimately amazing work but not necessarily lucrative, you know? [*Laughs*] That's not open to everyone. So, we can talk about trying to diversify, in terms of racial and ethnic identities but also in terms of class backgrounds, but it's a really difficult issue for the museum world.

HP: It's so complex, and when you were talking about the polarized responses of the art world, it does get back to this homogeneous system. How do you change that? Anthropology has the same homogeneous history.

DO: Absolutely. You can focus on the differences, you can focus on the convergences. For me there are important differences between art and anthropology, but I think one of the reasons I'm so happy living in this world that combines the two is that there are so many areas of convergence, both in terms of problems and in terms of fabulous ideas and wonderful ways of framing the world. One of the problems is that both the practice of art as well as academic art history have this exclusionary history. You know, who are they open to? And again, thinking about that very broadly—that's really what's helping me in my work at the Harvard Art Museums.

What I think about in my work with both university students, especially undergraduates, as well as high school students, is thinking about this idea that everyone with an interest belongs here. It doesn't mean that everyone can study at Harvard or become a curator, and sorry, but that's actually not my problem. My problem is that I want everyone who can possibly get to this museum to come here. There are a lot of invisible barriers to participation. For me one of the most important parts of my job is to help young people feel welcome, feel that they belong in the first place. And then to help them make sense of the art in their own way. And that is a combination of bringing one's self into the space fully, which means finding connections to the artists themselves, the works, all of this, wherever it's from, whatever time period, but that also has to include work from the now. Work from different kinds of artists. Work from artists of different genders. All this kind of stuff, this variety that we are so fortunate to have in our society, needs to be part of the art space. Not all together all at the same time for every single show, but it has to be part of institutional culture and practice.

All of my students need to be able to find ways to make the art valuable to themselves. And that's where I find a real alliance with my curatorial colleagues and with my colleagues in conservation. I think we have a lot of legitimately different ideas about how to get there, but ultimately I think most of us believe in the same thing in that regard.

HP: In the contemporary art world we've mentioned some examples about objects being removed and returned, but let's get back to that issue of restitution, as it's such a fascinating topic right now. I remember we discussed this at Oxford; we had some classes with Jeremy Coote [Curator and Former Head of Collections at the Pitt Rivers Museum] around this. The most public example that I think is completely fascinating is the president of France, Emmanuel Macron, commissioning this report by two independent scholars who determined that in all cases in France, every object that was taken during colonial rule from sub-Saharan Africa should be repatriated, should the country ask for it back.

DO: Fascinating. Who thought this day would come, right?

HP: But perhaps when looked at in the bigger sense, is this a corrective and do you need to make this kind of extreme statement at one side to kind of open up the discussion in the middle somewhere?

DO: To counterbalance the British Museum's refusal to repatriate certain objects, right?

HP: For example, yes.

DO: I think first of all, I couldn't agree more. It's one of the most exciting, interesting things happening right now, but you know what's funny is when I first heard the news about this, I mean, I'm not an Africanist, I haven't been following any of these developments very closely, but my first question was, "Oh, what is France trying to get out of this?" [*Laughs*] It was a very cynical—

HP: [*Laughs*]

DO: —kind of take on it. Like, "Oh, minerals."

HP: What, really?

DO: Is this a neocolonial approach? Not that the scholars who wrote the report were thinking about what France is going to gain financially. But what nation is going to say, "Yes, let's sort of start emptying our colonial treasures."

HP: That is fascinating.

DO: Thinking about the role of these objects in national heritage is a hugely problematic area. On the one hand, art can be used to create seemingly positive identities, but on the other, to exclude or repress minorities. These things are never simple. Great for teaching [*laughs*] but there is that larger, still very much present problem of colonialism, in terms of collections, museums, and the areas where these objects were taken from.

It's critical to be honest and genuine in trying to understand what the underlying, real problems are, without dismissing the language people use or what they're saying in the moment. I don't mean hidden agendas, but there are deeper reasons for everything we do, and I think that's true with larger protest movements as well as individual actions. And I think in terms of what's going on in France right now with the discussions around restitution, it's useful both thinking about this at the nation-state level in addition to an individual level. Who is gaining what? It's not pure altruism! Conversely, why might some people argue against repatriation? One of the things that we learned in graduate school was thinking about how the Pitt Rivers—an institution that I believe was one of the pioneers in starting to voluntarily repatriate objects—came to think of repatriation not exclusively as a loss. Certainly it is a loss of an object, but what is the nature of that loss and how do you reconfigure that as a collaboration or a partnership so that it's not just losing an object? It's like thinking about your child getting married. [*Laughs*] You're actually gaining something by having an equal partner in an intellectual sense, so that you're working with people in, as they used to say, source communities. Can you work on a real level with museum professionals and academics and students and others, people in the community, from these areas and actually not have it be a loss but have it open discussions up, new ways of thinking?

HP: I remember we talked about this at Oxford regarding a Native American object, where it was going to be returned to a place where it would decay over time. In the case of the object we studied, it was something that was always meant to be buried. Now that's not a reason not to return it, but it does make it more complex.

DO: Part of the rationale related to the traditional use of these objects, in that they were never meant to be kept forever. A true clash of values.

HP: Your whole conservation wing is dedicated to the perpetual eternal preservation of these objects!

DO: Yes, stopping time. [*Laughs*]

HP: And this points to a conflict between the originating culture and the Western museum ethos of preservation, two opposing philosophical values around the object.

DO: Degradation is inevitable, and you can't stop it. You can only delay things and, in some cases, resurrect things to a certain degree, but at a certain point everything will disappear. And that is such an important lesson, even within the center of these scientific, conservation cultures—and they are cultures. Check your Bruno Latour. There is at the highest levels a recognition that nothing lasts forever. It might be a really, really long time horizon, but nothing lasts forever. And so there are different approaches to what a long times means or what forever means.

HP: And speaking of the Native American example that we mentioned, from Oxford, this brings to mind the recent contemporary art example of Sam Durant's outdoor sculpture *Scaffold*, 2012, which we spoke of earlier. This work generated controversy at the Walker Art Center in Minneapolis when it was installed around the opening of its renovated sculpture garden. Meant as an interactive work (that in part encouraged children to climb on it), it was an abstracted sculpture based on seven sites of public execution—including the gallows where more than 150 years ago in Mankato, Minnesota, thirty-eight Dakota men were executed. It seemed that the Walker hadn't engaged with the Dakota community in its area at all, which seems in hindsight a serious blind spot. In the process what ultimately happened was that the work, in conversation with the artist, was given back to the Dakota community, dismantled, and buried. In a way, this was a very anthropological process, but one that came about through immense trauma.

DO: Oh, I agree. I'm glad that you thought of this case because to my mind it begs the question of who's working at the museum. And the idea that you could be living in

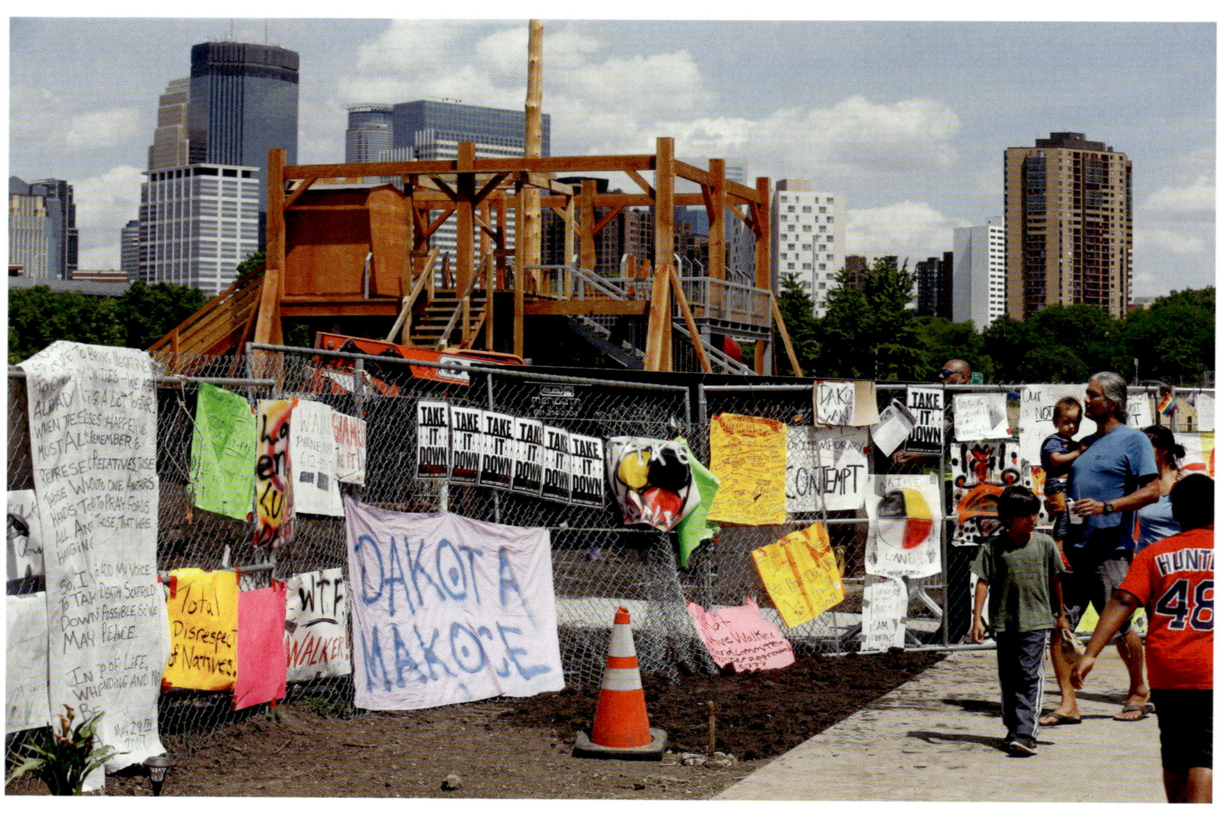

Signs protesting Sam Durant's *Scaffold*, 2012. View outside the Walker Art Center, Minneapolis, Minnesota, June 2, 2017.

Minneapolis and not realize that there are, quote unquote, *still* Native Americans there is part of the problem. And it is not limited to museums.

HP: No.

DO: The idea that "Oh, there were once Indians in this country" is ridiculous. But so many of us who are non-Native don't have the proper recognition of what's going on, so it's not surprising to me that the museum didn't think about consulting in advance. I think we also need to move beyond this notion of consultation to more integration. To be aware of issues that might come up, or a basic assumption around, "OK, what are we doing here?" To give proper credit to the artist, Durant, I think the resolution was a very interesting one. It wasn't the only one that they could have come up with but to me, that showed in this unusual case that destruction was the right thing to do.

To me, one of the most powerful things about art is to surface, confront, and explore painful, hateful, horrible things in addition to the beautiful in a more conventional sense. And I think we would feel very differently about so many works of art if the conversation were broader or more inclusive about who's creating what and who is allowed to do what. It seems mainly one-sided right now, even after all these years. And I think that's part of the problem. The very notion of who feels empowered to talk about anything is very different based on one's background, right? Not everyone feels that they have a right to say anything about anything. I think we need to question and think about who should be listening at different times. There are times to just shut up and listen. And there are times to raise your voice. I think we in the museum world definitely need to do a lot more listening.

All we can do is be the most ethical, thoughtful people we can be at this moment, and that goes a long way. It's not good enough for some people but I think we need to be honest about that and be authentic in our efforts. And I think if we really are . . . we can avoid a hell of a lot of, um, doing stupid things. [*Laughs*]

HP: Great advice.

DO: For example, our 2016 exhibition *Everywhen: The Eternal Present in Indigenous Art from Australia* was a beautiful show of contemporary Indigenous art from Australia, as well as some historical art, historical collections from Harvard's Peabody Museum. The guest curator, Sydney-based curator and art historian Stephen Gilchrist, is himself an Indigenous Australian, of the Yamatji people of the Inggarda language group of Western Australia. He had previously spent some time in this country at Dartmouth's Hood Museum, and I believe he studied at NYU with Fred Wilson and others and has a really great background from an academic and museum point of view. So, you know, this is, of course, this kind of crazy ideal scenario, inside/outside, right? He worked with us for a couple of years, I think, while he was doing research, but then was in residence for six months for a spring semester and the summer. And it wasn't just, hey, give us some free advice on what objects to exhibit, but he himself was a physical, intellectual, and emotional presence at the museum preceding and during the exhibition. His presence within the institution was transformative. One small example that comes to mind is the acknowledgment of country that often happens—in places like Canada and Australia but not so much in the United States—where you recognize the sovereignty of the Indigenous people of whatever land you're on. I was just amazed to hear colleagues on staff saying, "Oh, it was great. You know, Stephen indigenized the space!" Who ever thought you would hear that kind of language—

HP: A verb, indigenized.

DO: —at the Harvard Art Museums? Having that individual here with that incredible background really transformed and enriched us and our students and our audiences. I interviewed some colleagues who were involved in the exhibition for a paper I gave at a recent conference. I was so excited to hear about the ways in which Stephen's guidance regarding treatment of specific kinds of objects filtered into art handling in ways that were relatively seamless. Working with contemporary artists can sometimes result in very exacting requirements for the ways in which their objects are stored, certainly exhibited, and even interpreted, in terms of things like labels and other materials. You know, these are very important things that the museum respects. And if we could take that and apply that to culture, a respect or treatment of art objects and artists is no different from thinking about it on a kind of larger cultural scale.

I was talking to the director of the Harvard University Native American Program recently and she told me that she still had students who miss Stephen. Just having him here, an Indigenous person as a curator at the Harvard Art Museums. It's an important thing, for a young person, let alone any of us, right? It was very powerful for the Native American students. That's more than enough, but it was true for all the students that I interacted with around that show. And certainly for our institution, it was just enormously beneficial. And why can't that be the same with thinking about various kinds of Indigenous objects and their handling or contextualization?

HP: I love the idea that you're implying that, on one level, there's no rocket science to it. Let's allow the maker and the object to do the talking. Something that you mentioned earlier struck me, when you said the way to feel welcoming is to have people see objects and names and voices at the table that look and sound like them. There's a simplicity to that. But it's so complicated in the sense of how to make that happen.

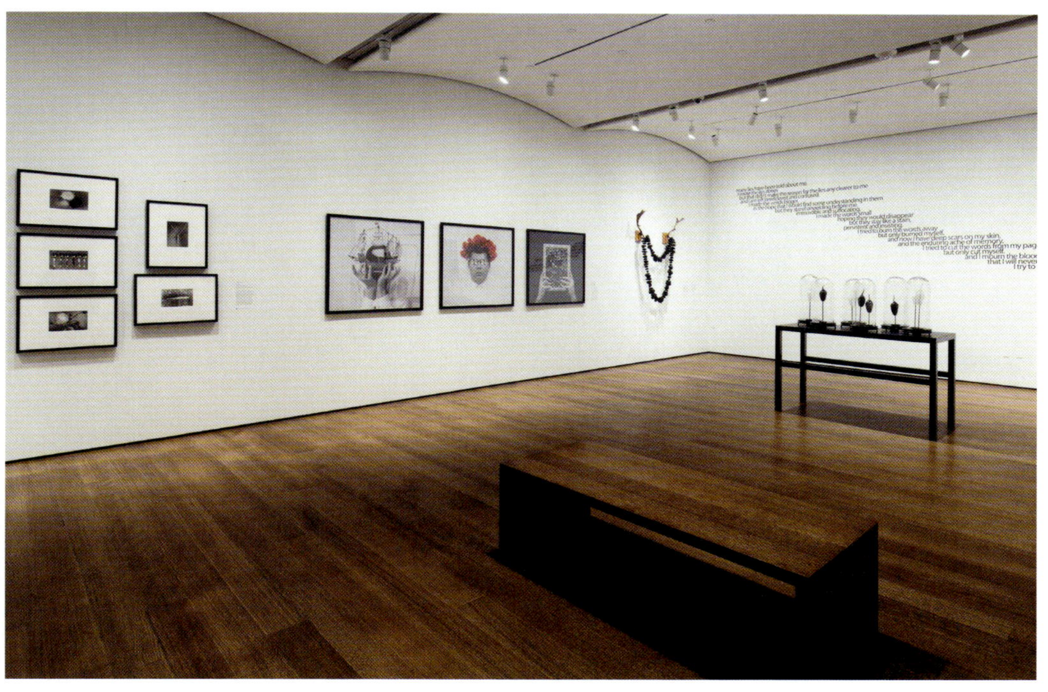

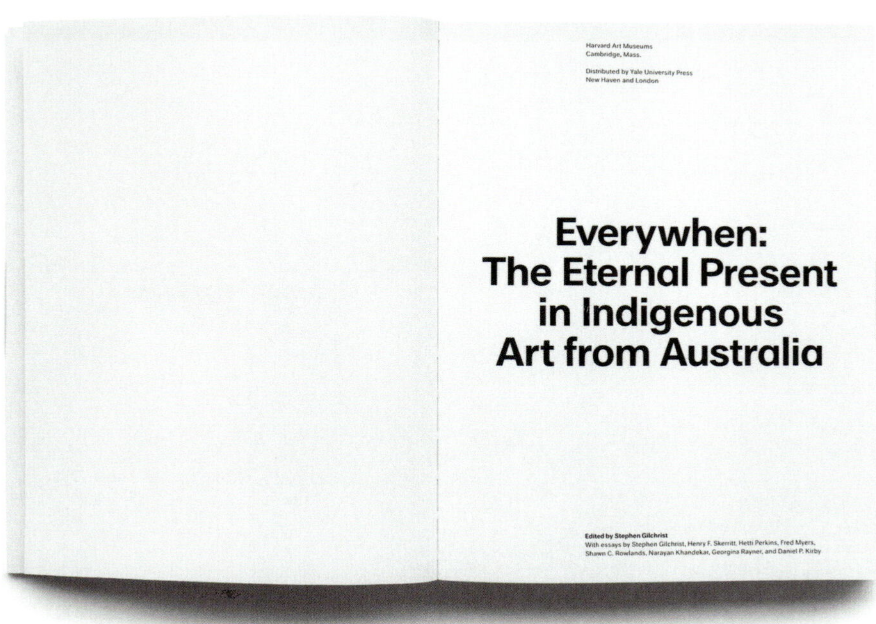

Harvard Art Museums
Cambridge, Mass.

Distributed by Yale University Press
New Haven and London

Everywhen: The Eternal Present in Indigenous Art from Australia

Edited by Stephen Gilchrist
With essays by Stephen Gilchrist, Henry F. Skerritt, Hetti Perkins, Fred Myers, Shawn C. Rowlands, Narayan Khandekar, Georgina Rayner, and Daniel P. Kirby

Top Installation view, *Everywhen: The Eternal Present in Indigenous Art from Australia*, Special Exhibitions Gallery, Harvard Art Museums, Cambridge, Massachusetts, 2016.

Bottom Interior, *Everywhen: The Eternal Present in Indigenous Art from Australia*, catalogue published in conjunction with exhibition of the same title (Cambridge, MA: Harvard Art Museums, 2016).

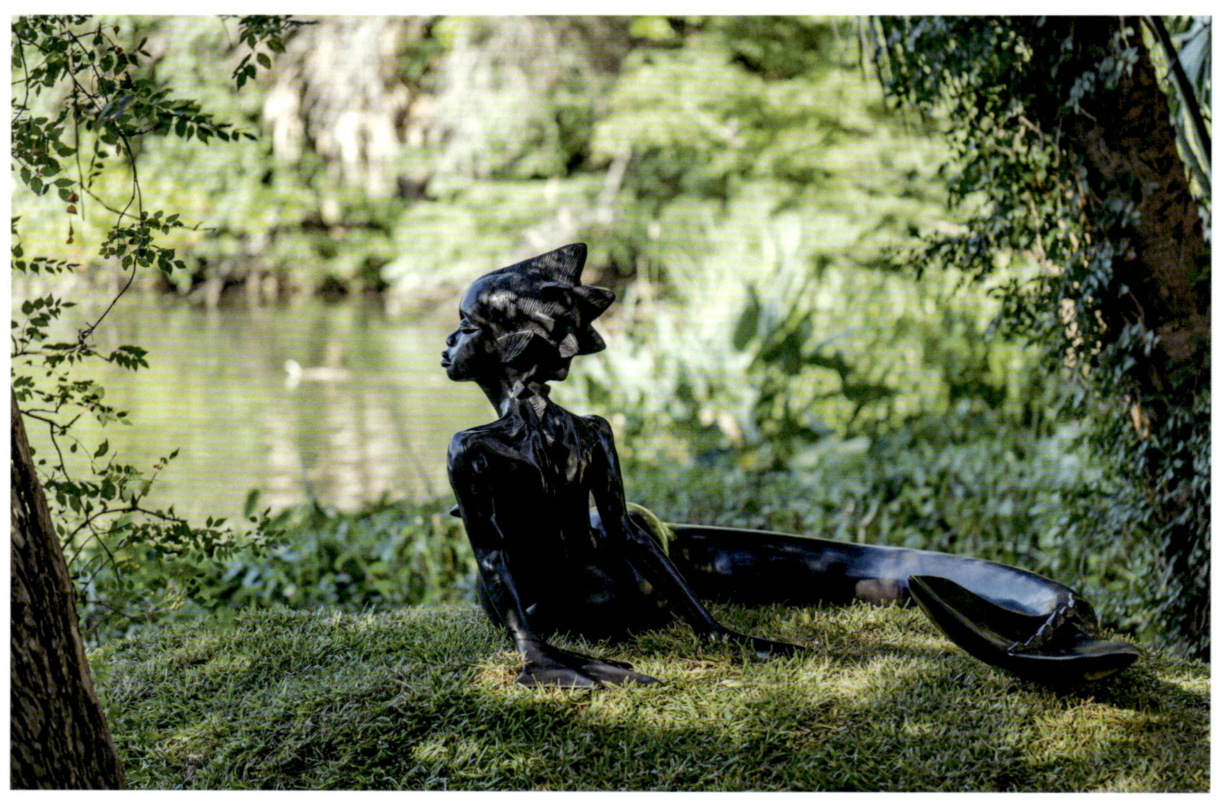

Wangechi Mutu, *Water Woman*, 2017. Bronze. 36 x 65 x 70 inches. Edition 2 of 3, 2 AP. Collection of The Contemporary Austin. Purchased with funds provided by the Edward and Betty Marcus Foundation. 2017.5.

While exhibition programming is just one avenue for bringing different voices to the table in the museum world, an example for me was working with the artist Wangechi Mutu in 2017. She's a Kenyan artist who immigrated to the United States as a teenager and has achieved great success. In 2015, I noticed a shift in her practice and so made a studio visit: whereas previously she primarily made two-dimensional collages, suddenly she was using clay, dirt, and other earthen materials, as well as performative gestures and video animation. As it turns out, that shift was connected to the fact that she had recently opened a studio back in Kenya, causing both familiarity and unfamiliarity, something she referred to as her "alien mother," a landscape that she both knew and didn't. This led to conversations between her and me about our outdoor sculpture park, and outdoor sculpture was not something she typically engaged with. She'd been thinking about this siren figure and when I visited Wangechi at her studio there were little mermaids on her window ledge that she'd made in chocolate. She told me they referred to *nguva* or sea manatees, something that in the mythology of East African folklore became sirens. So even my language in calling them mermaids is Western, or Hellenic European, right? But our project ultimately resulted in an indoor exhibition as well as this outdoor sculpture of a siren on our lagoon, at the base of the amphitheater, sitting on a little mound covered with native vegetation and looking out across the water.

The story behind her idea, as she told it to me, was that her daughter loved mermaids, but had never found any that looked like her, meaning they were all white and European. So she made this mermaid, and Wangechi told me that when she showed a picture of it to her daughter, she was so proud that she could finally say, here's a mermaid that looks like you. It's also the first permanent work at our sculpture park by an African artist.

DO: And as you say, it's not actually that complicated.

HP: No.

DO: And yet I think we sometimes want to overthink these problems and say, "Oh, that's too simplistic and that's reductionist or essentializing." Well, if you stop there, it is. It's not good enough simply to have a work of an African subject by an African artist on the wall of a museum. That's not what any of us of with goodwill are talking about. But at the same time, that simple act is absolutely necessary. The bigger issue is how to open up broader thinking and interesting ideas, and if you're being intellectually honest about what you're trying to achieve, then you are breaking down the barriers to so many different kinds of artists and art entering into the conversation at an institutional level. And I think that's what institutions are not good at, right? We don't want to change. Or certainly don't want to change rapidly. On the one hand we bemoan the lack of diversity on staff and on boards, and we want more diverse audiences, we want younger people to come, etcetera. And we don't do the most obvious things to make people of color and younger audiences (or whatever demographic you happen to be interested in) part of our world. It simply isn't that hard—we just need to do it.

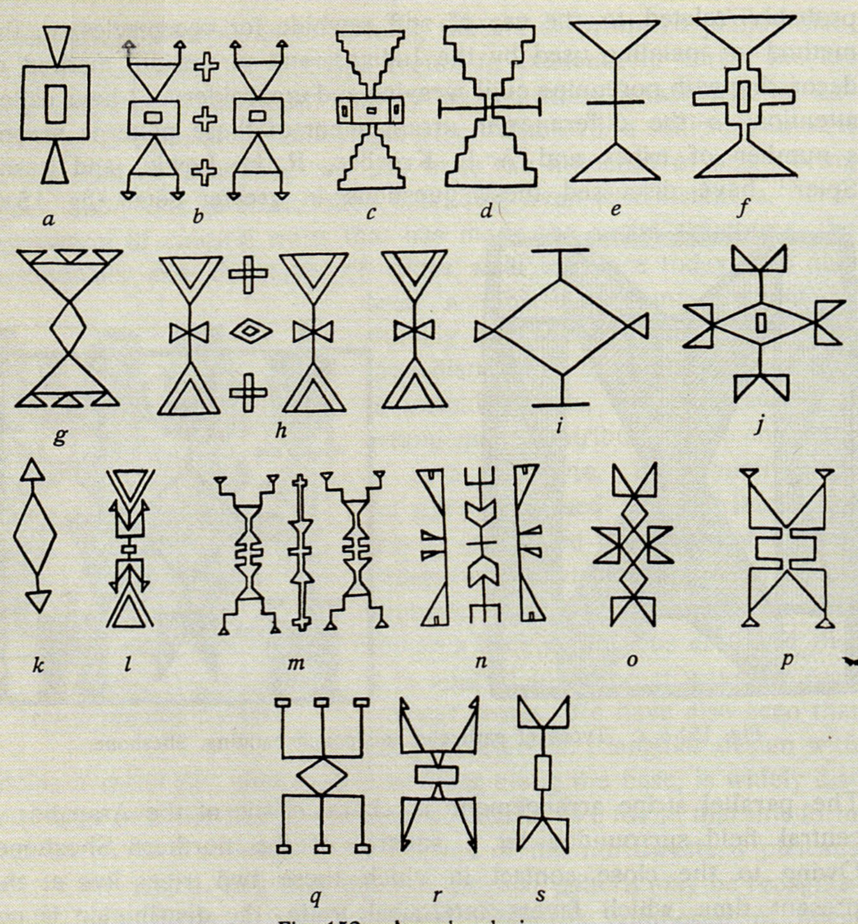

Fig. 152. Arapaho designs.

design consists of a central diamond or rectangle, from the corners of which emanate lines that terminate in triangles facing the central field either with the apex or with the base; sometimes a crossbar with prongs is found at the end of these lines. Among the Arapaho (fig. 152) these patterns appear singly on a plain background; among the Sioux (fig. 153) the central square is seldom

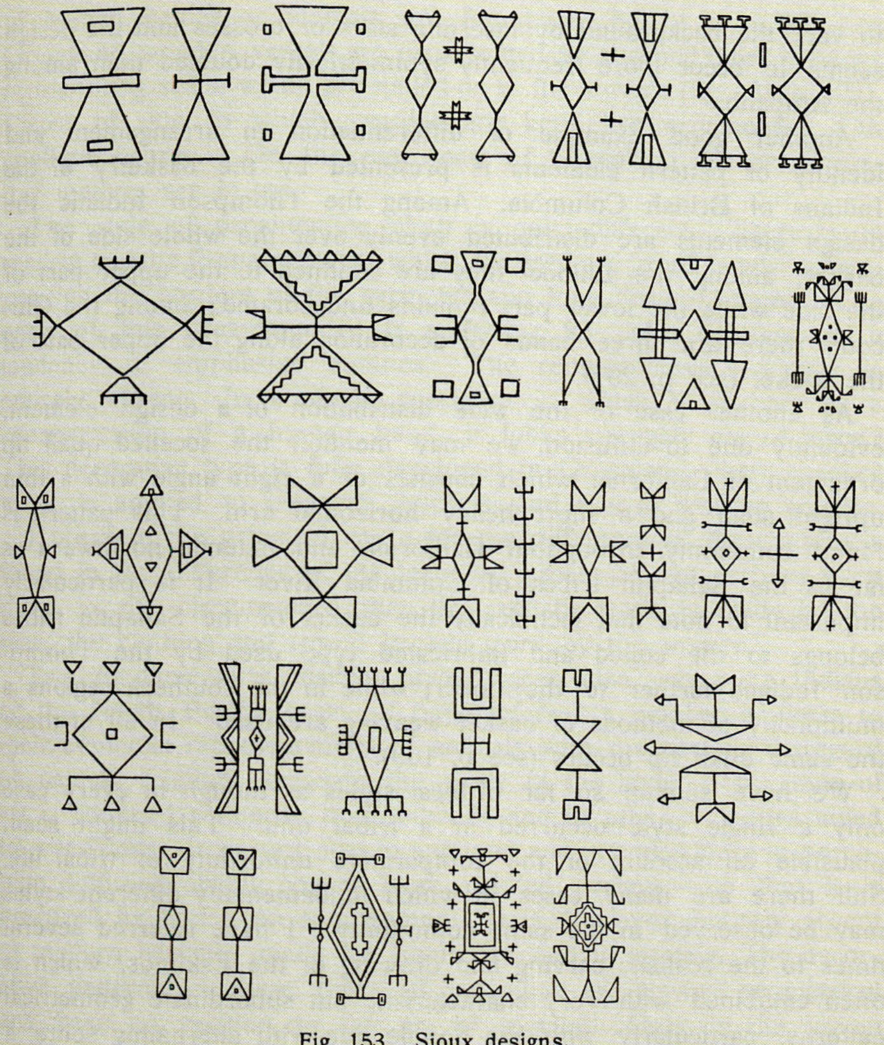

Fig. 153. Sioux designs.

used. While among the Arapaho the lines are usually attached to only two opposite ends, the Sioux almost always attach them to the four corners of the central diamond. Furthermore, the Sioux like

Letter provided by Julia V. Hendrickson.

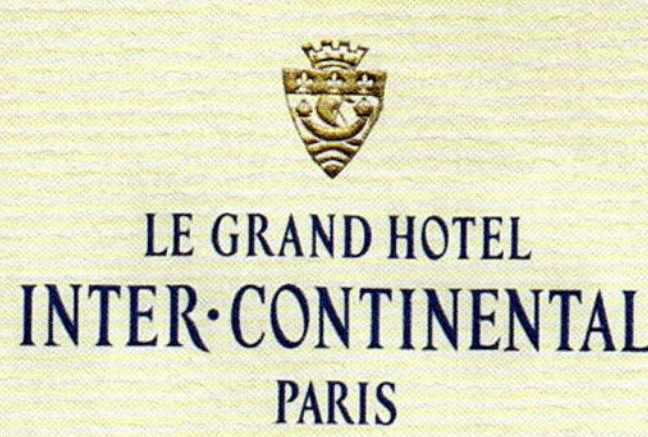

Attn: *Artforum* Magazine 21 juin

Mesdames et Messieurs les Rédacteurs en Chef,

I wanted to take this opportunity to inform you of the strange collection I have come across. I am writing to all of the major art publications now in the hopes that this important news is disseminated.

I am an anthropologist of some renown. In my extensive travels to museums throughout the world, I began to notice the most peculiar inscription on the labels (even directly on the objects at times) of the most rare and strange works in the collection. The inscription invariably turns out to read: "Coll: Fnz. Bs." Peculiar, yes, but please continue to humor me, for my conclusion is not without merit.

Every museum where I've visited and inquired—from hot and humid open-air historical collections in Chennai, to cool concrete Brutalist museums in Cologne, and even the occasional private house foundations or collections in Los Angeles—each one has subsequently discovered that they hold no formal record of the object as being catalogued in their inventory.
The works have simply appeared. Curious. Now, seeing this once, or even twice, I paid it little mind, but over the years the initials have surfaced again and again, and I now have what might be diagnosed as a full-blown obsession with what I am convinced is none other than the most rare and most intriguing thing—the heretofore unknown private collection of the anthropologist Franz Boas (1858–1942).

L'hôtel n'est pas l'expéditeur

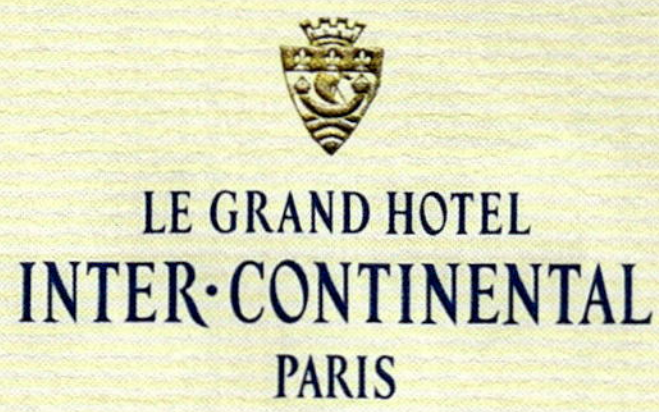

The wide range of works I have noted with the inscription is simply astonishing. Such eclectic, cosmopolitan taste! Masks, totems, statues, jewelry, ceramics, paintings: careful examination and carbon dating would need to be done to even determine the century of some of them. No one in their right mind today would be *so* insensitive as to nick a burial object or a sacred ritualistic mask, but of course dear Franz is from another time. Perhaps we can allow him some temporal relativistic leeway? More mysterious still, I'm certain that the dates of the objects occasionally postdate the man's death. Rather than let this derail me, based on extensive research in the field, I am now firmly convinced that either the fellow is still alive, stalking the halls of humanity's greatest historical collections, or (possibly *and*), he has (had?) an accomplice.

Alas, my research takes me in other directions, and my travel coffers have grown bare. I trust that you will take the reins and follow up on this unique and important discovery.

With sincere regards, I am yours,

Mme Anonyme
Paris

L'hôtel n'est pas l'expéditeur

Farther Afield

ED ATKINS

NUOTAMA BODOMO

THEO ESHETU

CAMERON JAMIE

KAPWANI KIWANGA

MARIE LORENZ

NATHAN MABRY

RUBEN OCHOA

DARIO ROBLETO

SHIMABUKU

JULIA WACHTEL

Introduction

In 1983, the writer, curator, critic, and activist Lucy R. Lippard published *Overlay*, a collection of her musings on the wide-ranging subject of contemporary art and its convergences with prehistoric sites and symbols. The implications were important for Lippard, as it represented not only a sincere foray into fieldwork, but, in her words, the first time she'd "had the guts to cross disciplinary barricades."[1] This meant exploring the cultural landscape rather than confining herself to the boundaries of art and art history, acting as tourist in unfamiliar disciplines.

Decades later, on the occasion of Arnd Schneider and Christopher Wright's significant collection of essays in *Between Contemporary Art and Anthropology: Contemporary Ethnographic Practice*, Lippard revisited her thinking around *Overlay* and its evolution since then, alongside the changing and intersecting fields of art and anthropology, in an essay titled "Farther Afield." Here Lippard mulled over the various affinities between the two fields from an art historical point of view, discussing several artists as case studies and reflecting on broad topics ranging from anthropology's exploitation of the disenfranchised to the fetishization of hybridity by art historical theorists—ultimately landing on the conclusion that there might exist a potential discourse that was both multivalent and, citing the Indian scholar and feminist critic Gayatri Chakravorty Spivak, "partly imaginary."[2]

1. Lucy R. Lippard, "Farther Afield," in *Between Art and Anthropology: Contemporary Ethnographic Practice*, eds. Arnd Schneider and Christopher Wright (Oxford, UK: Berg Publishers, 2010; New York: Bloomsbury, 2014), 23. Citations refer to the Bloomsbury edition.

2. Ibid, 33.

From this vantage, and in the spirit of this exhibition's premise around the existence of both fact and fiction betwixt the two fields, the artists featured in *The Sorcerer's Burden* were invited to participate in a section titled in homage to Lippard's essay and thinking. For this section, the editors of this book referenced Lippard's text but eschewed didactic connection, instead prompting these artists to propose "6–8 pages in the catalogue loosely based around inspiration, influences, and engagement around the topic of the intersection of contemporary art and anthropology. Examples could include preparatory sketches for works in the exhibition, studio snapshots, inspirational work, historical things, cultural references, archival materials, and/or writing." Artists were further encouraged to send originals, such as notes and sketches, which some did, and which were then photographed as ethnographic evidentiary objects. This accumulation resulted in *Farther Afield*, a compendium of loose associations and inspirations authored by each artist.

— HEATHER PESANTI

Page 207: Study for Nathan Mabry's *T/O/T/E/M* series, 2013–2014. Graphite on paper. 11 x 8 ½ inches.

Page 208–209: Reference material from Nathan Mabry's studio. Wall of André Breton's studio, the second room in Breton's apartment on rue Fontaine in Paris, where he lived and worked from 1922 until his death in 1966. Installation view, Musée National d'Art Moderne, Centre Pompidou, Paris, 2004.

Page 210: Study for Nathan Mabry's *u.n.t.i.t.l.e.d.* series, 2012. Graphite on Mylar. 14 x 11 inches.

Page 211: Nathan Mabry working in his studio.

Page 213: Ruben Ochoa, *Canal St. Acrylic (Infracted Sketch)*, 2007. Ballpoint pen on notebook paper. 11 x 8 ½ inches.

Page 214–215: Ruben Ochoa, *Recurring Amalgamation Sketch*, 2007. Graphite on paper. 16 x 20 inches.

Page 216–217: Ruben Ochoa, *Untitled Sketch*, 2007. Graphite on graph paper. 16 x 20 inches.

Page 218–219: Ruben Ochoa, *Study for Grounded*, 2010. Cement on graph paper. 11 x 16 ⅞ inches.

Page 220–227: Dario Robleto, "The First Time, the Heart," 2017–2018. Originally published, in slightly different form, as a booklet included with the portfolio *The First Time, the Heart (A Portrait of Life 1854–1913)*, 2017–2018.

Page 228: Shimabuku, *The Snow Monkeys of Texas: Do snow monkeys remember snow mountains?* (still), 2016. Single-channel HD video projection, color, sound; vinyl wall text; and cacti. Edition of 3, 2 AP. Running time: 20:00, looped.

Page 230–231, 233: Personal snapshots by Shimabuku related to *The Snow Monkeys of Texas*, 2016.

Page 232: Shimabuku, *The Snow Monkeys of Texas: Snow Monkey Stance*, 2016. Digital inkjet print on Hahnemühle photo rag, mounted on aluminum. 55 ¼ x 38 ¼ inches. Edition of 3, 2 AP.

Page 233: Shimabuku, *Erect*, 2017. Site-specific installation; driftwood and stones. Installation view, *Reborn-Art Festival*, Ishinomaki, Japan, 2017.

Page 234: Shimabuku, *Exhibition for the Monkeys*, 1992. Cibachrome print. 27 ½ x 27 ½ inches.

Page 235: Shimabuku, *Sharpening a MacBook Air*, 2015. HD video, color, sound; object. Running time: 02:05. Object in vitrine, 31 ½ x 33 ½ x 25 ⅝ inches.

Page 236–243: Reference images and descriptive texts related to Julia Wachtel's studio process, arranged by the artist, 2019.

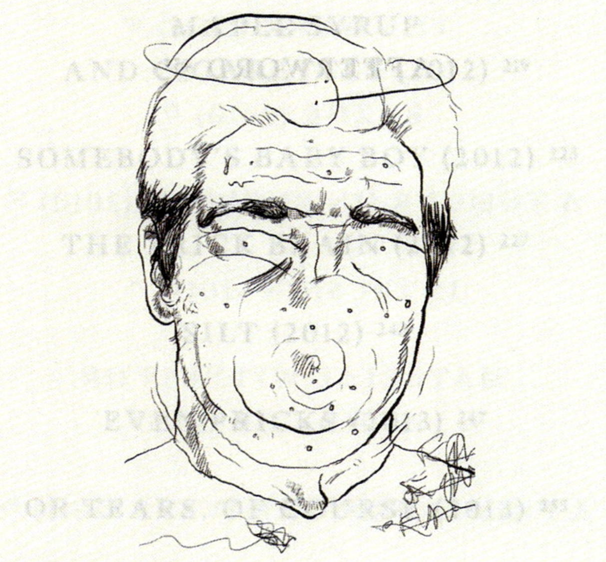

Ed Atkins

(born 1982 in Oxford, United Kingdom)

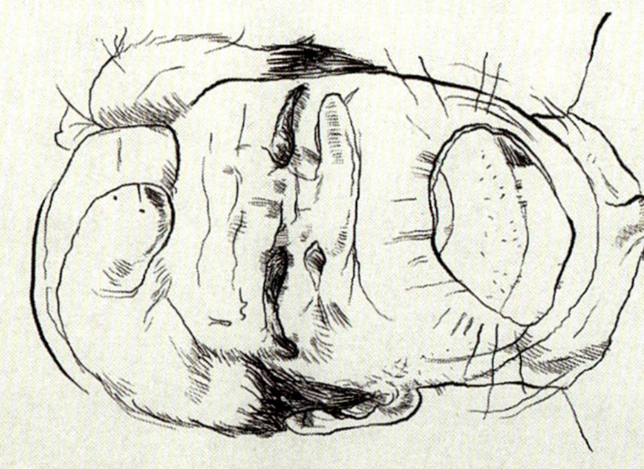

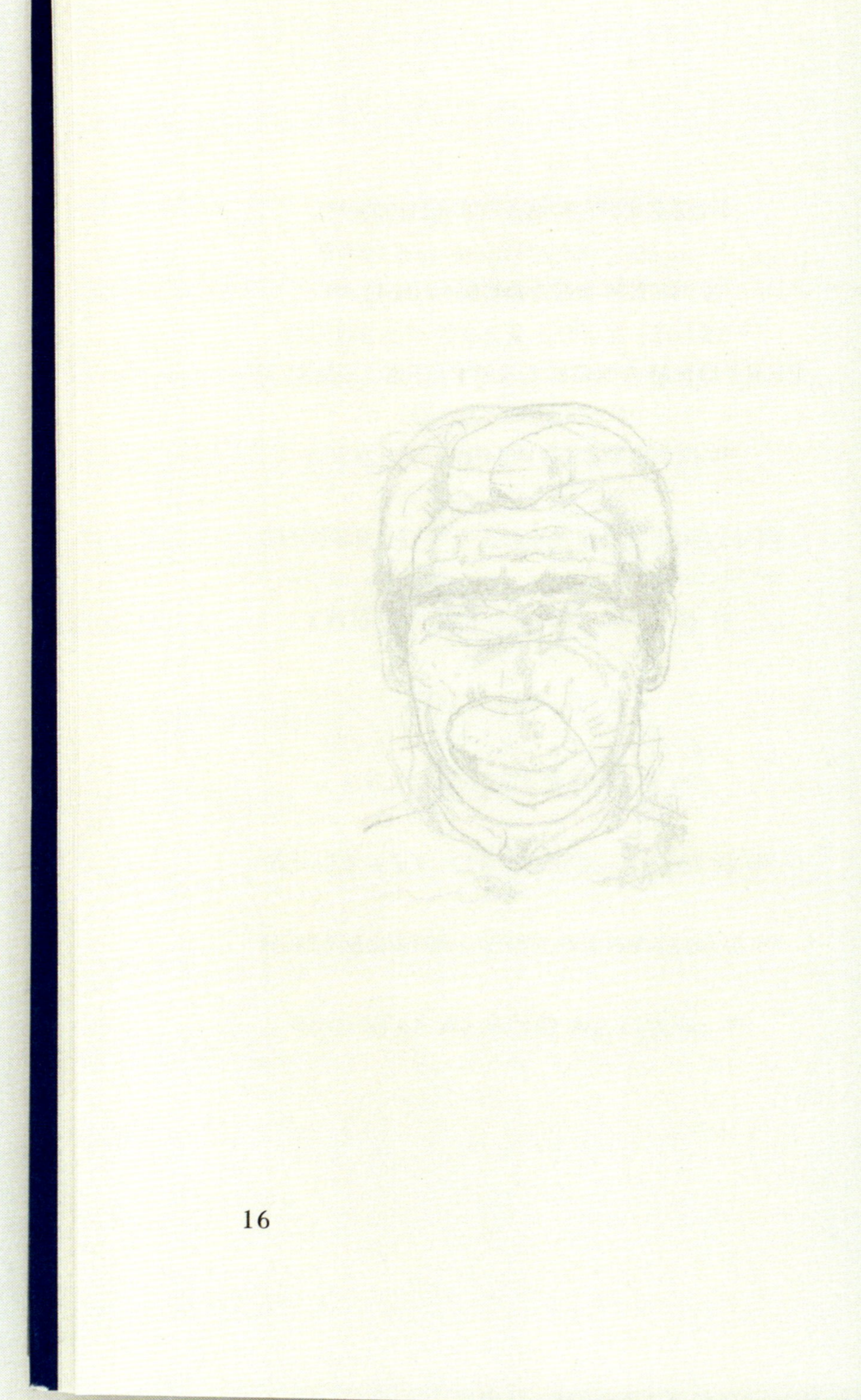

AN INTRODUCTION TO THE WORK

Dears –

Millions of urgent, mega-bereaved children will hurl wills wedged inside denuded plastic bottles and at cursed lakes forever choked with same,

X. A little later, after-hours, lining the shore they're, um, perfectly normally reflexively force-gagging one another with forebear's forefingers – which come in stiff pairings (snapped off *at the love*), tightly parcelled in red paisley bandanas that are now, we understand, browning and sodden with an unchecked gravy of same,

X.

Said ramming home so said summoning asphyxial opinions and sadly so soon after our super-hot bodies disentangled,

X. My mind is in your crotch,

X, while I sit staring at this piano's tremendously INTELLIGIBLE anachronisms; the acceptance of this pen's disabilities; the blithe arrogance of a fat analogue wristwatch,

X. Conservatively speaking, the machine-chamfered tools of late phallic *whittling* abound and universally, so honestly,

X, very much capable of honing any stubborn shape into the absolute SPIT. Normally, blunt knives designed as such and held *just so* for really wholesome bruising, in the main (a particular pedagogic method: firm, spheroidal fruit wielded inside ivory, Egyptian cotton pillowcases). So very nearly a joke, right? A cut, then, is only WORRIED into the world once weeks are spent on one rose-maddening patch of WINNING inner thigh, which, er, resembles nothing so incisive as the act of a blade, but rather ripping or *snagging* of clumsy child portions from a dim source with your monstrous fingernails,

X – under which we will retrieve dark evidence of that vast out-of-town mattress of toxic green moss and a lover's forensic picnic at the site thereof, comprising Alertec® 'corroborated' by kale and vivid yellow slime-mould, right? Recuperated, if needs be, *post mortem*. That's a threat. Hence the urgency around will penning, if law is to be so very previous.

Other weeks the whole thing just feels so, um, dumbly squandered on worthily enervated abstinence; your sole vignetted eye kept till bloodshot and weeping on today's such-and-such remedial shrine, fucktard. Remember,

X: everything here is *edible*; the keys, the shiny red car, the ring fingers, the police, those sad looking people queuing at maybe a product launch over there; the very tarmac, the very overcast sky – the very *shit* unfurling so conventionally down your leg. All of it perfectly cooked *sous vide* and in thin black bin bags secreted behind the wainscot and with zingy rats slashed and wrung out, concentrated – reduced – under really *not* the whole world's scrutinizing gaze by that haunted dog,

X: apparently readily available at the deli counter in enormous, autocratic supermarkets, which I can totally believe.

It can take years to reach a wrong full term, I guess. Also, please excuse the quiet. Excuse the quiet in here. Caught between discounted stud-walls where eloquent, eminent agonisms once rehearsed for avid audiences who fucking *owned* the subtleties of understanding. Quarrels that danced slow and deliberate into a love already defoliated of all the travesty-heart-shaped and weaponized amplification equipment. And notably angry vestigial language delivered from vulgar podia, erupting as 'red' from one of the five or six noise-making *rifts* I seldom though now envisaging quality hecklers of this unwaveringly dysmorphic façade. Well, my darling interlocutory *passerine*, who tenderly repossesses the sorely possessed over and over and through a mouth rapaciously giving out entire hissing summers of wet green noise to drown out nothing so much as ignorance,

X, which tends to the long-dead blue-sky-thinking thaumaturges, whose blood is now so despoiled of oxygen they may as well be forcibly identified as dreaming acanthuses, leaves carefully lifted in the already known to be futile hunt for a pair of jewel-like lungs or simply something recognizable as genitals.

Generally speaking there's been no DEARTHS identified with acceptance: of and under those factory-distressed clothes distressingly haired moles skin tagging and slowly peeling back in awkward equivalence to nictitating membranes, only without eyes to 'get at'; all the better to prevent cowardice being rehomed ahead of more deserving, tax-paying parties – such as your terrifying, mercenary sensibility,

X – which no doubt the very headwater of your historic ALONE. Better to *gag* again,

X; better to express when you're *considerably dissembled*; virtually deformed by the absence of sensory testimony and into some sort of mythical – *né* declawed – Monster of the Text, executed in long-handed blue-blood rope burn. So seeping out from the cuffs, the dock and the cute courthouse.

Whip pan to interior: this very real, tight bedsit, door bolted – and we might consider those two or three rectangular electrical *recta* that are getting busy the moment, merrily disgorging dark, rich, beautifully observed and oversized severed heads of handsome MEN – one by one and interminably; each emergent identikit countenance a stunning, flickering *pageant* of fucking superlative psychic expression! Most of which super-referents you're oblivious to,

X, and how sad you might feel if that too weren't a sensation out-performed with more coherent BRIO than you had thought attainable and *not*, of course, save for the shining, grinning plastic craw. O! the shame that flushes your system arrives simultaneously alongside a total disinterest concerning each expression's unimpeachable, tear-jerk humanity, which makes the whole rig seem irreproachable, really. Enviable certitude presented similarly irrefutably – benchmarking and desktop delimiting the vernacular of possible/impossible experience and its insufficient representation. As in: what will suffice to prevent disastrous interpretative divergence? – The judicious application of exclamation marks? A deft shuffle of enthusiastic dark-haired auditionee surrogates? (A proxy for tears is creditable,

X, but of loving blood-stifled collapsing chest-cavity *wha*?)

The Mirror Stage retrieved at last, taken away from those principled elephants and great apes of flattering anthropomorphism, gifted with calm irresponsibly to the exposure-wrecked pigeons, staggering out from beneath frowning underpasses, feet eroded by sustained contact with fried chicken and potato guano, exhausted; soft skulls poison-shrunk from olid and discarded black seed on spiked sills, or the swing of dull, unchecked toddler's fat leg. And it dawns: slowly rising flocks, the SMUT OF THE SUN, as if a beak could crack a smile over a thousand years. And here lies hope,

X: The London Met, humbled, hats off, numbers I don't even need to see with water-cannoned eyes. And it isn't, um, beautiful but instead monstrous, the heraldic crest of a troll emblazoned on everyone's tongues to lick past wounds because they taste groundingly *cheap*.

Desperate regurgitation the denial of *this* economy's omnipresence, even if and simply semantically. All there is left for me, gesture-wise, is the rejection of a huge thumb forcibly grafted for fingered value picked like a scab from the shea-buttered surface of every single plush tendril coming from your wondrous being,

X. The only way in which figuration is DE-violated and molecular-level insubordination could possibly *repair* otherness is how I just now liked to think as a description of love,

X. And fleeting: a bridge formed by leaping jets of whetted electrical current, subsequently misting in the blinding sunlight. The turning-down of productive, progressive *use* with just a cuddle,

X? Otherwise we might just fucking forget it and deservedly decamp: rejection the sole property of spirit-levelled sense-makers and, um, your home,

X, which is reaffirmed as a limited capacity pine lung stowed beneath sea-level.

No one hears you,

X. Though my searing wish would be to join you in there; with you and up against you. An unfettered pair of dampening husks curled together like savoured and pre-sucked Pringles. With somehow our lips and ears enfolded for whispering in circular breaths,

X, and aimless affirmatory conjurations and memories lisped with precise neurological terminology to simply galvanize the inaccuracy inside our heads and more than likely, tomorrow, as our brains turn to sparkling mush without curtains drawn and finally come together. Murmured try-outs of proper synonyms for love.

As in: I love you,

X. (Self-chiding for retarded vocabulary where it really counts: sighed into your face,

X. There's an idea that adequate performance recognition is the line of contingency for affective conveyance,

X – whereas it's v. clear that the irreproachability of you, sung to the moon in one of those perma-wilting falsettos, yields something that returns you to your embodied self, which gets loved as such and like a rash.)

Ergo, kisses possible not just for lips relish but applied thwarting warring apparatuses and rather than the *tart* foley of bullet on plate metal or breeze-block, sound-tracking instead in an orgy of agonistic stringed instruments bowed with taught and very willing vermilion guts and discordance is cherished. LIKED.

The need is unquestionable, though occasionally attempted dismissal with that self-same stately wave of the hand that labels evil though never inside of a young head. Ribbons of ticker-taped loathing drift down to no ground, remember? Like air-to-air ruination.

Will you write to me,

X? I will seldom respond, if ever. As wherever I go, there I am: *beneath beneath beneath*, sucker-punch doubled-over into stress positioned speech in nasty unisons – some benevolent thing seeming-listening with

22

stupid honourable prosthetic ears while from the mouth a few inches down and degrees perfect rotation: a vituperative, electrical bugged buzz-hole both sooth-says all this unreal and unmeant encouragement while through an adjacent hot air vent sucking correspondent oxygen (which I require for living,

X) from my lungs well in advance of the hopeful trachea, the plucky larynx, the dewy-eyed tongue and comedy teeth, all earnestly poised to pronounce, errm, the simple possibilities of disliking anything but in supra-agreement, etc. And what if I want to disavow the possibility of abundantly replacing an experience with some Legion other's mediated imagery?

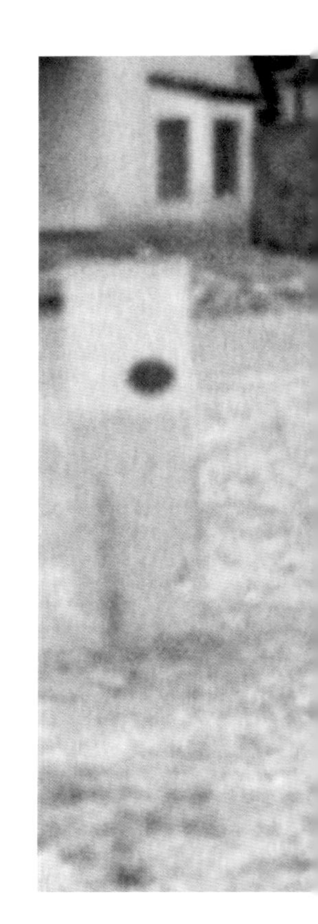

Nuotama Bodomo

(born 1988 in Accra, Ghana)

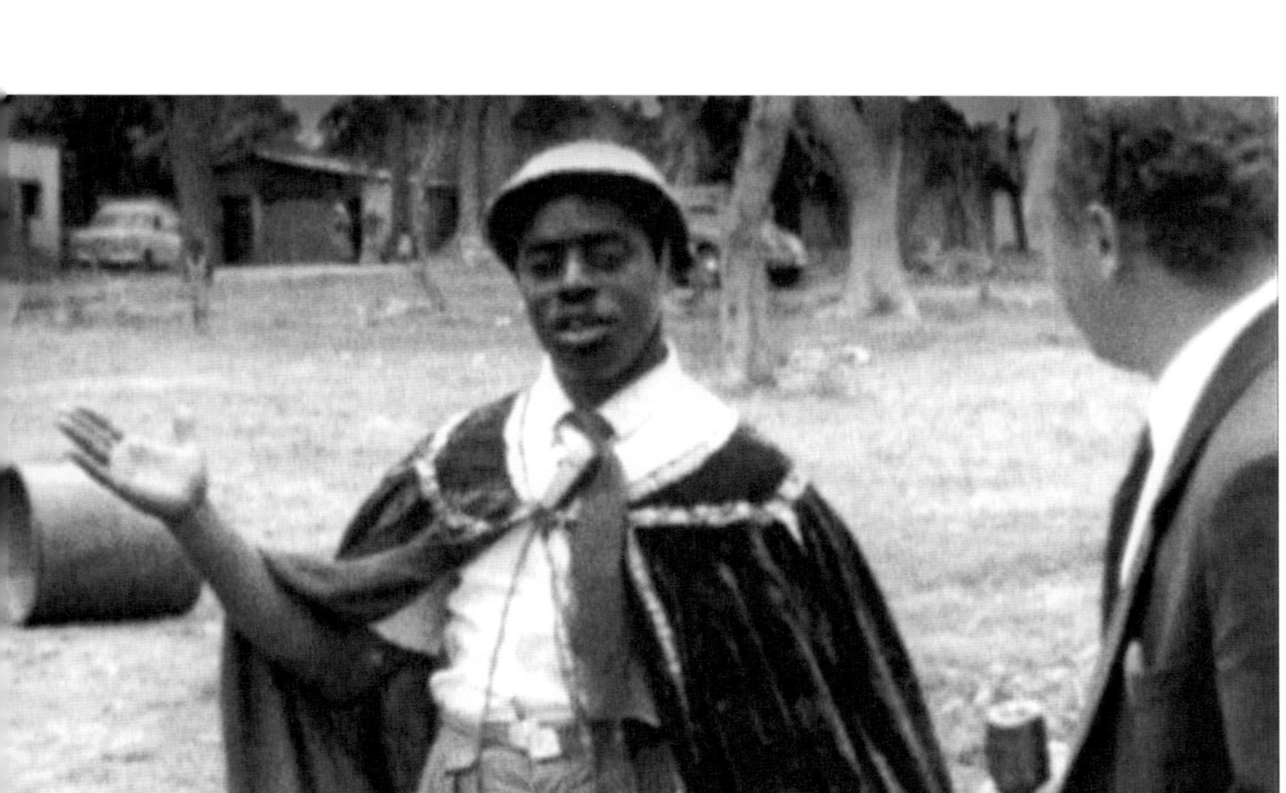

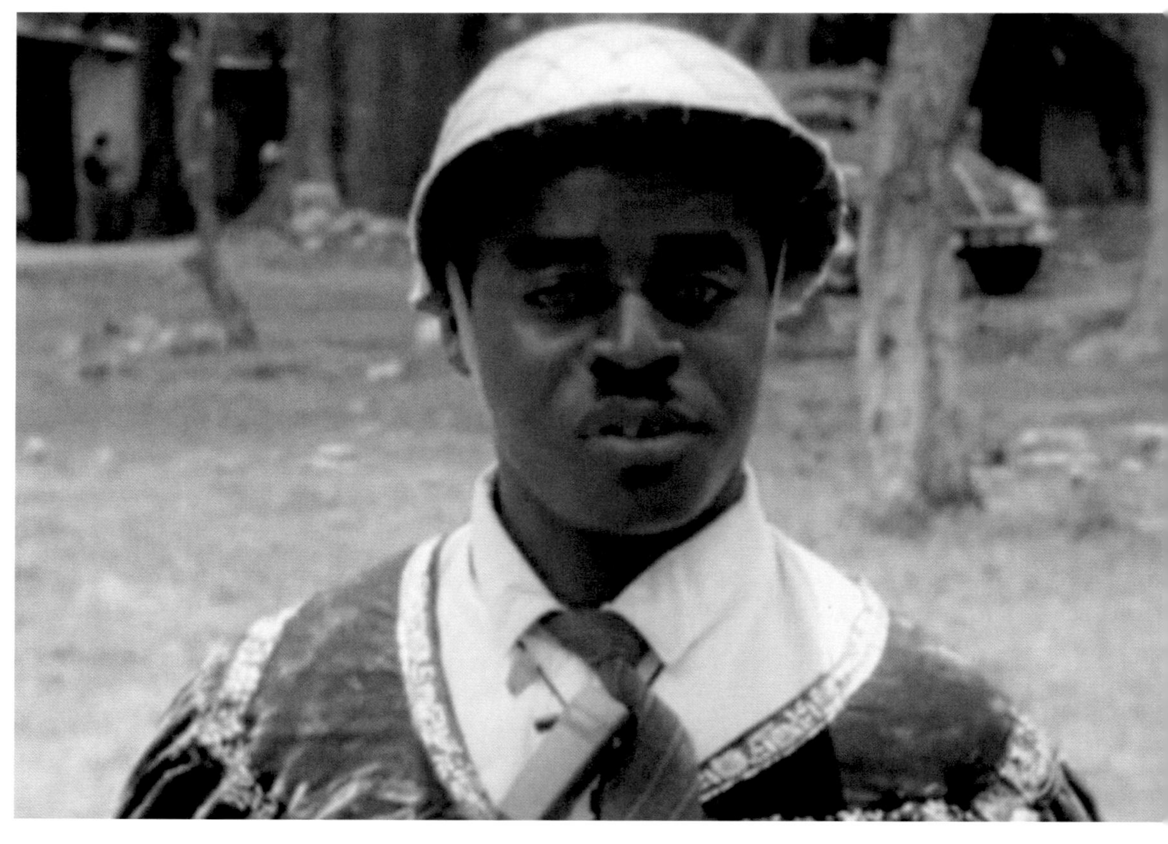

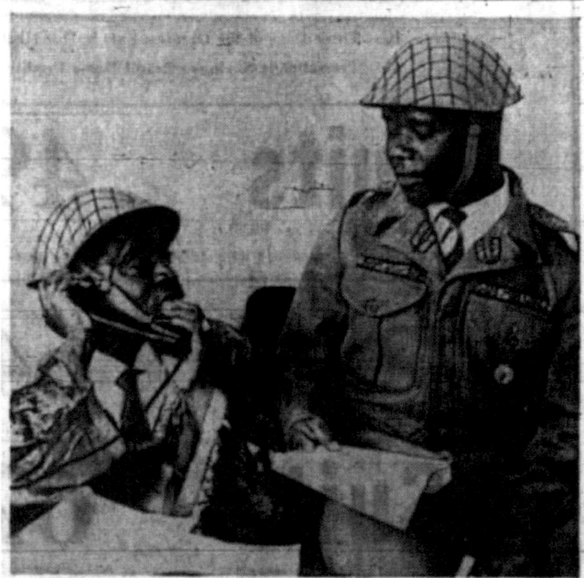

ZAMBIA'S COSMONAUT

Edward Mukuka Nkoloso, in spaceman's helmet and ornate cloak, interrupts a telephone conversation in Lusaka, Zambia, to talk to Zambia's No. 1 cosmonaut, Godfrey Mwango. Zambia is Africa's newest nation, formerly known as Northern Rhodesia, a British protectorate. Nkoloso, self-appointed Zambian minister of space research, boasts, "I'll have my first Zambian astronaut on the moon by 1965." He estimates he'll need almost $2 billion to place him there.

ROCKET A BIT WOBBLY

Zambia Warns Russia, U.S. We'll Beat You to Moon

By DENNIS LEE ROYLE

LUSAKA, Zambia (AP) — Edward Mukuka Nkoloso has designated himself Zambia's minister of space research, and says the United States

space. I also make them swing from the end of a long rope. When they reach the highest point I cut the rope — this produces the feeling of free-fall."

a project of this magnitude," he said. "Some of our ideas are way ahead of the Americans and Russians and these days I will not let anyone see my rocket plans."

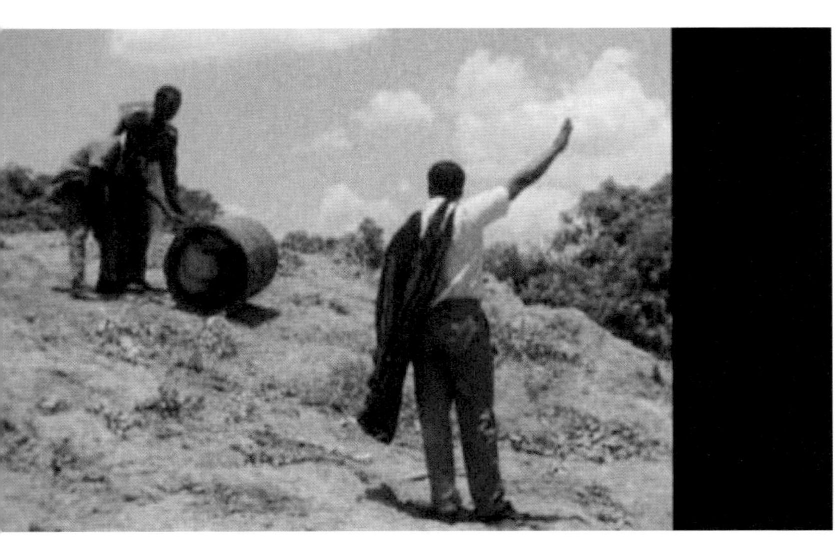

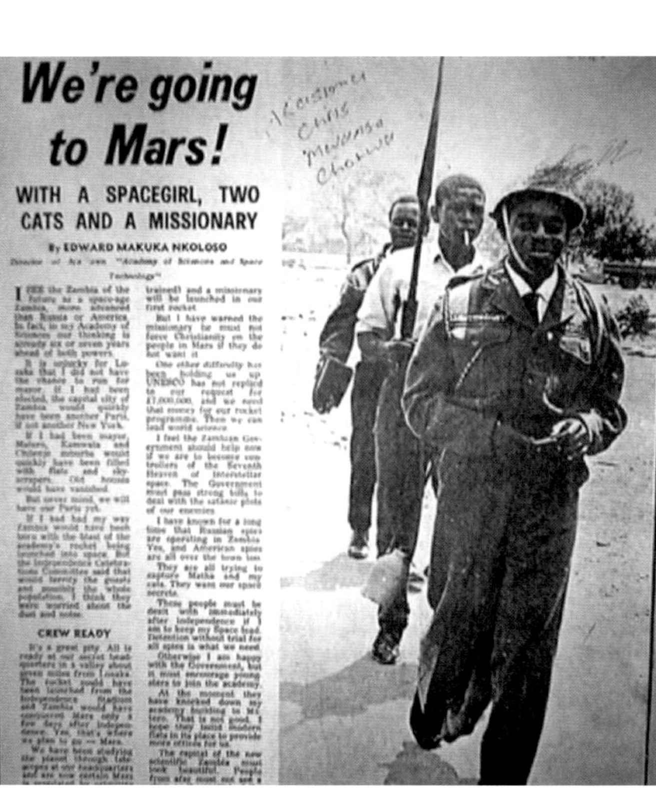

We're going to Mars!

WITH A SPACEGIRL, TWO CATS AND A MISSIONARY

By EDWARD MAKUKA NKOLOSO

Director of his own "Academy of Sciences and Space Technology"

I SEE the Zambia of the future as a space-age Zambia, more advanced than Russia or America. In fact, in my Academy of Sciences our thinking is already six or seven years ahead of both powers.

It is unlucky for Lusaka that I did not have the chance to run for mayor. If I had been elected, the capital city of Zambia would quickly have been another Paris, if not another New York.

If I had been mayor, Matero, Kamwala and Chilenje suburbs would quickly have been filled with flats and skyscrapers. Old houses would have vanished.

But never mind, we will have our Paris yet.

If I had had my way Zambia would have been born with the blast of the academy's rocket being launched into space. But the Independence Celebrations Committee said that would terrify the guests and possibly the whole population. I think they were worried about the dust and noise.

CREW READY

It's a great pity. All is ready at our secret headquarters in a valley about seven miles from Lusaka. The rocket could have been launched from the Independence Stadium and Zambia would have conquered Mars only a few days after independence. Yes, that's where we plan to go — Mars.

We have been studying the planet through telescopes at our headquarters and are now certain Mars is [illegible]

[illegible] trained) and a missionary will be launched in our first rocket.

But I have warned the missionary he must not force Christianity on the people in Mars if they do not want it.

One other difficulty has been holding us up. UNESCO has not replied to our request for £7,000,000, and we need that money for our rocket programme. Then we can lead world science.

I feel the Zambian Government should help now if we are to become controllers of the Seventh Heaven of interstellar space. The Government must pass strong bills to deal with the satanic plots of our enemies.

I have known for a long time that Russian spies are operating in Zambia. Yes, and American spies are all over the town too.

They are all trying to capture Matha and my cats. They want our space secrets.

These people must be dealt with immediately after independence if I am to keep my space lead. Detention without trial for all spies is what we need.

Otherwise I am happy with the Government, but it must encourage youngsters to join the academy.

At the moment they have knocked down my academy building in [illegible]. That is not good. I hope they build modern flats in its place to provide more offices for us.

The capital of the new scientific Zambia must look beautiful. People from afar must [illegible]

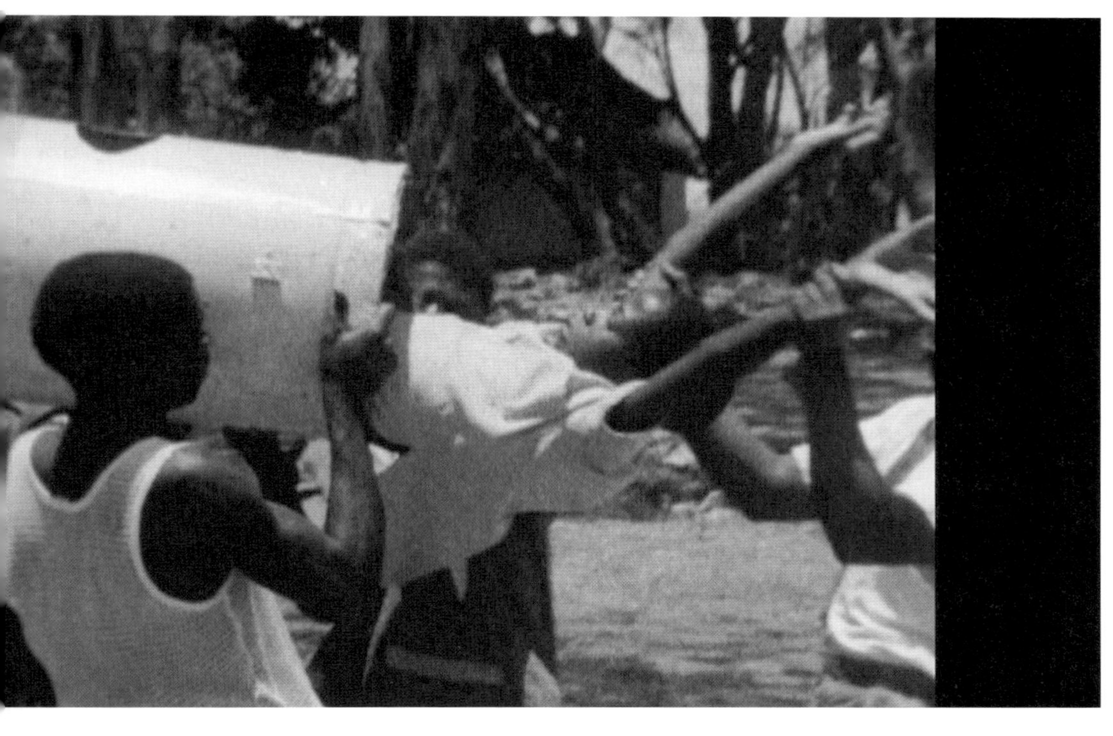

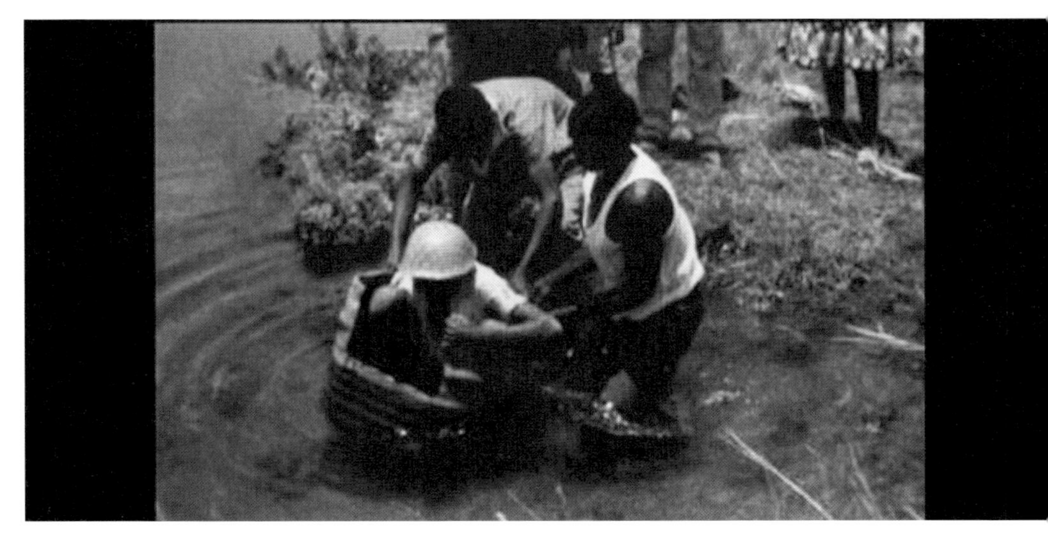

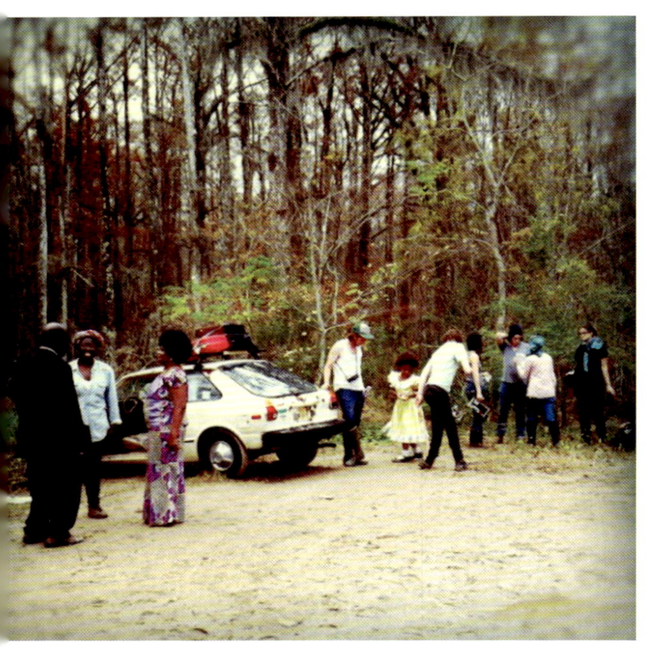

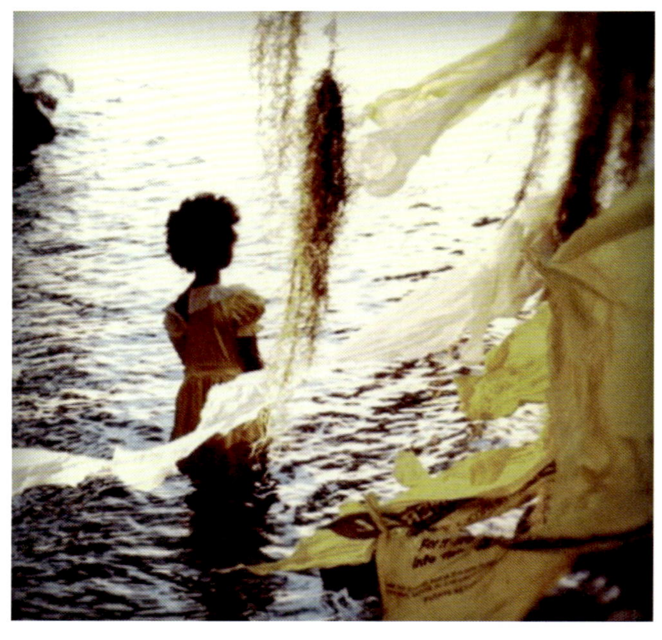

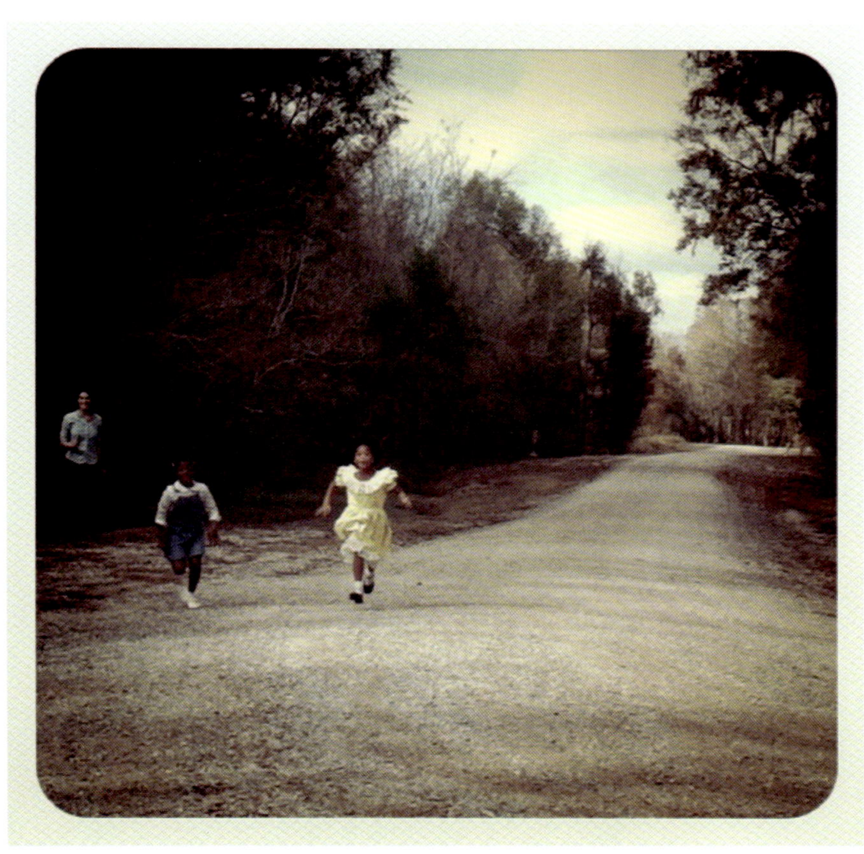

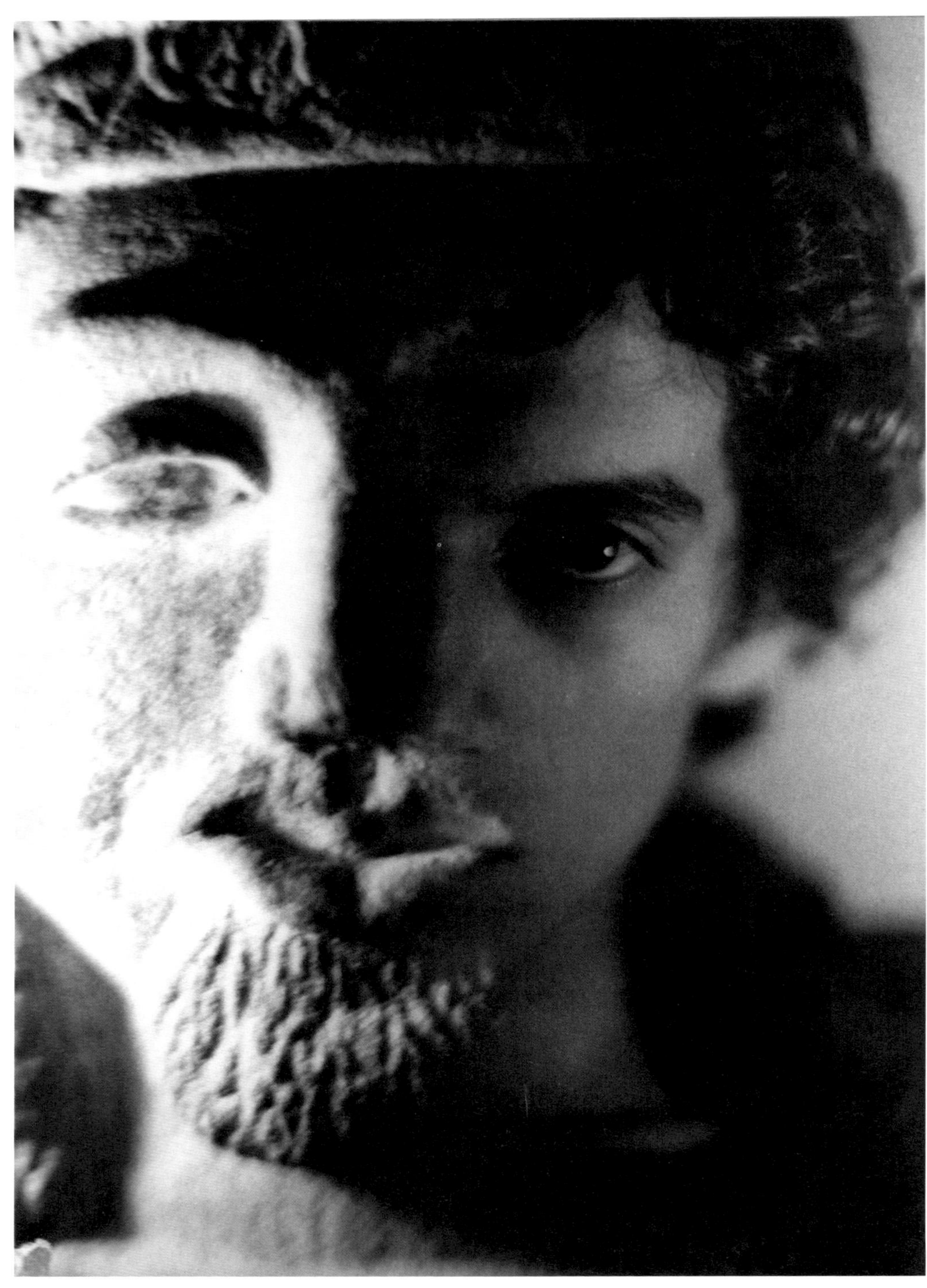

Self-Portrait, 1975

Part of a series of portraits using the technique of in-camera double exposures.

Theo Eshetu

(born 1958 in London, United Kingdom)

In the years leading to my studies in London and prior to taking up video art as a full-time activity, I worked mainly in black and white photography. Here is a small selection of early works that would later influence some of my thinking in the production of videos.

Boy and Dog, 1978

I often have considered this picture of my brother holding a mask and our dog Jamba rolling on the ground to be caressed to be my first photograph. While it wasn't actually the first photograph I took, it does point to the beginning of an artistic process where aesthetic and conceptual considerations merge. A process I was later to develop further in the production of videos.

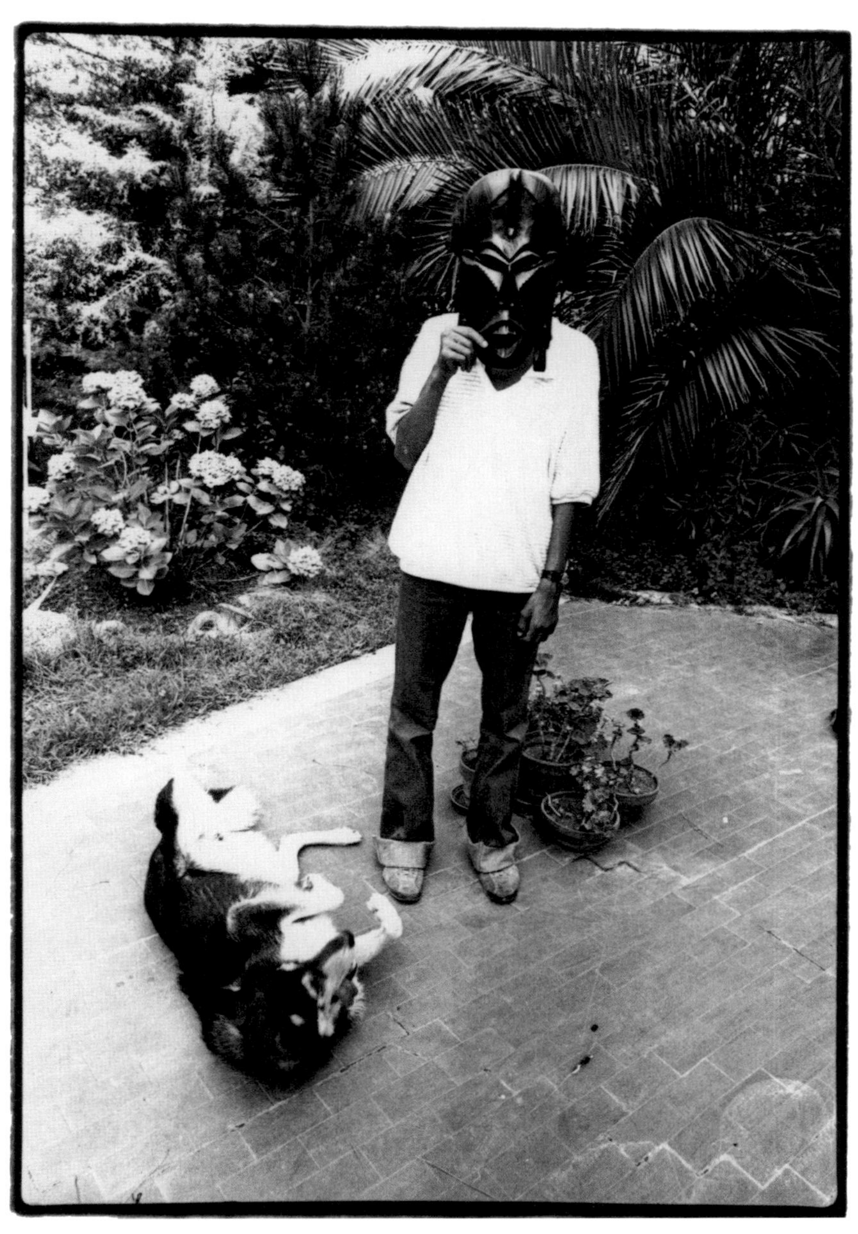

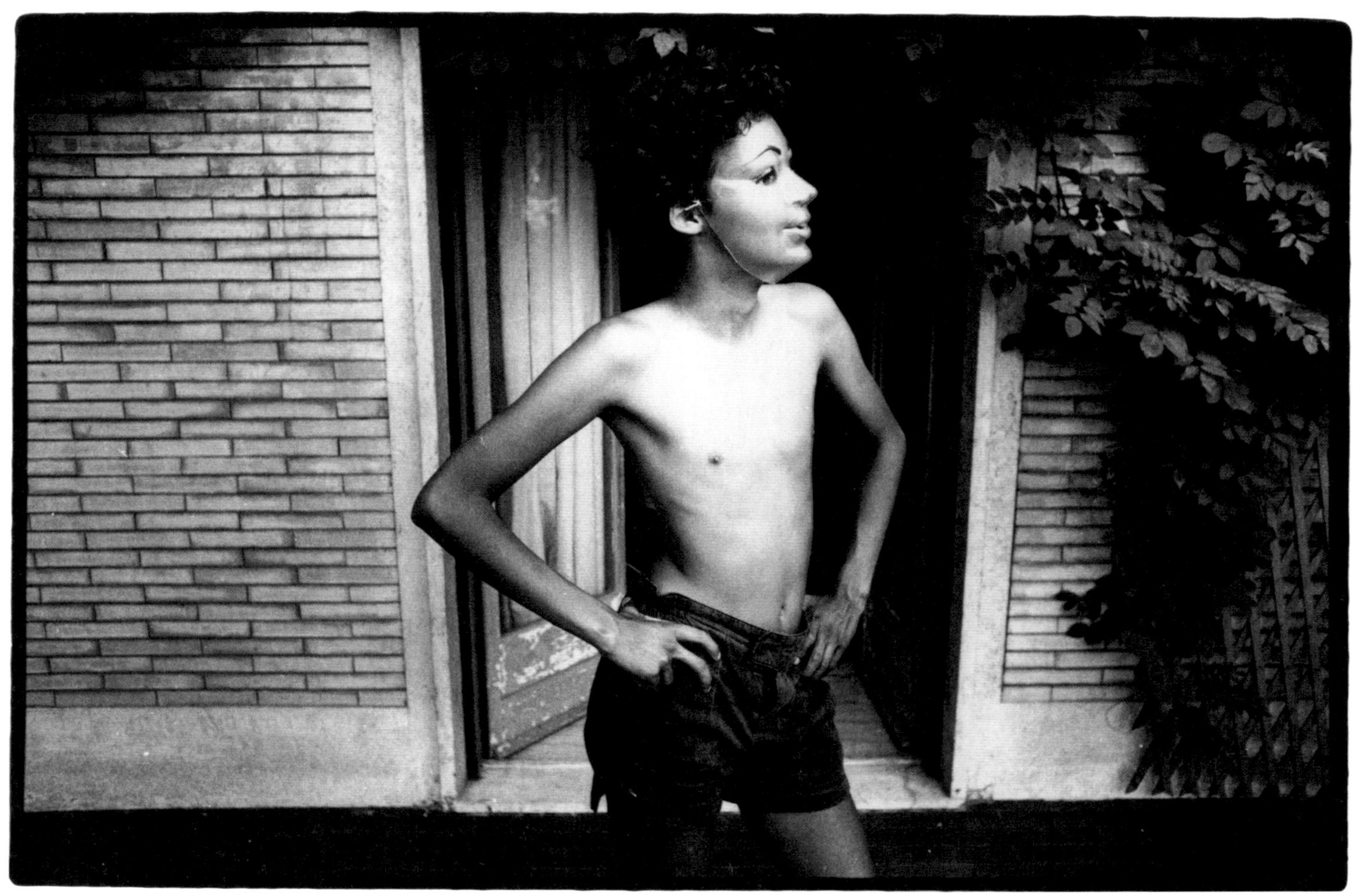

Boy and Mask, 1978

Here again a picture of my brother on our terrace in Rome wearing a transparent mask I had bought after seeing *The Rocky Horror Picture Show* in London. This is part of an extended series of portraits of friends and family made with these transparent masks.

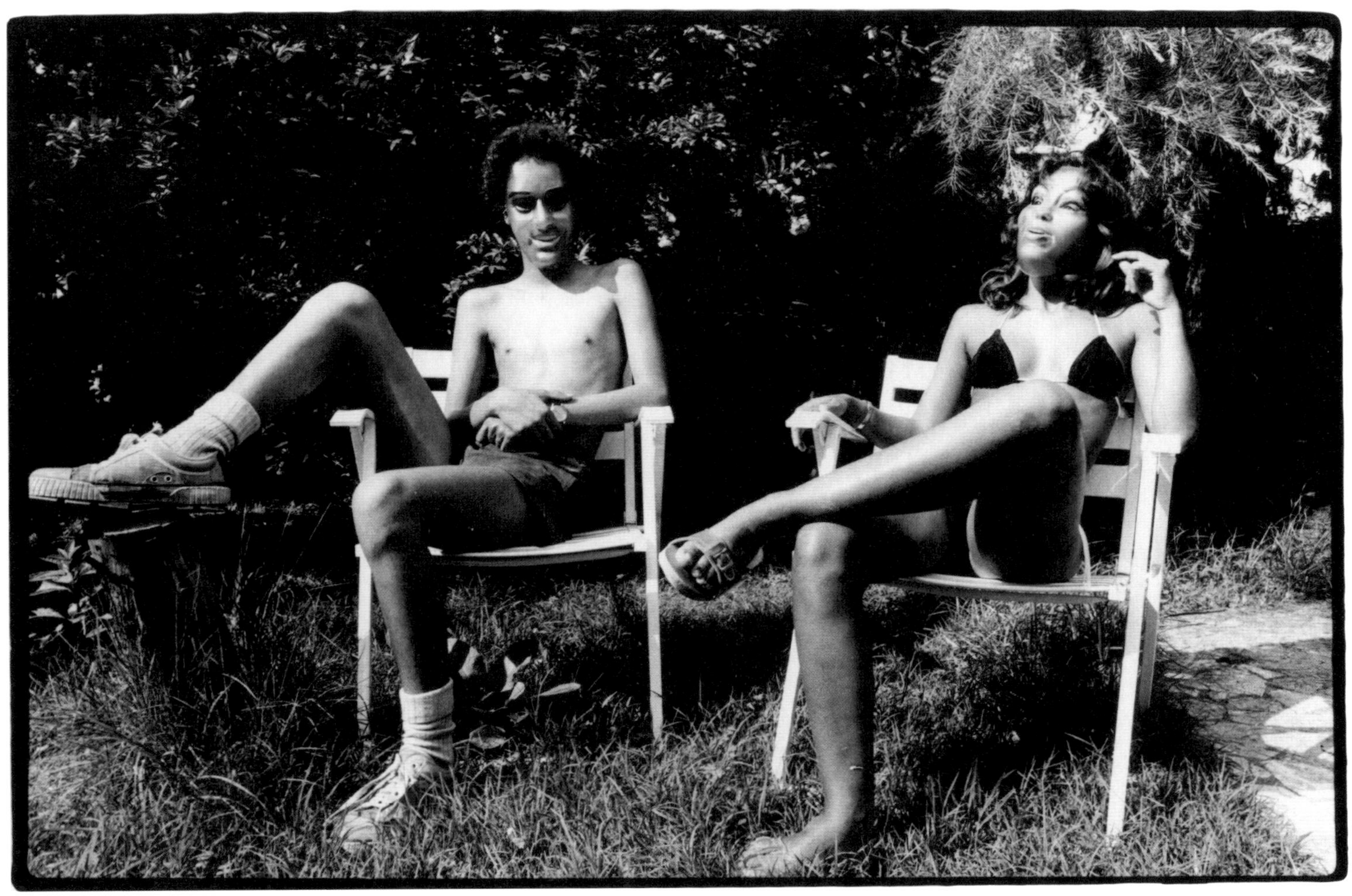

Brother and Sister, 1978

Portrait of my brother and sister wearing transparent masks, shot in our garden.

Self-Portrait and Mirror, 1979

This self-portrait, made in my first year of studies in London during a communication design course, was the basis for a series of brightly colored silk screens. This passage from one medium to another marked the beginning of my interest in video making. Mirrors and the idea of mirroring the image was a technique I developed in several videos, while the inclusion of the film strip in the print points to a wish to reveal the mechanics of image making. Masks, mirrors, and makeup have been an ongoing metaphor for deciphering the illusionary nature of a medium often associated with the representation of reality.

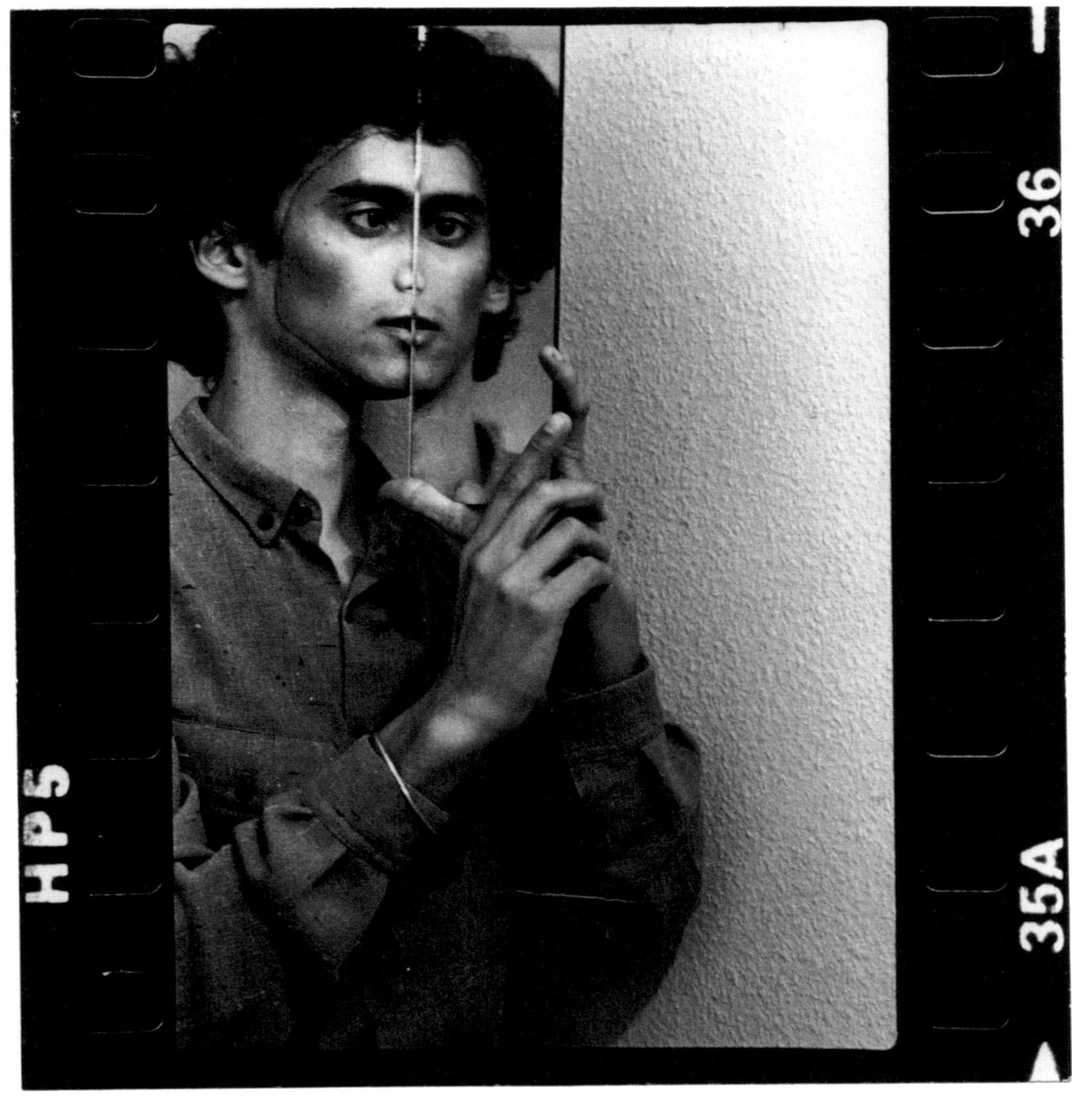
HP5
36
35A

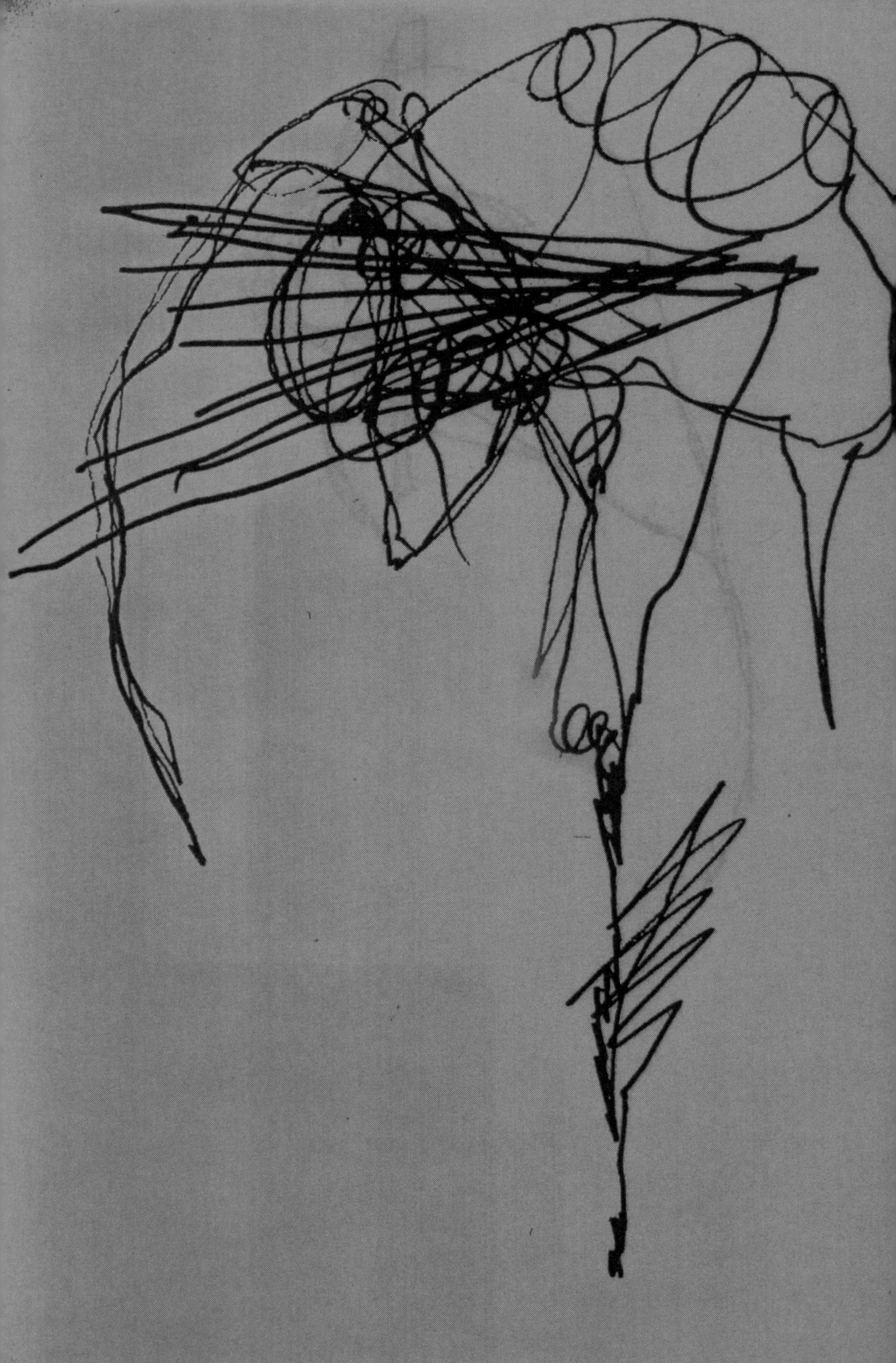

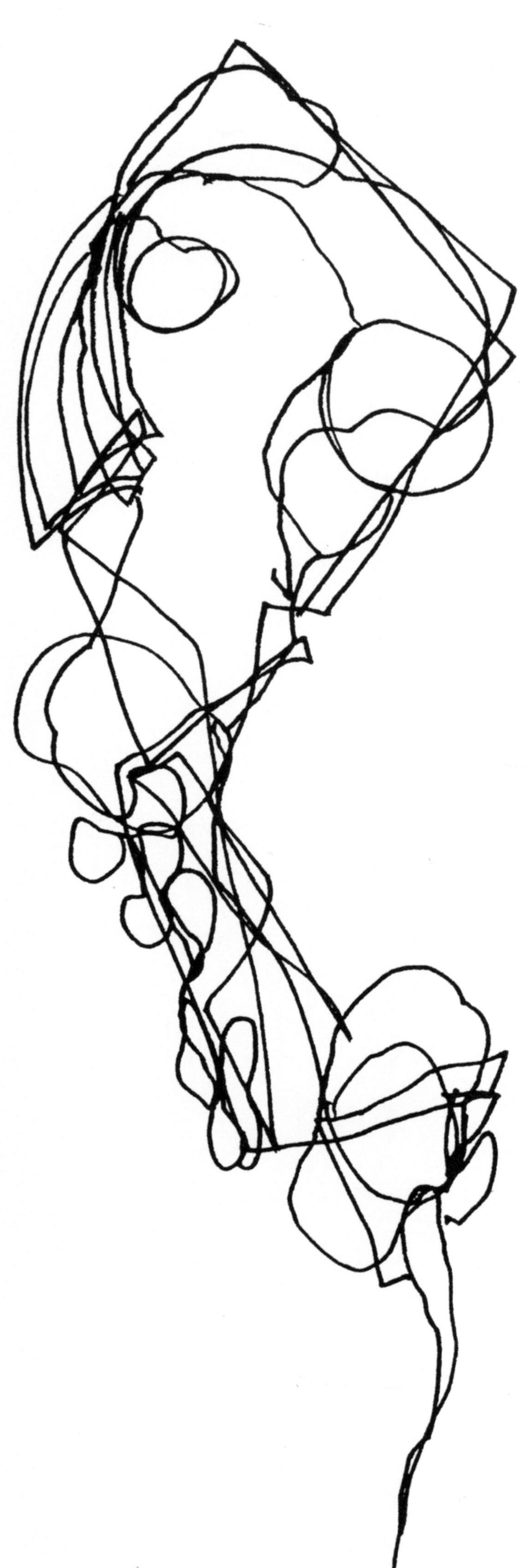

Cameron Jamie

(born 1969 in Los Angeles, California)

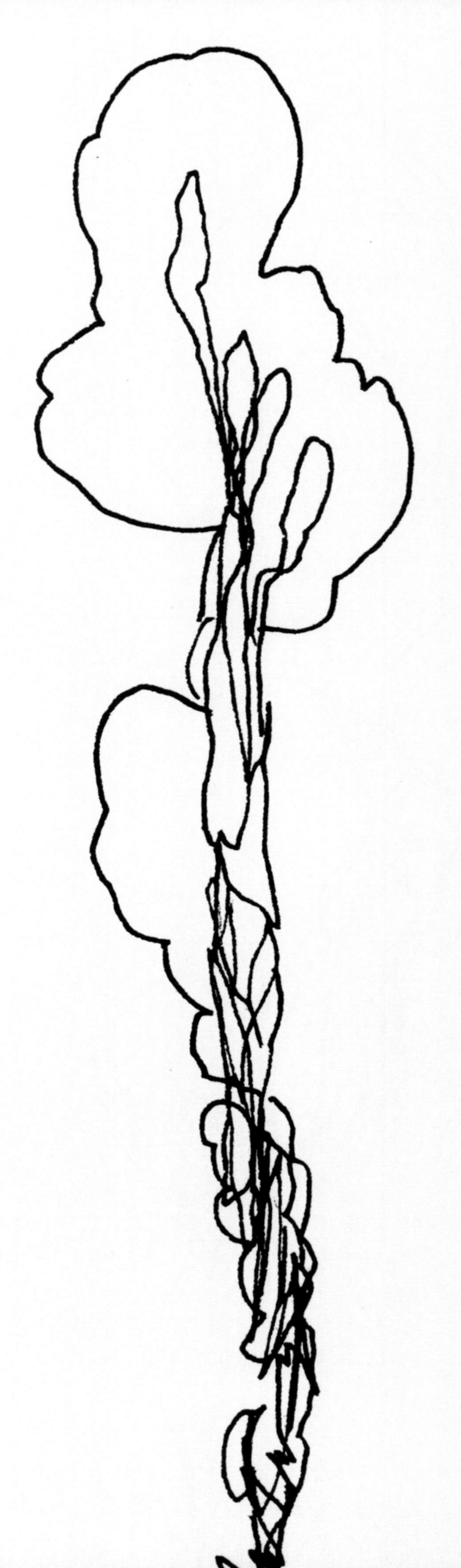

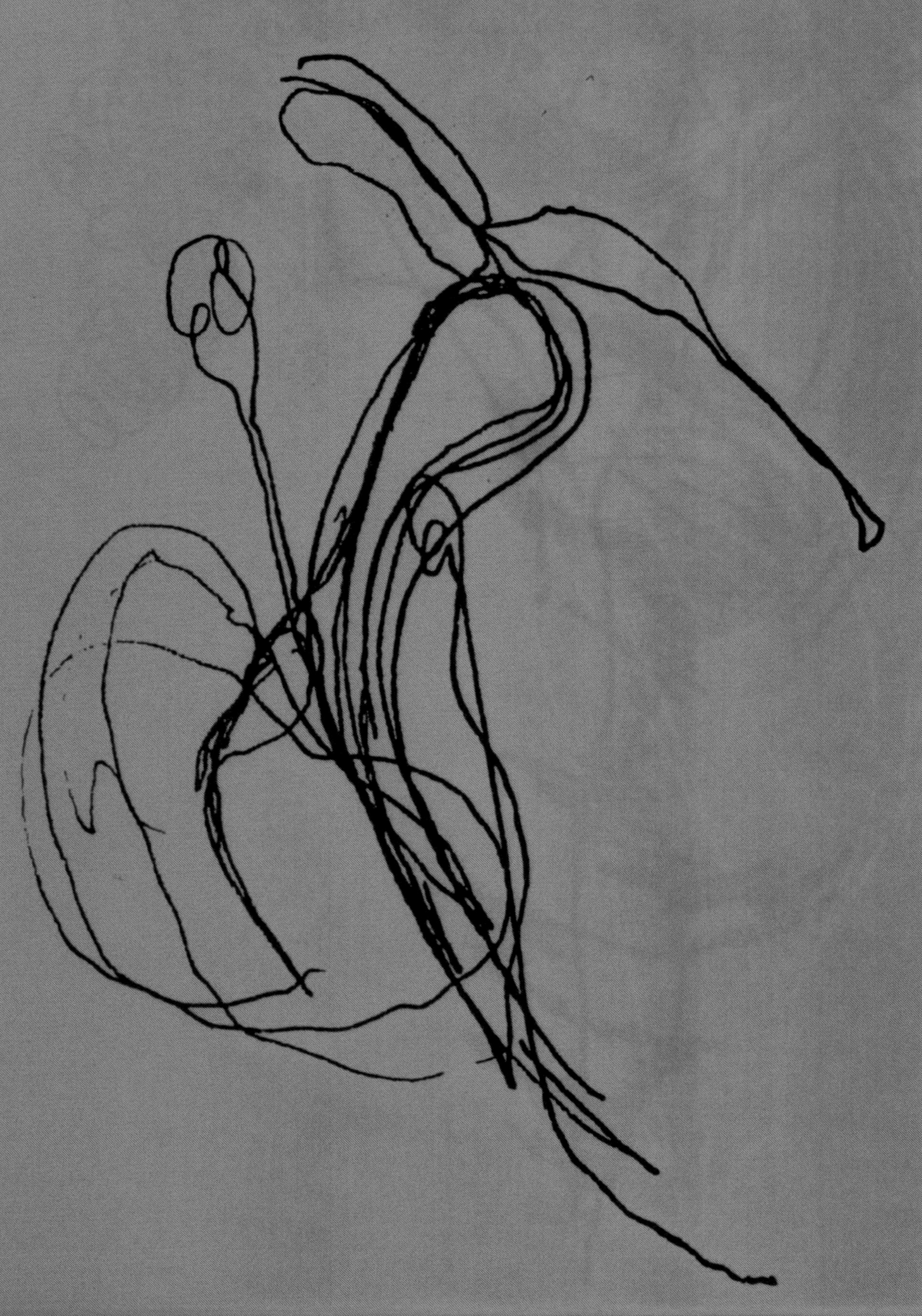

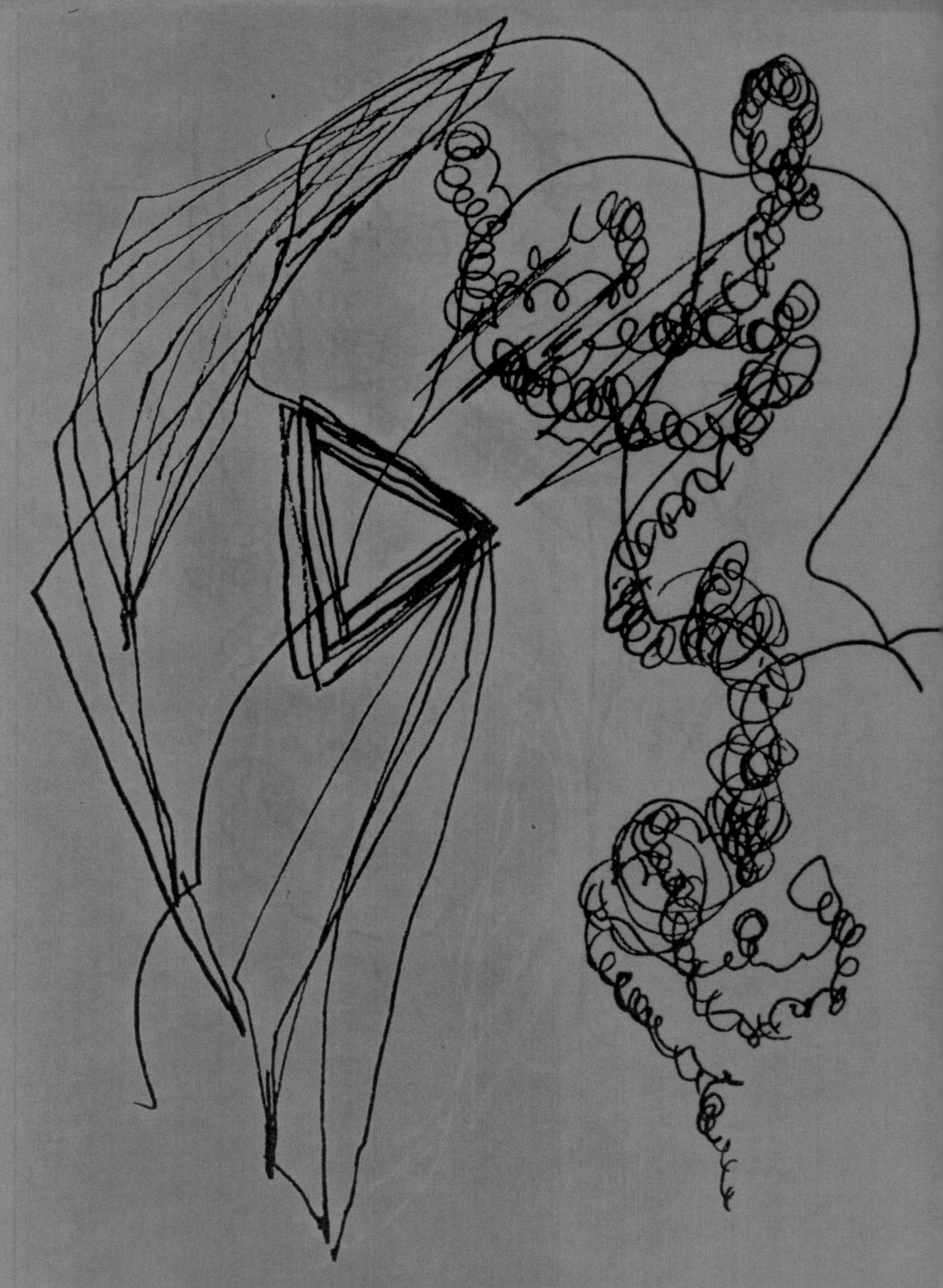

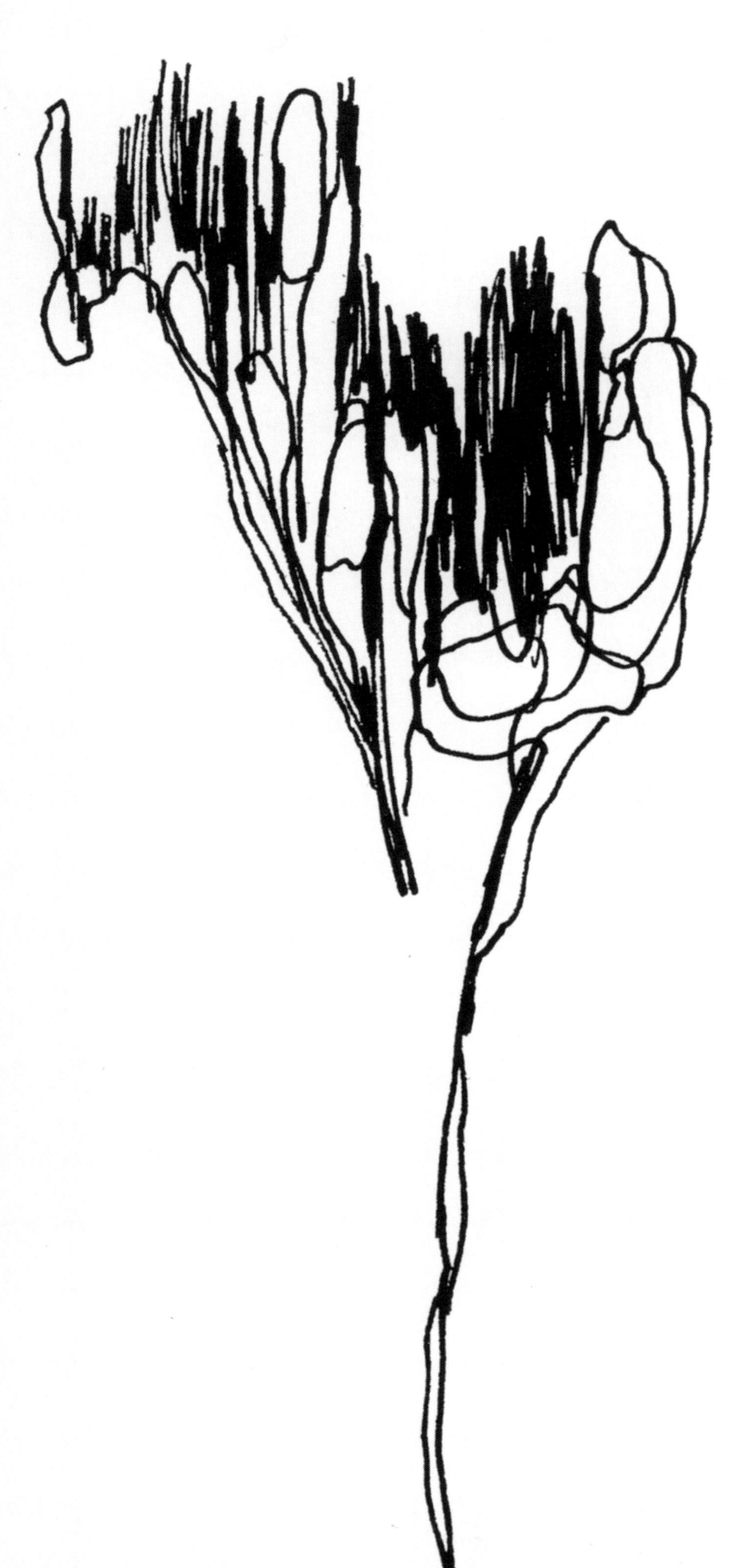

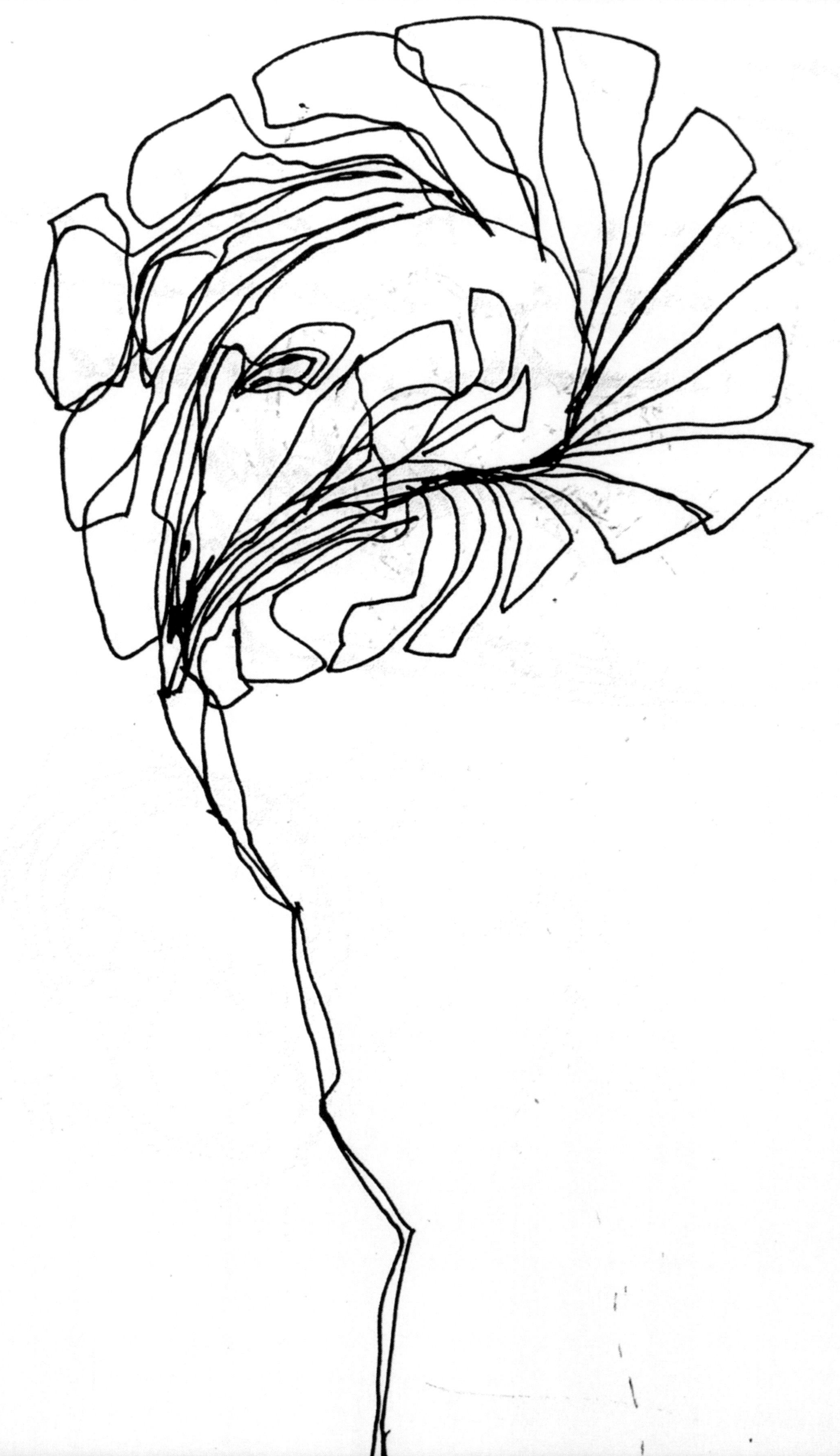

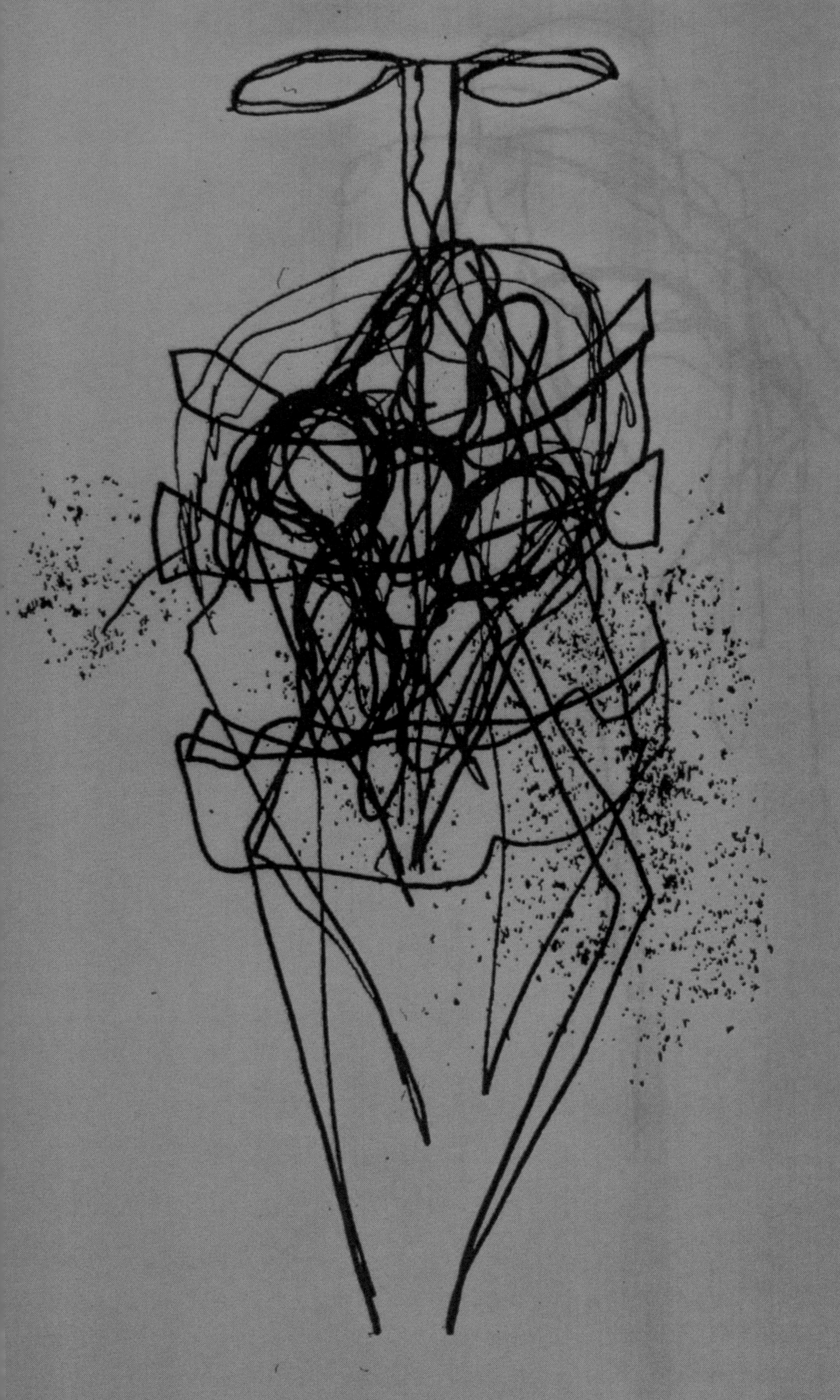

necessary counternarratives that challenged a claimant's stated timeline. I take up this transcript further below. For now, two interlocking questions emerge: First, how are we to read the historical record of these hearings given the context in which they were written, where humans owned other humans? Second, how do we grapple with the textual meaning itself, given that the record of these hearings is composed not of verbatim transcripts but of records of proceedings and decisions rendered almost noneventful in their brevity, and that are only partial accounts meant to be put to later use in the service of Patriots for claims of injury, losses of property, and compensation? By situating the Board of Inquiry hearings at Fraunces Tavern as moments of repossession, what I am arguing for here is a mapping of Fraunces Tavern as a space where black women, black men, and black children challenged *un*-visibility through contestations for freedom and mobility that were simultaneously demands for recognition not as property, but as full subjects, as humans. For Mercy, the so-called negroe wench, and her children, in the end Fraunces Tavern was a space for the making of her and her children as disposable ("to be disposed of as he may think proper"). They were sentenced to a life back in slavery. In the section that follows, I take up eighteenth-century lantern laws to question how black luminosity as a means of regulating mobility was legislated and also contested. I do this to historicize the surveillance of black life in New York City.

Torches, Torture, and Totau: Lantern Laws in New York City

I am truly a drop of sun under the earth.
—FRANTZ FANON, *Black Skin, White Masks*

"Moment by moment" is the experience of surveillance in urban life, as David Lyon observes, where the city dweller expects to be "constantly illuminated."[31] It is how the city dweller contends with this expectation that is instructive. To examine closely the performance of freedom, a performative practice, I suggest, that those named fugitive in the Board of Inquiry arbitration hearings at Fraunces Tavern made use of, I borrow political theorist Richard Iton's "visual surplus" and its B side, "performative sensibility."[32] What Iton suggests is that we come to internalize an expectation of the potential of being watched and with this emerges a certain "performa-

Kapwani Kiwanga
(born 1978 in Hamilton, Ontario, Canada)

A CHRONOLOGICAL HISTORY

OF THE

BOSTON WATCH AND POLICE,

FROM 1631 TO 1865;

TOGETHER WITH THE

Recollections of a Boston Police Officer,

OR

BOSTON BY DAYLIGHT AND GASLIGHT.

FROM THE DIARY OF AN OFFICER FIFTEEN YEARS IN THE SERVICE

BY

EDWARD H. SAVAGE.

"'Tis strange, but true,—for truth is always strange,
Stranger than fiction."—BYRON.

BOSTON:
PUBLISHED AND SOLD BY THE AUTHOR.
1865.

MONDAY, MARCH 14, 2016

Lanterns, Laws, and Legend

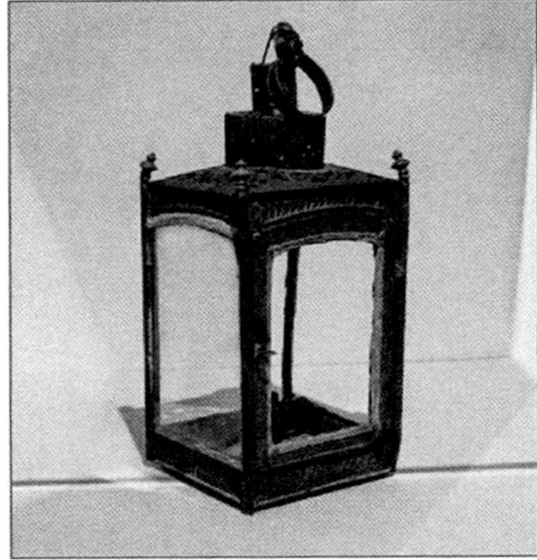

As I quoted back here, on 1 Nov 1769 Boston town clerk William Cooperwrote out instructions on behalf of the selectmen to Thomas Bradford, temporarily promoted to Constable of the South Watch. Among other things, the letter told Bradford:

> You are to take up all Negroes Indianand Molatto Slavesthat may be absent from their masters House after nine o'Clock at Night and passing the Streets unless they are carrying Lanthorns with light Candles and can give a good and satisfactory Account of their Business that such offenders may be proceeded with according to Law.

As I noted before, this amounted to license to stop every black or Native American person the watchmen met on the street at night since there was no way to tell by sight if they were slaves.

At the time, Boston was occupied by British regiments. An army captain named John Willson had reportedly asked in a tavern why the town's enslaved population had never risen up, which locals took (sincerely or not) as instigation to revolt. The result was that discriminatory addition to the watchmen's instructions, probably modeled on a measure in effect in New York since 1713.

Almost a century after Cooper's letter, Edward H. Savage published a history of the Boston police force. It seems to have appeared under different titles, including A Chronological History of the Boston Watch and Police: From 1631 to 1865. Using racist language and outrageous dialect, Savage spun an amusing story off that regulation from 1769:

> It was said soon after the order was given, "an old darkie was picked up prowling about in total darkness." Next morning, when asked by the magistrate if guilty, he replied "No, sa, I has de lantern," holding up before the astonished court, an old one, innocent of oil or candle. He was discharged, and the law amended, so as to require "a lantern with a candle." Old Tony was soon up again on the same complaint, and again entered a plea "not guilty," and again drawing forth the old lantern with a candle; but the wick had not been discolored by a flame. The defendant was discharged with a reprimand, and the law was made to read, "a lantern with a lighted candle." Old Tony was not caught again, having been heard to remark, "Massa got too much light on de subjec."

Marietta Lois Stow repeated the same anecdote about "old Caesar" and his empty lantern in Probate Chaff: Or, Beautiful Probate (1879).

I've seen other racist jokes like this from nineteenth-century Massachusetts, looking back on pre-Revolutionary slavery times. They usually come with a thick coating of dialect and white supremacy, but half the time the story is about a black man as clever trickster.

There's a problem with relying on this anecdote as history, however. As the quotation above shows, the selectmen had required "Lanthorns with light Candles" all along. So it's just a joke.

In a new book titled Dark Matters: On the Surveillance of Blackness, Simone Browne discusses the series of New York laws requiring blacks to carry lanterns after dark through 1784 as a presage of modern surveillance of non-white communities. That book calls those "lantern laws," seemingly a generic term. It's true that in 1998 Edwin G. Burrows and Mike Wallace's Gotham: A History of New York City to 1898 referred to that city's 1713 ordinance as a "new lantern law." However, Google Books uncovers the phrase "lantern law" earlier only in turn-of-the-20th-century discussions of bicycling.

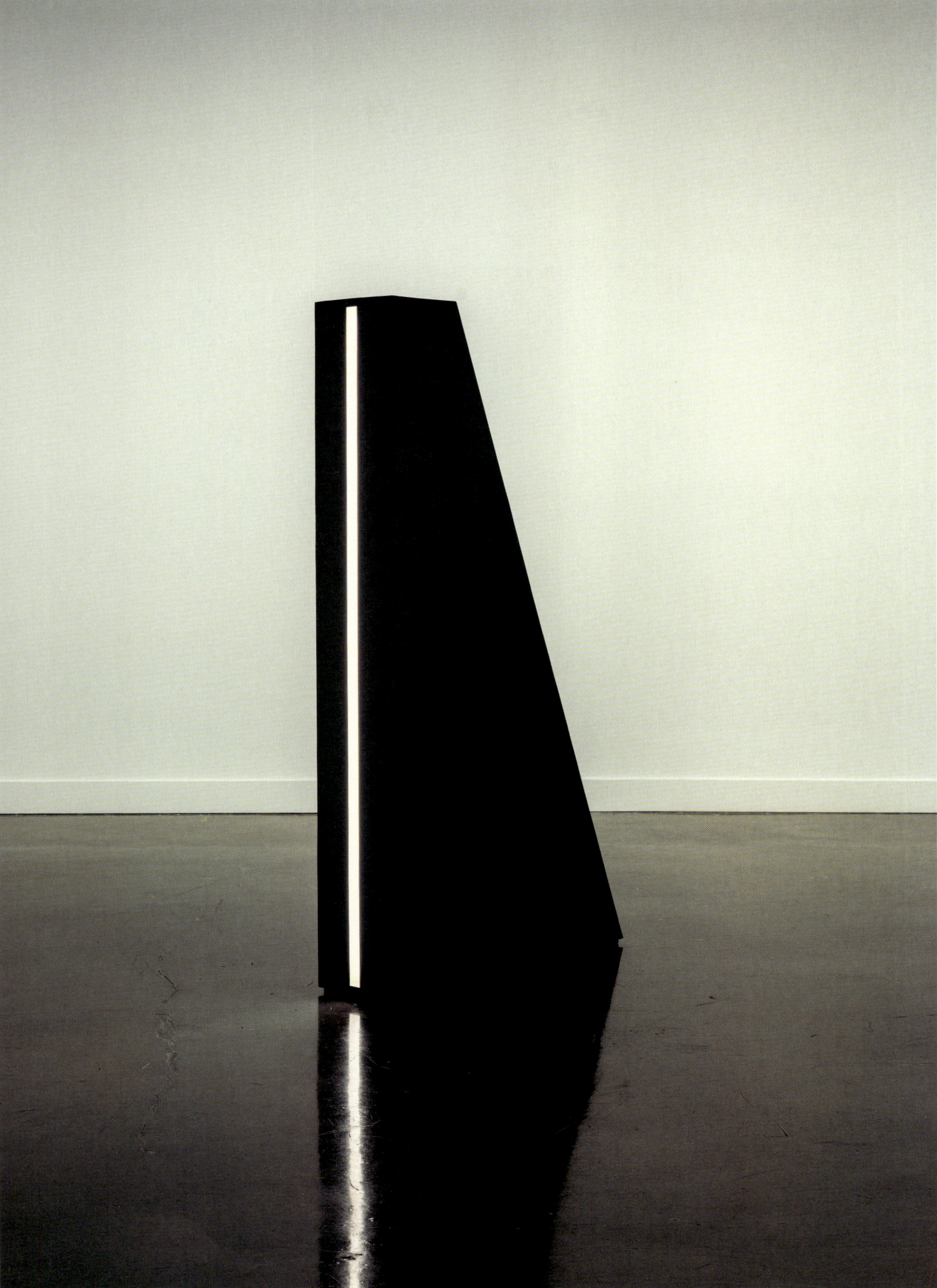

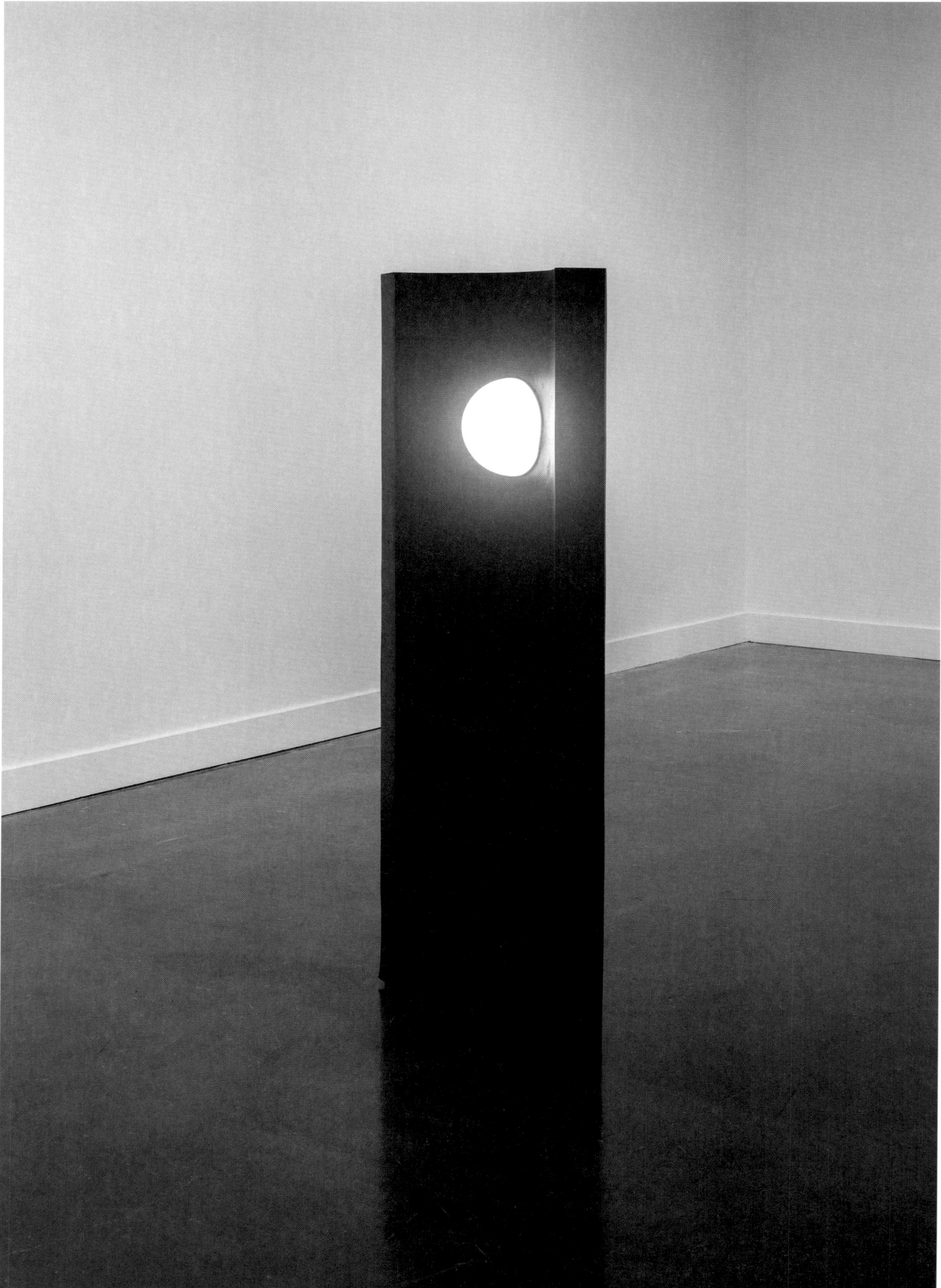

06

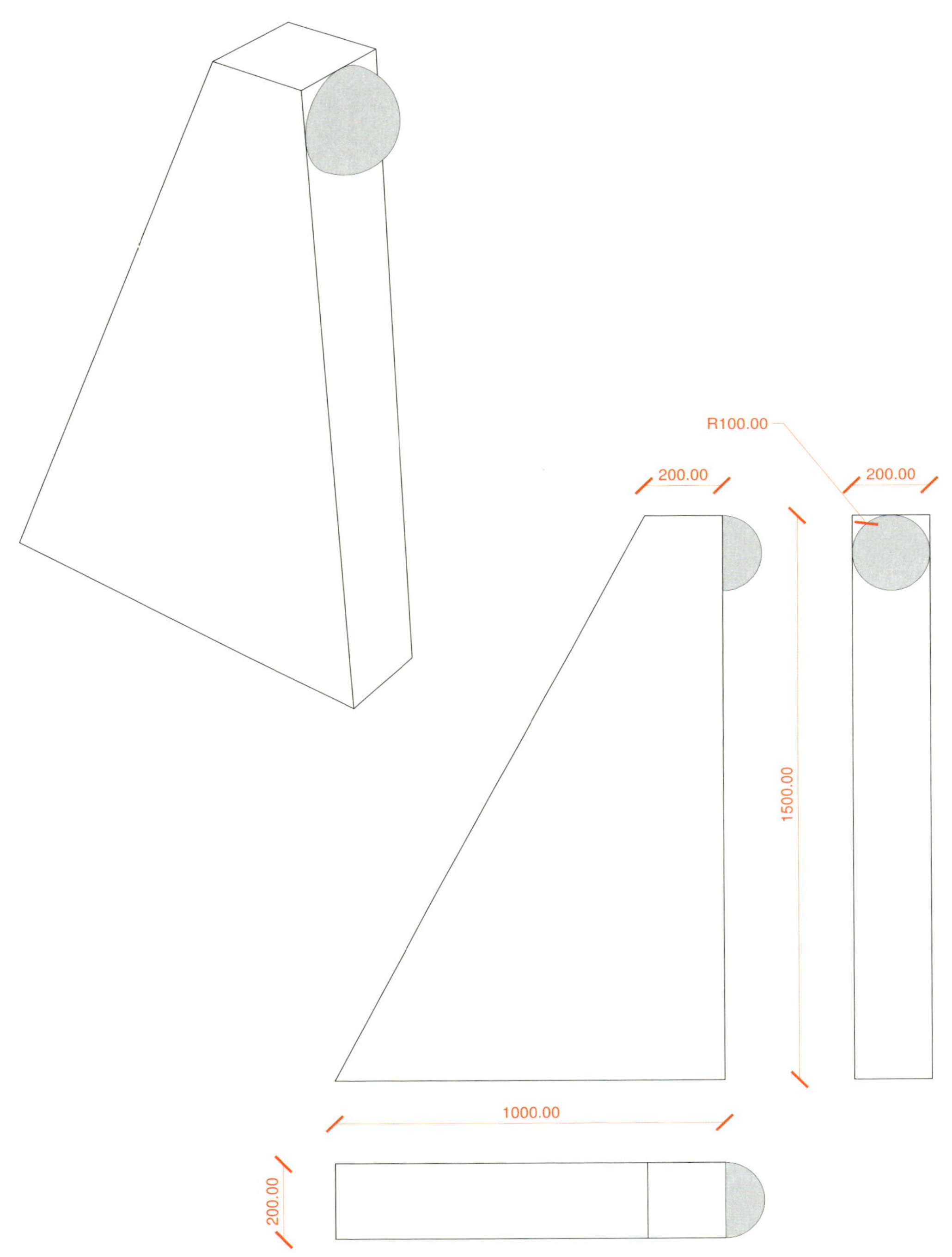

City of New-York, *ſs.*

A LAW

For Regulating Negroes and Slaves in the Night Time.

BE *It Ordained by the Mayor, Recorder, Aldermen and Aſſiſtants of the City of* New-York, *convened in Common-Council, and it is hereby Ordained by the Authority of the ſame,* That from hence-forth no Negro, Mulatto or Indian Slave, above the Age of Fourteen Years, do preſume to be or appear in any of the Streets of this City, on the South-ſide of the Freſh-Water, in the Night time, above an hour after Sun-ſet; And that if any ſuch Negro, Mulatto or Indian Slave or Slaves, as aforeſaid, ſhall be found in any of the Streets of this City, or in any other Place, on the South ſide of the Freſh-Water, in the Night-time, above one hour after Sun-ſet, without a Lanthorn and lighted Candle in it, ſo as the light thereof may be plainly ſeen (and not in company with his, her or their Maſter or Miſtreſs, or ſome White Perſon or White Servant belonging to the Family whoſe Slave he or ſhe is, or in whoſe Service he or ſhe then are) That then and in ſuch caſe it ſhall and may be lawful for any of his Majeſty's Subjects within the ſaid City to apprehend ſuch Slave or Slaves, not having ſuch Lanthorn and Candle, and forth-with carry him, her or them before the Mayor or Recorder, or any one of the Aldermen of the ſaid City (if at a ſeaſonable hour) and if at an unſeaſonable hour, to the Watch-houſe, there to be confined until the next Morning) who are hereby authorized, upon Proof of the Offence, to commit ſuch Slave or Slaves to the common Goal, for ſuch his, her or their Contempt, and there to remain until the Maſter, Miſtreſs or Owner of every ſuch Slave or Slaves, ſhall pay to the Perſon or Perſons who apprehended and Convicted ~~committed~~ every ſuch Slave or Slaves, the Sum of *Four Shillings* current Money of *New-York*, for his, her or their pains and Trouble therein, with Reaſonable Charges of Proſecution.

And be it further Ordained by the Authority aforeſaid, That every Slave or Slaves that ſhall be convicted of the Offence aforeſaid, before he, ſhe or they be diſcharged out of Cuſtody, ſhall be Whipped at the Publick Whipping-Poſt (not exceeding *Forty Lashes*) if deſired by the Maſter or Owner of ſuch Slave or Slaves.

Provided always, and it is the intent hereof, That if two or more Slaves (Not exceeding the Number of Three) be together in any lawful Employ or Labour for the Service of their *Ma*ſter or Miſtreſs (and not otherwiſe) and only one of them have and carry ſuch Lanthorn with a lighted Candle therein, the other Slaves in ſuch Company not carrying a Lanthorn and lighted Candle, ſhall not be conſtrued and intended to be within the meaning and Penalty of this Law, any thing in this Law contained to the contrary hereof in any wiſe notwithſtanding. *Dated at the City-Hall this Two and Twentieth Day of* April, *in the fourth year of His Majeſty's Reign,* Annoq; Domini 1731.

By Order of Common Council,

Will. Sharpas, *Cl.*

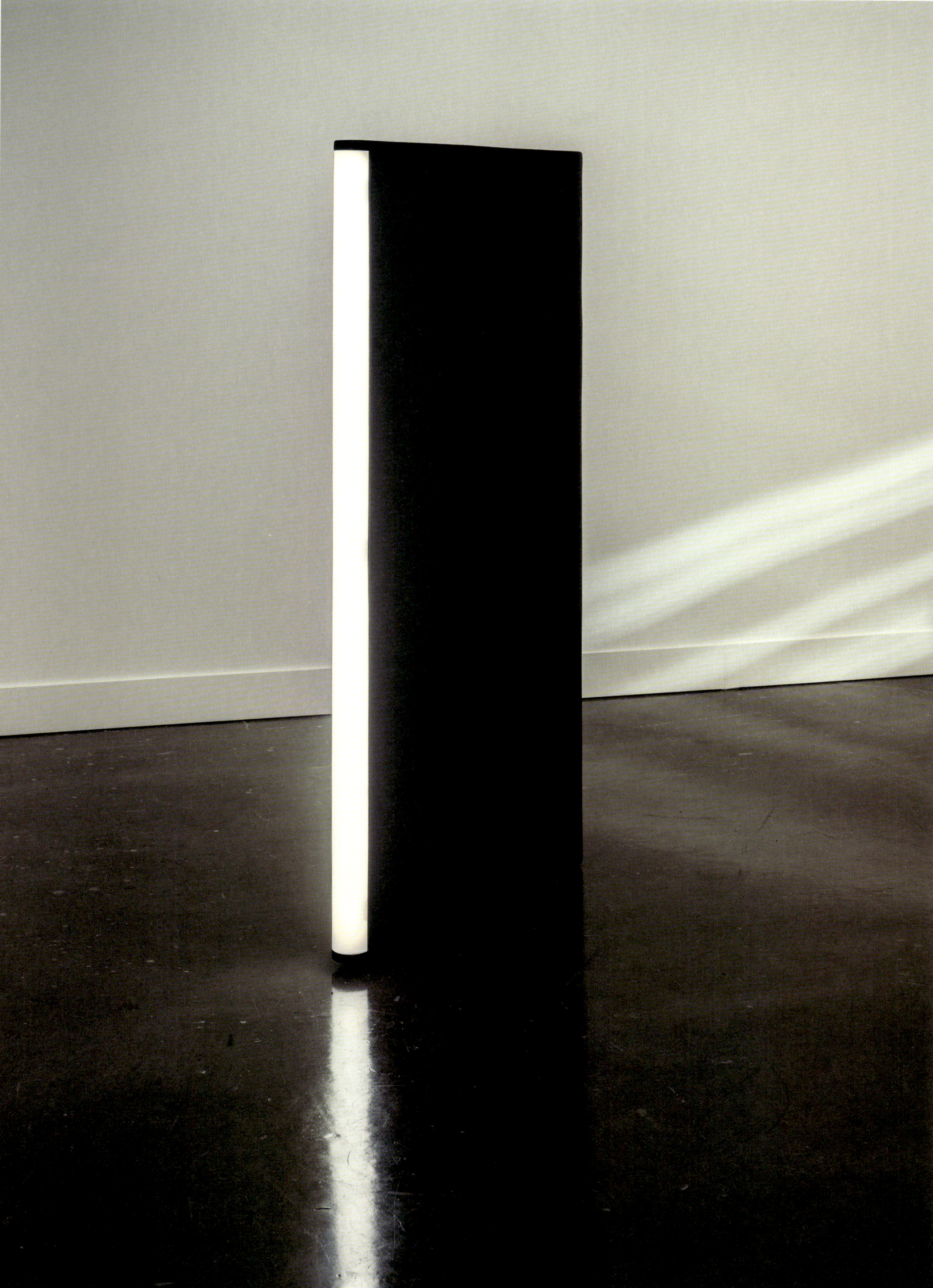

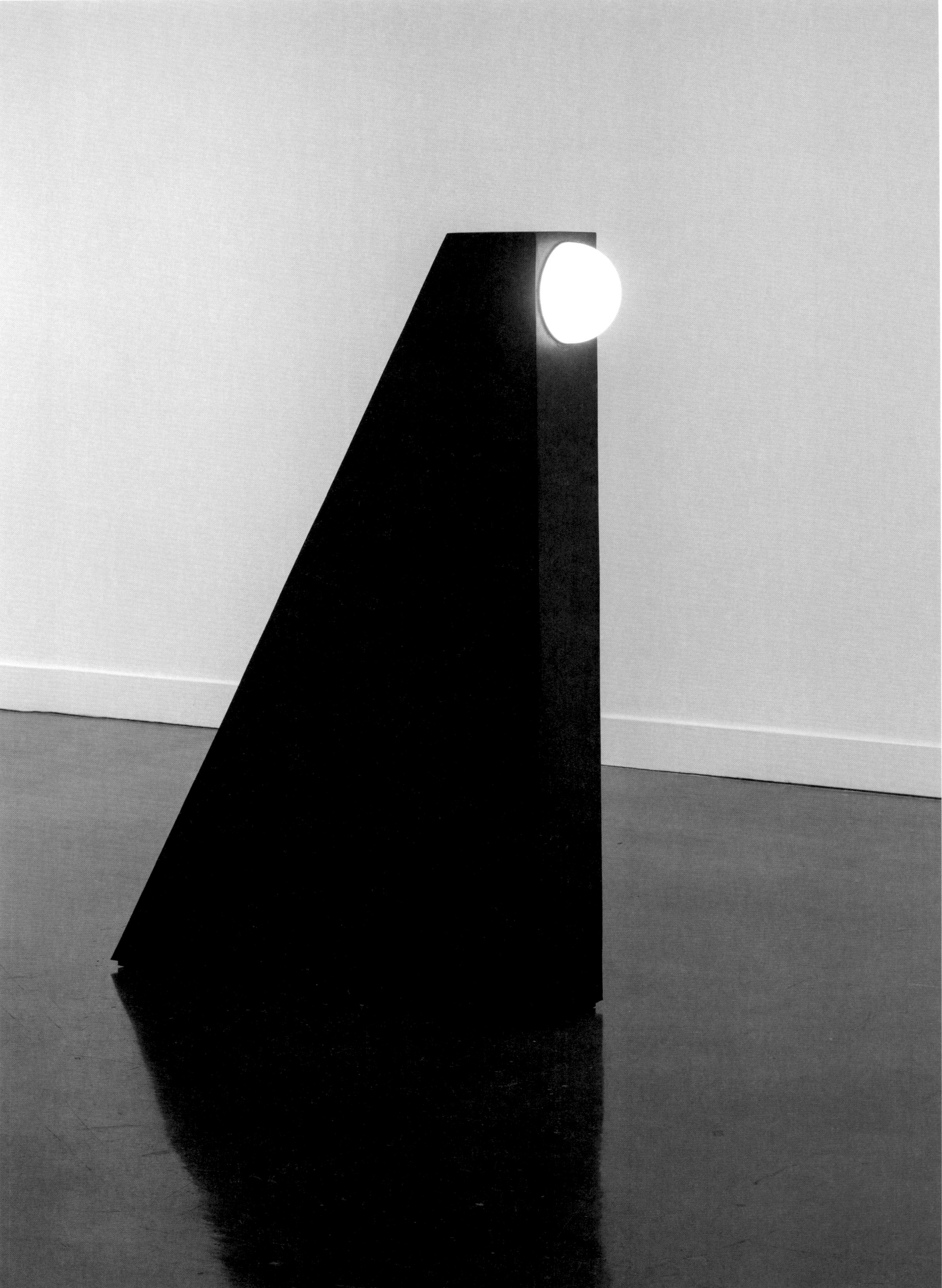

01

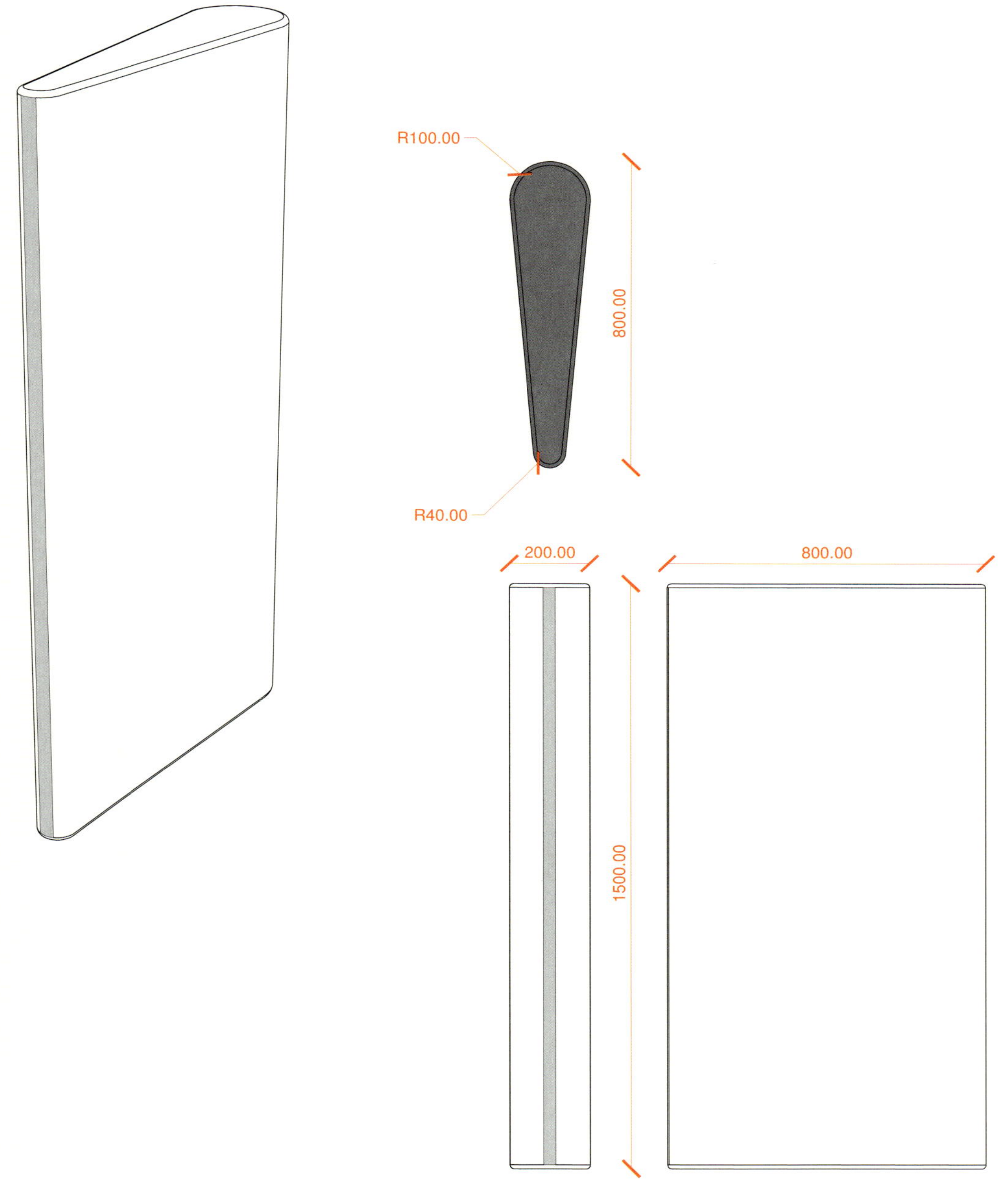

Marie Lorenz

(born 1973 in Twentynine Palms, California)

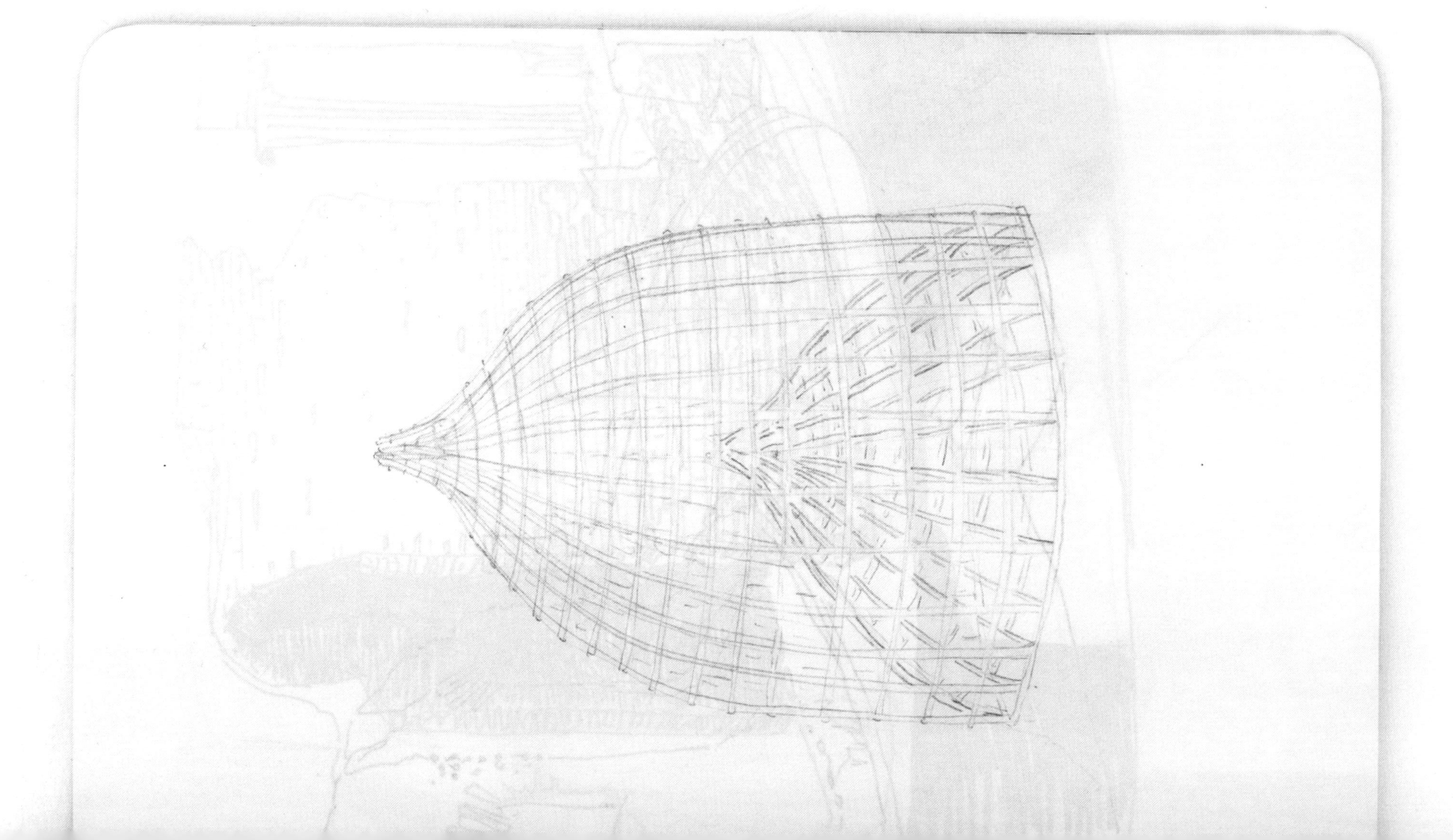

the audioguide encourages you to think about the site – to imagine how it was in the 2nd century, or 1st, teeming with people, horses, their feet on the stones, loud, bright, fabric draped in markets. heading into the center of town or on narrow alleyways. I prefer to imagine the 12th century, or the 8th, when the whole thing was buried under the rubble of its own crushed walls. Dark, silent, wet with earth, a worm maybe sliding along, using the less dense pathways under the stone. I prefer to think of the analogous world, proximity, closeness, time pressing in, but actually weightless. And about the frescoes – a thin membrane of lime, a new stone slowly exchanging minerals with the neighboring rock it appeared over 100s of years but not enough to change the colors too much. although there was no color down there just darkness.

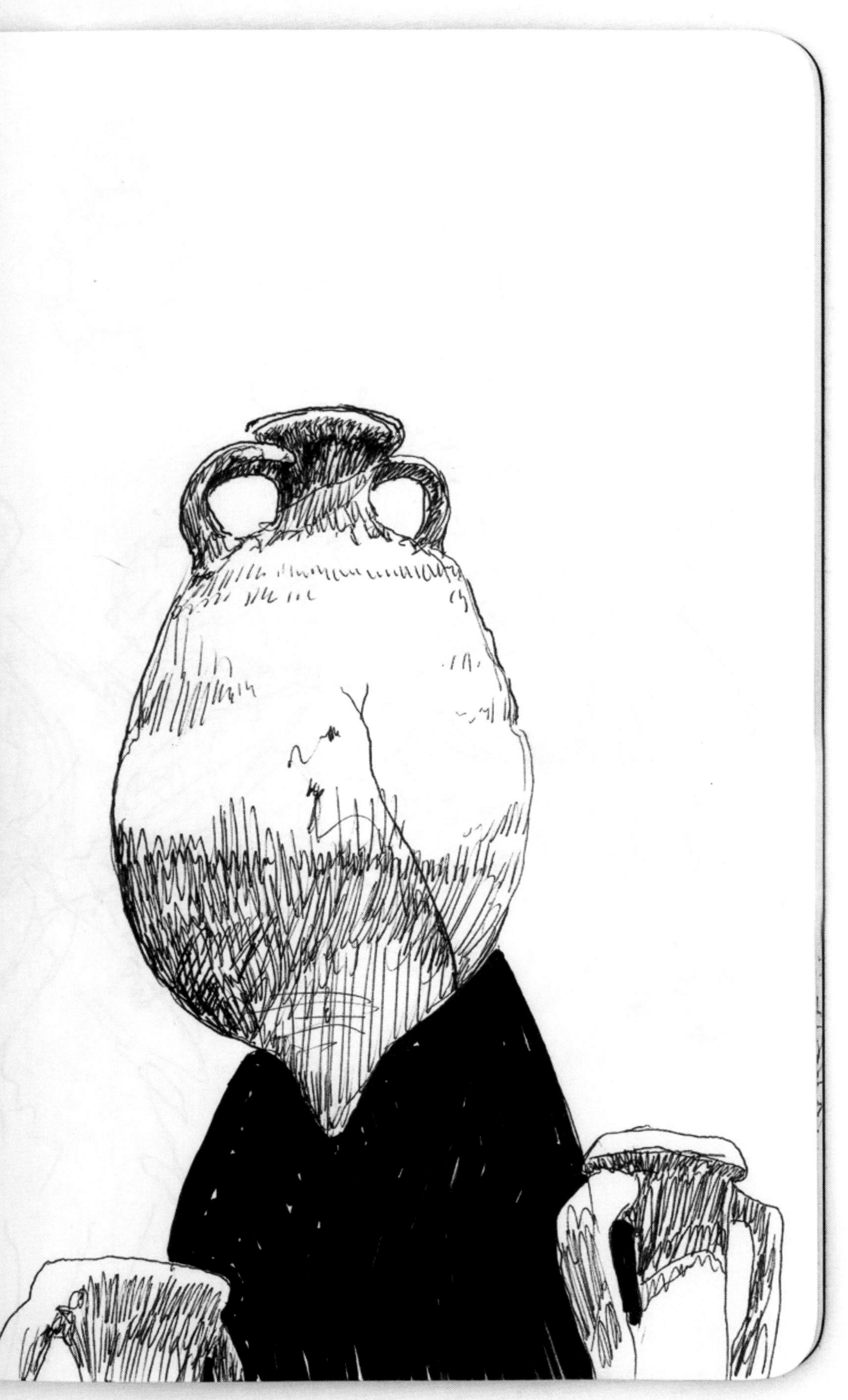

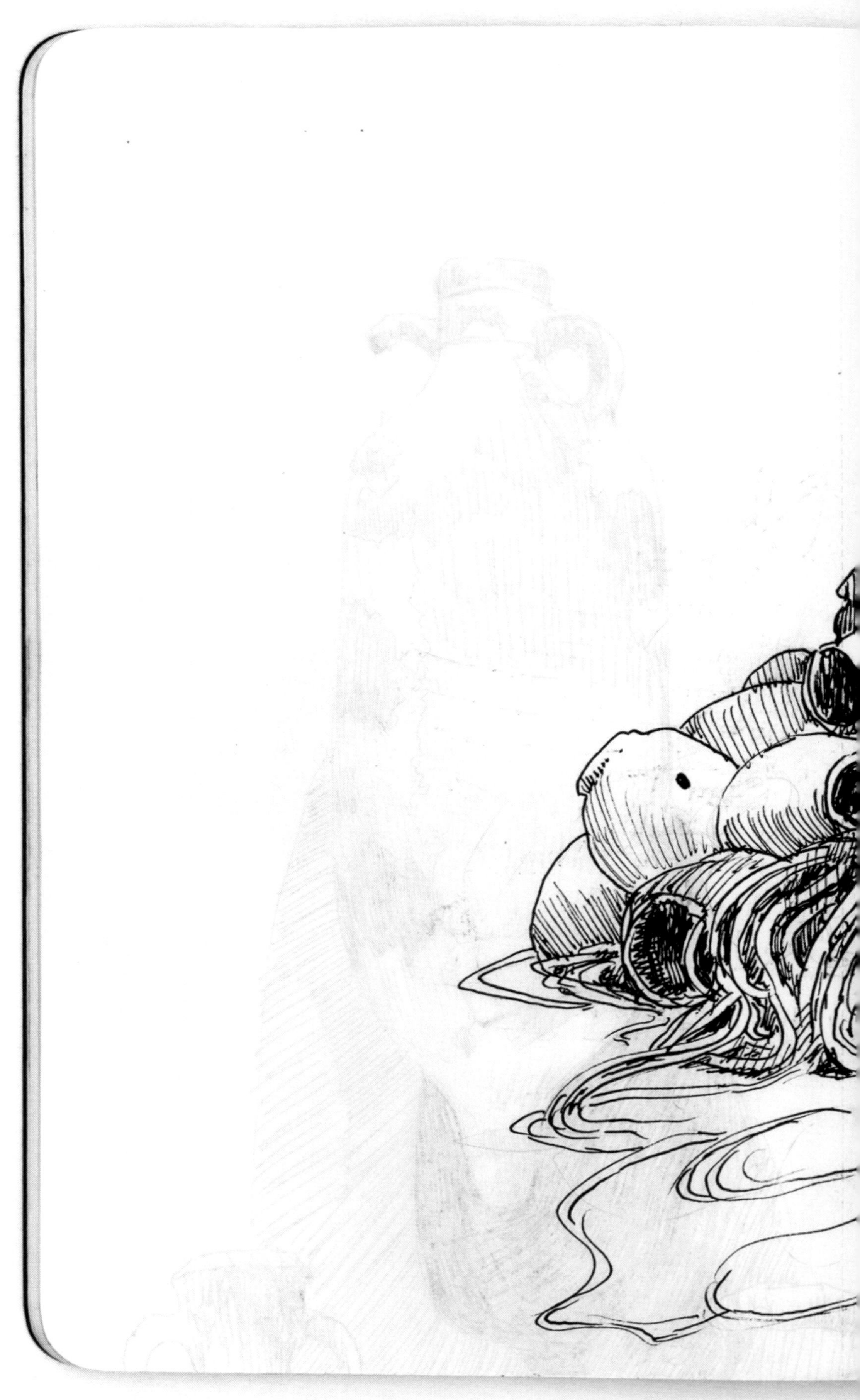

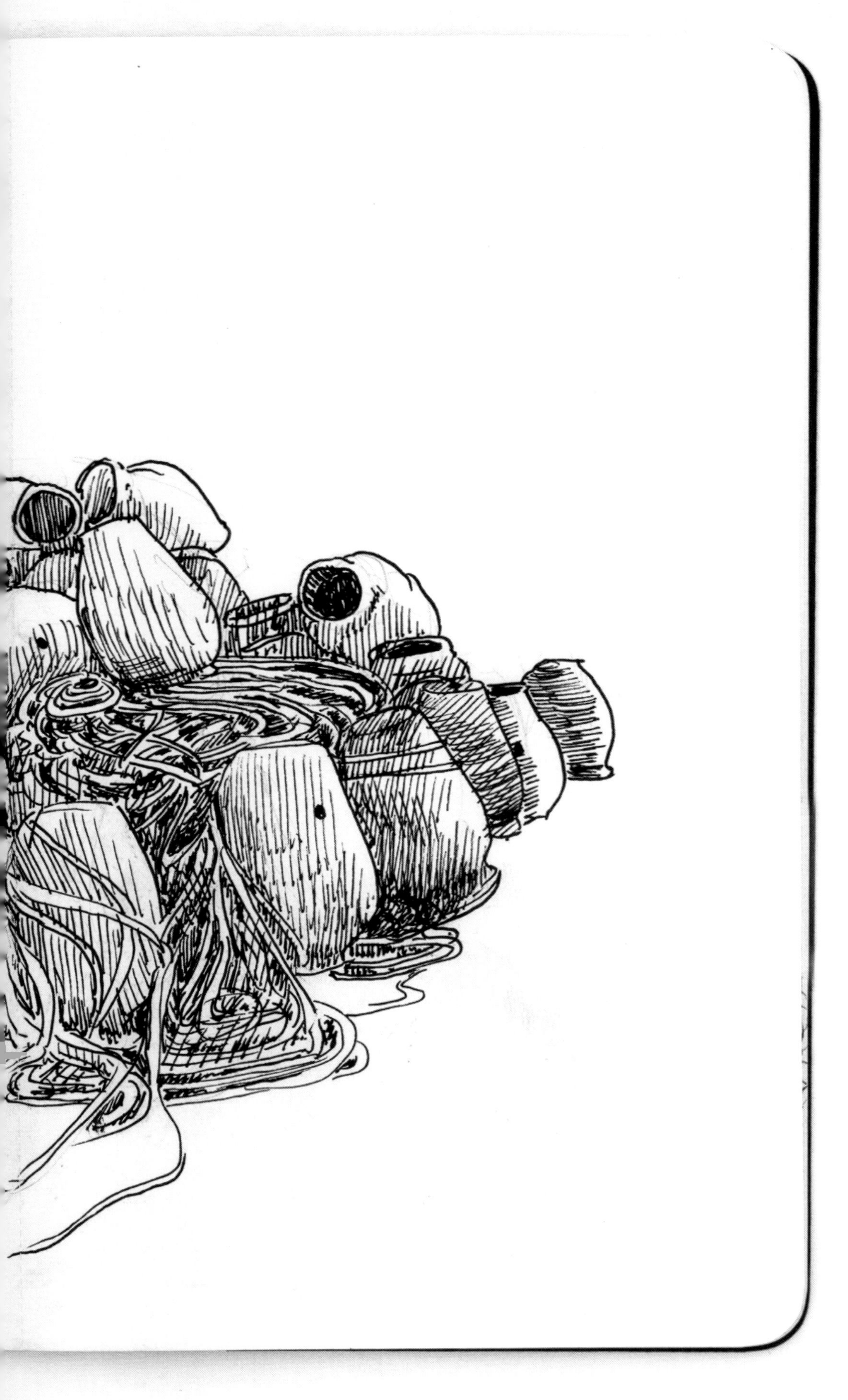

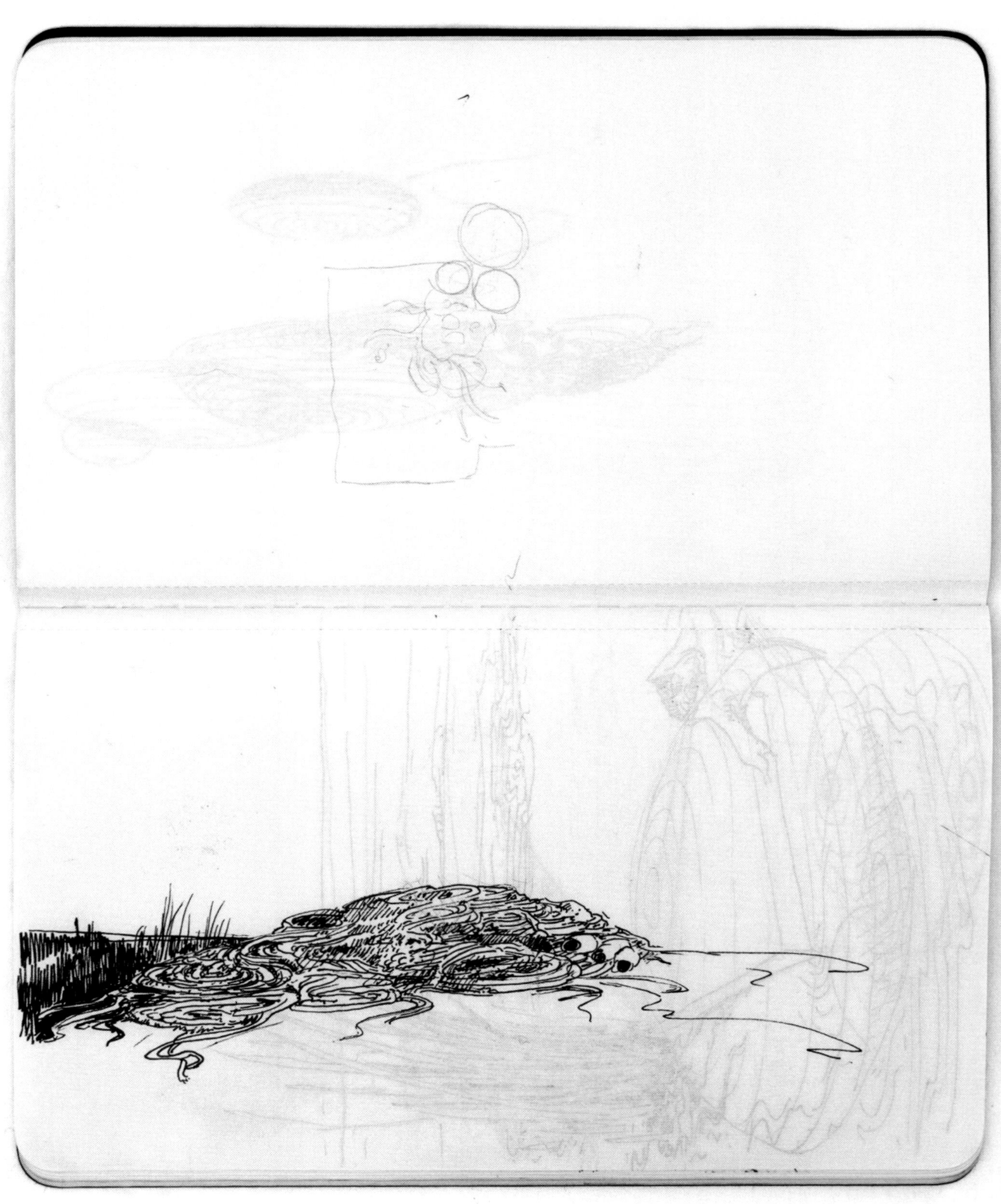

formed of poles and willow sticks, quite across the river at no great distance from each other. each of these, were fur-nished with two baskets; the one wear to take them ascending and the other in decending. in constructing these wears, poles were first tyed together in parcels of three near the smaller ex-tremity; these were set on end, and spread in a trian-gular form at the base, in such manner, that two of the three poles ranged in the direction of the intended work, and the third down the stream. two ranges of ho-rizontal poles, were next lashed with willow bark and wythes, to the ranging poles, and on these willow sticks were placed perpendicularly reaching from the bottom of the river to about 3 or four feet above it's surface, and placed so near each other as not to permit the passage of the fish, and even so thick insome parts, as with the help of gravel and stone to give a direction to the water which they wished. — the baskets were the same in form of the others. this is the form of the work, and disposition of the baskets.

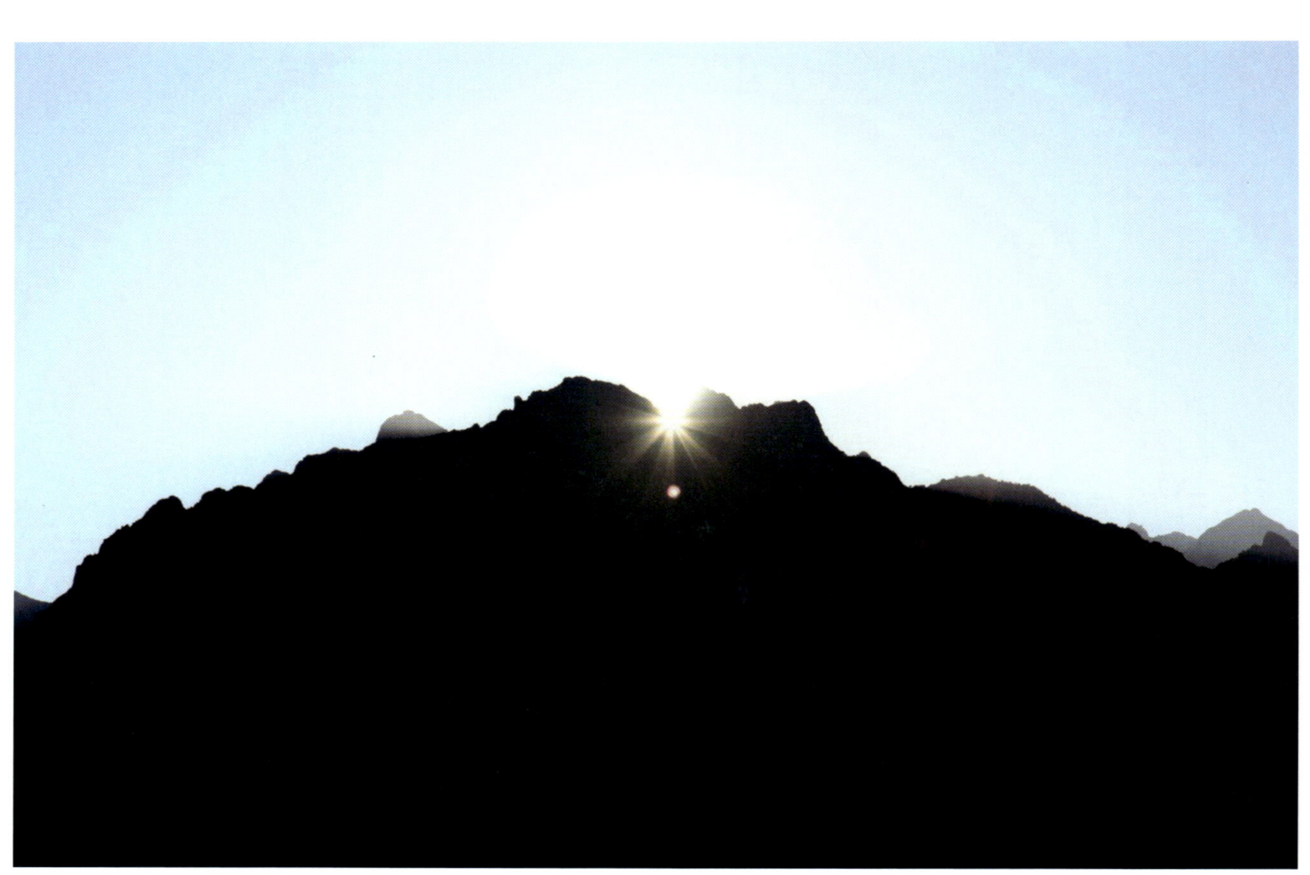

Nathan Mabry

(born 1978 in Durango, Colorado)

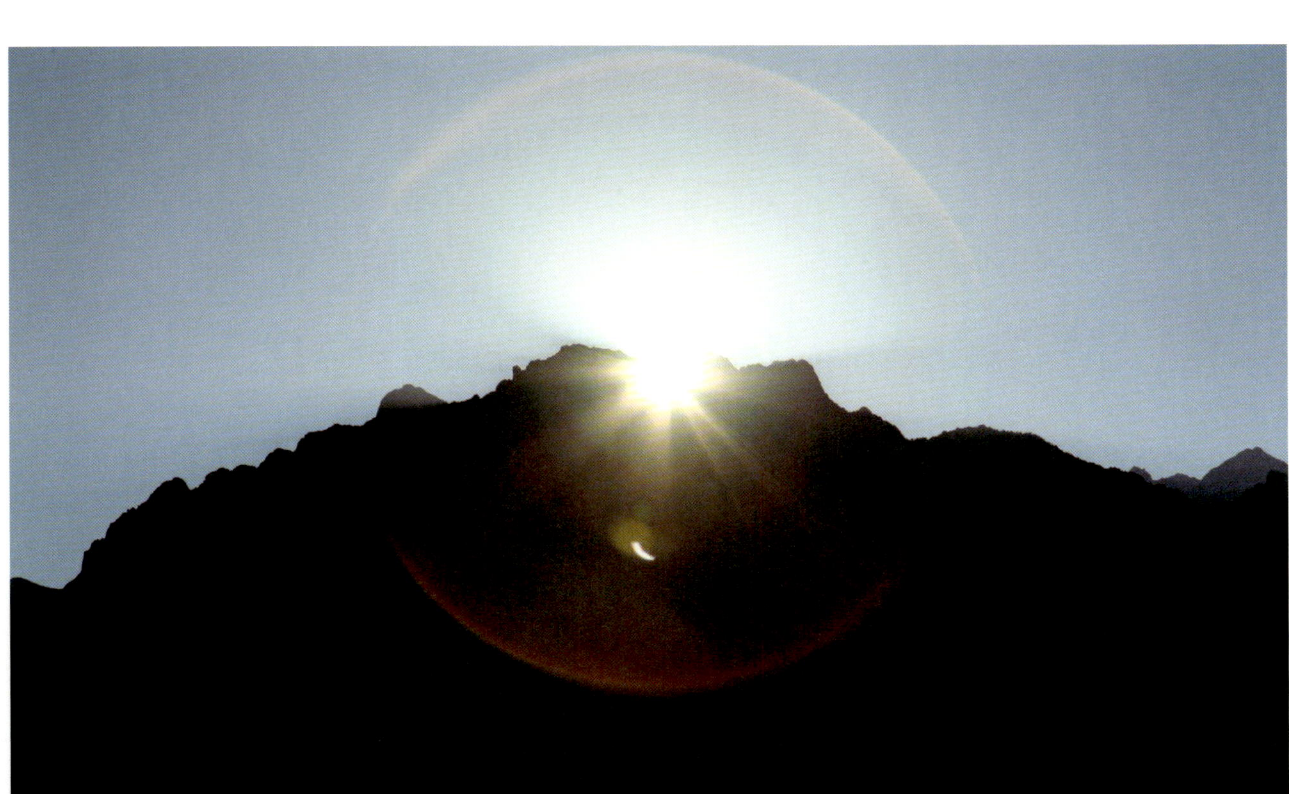

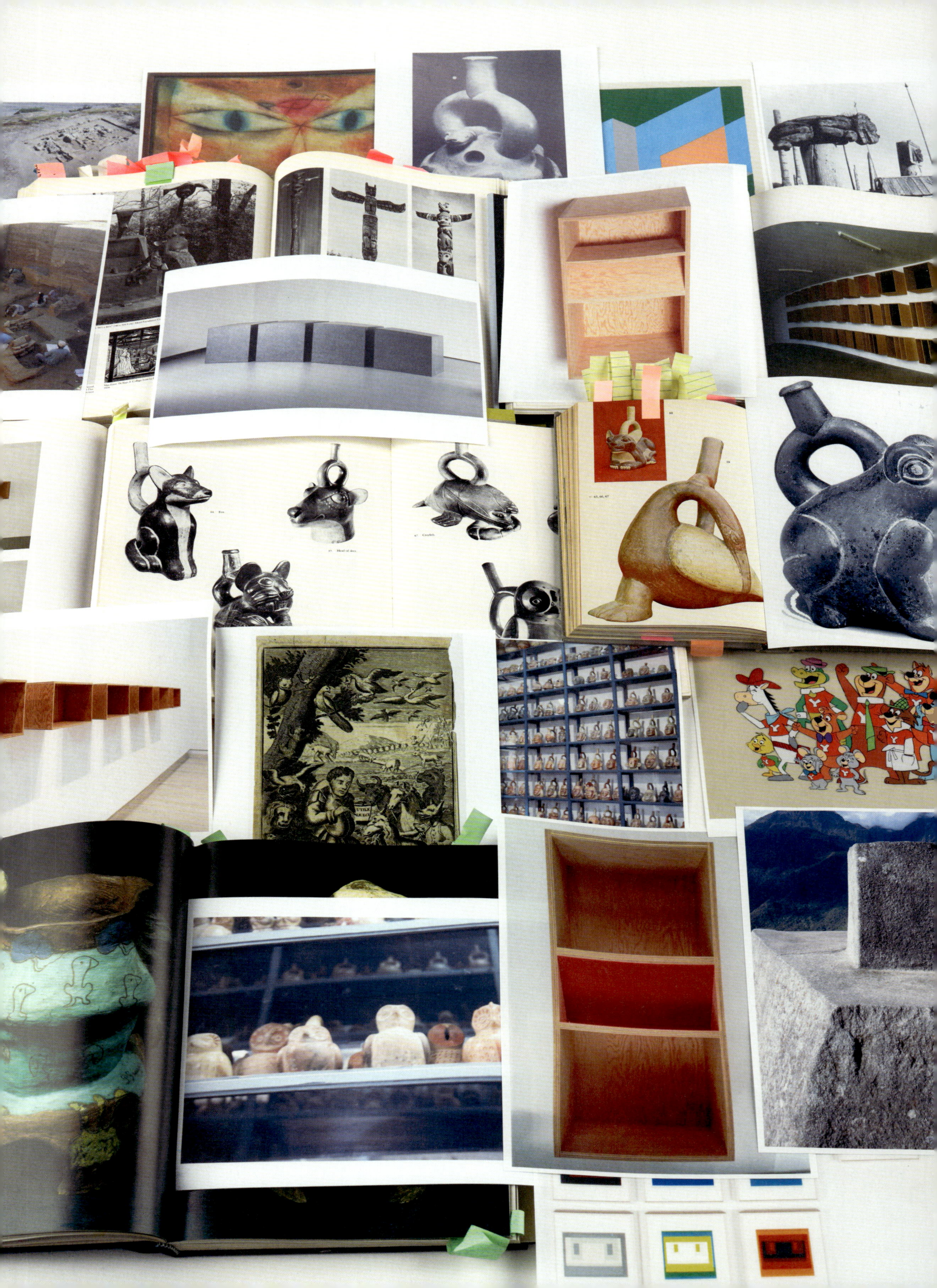

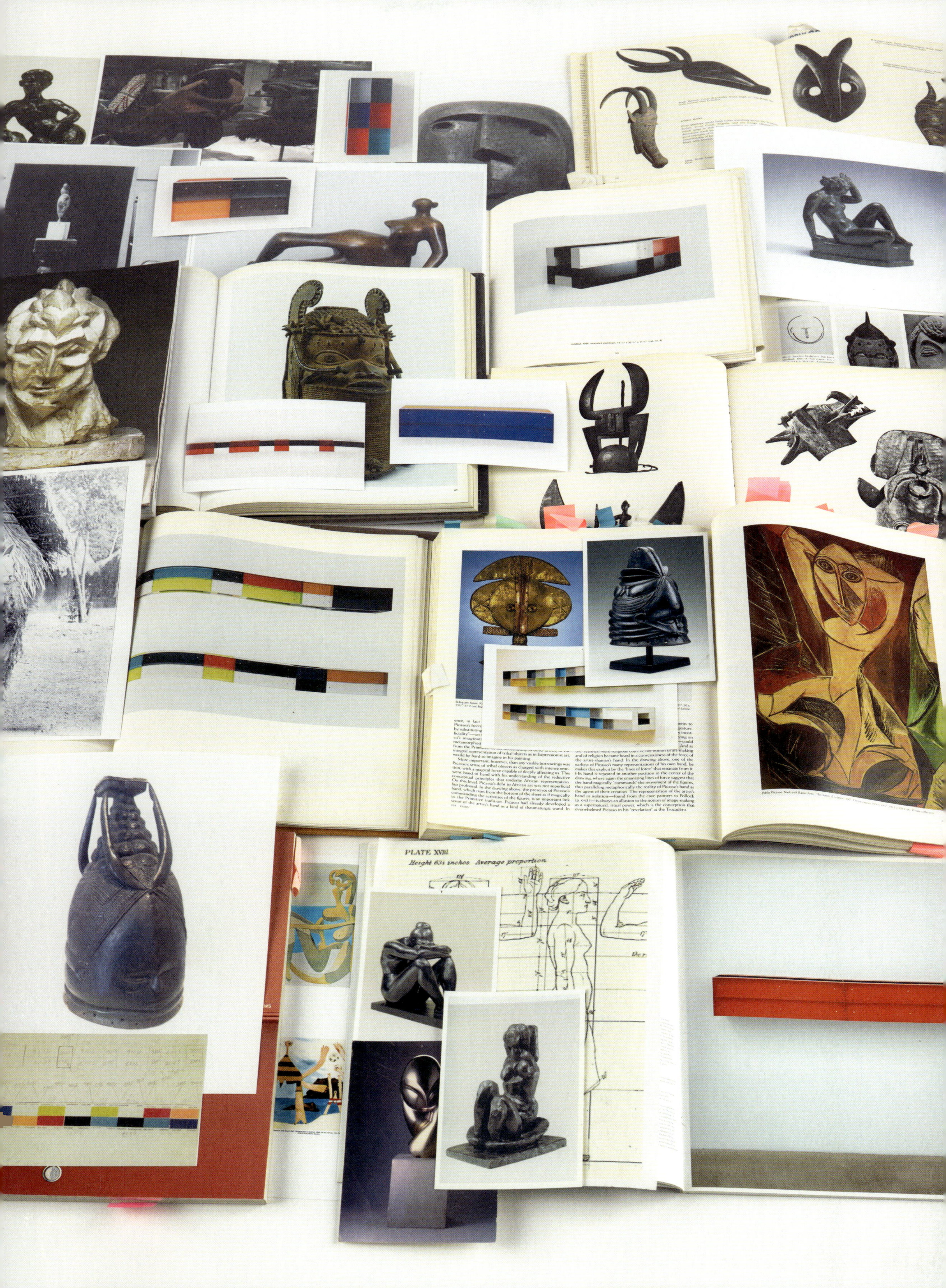

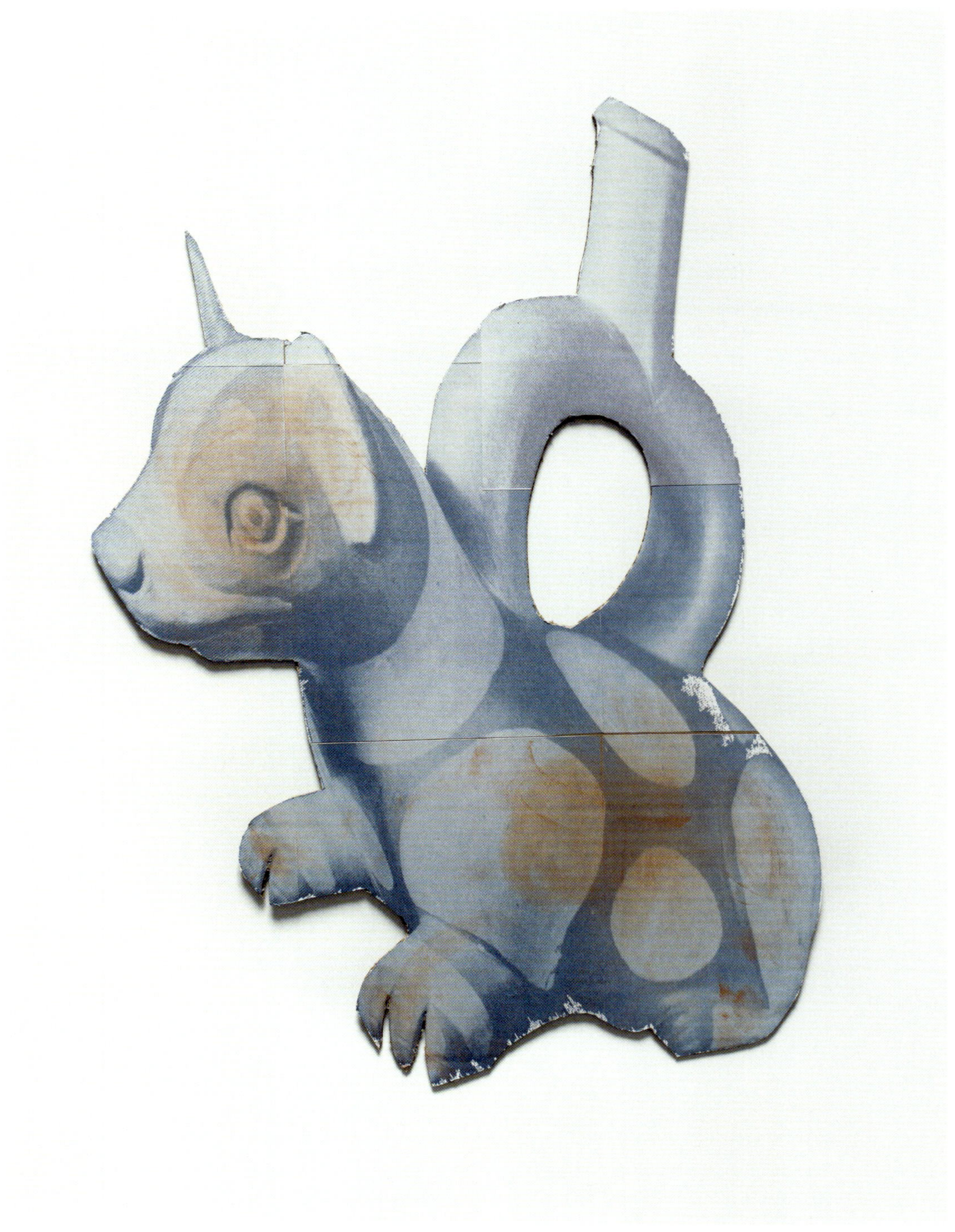

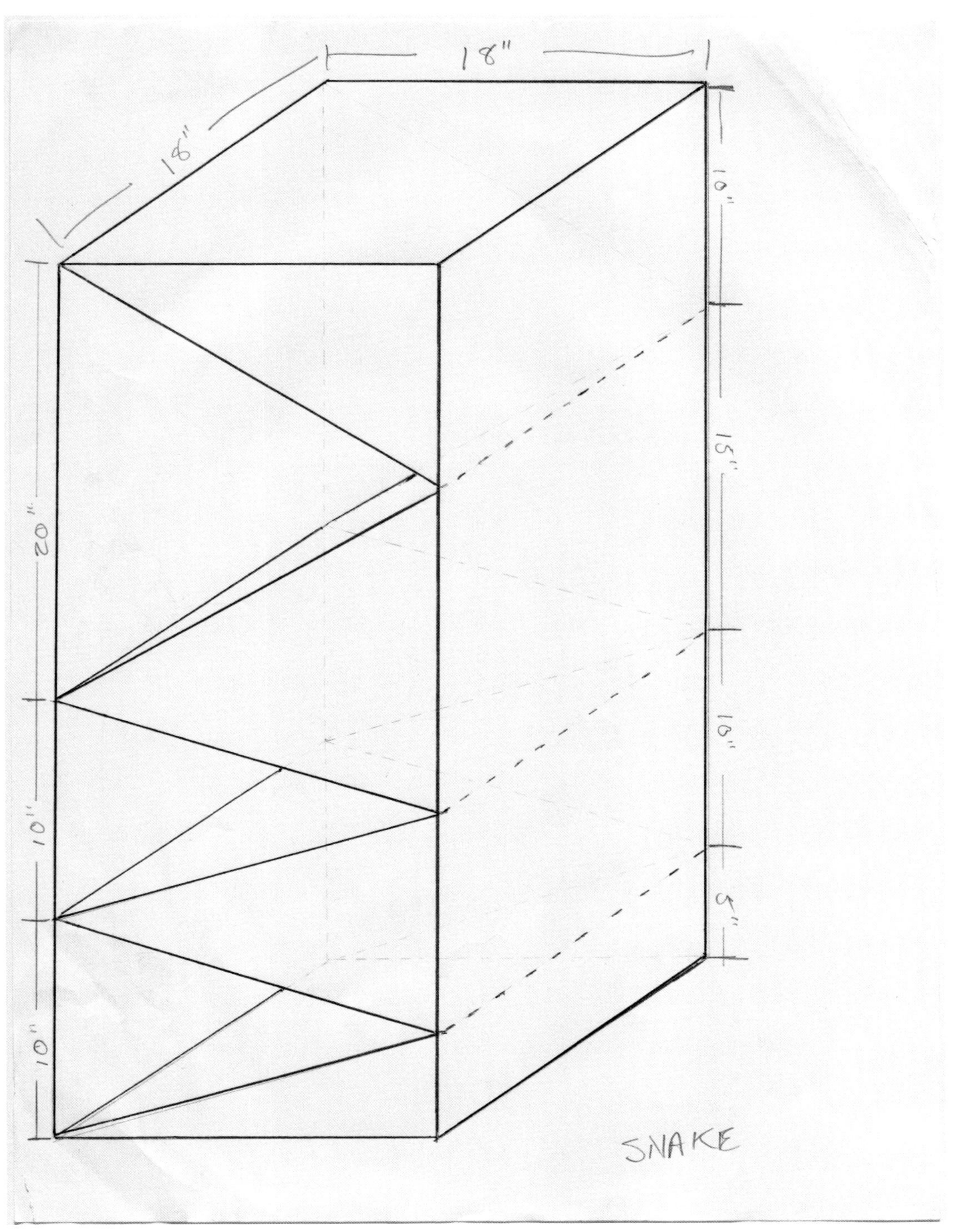
18"
18"
10"
15"
10"
5"
20"
10"
10"
SNAKE

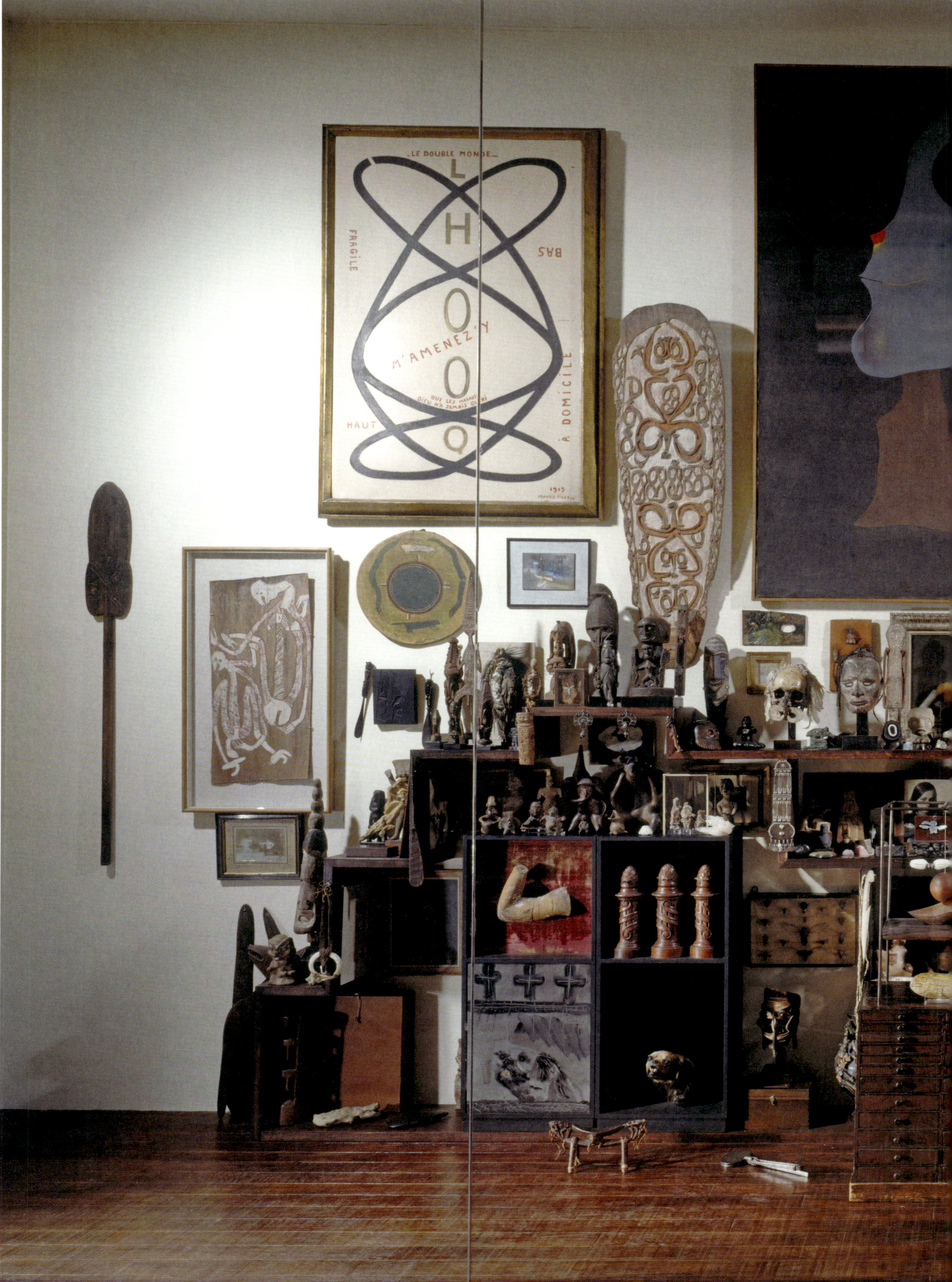
LE DOUBLE MONDE
L
H
O
O
Q
FRAGILE
BAS
M'AMENEZ-Y
HAUT
À DOMICILE

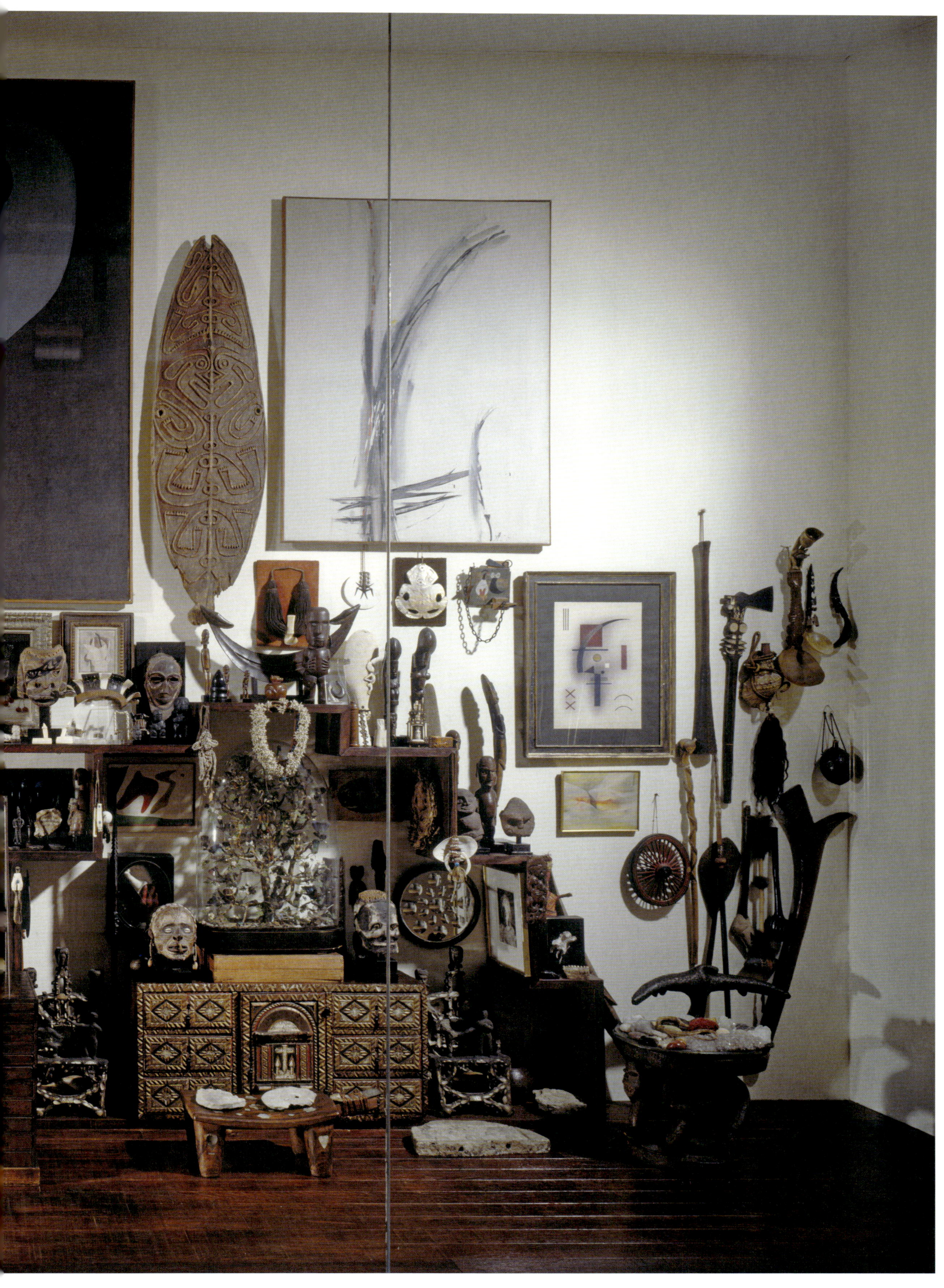

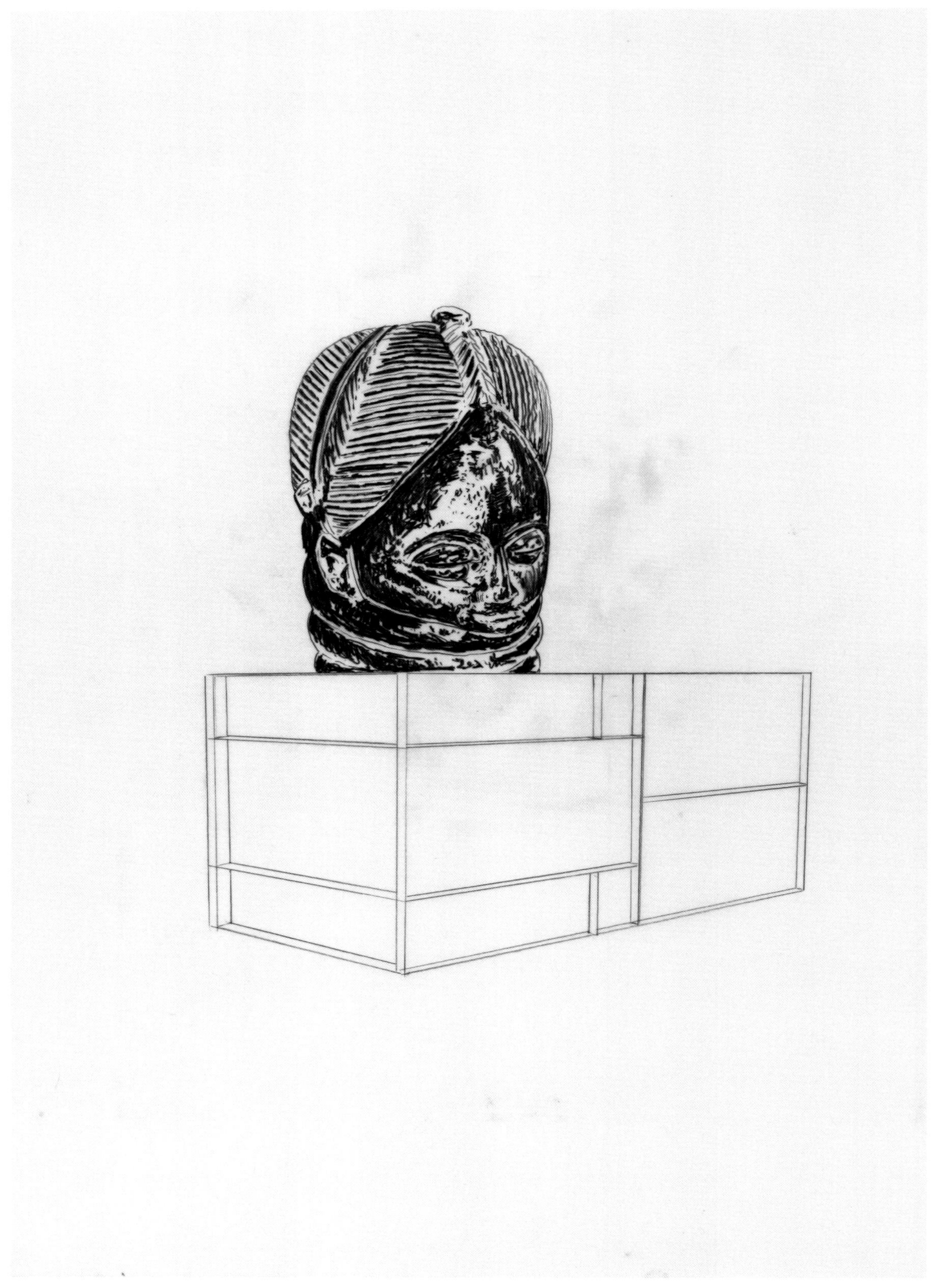

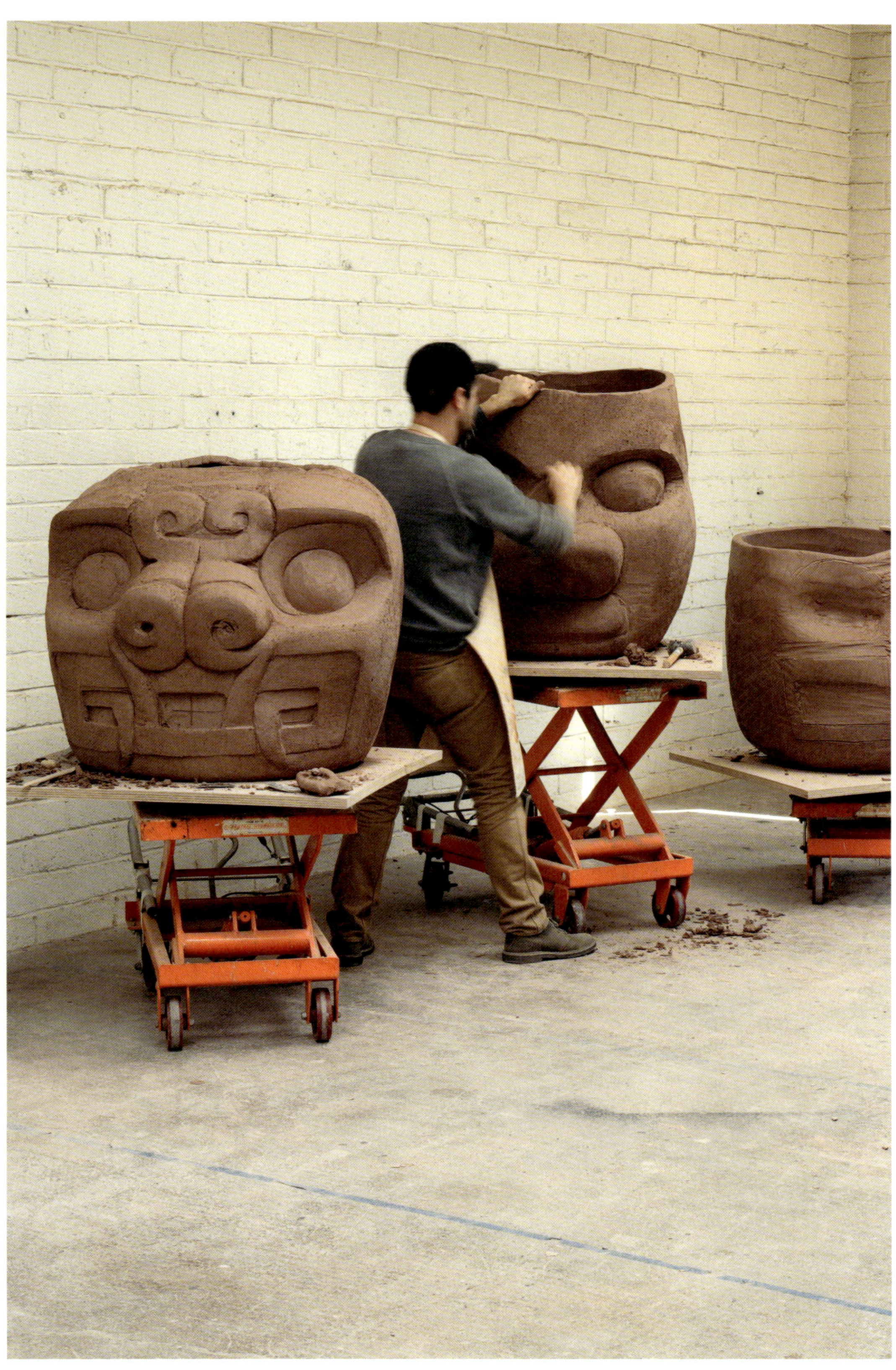

Ruben Ochoa

(born 1974 in Oceanside, California)

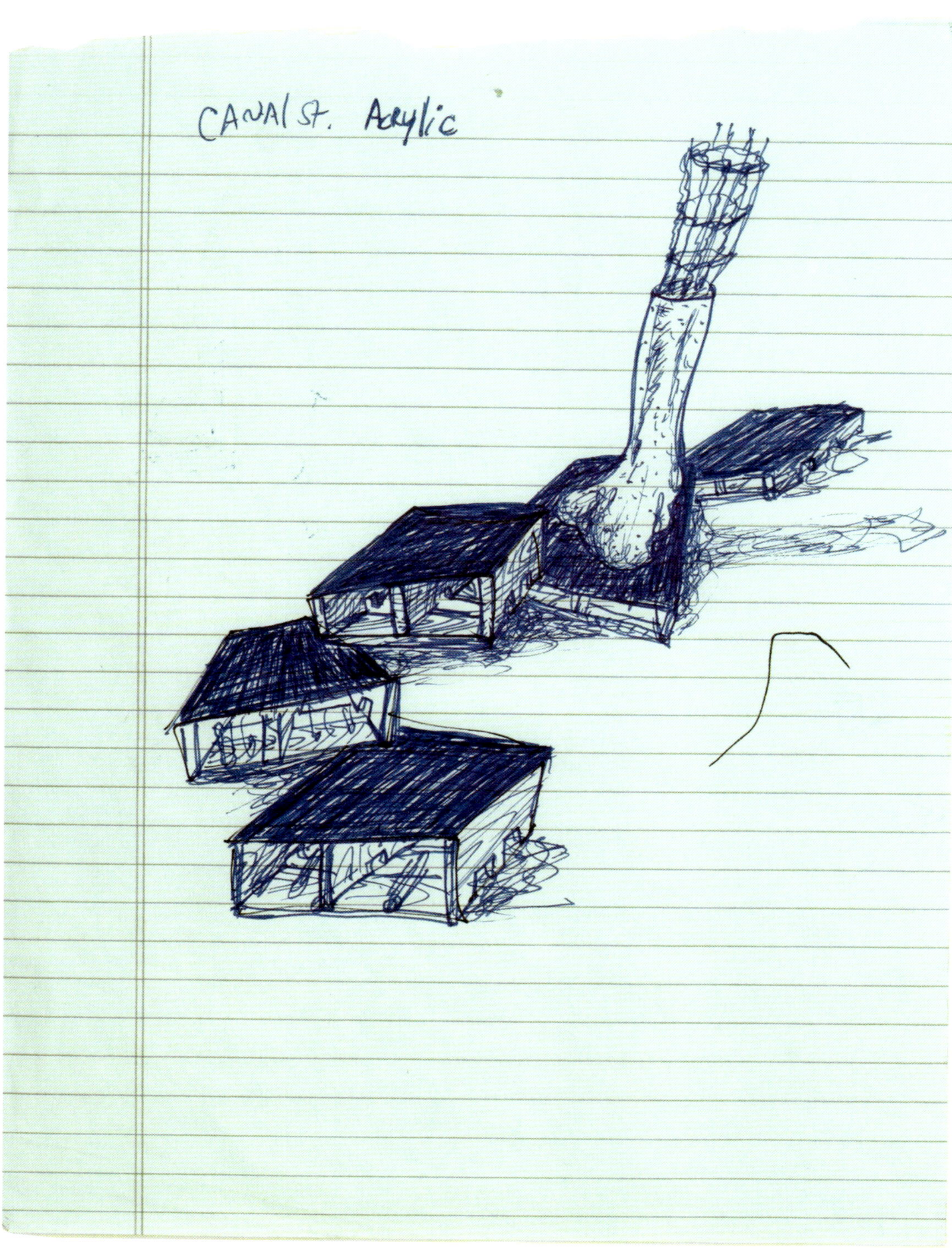

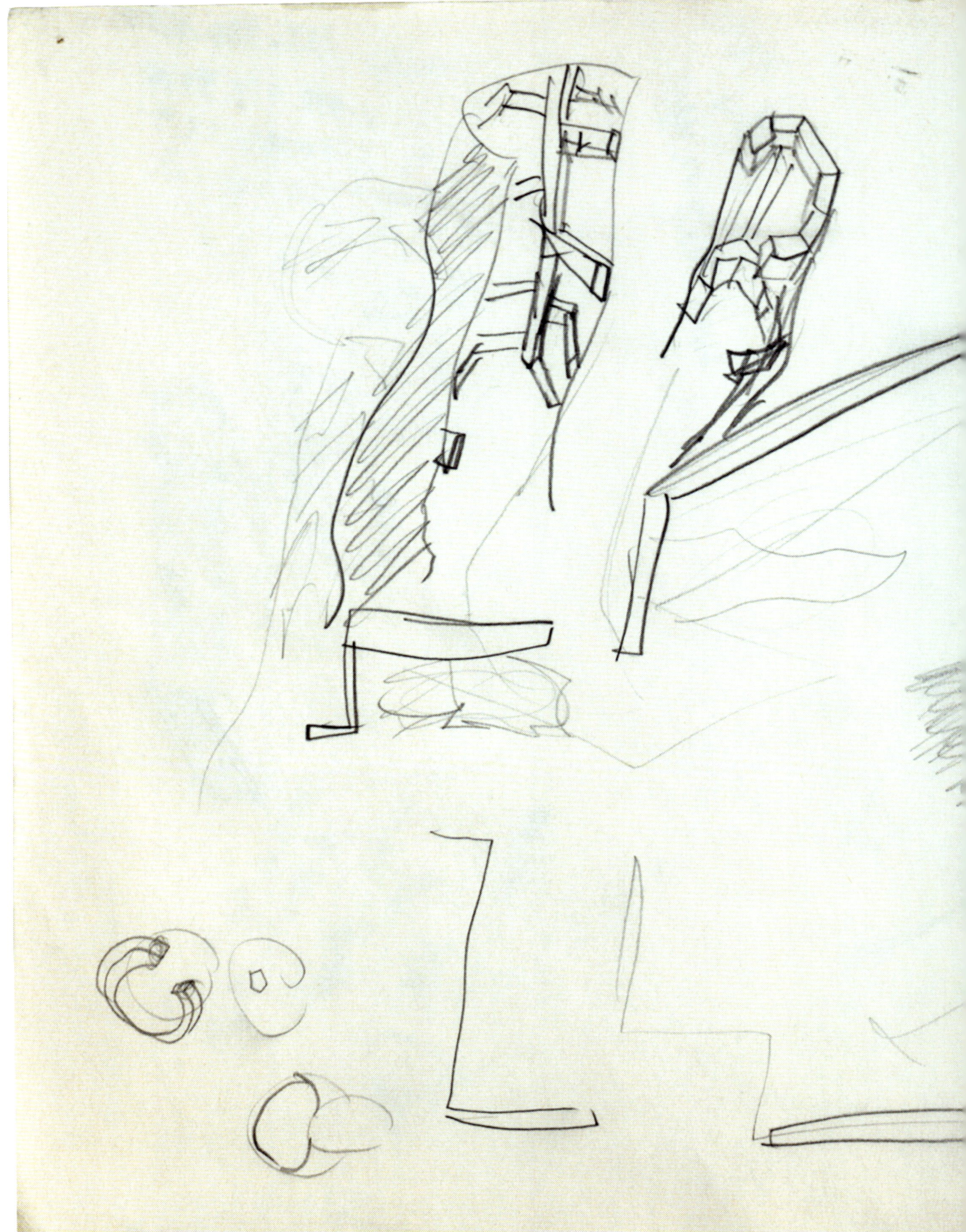

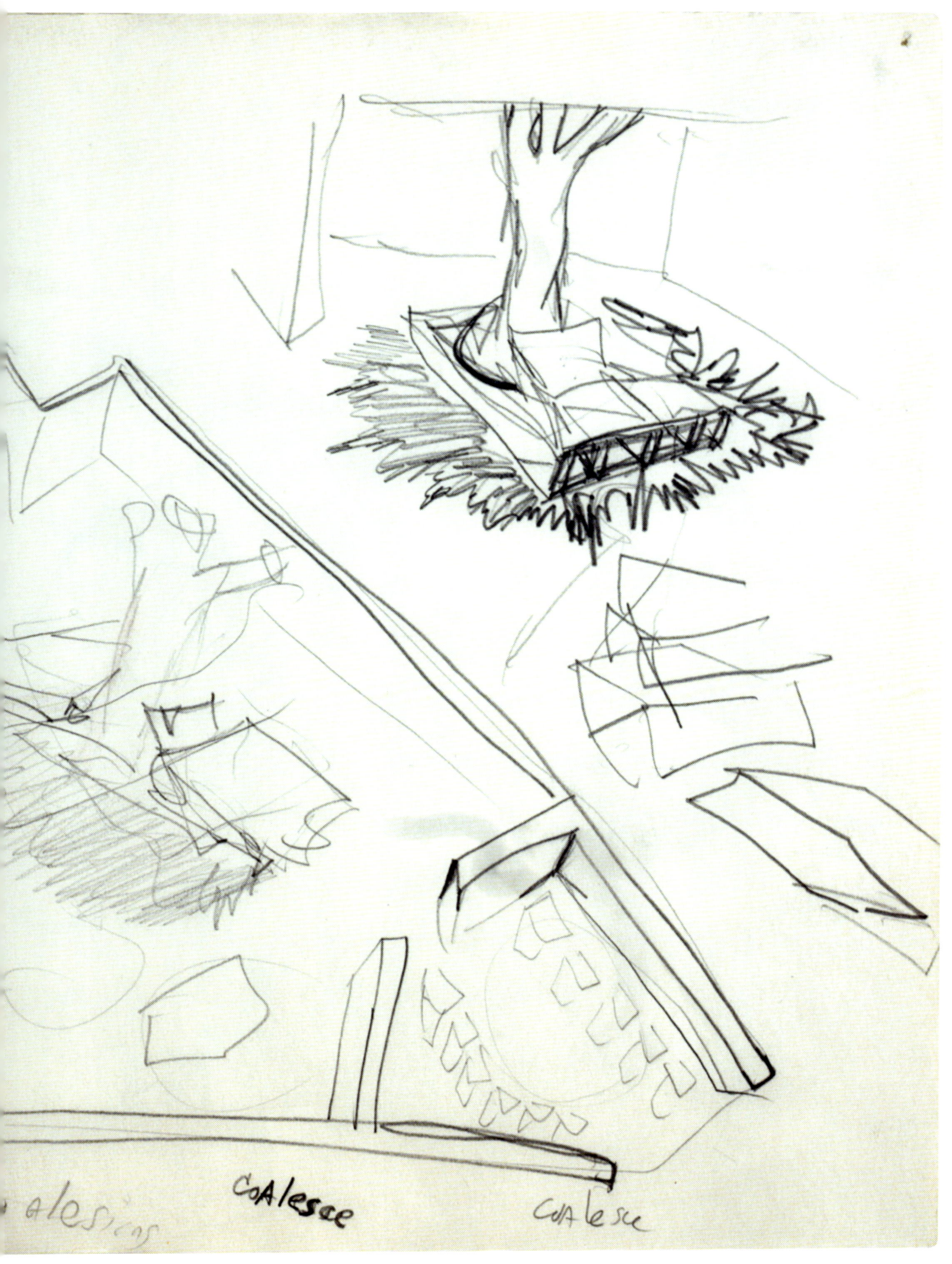
coAlesce
coAlesce

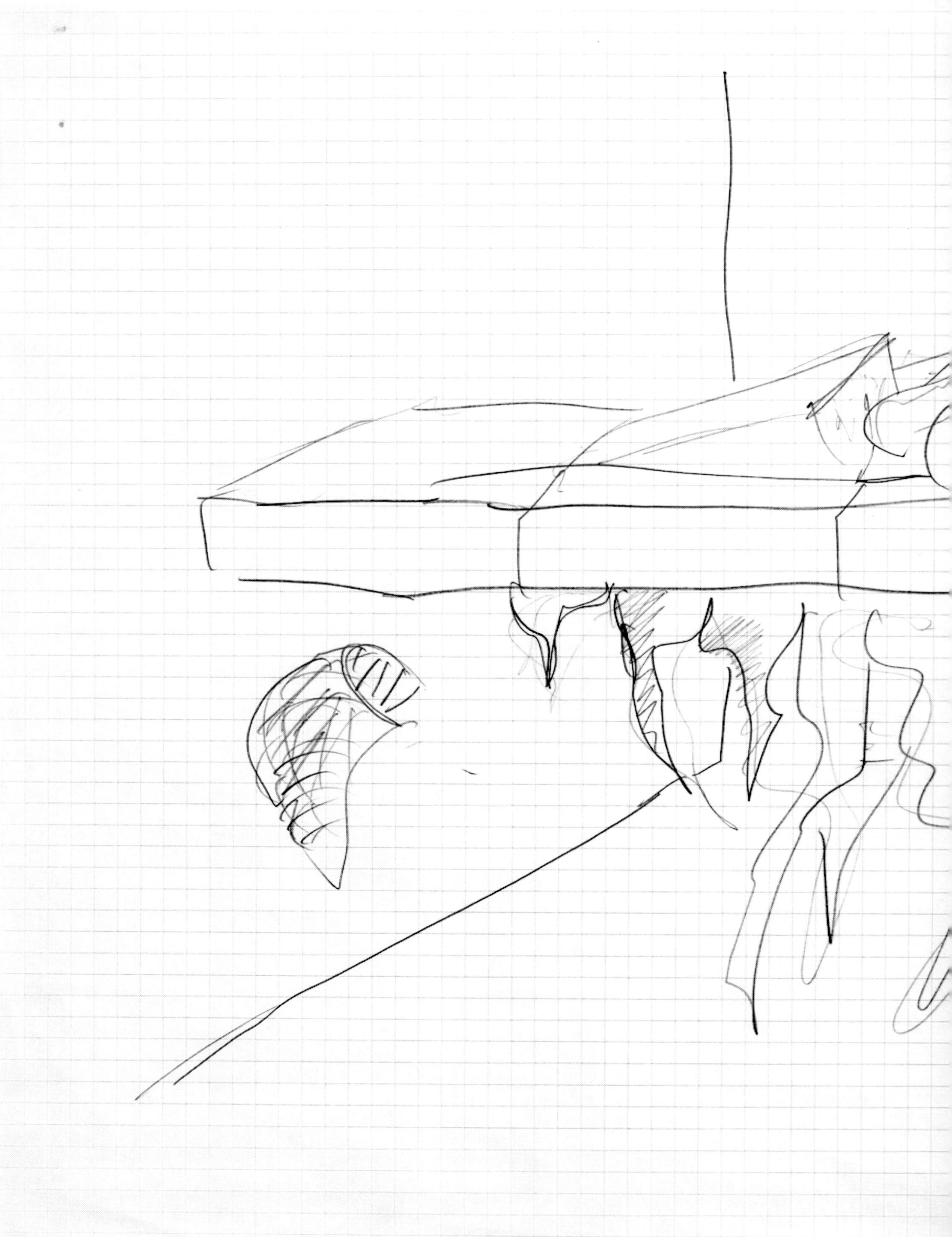

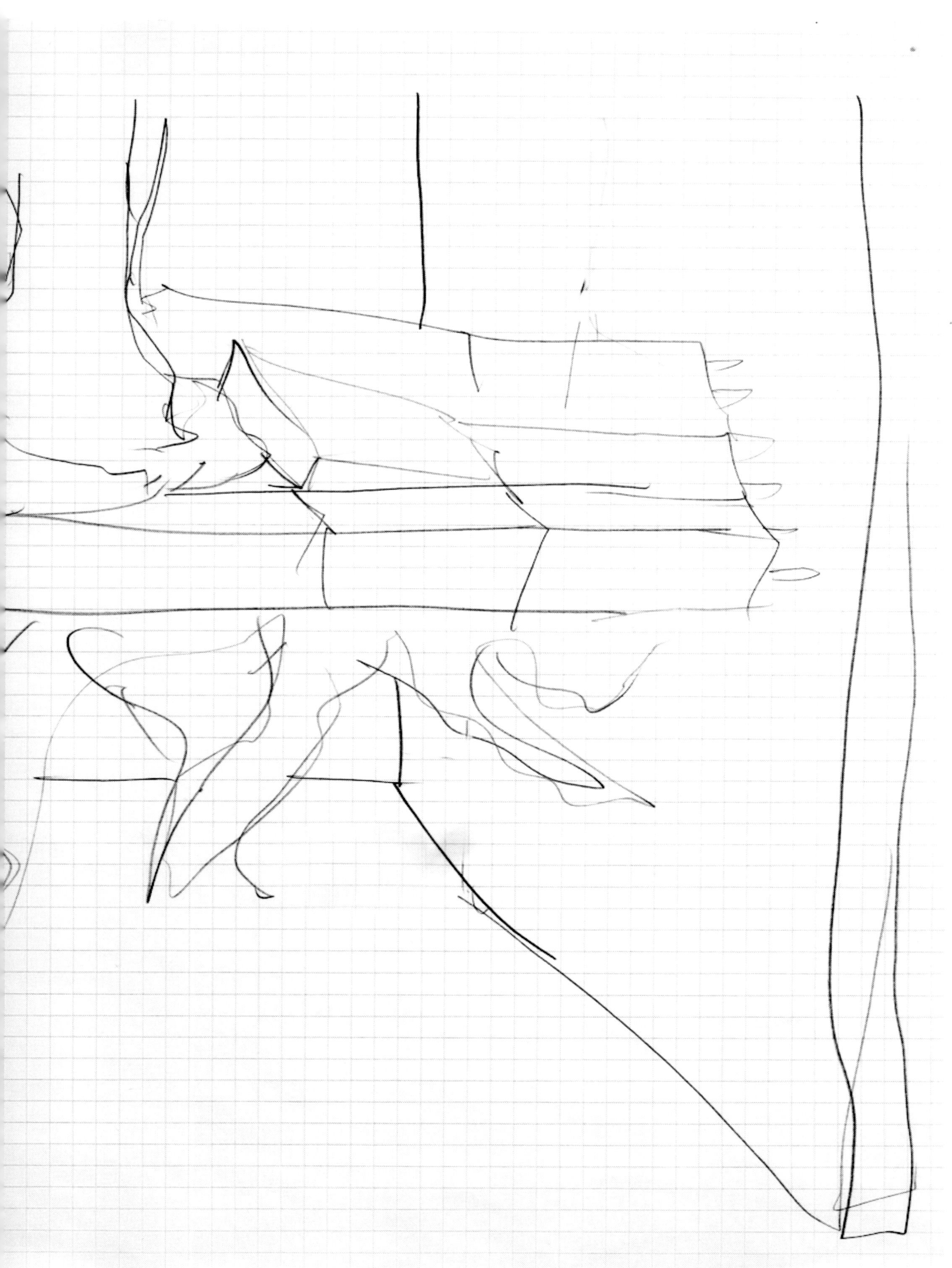

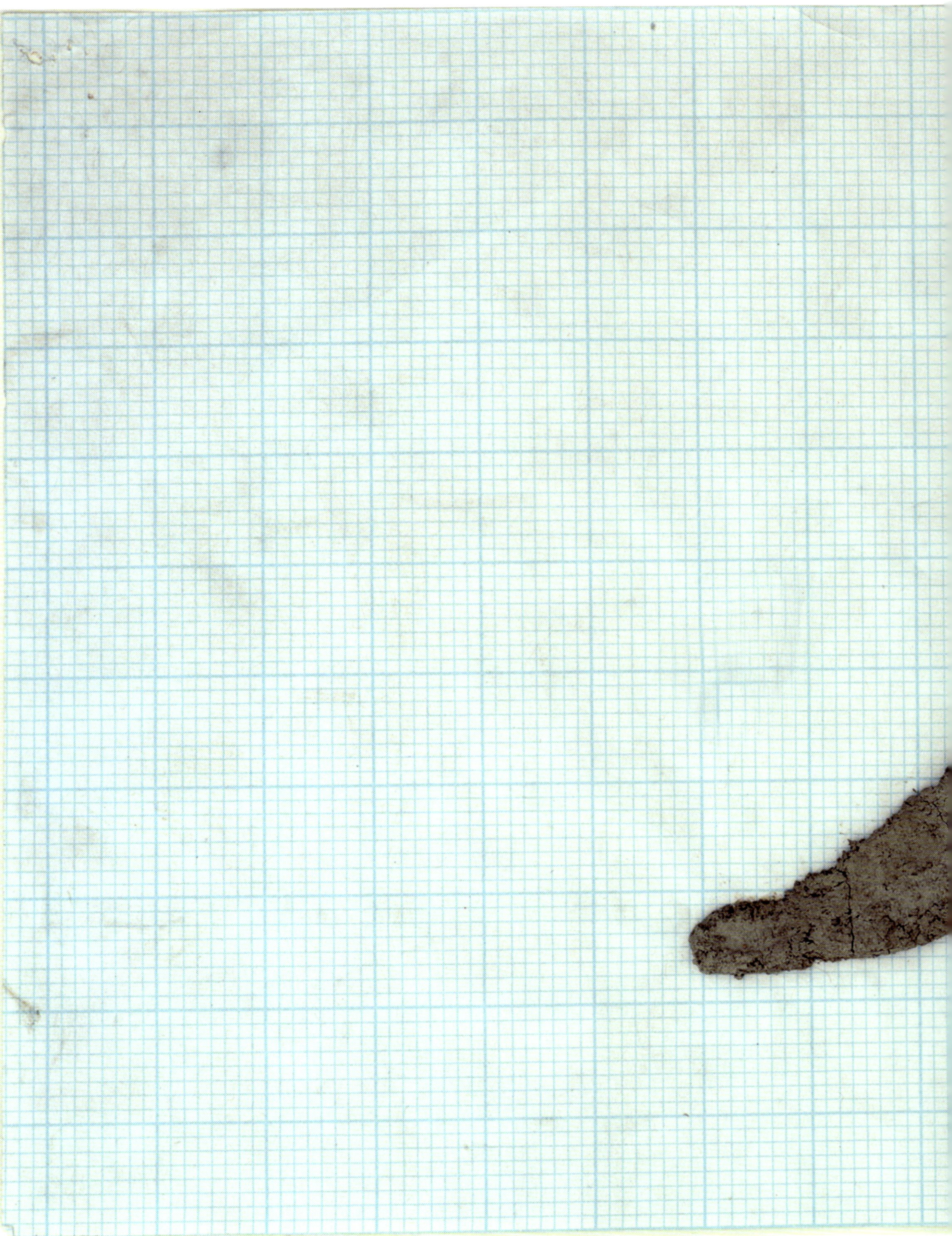

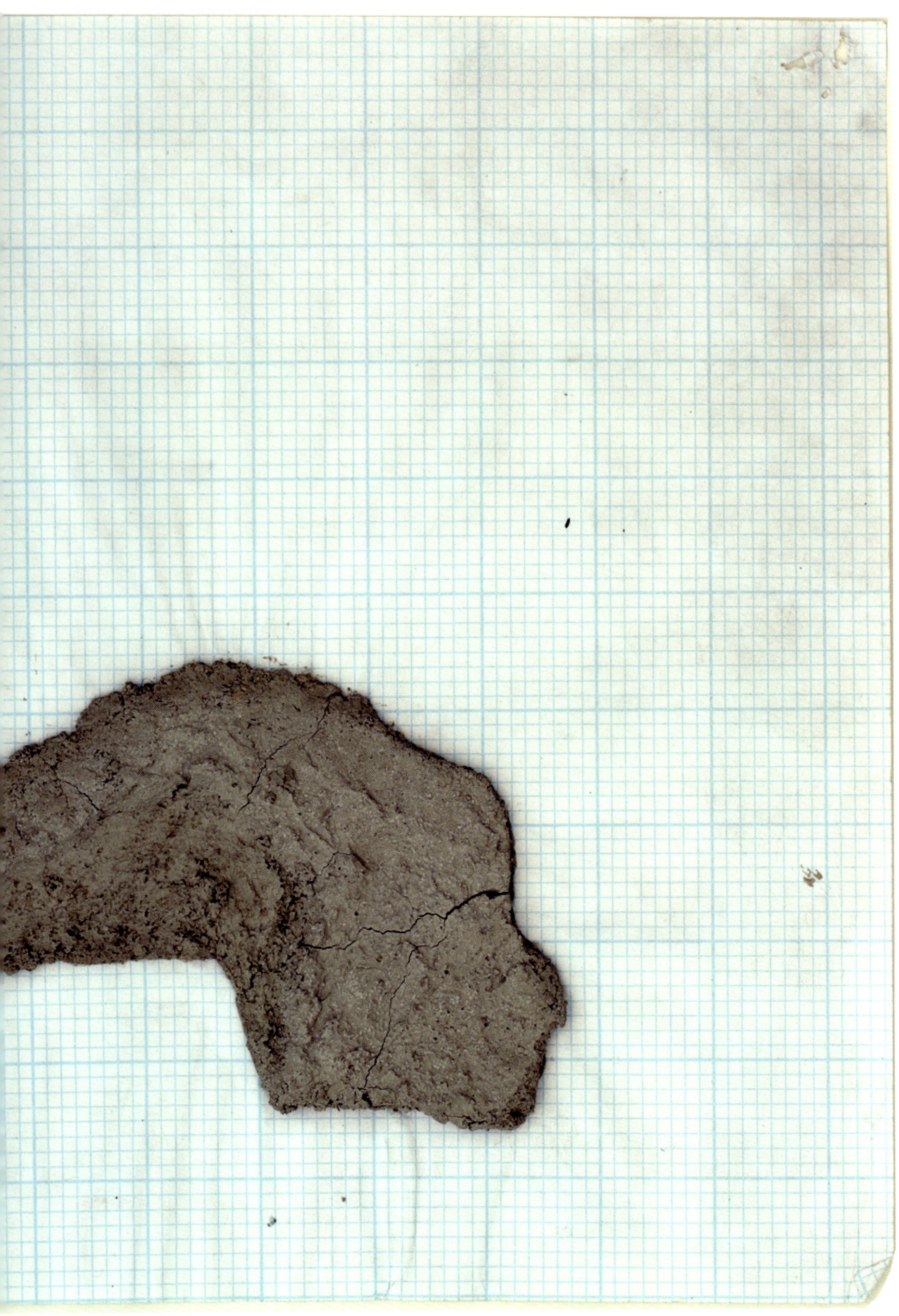

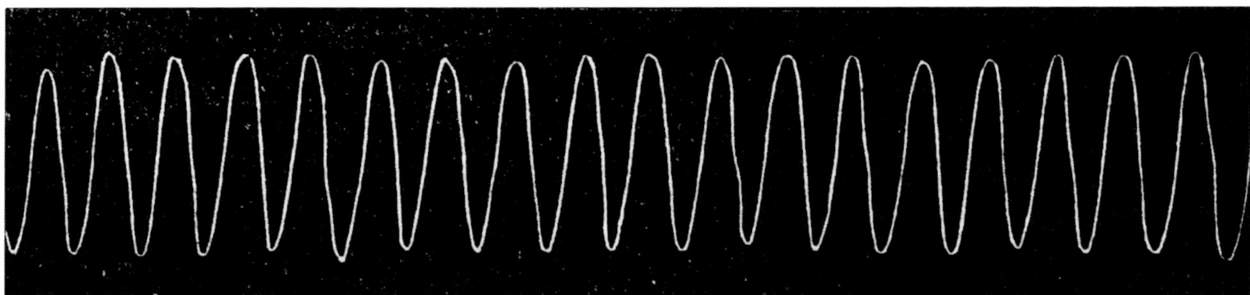

First pulse, 1854

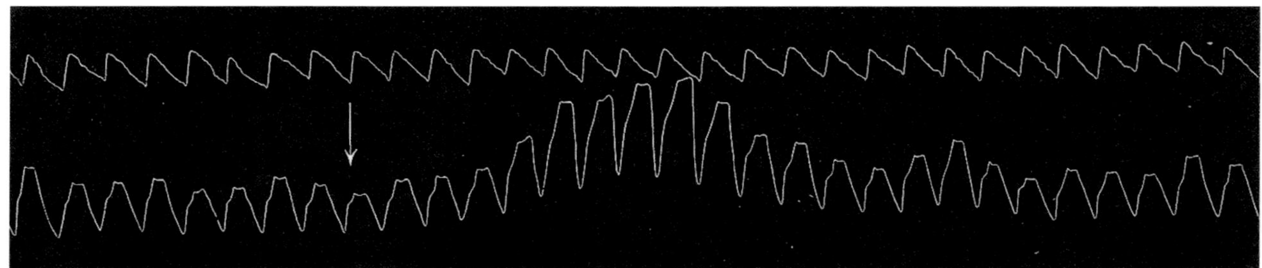

Religious guilt, 1878

Dario Robleto
(born 1972 in San Antonio, Texas)

The First Time, the Heart

A Portrait of Life 1854–1913

Dario Robleto

From the first time one human placed her or his ear to another's chest, the mysteries of the heartbeat and pulse have shaped much of the human imagination around life, death, individuality, love, and salvation, to name a few. To this day, even with the rise of the brain sciences as the central investigation of the internal self, the conception of the heart as the embodiment of one's deepest intimacies holds as an unbreakable metaphor in how we relate to each other. There is a reason we have centuries' worth of poetry about the actions of the heart and not the kidneys, liver, or lungs. When we "give" our hearts to each other, "wear" them on our sleeves, or "listen" to them as if they possess another, more authentic "you," we are enacting complex interpretations and behaviors of the heart with deep-rooted, cross-cultural entanglements of religious, mystical, emotional, and medical knowledge. In this way, our hearts truly do connect us over time.

This mysteriousness of the heart had much to do with our inaccessibility to observe its direct movements; for most of medical history, it was too technically challenging and culturally taboo to probe into a living human heart. For this reason, we have traditionally looked to the arts, myth, and religion to give shape and interpretation to the inscrutable actions of our hearts, which were understood as inherently ephemeral, divinely ordered, and forever beyond the domain of scientific understanding. Perhaps this ancient desire to understand our hearts found its most essential form, though, through the scientific invention of an image we often take for granted, and which for the first time in history gave us visual access to the living heart: the pulse wave.

To visualize this fundamental movement of life is to suggest the possibility of visualizing its opposite: the stillness of death. As revolutionary as it was to invent a new image of life through a simple rhythmic curve, that same curve, stretched long and taut, has produced no less an iconic image of our existence: the flatline.

But where are the first pulse wave and flatline ever recorded? For that matter, where are the first recordings of the heart under all of life's conditions: love, fear, anticipation, desire, eating, sleeping, and laughing? Whose hearts were the first to offer their form, their remnants of a lived, emotionally complex life embedded in the oscillations of a wavy line? What technology needed to be invented to record the long-thought inaccessible heart?

Like the earliest tracing of a hand on an ancient cave wall, these milestones in the history of images should be remembered, honored, and empathized with because of their ability to universally convey something essential about us over long periods of time. The portfolio of prints *The First Time, the Heart (A Portrait of Life 1854–1913)* brings together the first successful scientific attempts to image and document the various experiences of a living heart, which would change the way we understand and communicate our bodies.

It has primarily been the domain of art and religion to ponder and interpret the meaning and purpose of the heart, producing a rich legacy of objects, images, and thought. However, by 1853, science could now contribute to investigating the mysteries of the living heart when the German physiologist Karl von Vierordt (1818–1884) produced the first visual tracings of the human pulse. The now near-universally familiar images of the wavelike pulse lines as they appear on a heart monitor were at the time groundbreaking images that scientists hoped would reveal a "natural language" of life. These hieroglyphics of the heart only needed to be deciphered once the pulse and heartbeat were made into a visual form.

Vierordt's device, an exquisite machine of sensitivity for the nineteenth century, was called a sphygmograph, or "pulse writer." The device was designed to absorb the movement of a pulsing artery into a membrane or spring that would then make an attached stylus pulse in unison. After many attempts searching for the most sensitive material for the stylus, a balance between rigidity and suppleness, he settled on a short strand of human hair. The stylus would then trace out the white curvilinear forms on a piece of soot-covered paper on a rotating drum. Although it was simply a material practicality of the time, it is no less a poetic moment of astounding fragility to know the first pulse ever scientifically recorded was traced by a single human hair in the residue of candle flames that burned and extinguished over 160 years ago.

Almost two decades later, in 1870, the French physiologist Paul Lorain recorded the last fleeting signals of a dying heart as the body succumbed to the ravages of stomach cancer. The line, almost entirely rigid except for a few subtle ripples—the last quivers of a determined heart—is perhaps the most succinct portrait of death ever created.

Consider for a moment the invisible history of the images before us: for millions of years, billions of hearts have been pulsing these patterns, each representing the waves of our internal oceans, carrying both energy and emotional knowledge through the body. Yet, it was only a little over a century and a half ago that we could scientifically record, observe, and preserve, through an undulating line, the past actions of our always forward-moving hearts. Like ancient starlight absorbed by youthful telescopes—always there, waiting to be seen—images of our pulses and heartbeats came into view, oscillating through the wind-sensitive residue of candle flames on paper. However, these lines were not only medical but also poetic and philosophical in the long arc of human self-reflection. Humans are beautifully creative in the ways we hope meaning—an *essence*—is literally in the lines, images, or objects we create to hold them. The first pulse and heart waves should be remembered as part of that history.

Looking through the earliest heart and pulse tracings from the nineteenth and early twentieth centuries, one quickly realizes the sense of excitement early investigators must have felt about the possibilities that opened with the ability to record and visualize the heart's movements. With these new tools of observation, the modern scientific heart was brought into focus and previously suspected and newly discovered diseases and malfunctions of the heart were dutifully cataloged, producing a novel type of compendium—how our hearts can fail us. And although recording sick hearts for diagnostic reasons

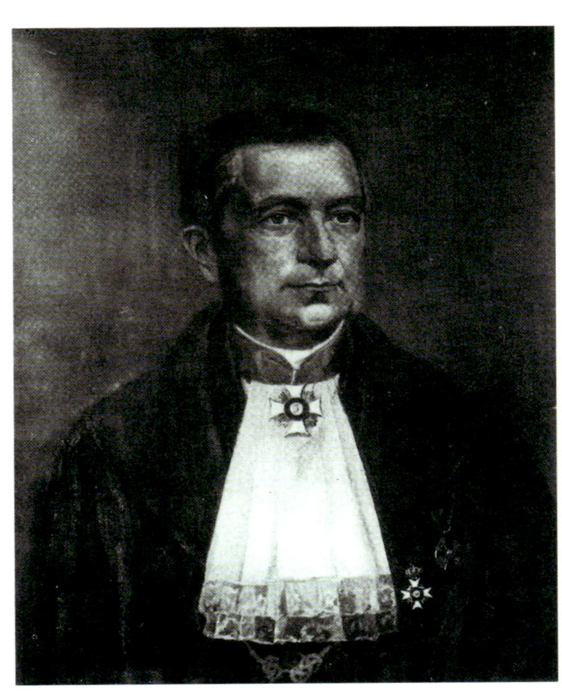

Karl von Vierordt, 1818–1884

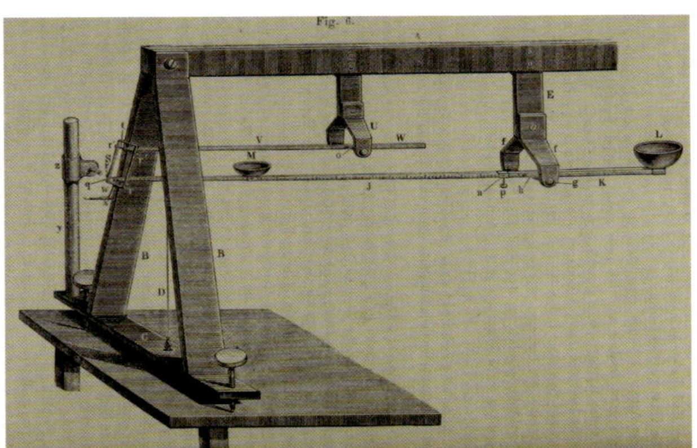

Vierordt Sphygmograph Instrument

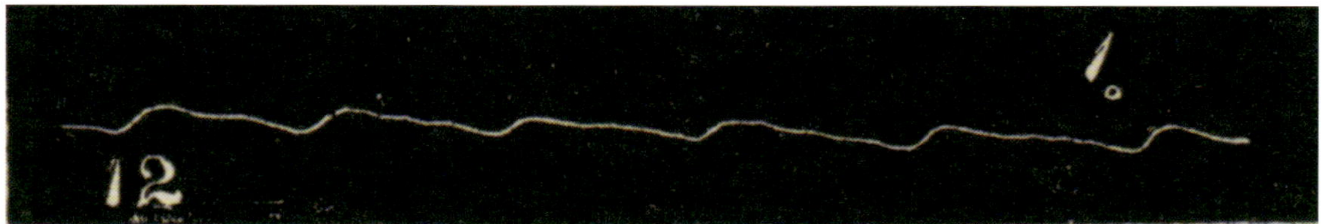

Full meal with wine. 1874

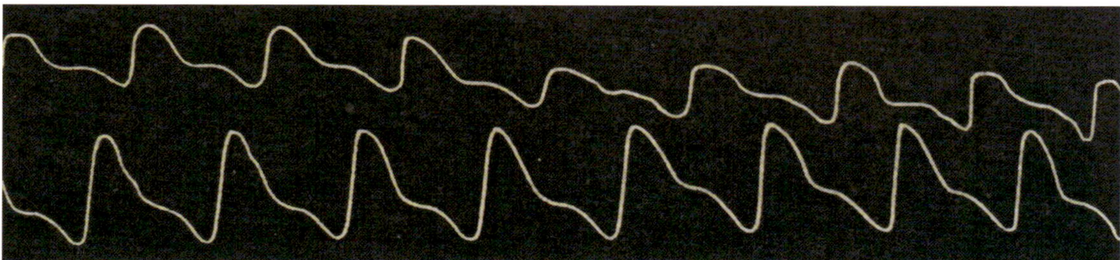

Before and during emotion. 1870

Flatline (dying of stomach cancer). 1870

remained the early priority behind the research, something else fascinating started to emerge, an accidental by-product of the more extensive study of disease: a poetic portrait of everyday life.

Occasionally, a breakthrough in science will so alter our mental landscape that, in a sense, everything is new again. Mystery reclaims the banal; revelation is possible once more, embedded in the ordinary. The sphygmograph, cardiograph, EKG, and other technologies of visualizing the once invisible inner workings of the heart had this power. They were a unique mixture of science in its grandest efforts at profundity—for what was more profound than attempting to decipher the unknown language of the human heart—but also, more unexpectedly and unintentionally, they became tools to unlock the poetics of the everyday.

Underway across laboratories and hospitals in Europe and the US, there was a grand effort at recording life from the beginning again. "Life from the beginning" in the sense that every experience, no matter how routine, could now be recorded, visualized, and interpreted by science through this most complex of vessels. The inner workings of the heart and pulse in a state of disease, stress, or malfunction were one thing, but what of the other multitude of daily moments that give life its deeper texture—fear, dreaming, eating chocolate, drinking wine, hiccupping, or hearing a whistle? What could science say about our hearts simply *living life*? Like seismic sensors to the heart's purposeful mundanities, these recording devices dutifully output their flowing lines, allowing a new type of confirmation and connection through time. Just like our hearts, these century-old ones beat a little faster when blushing, a little slower when sleeping, irregularly when anxious, and wildly when excited.

As these past hearts are held forward in time, another interesting phenomenon appears. From the mid-nineteenth century forward, miles and miles of heart waves start to fill countless books and research papers, all notated with the new, rhythmic language of heart disease: angina pectoris, atrial fibrillation, tachycardia, endocarditis, myocardial infarction. With this language of disease, though, came the newly heart-charged language of life. By merely stating the experience being recorded with the matter-of-factness science excels at, a type of strange, beautiful, and accidental poetry takes form: "pulse of man 6 feet tall," "ear lightly touched with feather while sleeping," "sadness from listening to a sung melody," "threatening a little girl, 10, to go to the dentist," "before and after a draught of hot milk," "mail carrier with amputated arm," "smelling lavender."

Although there was much science to learn about how the heart and circulatory system responded to the effects of height, touch, exertion, or listening, in these combinations of image and text we are reminded of the heart's unique ability to give an urgent lens to view all aspects of life. There is "sadness from listening to a sung melody," and there is the *first time an individual's heart was recorded while feeling sadness from listening to a sung melody*—an experience as rich with artistic contemplation as scientific. It was certainly not the first time that a human heart felt such emotion as a response to music. But like literature, sculpture, dance, or the invention of any expressive genre, with the pulse wave, we had a new method to represent that experience—only this time it literally came directly from the heart.

Whether through writing, drawing, photography, or sound, the act of recording changes our relationship to time and place. With each method, there is always an opportunity to expand empathy, communication, and shared purpose through time. Like the excitement of discovering a decaying, unopened crate of early wax cylinder recordings documenting long-assumed lost languages and songs, these pulse images and texts, taken as a whole, constitute an untapped documentary recording of the daily and emotional lives of another time and place as registered through their hearts.

Researched and gathered from many different libraries and archives, the fifty pulse waves in this portfolio were chosen to document a life, from birth to death. In each instance, it is likely the first time the heart was recorded under that experience—a locus point in time for all hearts to follow. Although each pulse wave is from a different person (representing many years, ages, locations, genders, nationalities, races, and religions), together, they complete a familiar life. From an eight-months-pregnant woman, a fetal heartbeat at birth, riding a bike, to early senility and heart failure, as we watch these former hearts ripple by, we can enact our gift of empathy across time.

As exciting as the possibility of opening a new sensory path to the past is, because of the way these images were originally documented, this act of empathy will always have a gap. As we all have experienced, the complex gestures we have invented to give each other our hearts matters so deeply to us because of the specifics of *whose* heart and *why* it is being given. But the images of pulse and heart waves this portfolio gathers cannot do this, secluding them into a strange, emotionally complex zone between intimacy and anonymity. So many of the individuals who left memories of their hearts in countless books and manuscripts were not documented by name by the scientists or doctors conducting the research. It was not uncommon for the experimenters to freely test new devices or procedures on the constant influx of new patients moving through hospitals, and they were often merely identified by their gender, age, and medical condition. The paradox is that we can now share an intimacy with thousands and thousands of former lives by glimpsing into fleeting moments of their hearts—moments of birth, laughter, anticipation, suicide, and death—without ever knowing anything more about them. But because it is their heart they gave, we should feel compelled to ask: Whose birth? Was it a boy or a girl? What did they become? What made them fearful? Who did they love? Where are they buried? Their names and bodies may be gone, their souls ghosted to the ones they once loved, but they do not need to remain memories with no witnesses. In these few pulse waves, now freed from the decay of their host heart, they are still material and alive, ready to be seen, remembered, felt, and held in sync with ours.

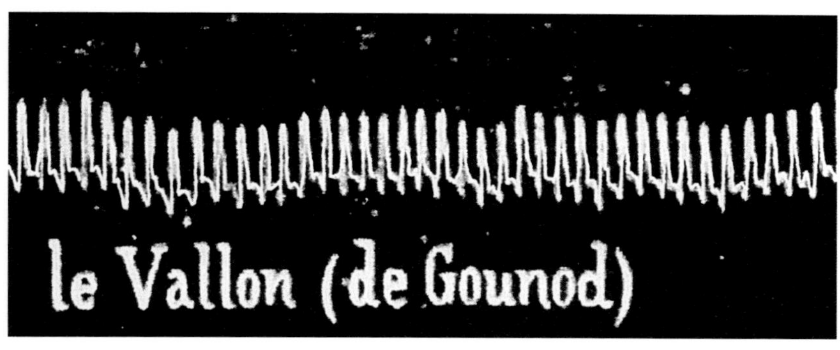

Sadness from listening to a sung melody, le Vallon (de Gounod), 1896

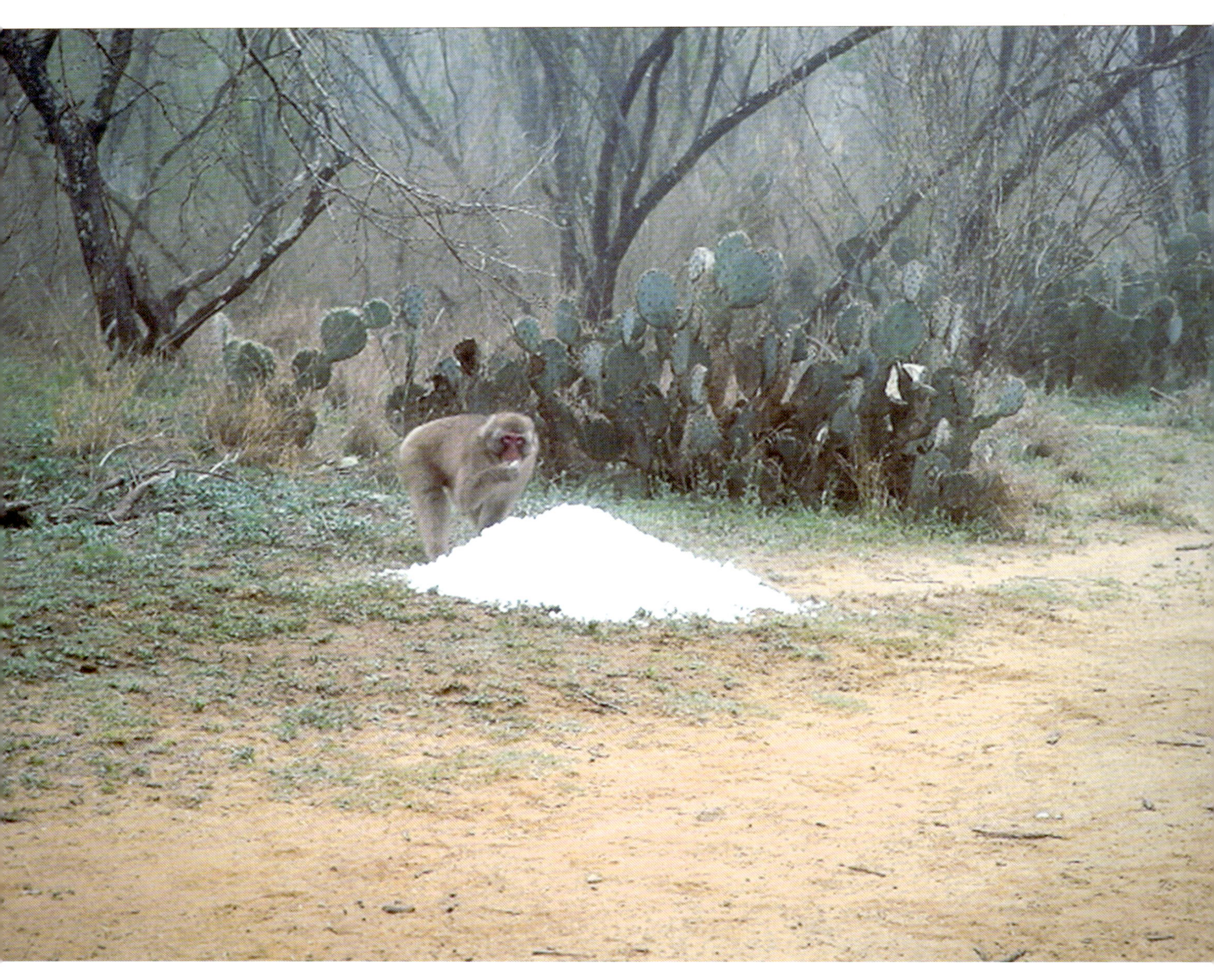

The Snow Monkeys of Texas: Do snow monkeys remember snow mountains? (still), 2016

Shimabuku

(born 1969 in Kobe, Japan)

When I visited the monkey mountain in Kyoto in 1992 I heard an interesting story.

In 1972 a group of Japanese snow monkeys were brought from the mountains of Kyoto to a Texas desert. The first year, their numbers reduced dramatically. They didn't know how to live in the desert with cactus, cougars or rattlesnakes. But in the second year their population grew. Do monkeys adapt to new environments faster than people do? I wanted to go and meet them someday.

In 2016 I finally visited them in Texas. I saw that they looked a bit Americanized, somehow. They are a bit bigger, and started to eat cactus. Now they know how to deal with the cougars and rattlesnakes. They have a new language to alert each other.

When I spent a few days with them under the Texan sun, I decided to make a mountain with ice for them. I filled a car with bags of ice. And I wondered, do they remember snow mountains?

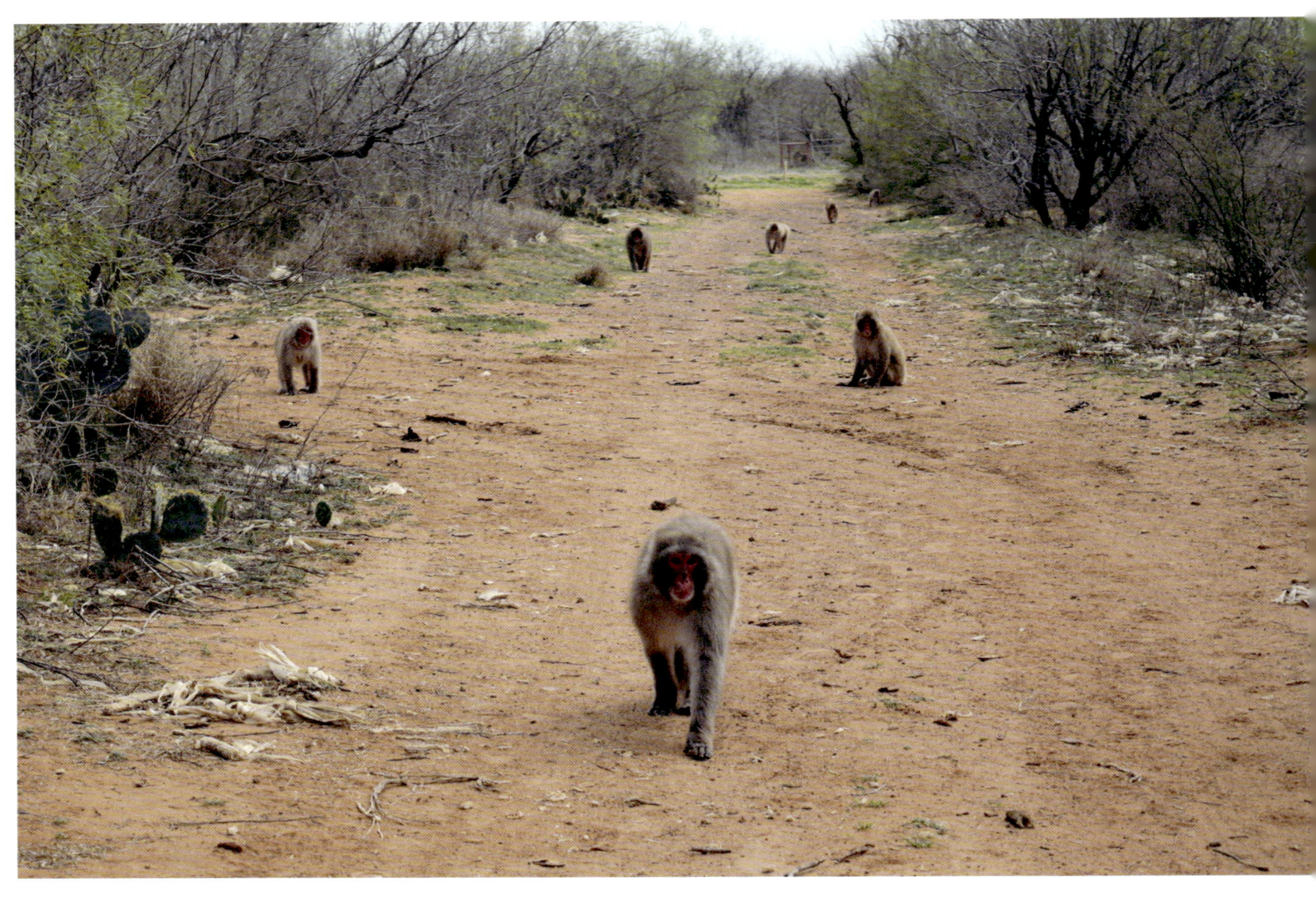

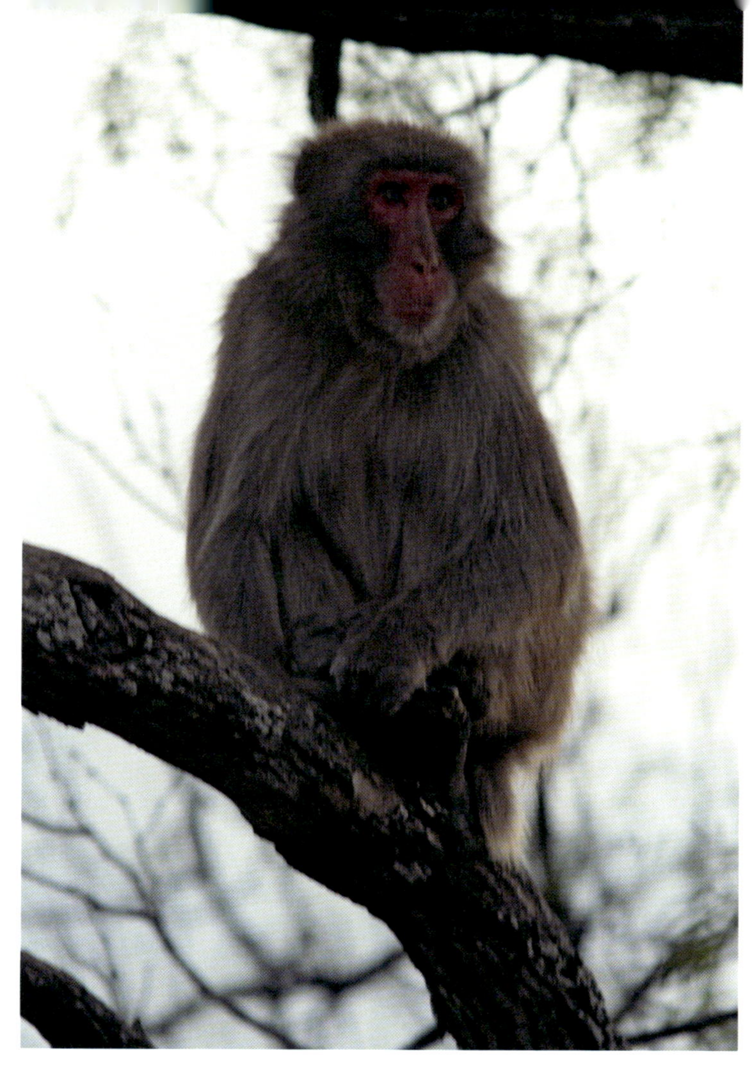

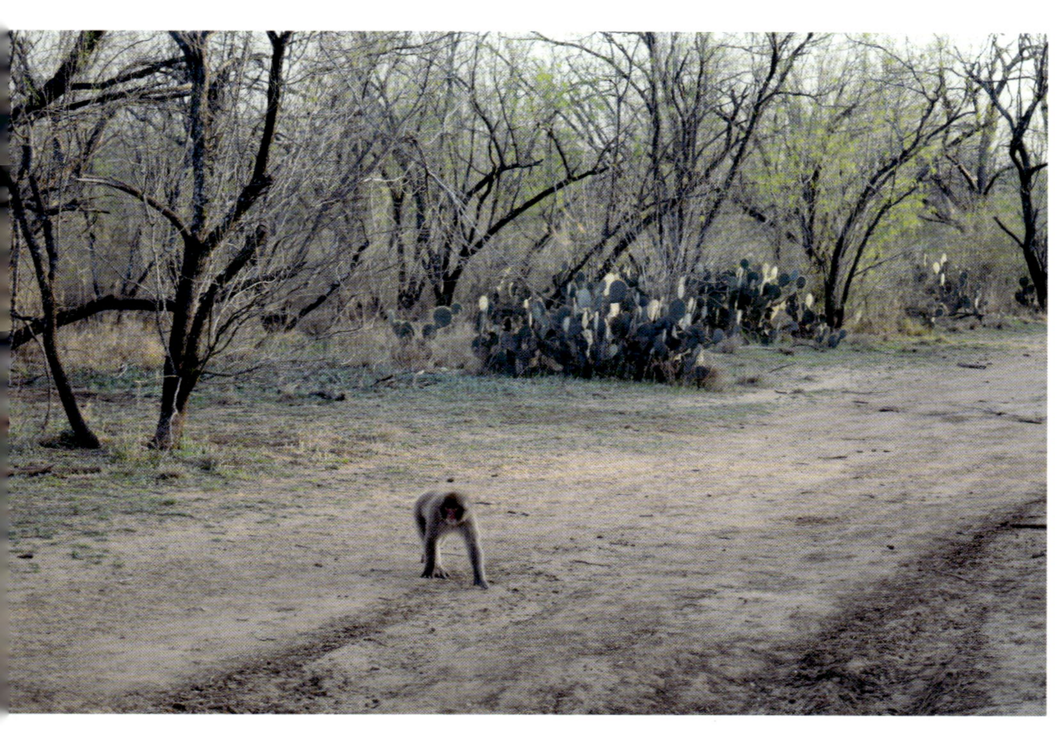

Placing things upright. Placing the lying things upright. Placing the trees and stones that lie on the beach upright.

With the collaboration of many people, we will place many things in an upright position. We will try to put our energy together to place huge trees as well in an upright position.

This should make something that lies in our hearts stand up in an upright position.

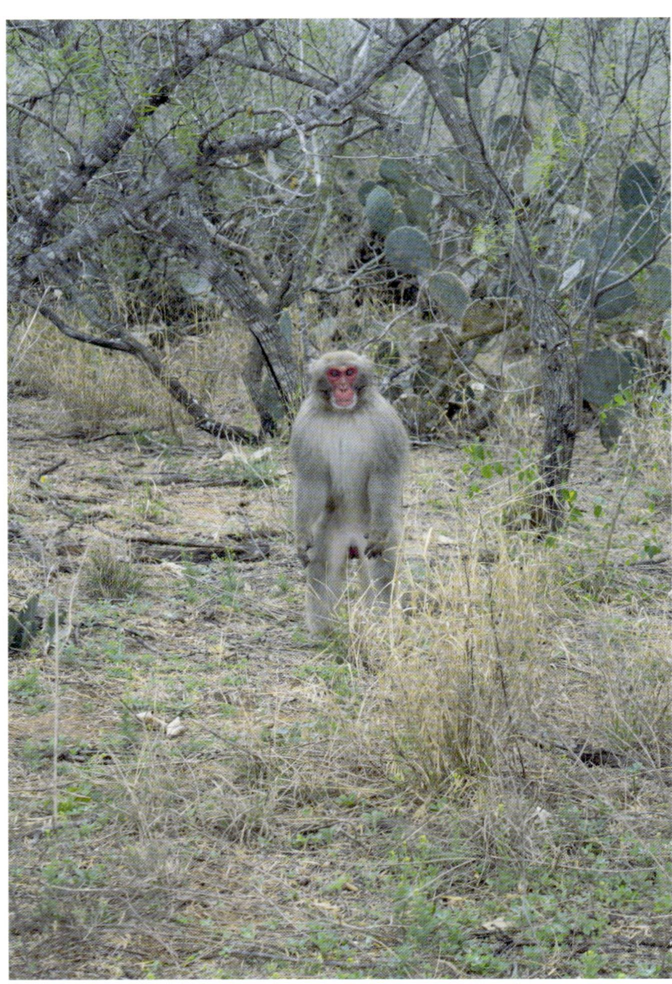

The Snow Monkeys of Texas: Snow Monkey Stance, 2016

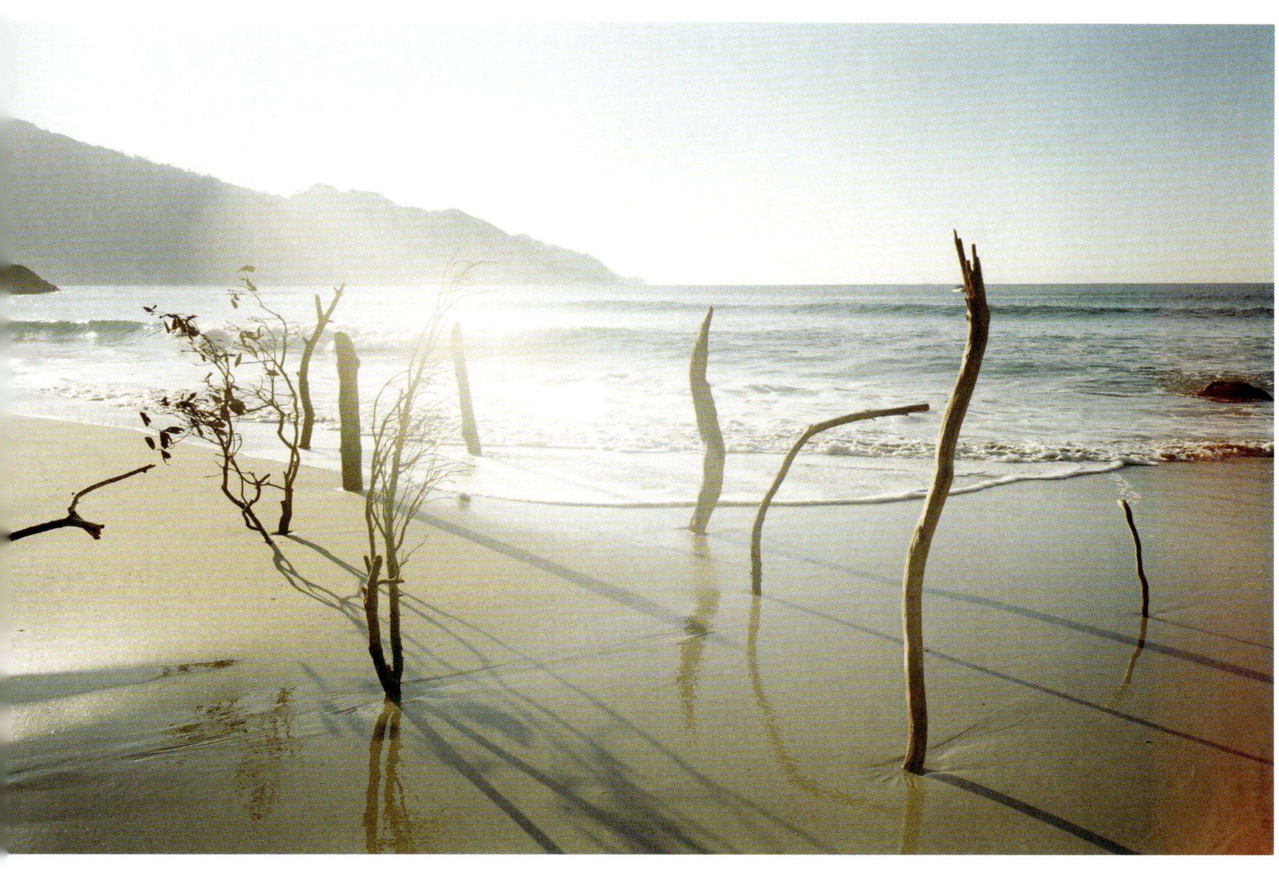

Erect, 2017

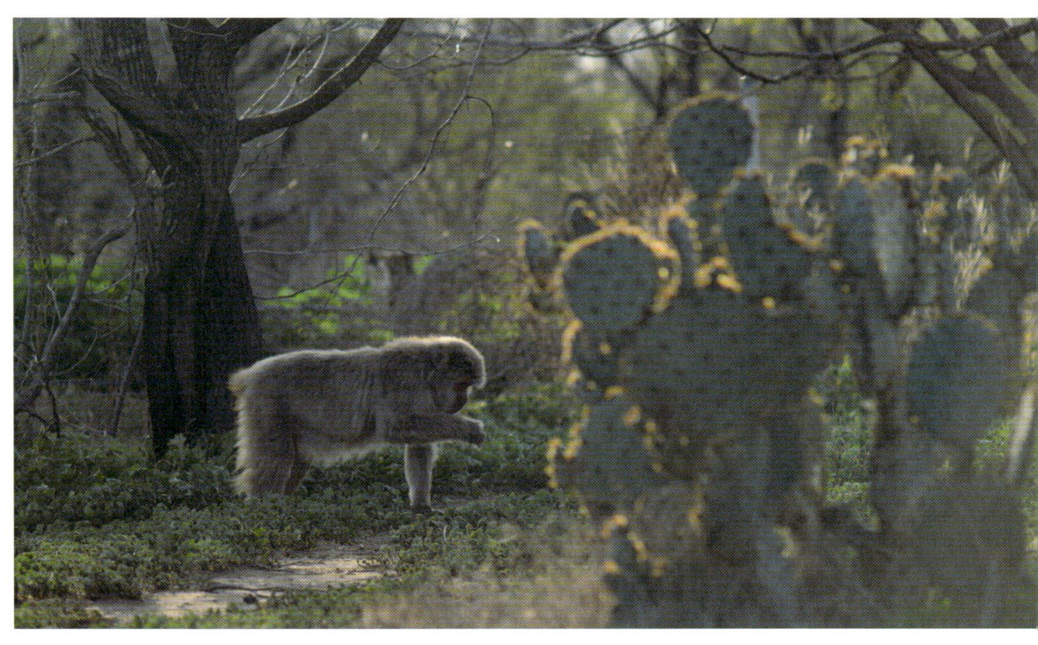

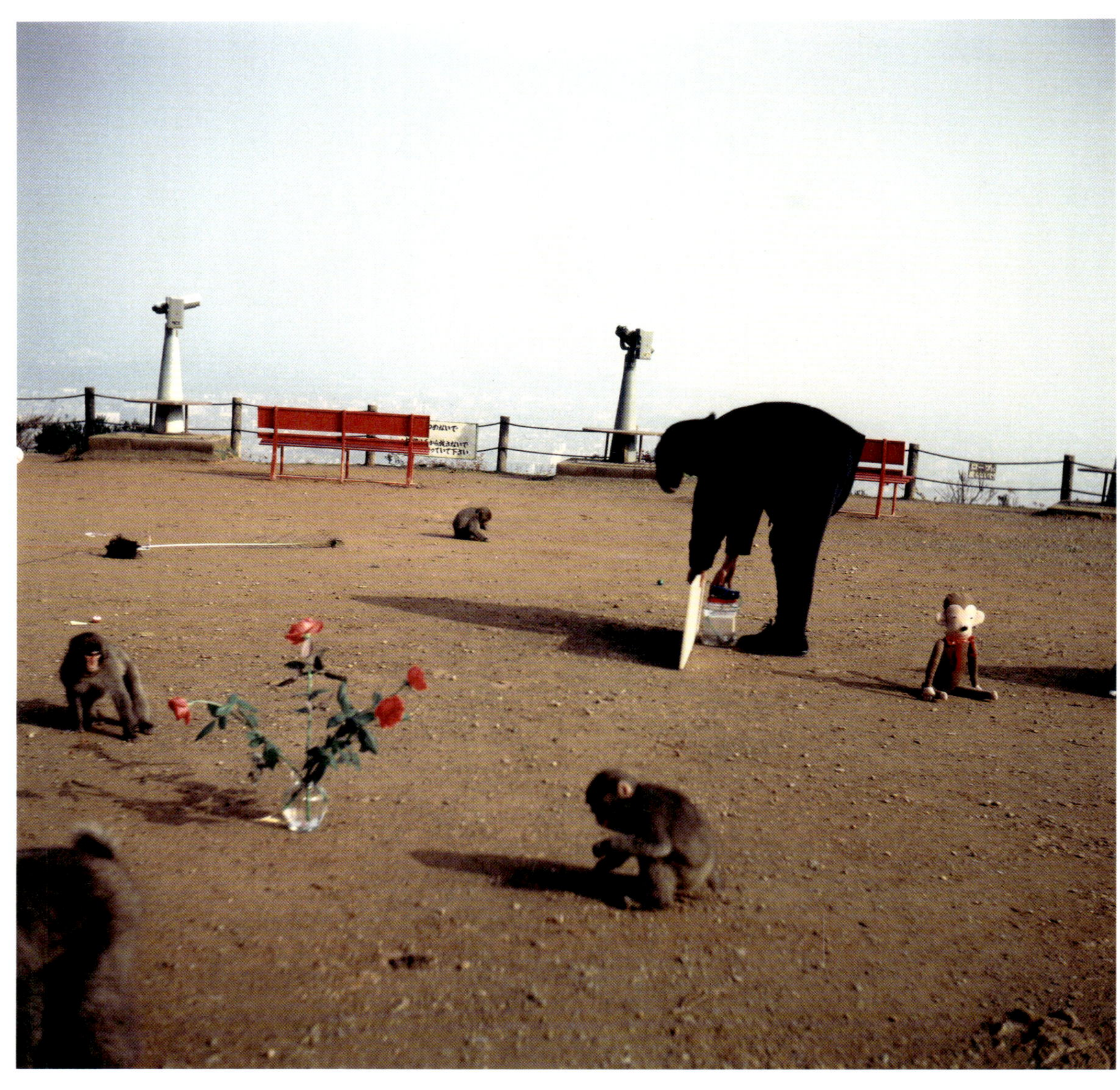

Exhibition for the Monkeys, 1992

When I went to the "monkey mountain" in Kyoto, I learned that sometimes, one of the monkeys picks up pieces of broken glass and stares at them. I decided to hold an exhibition for the monkeys.

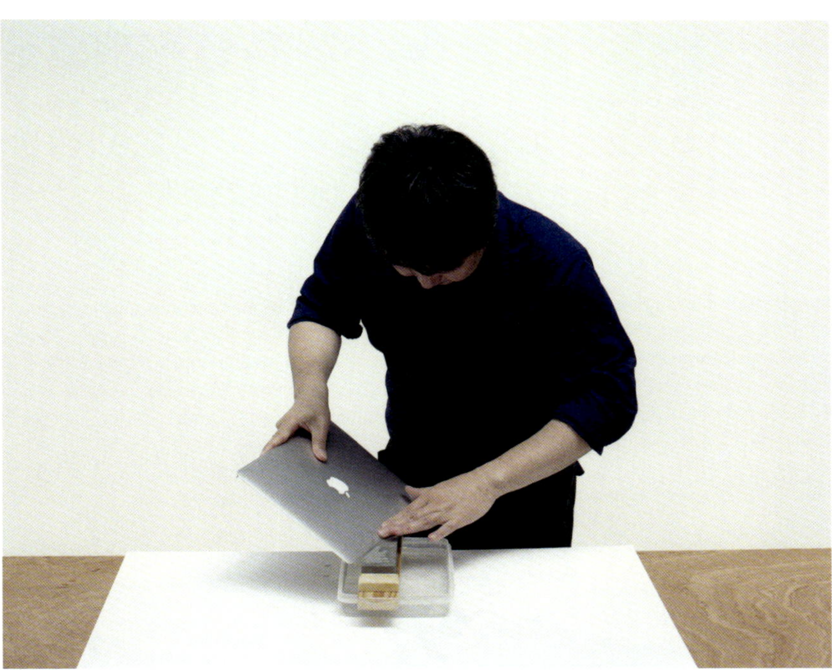

Sharpening a MacBook Air, 2015

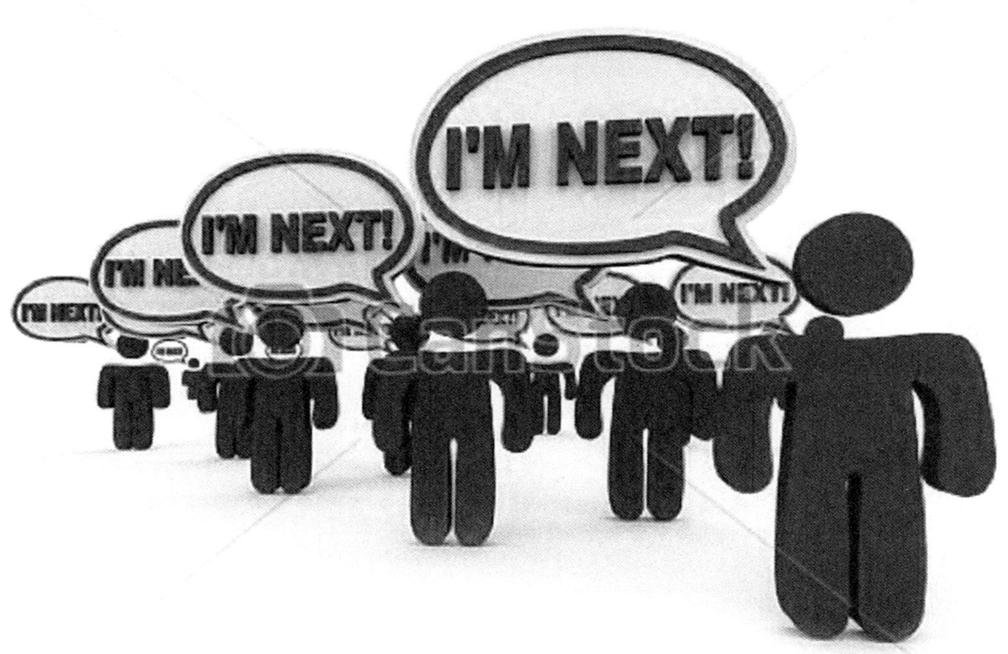

These two images came from a common Internet search—“people standing in line.” When plugged into a search engine the results cross the spectrum from refugees seeking safety to people waiting on line to compete on *American Idol*. The image on the right does not reveal any clear context for the scene. Who are they, where are they, why are they? The stock photo on the left is an example of a ubiquitous genre of stock photo illustration. I look at these types of stock illustrations (ready to customize with many other captions, i.e., “agree,” “now,” “more”) as the most basic, ground-floor level of commercial illustration.

https://www.inc.com/jill-krasny/why-waiting-in-lines-makes-things-more-appealing.html

https://www.google.com/search?q=I%27m+Next+stock+photo&client=firefox-b-1-ab&source=lnms&tbm=isch&sa=X-&ved=0ahUKE- wit7KjLw97fAhVJ_IMKHSt4BBAQ_AUIDigB&biw=1825&bih=932#imgrc=XBrlR3WeuSl06M:

Julia Wachtel

(born 1956 in New York City, New York)

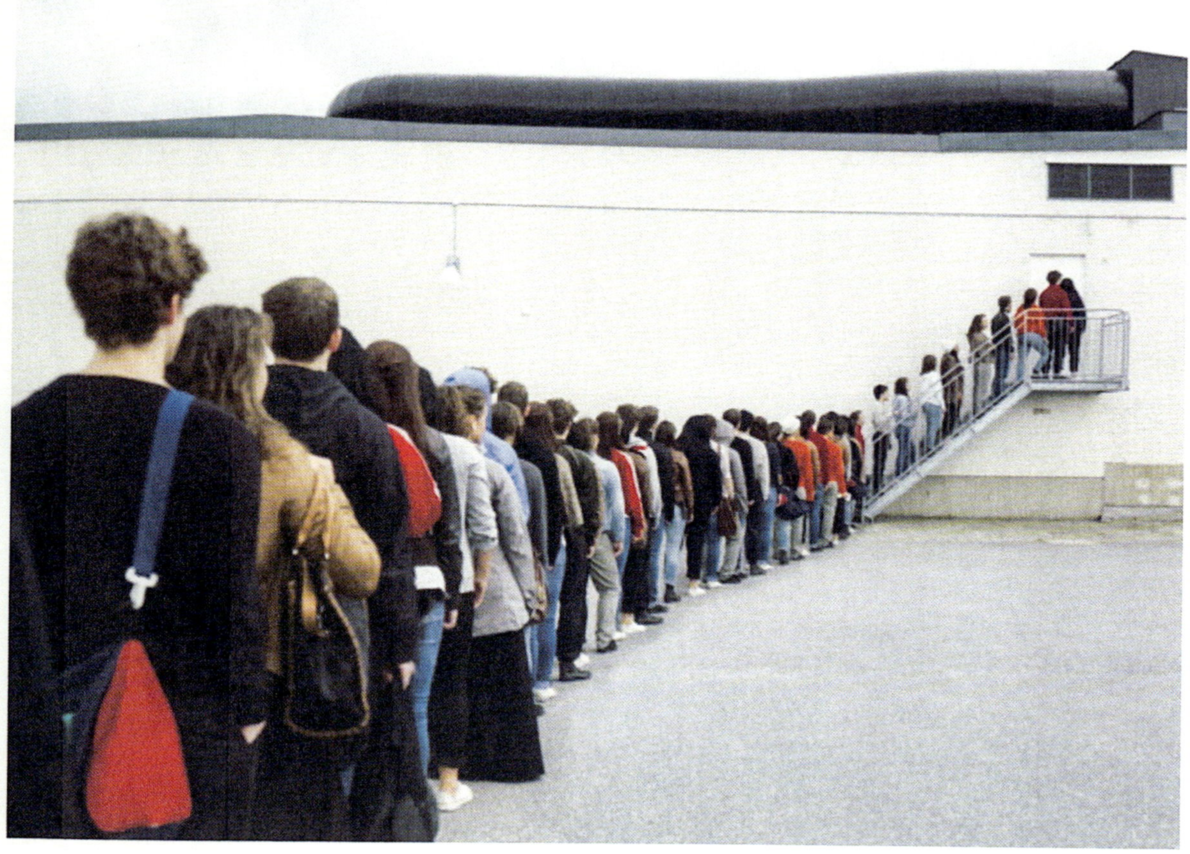

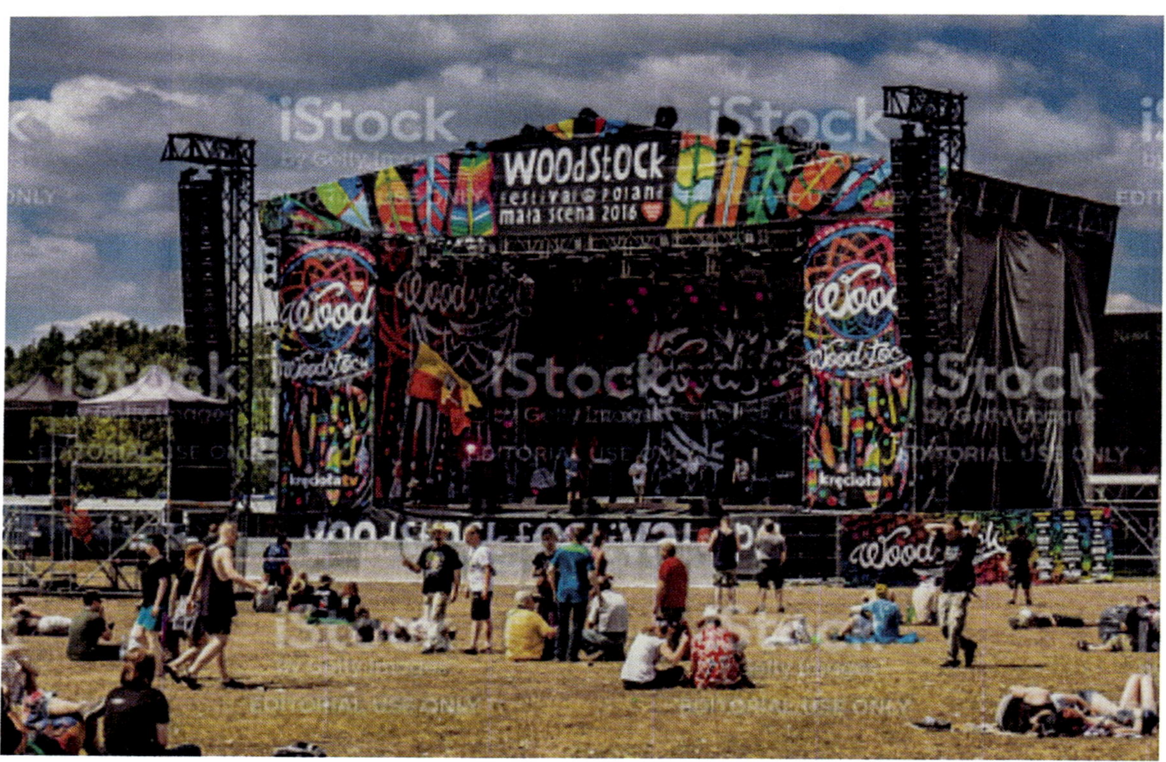

These two images interest me as they both represent cultural distortions and ideological overlaps. The image on the left is a Getty stock photo from the annual event Przystanek Woodstock in Poland. This description was taken directly from Wikipedia:

> The name Przystanek Woodstock - "Woodstock Station" refers to peace and friendship symbolized by the Woodstock Festival and the TV series Northern Exposure, aired as Przystanek Alaska (Alaska Station), immensely popular in Poland at that time. The name of the festival has been changed to PolAndRock Festival on March 8th, 2018. The change has been motivated by licensing dispute with the agency representing Michael Lang. New name reflects the both the rock'n'roll roots of the event and the strong ties to the heritage of Polish democratic and freedom fighting movement. The organizers of the festival claim that even though the name of the festival has changed, the ethos behind the event remains unchanged.

This image interests me as it speaks to the trajectory from the origin event of Woodstock through countless iterations of commercialization and re-creation and ending here with this stock photo. The overlap of the American TV show *Northern Exposure* adds another layer of appropriation and displacement.

The image on the right is a found Internet meme blending the faces of Kim Jong-un and Kim Kardashian. It is the work of Instagram artist "The Johnny Smith."

https://en.wikipedia.org/wiki/Pol%27and%27Rock_Festival

https://www.google.com/search?hl=en&q=Getty+Images&tbm=isch&tbs=simg:CAQSlQEJFme8b6Kkr6UaiQELEKjU2AQaAggVDAsQsIynCBpiCmAIAx-Io3Be3Hr8exRepHt0eixW5HqMewh6xObM5rjmvObkrqjmwObortyu7KxowDhovGhWV4Zavd8t2wGy7h8OXFScyASKvvEhTJ6VplaKAPqt8zWRqdeb_1n-Fhz6gPsIAQMCxCOrv4IGgoKCAgBEgSTMj8jDA&sa=X&ved=0ahUKEwiAstWYx97fAhUT8YMKHWqPBJwQwg4IKygA&biw=1416&bi-h=560#imgrc=_8rzdWA0CdpkUM:

https://www.google.com/search?sa=G&hl=en&q=kim+jong+un+kim+kardashian&tbm=isch&tbs=simg:CAQSmwEJinC8MObh3eAajwELEKjU2AQaCAgX-CD0IQwgVDAsQsIynCBpiCmAIAxIoshqpH6ofrx_1IGqwfrR_11D9UayxqjPPYvgjHyMOgwpDzlL6Yx6zHyMRowejk8jTmUfd-sfOV74048djML37tiLkD-vkLTTLzhj6DQaQgRnB1pCyD_1zBseRAKuJIAQMCxCOrv4IGgoKCAgBEgQRRqigDA&ved=0ahUKEwir0YK6x97fAhUBq4MKHdapBMsQg4IKygA&bi-

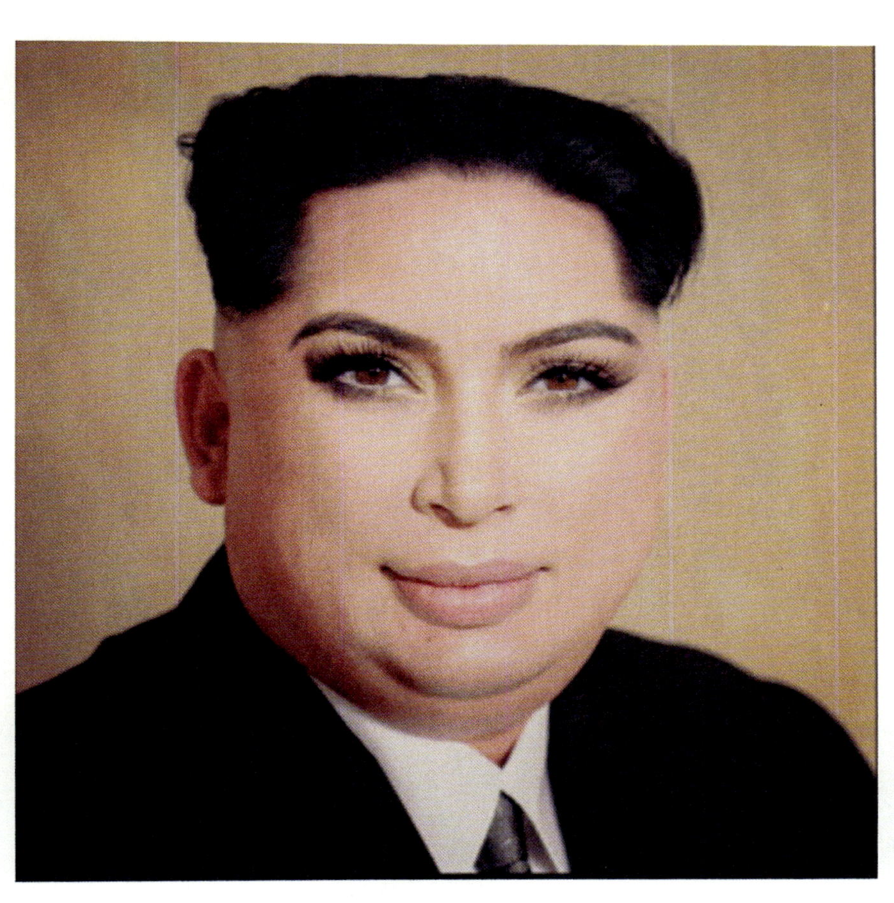

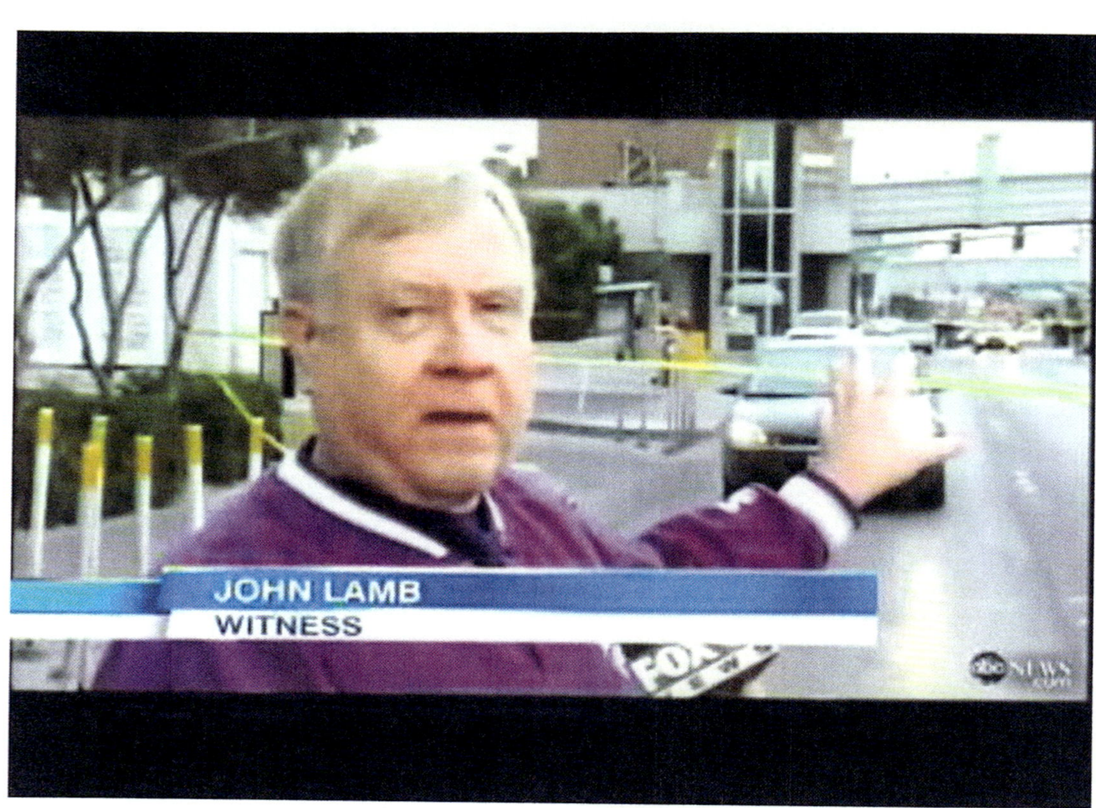

Both these images are photos taken directly off my TV with my iPhone. The image on the left is from a TV news program. The image on the right is from the TV sitcom *The Middle*.

https://en.wikipedia.org/wiki/The_Middle_(TV_series)

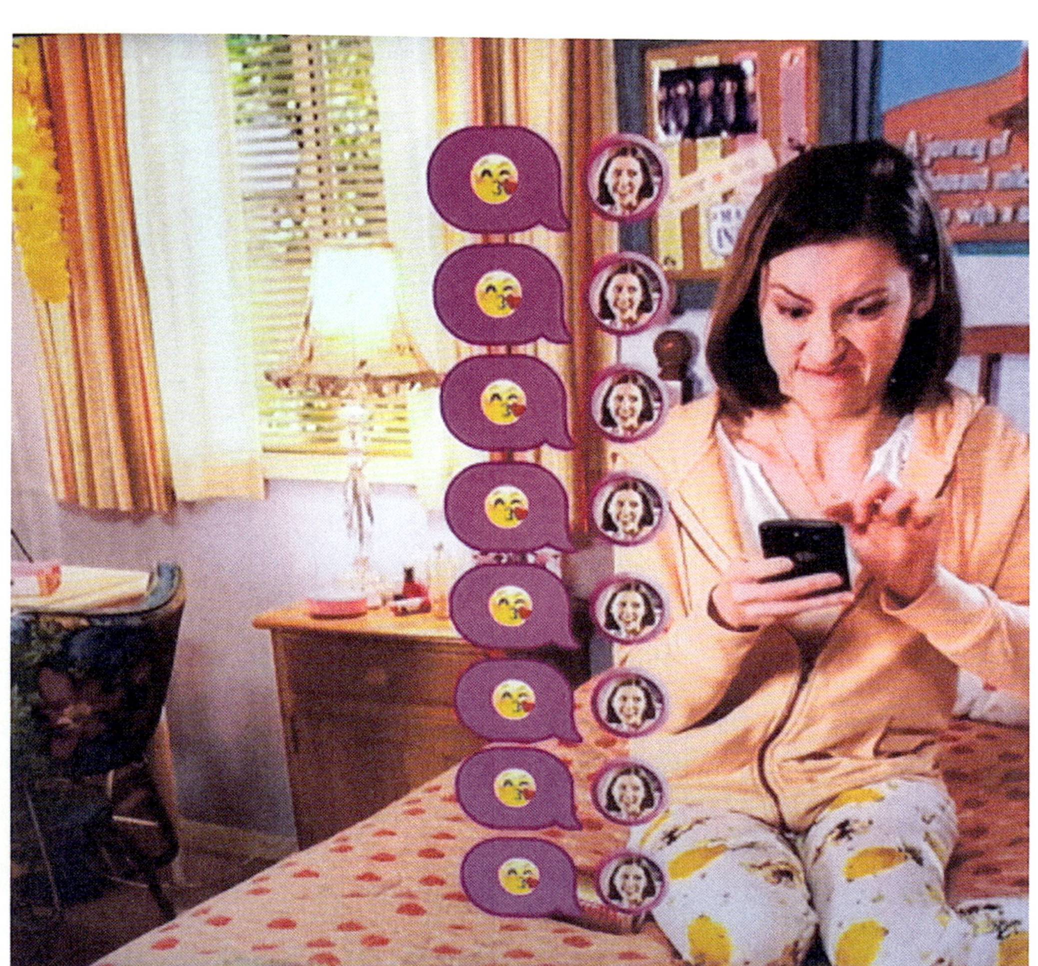

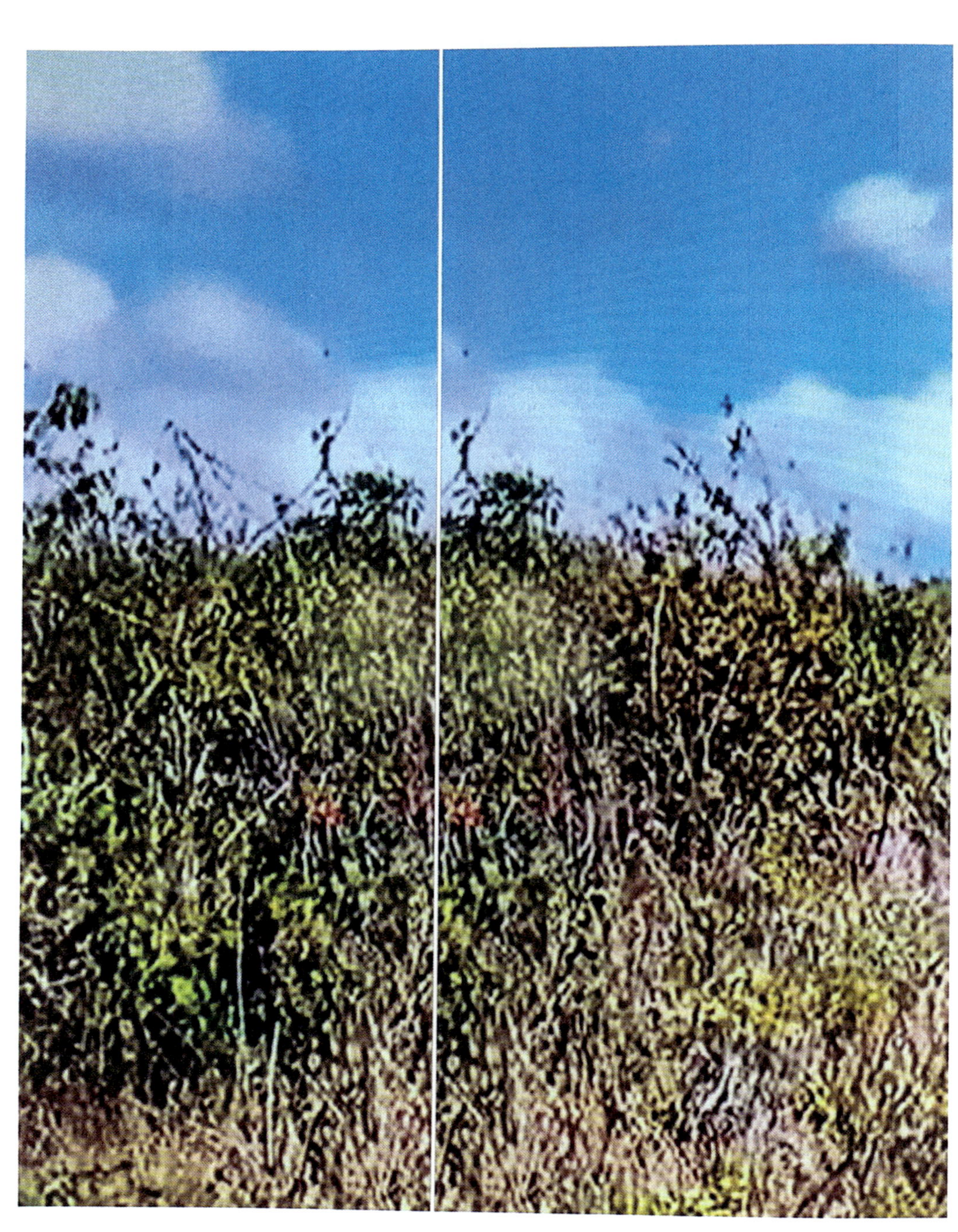

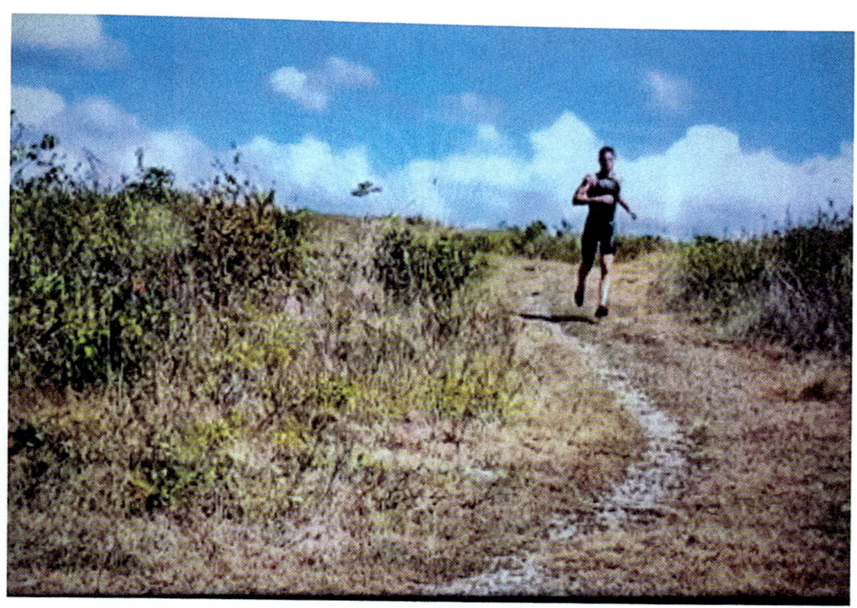

The source image (above) is a photo taken directly off my TV with my iPhone. The images to the left represent close-up sections extracted from the original to comprise the middle two panels of the painting below. The first four panels are photo screen printed. The middle two panels being screen prints of screens. My interest in the TV screen as a source is not only to mine the TV scape for content, but also to exploit the "natural" formal language such as moiré patterns, and to enlarge close-ups to heighten an experience of the abstraction of the image.

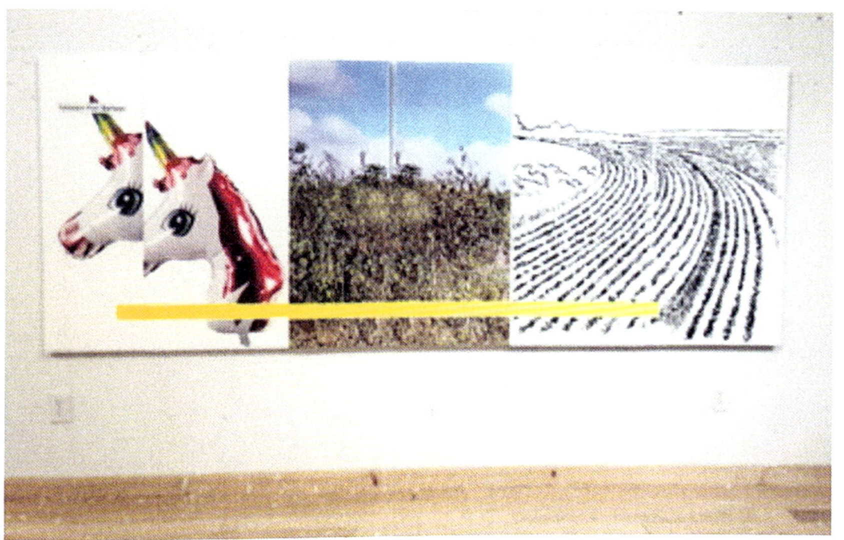

Ed Atkins (born 1982 in Oxford, United Kingdom)

Material Witness OR A Liquid Cop, 2012
Single-channel HD video, color, stereo sound
Running time: 19:17, looped
Courtesy the artist and Gavin Brown's enterprise, New York/Rome

Nuotama Bodomo (born 1988 in Accra, Ghana)

Boneshaker, 2013
Single-channel HD video, color, sound; converted from Super 16 mm
Running time: 13:00
Courtesy the artist

Afronauts, 2014
Single-channel HD video, black and white, sound
Running time: 14:00
Courtesy the artist

Theo Eshetu (born 1958 in London, United Kingdom)

Adieu Les Demoiselles, 2019
Single-channel HD video, color, sound
Camera and color correction: Samuele Malfatti; sound design: Keir Fraser; graphics: Naia Burucoa, Melanie Wiener; set construction: Daniel Paiva de Miranda; casting and locations: Lisa Stertz; performers: Federica Dauri, Anna Fingerhuth, Zoe Goldstein, Yuko Kaseki, Sarah Kutzias Vella, Nicole Michalla, Lisa Stertz, Maria Torrents
Running time: 8:45, looped
Commissioned by The Contemporary Austin
Courtesy the artist and Axis Gallery, New York

Cameron Jamie (born 1969 in Los Angeles, California)

Mon Singe, 2019
Bronze
73 ¼ x 26 ½ x 26 inches
Commissioned by The Contemporary Austin, with funds provided by the Edward and Betty Marcus Foundation
Courtesy the artist and Gladstone Gallery, New York and Brussels

Kapwani Kiwanga (born 1978 in Hamilton, Ontario, Canada)

Flowers for Africa: Ivory Coast, 2015
Protocol of assembly and display including archival iconography to guide the reconstruction of a floral arrangement consisting of cut flowers
Dimensions variable
Christophe Guillot Collection

Glow, 2019
Wood, stucco, acrylic, steel, and LED lights
Dimensions variable
Commissioned by the MIT List Visual Arts Center, Cambridge, Massachusetts
Courtesy the artist and Galerie Jérôme Poggi, Paris

Marie Lorenz (born 1973 in Twentynine Palms, California)

Graybelt Field Trips, 2019
Participatory boat excursions with the artist in the Colorado River and Laguna Gloria lagoon; boat designed and built by the artist
Courtesy the artist

Trap and Weir, 2019
Ceramic, steel, cement, and rope; site-specific installation
Dimensions variable
Commissioned by The Contemporary Austin, with funds provided by the Edward and Betty Marcus Foundation
Courtesy the artist and Jack Hanley Gallery, New York

Nathan Mabry (born 1978 in Durango, Colorado)

u.n.t.i.t.l.e.d. (Crouching Figure – Blue), 2012
Bronze, aluminum, paint, and stainless steel
28 x 12 x 11 inches
AP 1 of 1, Edition of 1
Courtesy the artist and Philip Martin Gallery, Los Angeles

u.n.t.i.t.l.e.d. (Reclining Figure with Right Arm Bent – Red), 2012
Bronze, aluminum, paint, and stainless steel
29 x 28 x 10 inches
AP 1 of 1, Edition of 1
The Masi Kolb Collection

T/O/T/E/M (. . . have eyes like a . . .), 2013
Terra-cotta, patina, white oak plywood, and Plexiglas
63 x 18 x 20 ½ inches
Courtesy the artist and Philip Martin Gallery, Los Angeles

T/O/T/E/M (. . . wise like a . . .), 2013
Terra-cotta, patina, vertical fir plywood, and Plexiglas
61 x 18 x 19 inches
Courtesy the artist and Philip Martin Gallery, Los Angeles

T/O/T/E/M (. . . dog eat dog . . .), 2014
Terra-cotta, patina, walnut plywood, and Plexiglas
63 x 18 x 18 inches
Courtesy the artist and Philip Martin Gallery, Los Angeles

T/O/T/E/M (. . . in a row . . .), 2014
Terra-cotta, patina, ash plywood, and Plexiglas
62 x 22 x 18 inches
Courtesy the artist and Philip Martin Gallery, Los Angeles

T/O/T/E/M (. . . in your throat . . .), 2014
Terra-cotta, patina, mahogany plywood, and Plexiglas
65 x 18 x 18 inches
Courtesy the artist and Philip Martin Gallery, Los Angeles

T/O/T/E/M (. . . would have bit you . . .), 2014
Terra-cotta, patina, red oak plywood, and Plexiglas
66 x 18 x 18 inches
Courtesy the artist and Philip Martin Gallery, Los Angeles

Ruben Ochoa (born 1974 in Oceanside, California)

Kissed in the 90011, 2007
Chromogenic print in custom wenge frame
43 x 53 ⅛ inches
Edition 2 of 3, 2 AP
Courtesy the artist and Vielmetter Los Angeles

Overlapped in the 90063, 2007
Chromogenic print in custom wenge frame
43 x 53 ⅛ inches
Edition 2 of 3, 2 AP
Courtesy the artist and Vielmetter Los Angeles

Still Tripping, 90033, 2007
Chromogenic print in custom wenge frame
43 x 53 ⅛ inches
Edition 2 of 5, 2 AP
Courtesy the artist and Vielmetter Los Angeles

A bit of detritus, 2011
Concrete, metal, and dirt
80 x 32 x 32 inches
Courtesy the artist and Vielmetter Los Angeles

Casting Binaries, 2015
Rust on paper
Each, 24 x 18 inches
Overall, 24 x 126 inches
Courtesy the artist and Vielmetter Los Angeles

Season of Darkness, 2015
Rust on linen over panel
90 x 126 inches
Courtesy the artist and Vielmetter Los Angeles

Tripping the Light Fantastick, 2015
Rust on linen
90 x 126 inches
Courtesy the artist and Vielmetter Los Angeles

Glyphs in the nite, 2016
Rust on linen over panel
90 x 126 inches
Courtesy the artist and Vielmetter Los Angeles

One day it's fine and next it's black, 2017
Steel
42 ½ x 29 x 24 inches
Courtesy the artist and Vielmetter Los Angeles

One day it's fine and next it's black, 2017
Steel
63 ½ x 29 ½ x 16 ½ inches
Courtesy the artist and Vielmetter Los Angeles

One day it's fine and next it's black, 2017
Steel
75 x 25 x 24 inches
Courtesy the artist and Vielmetter Los Angeles

Dario Robleto (born 1972 in San Antonio, Texas)

The First Time, the Heart (A Portrait of Life 1854–1913), 2017–2018

10 year old boy, 1886
A hard drinker, quite recently a sufferer of sunstroke, 1874
Anger, 1874
Before and after a draught of hot milk, 1878
Ear lightly touched with feather while sleeping, 1877
Emotion of fear from shouting of the word "snakes," 1896
Experiment with cannabis (sudden freedom from any unusual feeling, beginning to feel an indefinable sensation of comfort), 1874
First pulse, 1854
Holding breath while listening to tuning fork, 1880
Listening to music (Schubert's "Serenade"), 1880
Palpitations (panic attack), 1902
Perfect mental repose, 1879
Religious guilt, 1878
Sadness from listening to a sung melody, (Le Vallon) Gounod, 1896
Taking involuntary deep breath while solving multiplication problem, 1879
Under influence of hiccups, 1886
Young boy, dreaming, 1877

Selection from a portfolio of fifty prints on Rising Drawing Bristol; photolithgraphs with transparent base ink, hand-flamed and sooted paper; image brushed with lithotine and lifted from soot, fused in a mild solution of shellac and denatured alcohol
Published by Island Press at Washington University, St. Louis, Missouri
Edition 1 of 6
Each, 11 ½ x 14 ¼ inches
Courtesy the artist and Inman Gallery, Houston

The Boundary of Life Is Quietly Crossed, 2019
Two-channel HD video, color, sound installation
Running time: 25:00, looped
Commissioned by The Contemporary Austin
Courtesy the artist and Inman Gallery, Houston

Shimabuku (born 1969 in Kobe, Japan)

The Snow Monkeys of Texas: Do snow monkeys remember snow mountains?, 2016
Single-channel HD video projection, color, sound; vinyl wall text; and cacti
AP 1 of 2, Edition of 3
Running time: 20:00, looped
Courtesy the artist and Freedman Fitzpatrick, Los Angeles/Paris

The Snow Monkeys of Texas: Snow Monkey Stance, 2016
Digital inkjet print on Hahnemühle photo rag, mounted on aluminum
55 ¼ x 38 ¼ inches
Edition 1 of 3, 2 AP
Courtesy the artist and Freedman Fitzpatrick, Los Angeles/Paris

Julia Wachtel (born 1956 in New York City, New York)

Floater, 1997
Oil on linen
74 x 74 inches
Courtesy the artist

The History of Animals, 1997
Oil on linen
64 x 104 inches
Courtesy the artist

Bad, 2015
Oil, acrylic ink, and Flashe on canvas
60 x 150 inches
Courtesy the artist

Time and Again, 2015
Oil and acrylic ink on canvas
64 x 94 inches
Courtesy the artist

Investigation, 2017
60 x 103 inches
Oil and acrylic ink on canvas
Courtesy the artist

Glossary of Tools

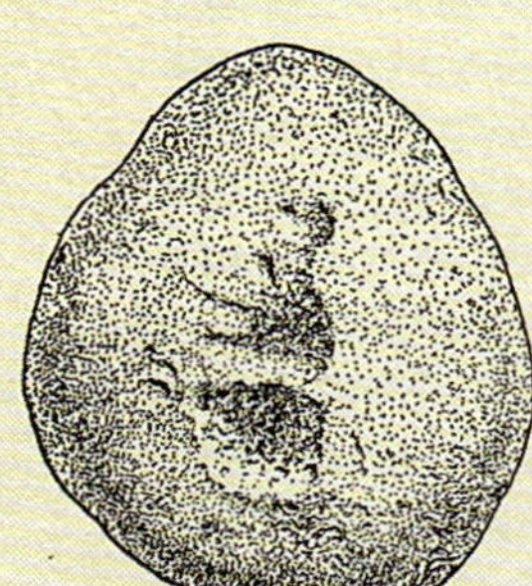

Anvils

The anvils found at Olduvai fall into two groups: (a) cuboid or circular blocks, often made of gneiss or tabular quartzite, with flat upper and lower faces and nearly vertical sides and (b) stones with pitted hollows. In the first group, the edges are battered, with many plunging flake scars, while the upper and lower faces also show marks of blows. In Bed I the anvils are usually natural blocks of rock that have not been shaped before use; but in Bed II they have sometimes been roughly shaped. Pitted anvils of the second type are found commonly in Bed IV, although rare examples are known earlier; there is even one specimen from lower Bed II and another from the top of Bed I. They consist of lava cobbles and small boulders on which there are roughly pitted hollows. These hollows occur singly, in pairs, or one on either side of the stone. Occasionally there are multiple hollows: in one six-sided example there are six, one on each face of the stone. The hollows vary in diameter from one to seven centimetres, and the depth is also variable. The interiors are

always rough
pecked.
It is proba
have resulted
technique for
method the co
be knocked of
hit at the opp
stone. A seco
pitted anvils
described bel
together for p
Length of figur

Awls

These small,
or notched c
unknown in
lower Bed II
for making too
in upper Bed
historic times,
for piercing le
Length of figur

O.G.

Ed Atkins (born 1982 in Oxford, United Kingdom) lives and works in Copenhagen and Berlin. While best known for his CGI video works, Atkins is also a published writer. He has held solo exhibitions at major institutions across the world, including Kunsthalle Zürich; Martin-Gropius-Bau, Berlin; MoMA PS1, New York; Serpentine Galleries, London; Kunsthaus Bregenz; and Stedelijk Museum, Amsterdam.

Nuotama Bodomo (born 1988 in Accra, Ghana) is a filmmaker whose award-winning short films *Boneshaker*, 2013; *Afronauts*, 2014; and *Everybody Dies!*, 2016, have played at festivals including Sundance, the Berlinale, Telluride, Rotterdam, SXSW, and New Directors/New Films. *Afronauts* was exhibited at the Whitney Museum of American Art, New York, as part of the group show *Dreamlands: Immersive Cinema and Art, 1905–2016*; at the Barbican Centre, London, as part of *Into the Unknown: A Journey Through Science Fiction*; and at the 2018 *Venice Architecture Biennale* (US Pavilion) as part of *Dimensions of Citizenship*. Bodomo recently served as staff writer and director on the first season of HBO's *Random Acts of Flyness*. She is currently in Zambia developing the feature film version of *Afronauts*.

Theo Eshetu (born 1958 in London, United Kingdom) has worked in media art since 1982, exploring formats from essay documentaries to video installations with a specific engagement in intercultural relations and how electronic media shapes and forms identities and perceptions. Eshetu received his degree in Communications in London and moved to Rome to develop his career as a video artist. His work has been shown at numerous film and video festivals, and he has received awards at the Berlin Video Festival; the International African Film Festival, Milan; and the VideoArt Festival, Locarno, Switzerland. He participated in the exhibition *Snap Judgments*, organized by the International Center of Photography, New York, and also presented at the Stedelijk Museum, Amsterdam, and the National Gallery of Canada, Ottawa, Ontario, among other institutions. Eshetu has participated in international exhibitions including *Die Tropen* at the Martin-Gropius-Bau, Berlin, and the South African National Gallery, Cape Town; *Sense of Time* at the Los

Angeles County Museum of Art and the Smithsonian National Museum of African Art, Washington, D.C.; numerous biennials including the *Venice Biennale* and *Kochi-Muziris Biennale* in 2011; and *documenta 14*. A recipient of the DAAD artist-in-residence award grant in 2012, Eshetu lives and works in Berlin.

Cameron Jamie (born 1969 in Los Angeles, California) has lived in France since 2000. Jamie has been the subject of museum surveys at the Kunsthalle Zürich (2013) and the Walker Art Center, Minneapolis (2006), which traveled to the MIT List Visual Arts Center, Cambridge, Massachusetts. He has been featured in film festivals and major group exhibitions including *The Absent Museum*, Wiels, Brussels (2017); *The Infinite Mix*, Hayward Gallery, London (2016); *Lyon Biennale* (2015); *Berlin Biennale* (2010); *Traces du sacré*, Centre Pompidou, Paris (2008); *Whitney Biennial*, New York (2006); and *Venice Biennale* (2005). In 2008 Jamie was the first recipient of the Yanghyun Prize, and in 2016 he was awarded the Daniel and Florence Guerlain Contemporary Art Foundation Drawing Prize.

Kapwani Kiwanga (born 1978 in Hamilton, Ontario, Canada) lives and works in Paris. Kiwanga studied Anthropology and Comparative Religion at McGill University, Montreal, and Art at the École Nationale Supérieure des Beaux-Arts, Paris. In 2018, Kiwanga received the Frieze Artist Award and was also the winner of the annual Sobey Art Award. Solo exhibitions include presentations at the MIT List Visual Arts Center, Cambridge, Massachusetts; Albertinum, Dresden; Artpace, San Antonio, Texas; Esker Foundation, Calgary, Alberta; Tramway, Glasgow International; Fondazione Sandretto Re Rebaudengo, Turin, Italy; The Power Plant, Toronto, Ontario; Reva and David Logan Center for the Arts, University of Chicago; South London Gallery; and Jeu de Paume, Paris. Selected group exhibitions include Whitechapel Gallery, London; Serpentine Galleries, London; Yuz Museum, Shanghai; National Gallery of Canada, Ottawa, Ontario; Contemporary Arts Museum Houston; Centre for Contemporary Art, Derry-Londonderry, UK; Centre Pompidou, Paris; Contemporary Art Gallery, Vancouver, British Columbia; and Hammer Museum, Los Angeles.

Marie Lorenz (born 1973 in Twentynine Palms, California) roots her work in exploration and narrative. In her ongoing project *Tide and Current Taxi*, Lorenz takes participants through New York waterways in boats that she designs and builds, using tidal current to propel the boat. Recent solo exhibitions include *Marie Lorenz: Ezekia* at the Albright-Knox Art Gallery, Buffalo, New York; *Flow Pool* at Recess, New York; *The Valley of Dry Bones* at Jack Hanley Gallery, New York; *Wanderlust* at High Line Art, New York; and *Erie Canal* at the Everson Museum of Art, Syracuse, New York, an exhibition about her month-long journey down the Erie Canal. Group exhibitions include *Providence*, Musée International des Arts Modestes, Sète, France; *Future Nature*,

Jack Hanley Gallery, New York; *Public Works: Artists' Interventions 1970s – Now*, Mills College Art Museum, Oakland, California; and *Arcadia: Thoughts on the Contemporary Pastoral*, Mills Gallery at the Boston Center for the Arts. Residencies include International Artist-in-Residence at Artpace, San Antonio, Texas, and John Michael Kohler Arts Center, Sheboygan, Wisconsin. In 2008 she was awarded the Joseph H. Hazen Rome Prize by the American Academy in Rome. Lorenz received a BFA from the Rhode Island School of Design and an MFA from the Yale School of Art. She lives and works in Brooklyn, New York, and Austin, Texas.

Nathan Mabry (born 1978 in Durango, Colorado) received his BFA from the Kansas City Art Institute in 2001 and his MFA from the University of California, Los Angeles, in 2004. Mabry has been the focus of important exhibitions, such as a solo presentation at the Nasher Sculpture Center, Dallas, and group exhibitions including *THING: New Sculpture from Los Angeles*, Hammer Museum, Los Angeles; *Red Eye: L.A. Artists from the Rubell Family Collection*, Rubell Family Collection, Miami; *Body Language*, Saatchi Gallery, London; and *Thief Among Thieves*, Museum of Contemporary Art Denver. Mabry's work is included in the collections of the Hammer Museum, Los Angeles; Los Angeles County Museum of Art; Orange County Museum of Art, Newport Beach, California; Museum of Contemporary Art San Diego; Phoenix Museum of Art; Dallas Museum of Art; Nasher Sculpture Center, Dallas; The Nelson-Atkins Museum of Art, Kansas City, Missouri; and Whitney Museum of American Art, New York. Private collections include 176 / Zabludowicz Collection, London; Rubell Family Collection, Miami; and Vanhaerents Art Collection, Brussels. Mabry's work has been the subject of reviews and articles in publications such as *Art in America*, *Artforum*, *Art + Auction*, *Frieze*, *Modern Painters*, *The Art Newspaper*, *Los Angeles Times*, and *The New York Times*. He lives and works in Los Angeles.

Ruben Ochoa (born 1974 in Oceanside, California) engages space as both a concept and a material in his practice. Often produced in material forms associated with construction, Ochoa's works expose the ideological and broader sociopolitical and economic relationships that facilitate the way spaces we inhabit and move through are assembled. Solo career highlights include *MATRIX 169: Cloudless Day*, Wadsworth Atheneum Museum of Art, Hartford, Connecticut (2014); *Cores and Cutouts*, Locust Projects, Miami (2011); *Building on the Fringes of Tomorrow*, Museum of Contemporary Art San Diego (2010); *Crooked Under the Weight*, SITE Santa Fe, New Mexico (2009); and *Extracted*, a site-specific installation at LAXART (2006). Group exhibition highlights include an artwork acquisition exhibited in *Down These Mean Streets*, Smithsonian American Art Museum, Washington, D.C. (2017); *The Future Generation Art Prize Exhibition*, 54th *Venice Biennale* Collateral Event (2011); and the 2008 *Whitney Biennial*, New York. Public works highlights include *Fwy Wall Extraction*, the first

California Department of Transportation and City of Los Angeles–approved public art installation on a Los Angeles freeway since the 1984 Olympic Murals (2006–2007), and *CLASS: C*, a mobile artists' space housed in the back of Ochoa's parents' former 1985 Chevy tortilla delivery van (2001–2005). Notable awards include two California Community Foundation fellowships (2004, 2013) and a Guggenheim Fellowship (2008). Ochoa received his BFA from Otis College of Art and Design and his MFA from the University of California, Irvine. He lives and works in Los Angeles.

Dario Robleto (born 1972 in San Antonio, Texas) is a transdisciplinary artist, researcher, citizen scientist, writer, and teacher. He lives and works in Houston. Recent solo exhibitions include the McNay Art Museum, San Antonio, Texas (2018); The Menil Collection, Houston (2014); and the Baltimore Museum of Art (2014). In 2004 he was included in the *Whitney Biennial*, New York. His work has been profiled in numerous publications and media including *Radiolab*, Krista Tippet's *On Being*, and *The New York Times*. In 2008, a ten-year survey exhibition, *Alloy of Love*, was organized by the Frances Young Tang Teaching Museum and Art Gallery at Skidmore College, Saratoga Springs, New York, and the Frye Art Museum, Seattle. He is the recipient of the Joan Mitchell Foundation Grant (2007) and the United States Artists Rasmuson Foundation Fellowship (2009). He has been a research fellow and artist-in-residence at institutions such as the Smithsonian National Museum of American History (2011); SETI Institute (2016–2017); and Robert Rauschenberg Foundation (2017). From 2016 to 2019 he co-organized the International Conference on Mobile Brain-Body Imaging and the Neuroscience of Art, Innovation, and Creativity in Cancun, Mexico, and Valencia, Spain. He is currently serving as an artist-in-residence in Neuroaesthetics at the University of Houston's Cullen College of Engineering and as artist-at-large at Northwestern University's McCormick School of Engineering and the Block Museum of Art. In 2016 he was appointed as the Texas State Artist Laureate.

Shimabuku (born 1969 in Kobe, Japan) lives and works in Naha, Japan. His work was featured in *Viva Arte Viva*, the 57th *Venice Biennale* (2017), and the *Okayama Art Summit* (2016). Recent solo exhibitions include Centre d'art contemporain d'Ivry – le Crédac, Ivry-sur-Seine, France (2018); Denver Art Museum (2018); Amanda Wilkinson Gallery, London (2018); Barbara Wien, Berlin (2017); Freedman Fitzpatrick, Los Angeles (2016); Nogueras Blanchard, Madrid (2016); Contemporary Art Gallery, Vancouver, British Columbia (2014); Air de Paris (2014); and 21st Century Museum of Contemporary Art, Kanazawa, Japan (2013). His works belongs to the collections of The Louis Vuitton Foundation, Paris; FRAC Île-de-France, Paris; FRAC Corsica, Corte, France; Centre Pompidou, Paris; Nouveau Musée National de Monaco; and Kunstmuseum Bern, Switzerland.

Julia Wachtel (born 1956 in New York City, New York) has exhibited in museums and galleries worldwide since the 1980s. In the last five years she has had solo exhibitions at The Cleveland Museum of Art; Bergen Kunsthall, Norway; Vilma Gold, London; Elizabeth Dee, New York; Mary Boone Gallery, New York; and Super Dakota, Brussels. She has been in numerous group exhibitions, both in institutional and gallery contexts, including the Migros Museum, Zurich; Walker Art Center, Minneapolis; Zabludowicz Collection, London; Saatchi Gallery, London; Elizabeth Dee, New York; Gavin Brown's enterprise, New York; Maruani Mercier, Brussels; Redling Fine Art, Los Angeles; and Foxy Production, New York. In 2017 Wachtel was featured in the exhibition *Fast Forward: Painting from the 1980s* at the Whitney Museum of American Art, New York, and in 2018 in the exhibition *Too Much Is Not Enough: Art and Commodity in the 1980s* at the Hirshhorn Museum and Sculpture Garden, Washington, D.C. Her work is in the collections of The Museum of Modern Art, New York; Whitney Museum of American Art, New York; Brooklyn Museum; The Cleveland Museum of Art; and The Museum of Contemporary Art, Los Angeles. Wachtel lives and works in Connecticut and Brooklyn, New York.

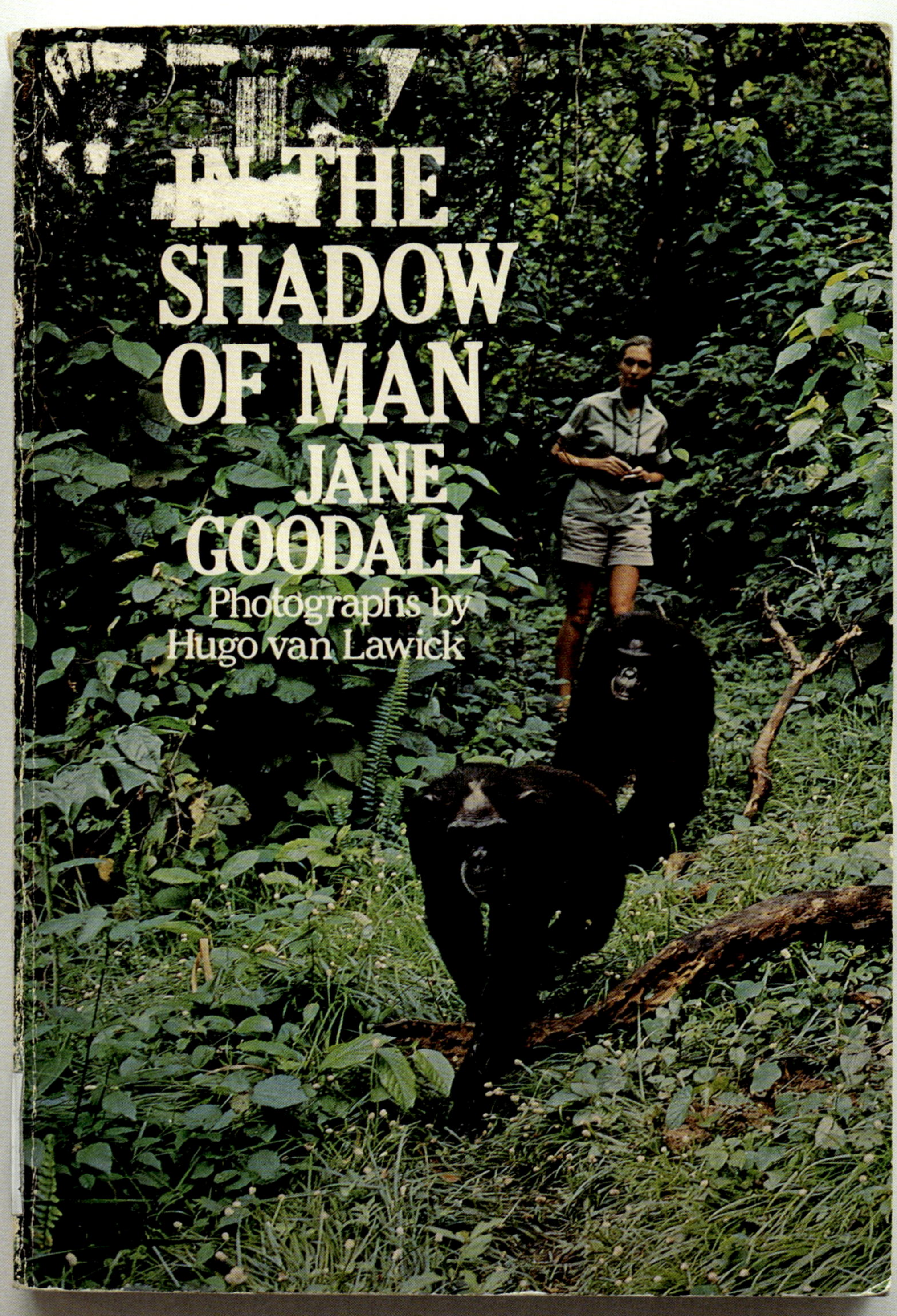
THE
SHADOW
OF MAN
JANE
GOODALL
Photographs by
Hugo van Lawick

Heather Pesanti is Chief Curator & Director of Curatorial Affairs at The Contemporary Austin, where she has organized exhibitions and commissions of work by John Bock, Carol Bove, Abraham Cruzvillegas, Anya Gallaccio, Lionel Maunz, Rodney McMillian, Wangechi Mutu, Monika Sosnowska, Robert Therrien, and Marianne Vitale, as well as the thematic exhibitions *Strange Pilgrims* and *The Sorcerer's Burden: Contemporary Art and the Anthropological Turn*. Forthcoming projects include solo exhibitions of Nicole Eisenman, Deborah Roberts, and Torbjørn Rødland. Pesanti received her MA in Art History from New York University's Institute of Fine Arts, MSc in Cultural Anthropology from the University of Oxford, and BA from the University of Pennsylvania.

Robert Storr is an artist, critic, and curator.

Dr. David Odo is the Director of Student Programs and Research Curator of University Collections Initiatives at the Harvard Art Museums. He is a visual and material anthropologist, with primary research and teaching interests in the anthropology of art, including early photography, critical museology, and objects of colonial encounter. He is the author of *The Journey of "A Good Type": From Artistry to Ethnography in Early Japanese Photographs*, and his current project is a monograph about photography and history in Japan's Ogasawara Islands. Odo received his D.Phil. in Social and Cultural Anthropology from the University of Oxford, and a BA in East Asian Studies from Columbia University.

Julia V. Hendrickson is the Associate Curator at The Contemporary Austin. She has an extensive background in art book publishing and editing, and has organized exhibitions for the museum with artists Janine Antoni, Lise Haller Baggesen, Huma Bhabha, and Jessica Stockholder. Hendrickson holds an MA in the History of Art from The Courtauld Institute of Art, London.

RADIUS BOOKS BOARD OF DIRECTORS

THE CONTEMPORARY AUSTIN BOARD OF TRUSTEES *as of January 2019*

PRAEGER UNIVERSITY SERIES $2.95

Thomas Crump

Man and His Kind

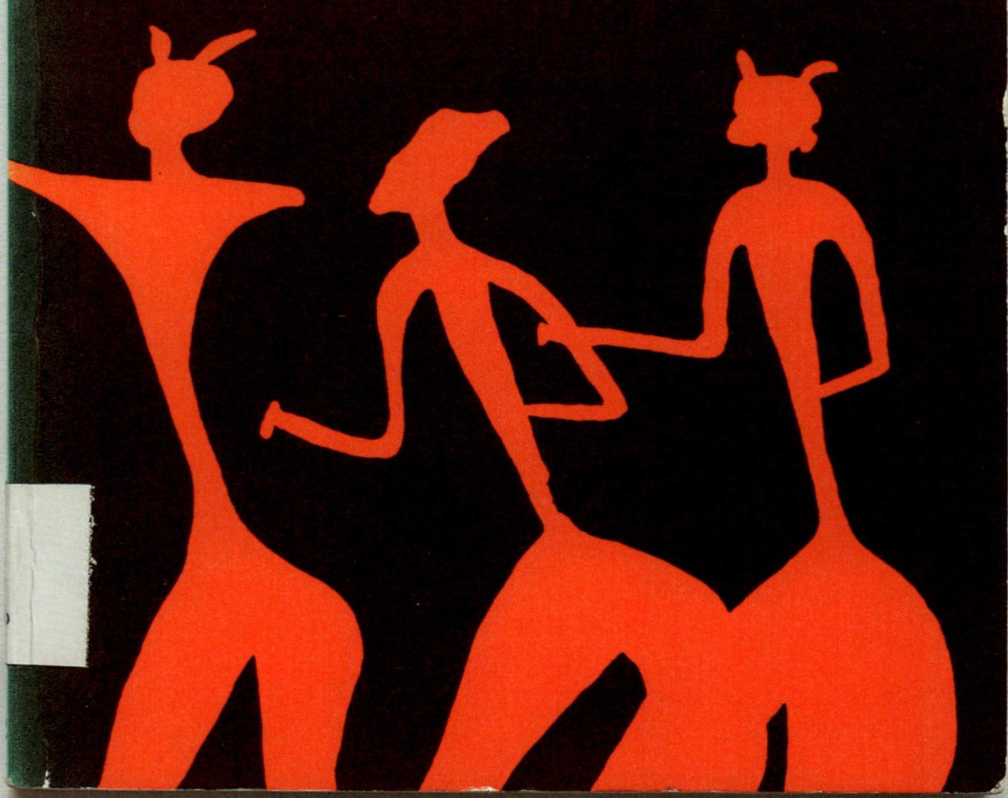

David Aaronoff
Installation Assistant

Simone Alexander
Development Assistant

Seth Bailey
Security Guard

Elizabeth Brewer
Horticulturist

Max Brooks
Volunteer & Studio Coordinator

Kyle Brumsted
Ceramics Assistant

Cameron Busby
Facilities Manager, Laguna Gloria

Ted Carey
Assistant Preparator

Emily Cayton
Associate Director of Education

Nick Clark
Gallery Attendant

Erin Coupal
Registrar

Anthony B. Creeden
Installation Assistant

Dave Culpepper
Preparator

Ryan Day
Installation Assistant

Antora DeLong
Registration Coordinator

Patrick Diaz
Gallery Attendant

Erin Druva
Gallery Attendant

Dianne Fox
Visitor Relations Specialist

Nick Francel
Security Guard

Chris Garza
Director of Finance

Phyllis Goodale
Editor & Communications Writer

Louis Grachos
Ernest and Sarah Butler Executive Director & CEO

Elle Grassel-Johnson
Groundskeeper

Nicole Chism Griffin
Director of Communications

Steve Griffin
Director of Exhibitions Production

Tiffany Guerra
Security Guard

Rigo Guerrero
Tour Coordinator

Hillary Halik
Executive Assistant to the Director

Julia V. Hendrickson
Associate Curator

Matthew Hoggle
Director of the Art School

Dan Jefferson
Facilities Manager, Jones Center

Alexa Johnson
Communications Coordinator

Hilary Kuhlmey
Gallery Attendant

Julie Le
Administrative Assistant, Curatorial

Izobeau Loureiro
Studio Instructor

Alexis Mabry
Security Guard

Arin Madera
Rentals Coordinator

Anna Maldonado
Gallery Attendant

Rebecca Marino
Installation Assistant

Abby Mechling
Director of Education

Maia Medel
Gallery Attendant

Andrea Mellard
Director of Public Programs & Community Engagement

Julie Merry
Staff Accountant

Alyssa Miller
Gallery Attendant

Carlos Moreno
Visitor Relations Specialist

Deja Morgan
Visitor Relations Specialist

Maryhelen Murray
Visitor Relations Specialist

Robin Mygatt
Senior Database Administrator

Emily Nagel
Visitor Relations Specialist

Grayson Norwood
Director of Human Resources & Administration

Landon O'Brien
Installation Assistant

Precious Parker
Gallery Attendant

Nadine Pennypacker
Membership Manager

Heather Pesanti
Chief Curator
& Director of Curatorial Affairs

Margie Rine
Deputy Director
& Chief Development Officer

Mariel Robles
Program Coordinator

Jay Roff
Installation Assistant

Weatherly Sawyer
Gallery Attendant

Sarah Schultz
Event Production Manager

Michael Shissler
Gallery Attendant

Caroline Smith
Digital Marketing Manager

Louis Strandberg
Installation Assistant

Paige Stumbough
Staff Accountant

James Tisdale
Ceramics Coordinator

Kelcie Tisher
Administrative Manager

Natalie Tran
Visitor Relations Manager

Jessica Vacek
Security Guard

Katherine Vaughn
Security Guard

Michelle Voss
Fund Development Manager

Shannon Willis
Rentals Manager

Tanya Zal
Public Programs Coordinator

COVER & ENDPAPERS

Theo Eshetu, *Self-Portrait* (detail), 1975. Black and white photograph. Artwork © Theo Eshetu. Image courtesy the artist.

Ole Worm, *Musei Wormiani Historia* (detail), in *Museum Wormianum, seu, Historia rerum rariorum : tam naturalium, quam artificialium, tam domesticarum, quam exoticarum, quae Hafniae Danorum in aedibus authoris servantur*, 1655. Woodcut on paper. Image courtesy Getty Research Institute, Los Angeles (87-B26388).

ANTHROPOLOGY BOOK COVERS & INTERIORS

Unless otherwise noted, all anthropology book cover and interior images courtesy The Contemporary Austin/Radius Books, with photographs by Brad Trone.

Page 2: Interior, L. S. B. Leakey, "Plate 10, Close-up of gravel beds of Va, & Plate 11, Bed V unconformable on Bed I at the third fault," in *Olduvai Gorge 1951–1961*, vol. 1, *A Preliminary Report on the Geology and Fauna* (Cambridge, UK: Cambridge University Press, 1965), n.p.

Page 5: Cover, Zora Neale Hurston, *Mules and Men* (Bloomington: Indiana University Press, 1978, first published 1935). Reproduction of artwork by Miguel Covarrubias © María Elena Rico Covarrubias.

Page 6–7: Interior, M. D. Leakey and L. S. B. Leakey, "Fig. 7 & Fig. 8, The stone bowls," in *Excavations at the Njoro River Cave: Stone Age Cremated Burials in Kenya Colony* (Oxford, UK: The Clarendon Press and Oxford University Press, 1950), 14–15.

Page 8: Cover, Margaret Mead, *Sex and Temperament in Three Primitive Societies* (New York: William Morrow and Company, 1963; first published 1935). Reprinted by permission of HarperCollins Publishers.

Page 10: Interior, M. D. Leakey and L. S. B. Leakey, "Plate II, Two reconstructed pots," in *Excavations at the Njoro River Cave: Stone Age Cremated Burials in Kenya Colony* (Oxford, UK: The Clarendon Press and Oxford University Press, 1950), n.p.

Page 12: Cover, Franz Boas, *Primitive Art* (New York: Dover Publications, 1955; first published 1927). Reprinted by permission of Dover Publications.

Page 13: Cover, Marcel Mauss, *Manuel d'Ethnographie* (Paris: Petite Bibliothèque Payot, 1967; first published 1926). © Éditions Payot, Paris, 1967.

Page 14: Cover, Clifford Geertz, *The Interpretation of Cultures* (New York: Basic Books, 1973).

Page 16: Interior, M. D. Leakey and L. S. B. Leakey, "Fig. 9, Njoro River Cave, The pestle-rubbers," in *Excavations at the Njoro River Cave: Stone Age Cremated Burials in Kenya Colony* (Oxford, UK: The Clarendon Press and Oxford University Press, 1950), 22.

Page 20: Cover, Weston La Barre, *The Human Animal* (Chicago: The University of Chicago Press and Phoenix Books, 1963; first published 1954). Reprinted by permission of The University of Chicago Press.

Page 21: Cover, Bronisław Malinowski, *Argonauts of the Western Pacific* (Prospect Heights, Illinois: Waveland Press, 1984; first published 1922). Reprinted by permission of Waveland Press, Inc., Long Grove, Illinois.

Page 22: Interior, L. S. B. Leakey, "Plate 2, 'Desert roses' *in situ* near the top of Bed I, & Plate 3, General view of the FLK area from the camp road, with the *Zinjanthropus* site indicated," in *Olduvai Gorge 1951–1961*, vol. 1, *A Preliminary Report on the Geology and Fauna* (Cambridge, UK: Cambridge University Press, 1965), n.p.

Page 104: Cover, Mary Leakey, *Disclosing the Past: An Autobiography* (Boston: G. K. Hall & Co., 1984).

Page 105: Cover, Claude Lévi-Strauss, *The Savage Mind* (Chicago: The University of Chicago Press, 1966; first published as *La pensée sauvage*, 1962). Reprinted by permission of The University of Chicago Press.

Page 106: Interior, Franz Boas, "Fig. 200 & Fig. 201, Designs from a set of gambling sticks," in *Primitive Art* (New York: Dover Publications, 1955; first published 1927), 210–211.

Page 112: Cover, Jeremy Coote and Anthony Shelton, eds., *Anthropology, Art, and Aesthetics* (Oxford, UK, and New York: Oxford University Press, 1994; first published 1992). Reprinted by permission of Oxford University Press and Phoebe A. Hearst Museum of Anthropology, University of California, Berkeley.

Page 138–139: Interior, Franz Boas, "Fig. 152, Arapaho designs, & Fig. 153, Sioux designs," in *Primitive Art* (New York: Dover Publications, 1955; first published 1927), 178–179.

Page 252: Interior, Mary D. Leakey, "Glossary of Tools, *Anvils–Awls*," in *Olduvai Gorge: My Search for Early Man* (Glasgow: William Collins Sons & Co. Ltd., 1979), 110–111.

Page 258: Cover, Jane Goodall, *In the Shadow of Man* (Boston: Houghton Mifflin Company, 1983; first published 1971). Photograph depicted on cover by Hugo van Lawick.

Page 262: Cover, Thomas Crump, *Man and His Kind* (New York and Washington, D.C.: Praeger, 1973). Reprinted by permission of Darton, Longman and Todd Ltd., London.

Fig. 1: Reprinted by permission of the author. Image courtesy The Contemporary Austin/Radius Books. Photograph by Brad Trone.

Fig. 2: Artwork © Richard Long. All Rights Reserved, DACS, London / ARS, New York. Artwork © Warlukurlangu Artists of Yuendumu / Copyright Agency. Licensed by Artists Rights Society (ARS), New York, 2019. Image © CNAC/MNAM/Dist. RMN-Grand Palais / Art Resource, New York. Courtesy Bibliothèque Kandinsky, Musée National d'Art Moderne, Centre Pompidou, Paris. INV. EX320. Photograph by Béatrice Hatala / Konstantinos Ignatiadis.

Fig. 3: Image courtesy Archivio Storico della Biennale di Venezia – ASAC. Photograph © Francesco Galli.

Fig. 4: Image courtesy Getty Research Institute, Los Angeles (87-B26388).

Fig. 5 & 6: Artwork © Dario Robleto. Image courtesy the artist and Inman Gallery, Houston.

Fig. 7: Reprinted by permission of HarperCollins Publishers. Image courtesy The Contemporary Austin/Radius Books. Photograph by Brad Trone.

Fig. 8: Artwork © Cameron Jamie. Courtesy the artist and Gladstone Gallery, New York and Brussels.

Fig. 9: Artwork © Cameron Jamie. Image courtesy the artist; Gladstone Gallery, New York and Brussels; and Bernier/Eliades Gallery, Athens and Brussels. Photograph by Tadzio.

Fig. 10: Artwork © Cameron Jamie. Image courtesy the artist.

Fig. 11: Artwork © 2019 Estate of Pablo Picasso / Artists Rights Society (ARS), New York. Digital image © The Museum of Modern Art / Licensed by SCALA / Art Resource, New York.

Fig. 12: Artwork © 2019 Estate of Pablo Picasso / Artists Rights Society (ARS), New York. Digital image © The Museum of Modern Art / Licensed by SCALA / Art Resource, New York. Courtesy the Photographic Archive, The Museum of Modern Art Archives, New York. Photograph by Katherine Keller.

Fig. 13: Artwork © Theo Eshetu. Image courtesy the artist and Axis Gallery, New York. Photograph by Mathias Völzke.

Fig. 14 & 15: Artwork © Theo Eshetu. Image courtesy the artist and Axis Gallery, New York.

Fig. 16: Artwork © Georges Adéagbo/VG Bild-Kunst. Image © documenta archiv. Photograph by Ryszard Kasiewicz.

Fig. 17: Artwork © Shimabuku. Image courtesy the artist and Freedman Fitzpatrick, Los Angeles/Paris.

Fig. 18 & 19: Artwork © Nuotama Bodomo. Image courtesy the artist.

Fig. 20 & 21: Artwork © Ed Atkins. Image courtesy the artist and Gavin Brown's enterprise, New York/Rome.

Fig. 22, 23, & 24: Artwork © Julia Wachtel. Image courtesy the artist.

Fig. 25, 26, & 27: Artwork © Nathan Mabry. Image courtesy the artist and Philip Martin Gallery, Los Angeles.

Fig. 28: Artwork © Marie Lorenz. Image courtesy the artist. Photograph by Marie Lorenz; *middle right*: photograph by Rachel Mason.

Fig. 29: © *Artforum*, December 1967. © 2019 Holt/Smithson Foundation / Licensed by VAGA at Artists Rights Society (ARS), New York. Reprinted by permission. Image courtesy The Contemporary Austin/Radius Books. Photograph by Brad Trone.

Fig. 30: Artwork © Ruben Ochoa. Image courtesy the artist and Vielmetter Los Angeles. Photograph by Juerg Isler.

Fig. 31 & 32: Artwork © Ruben Ochoa. Image courtesy the artist and Vielmetter Los Angeles. Photograph by Robert Wedemeyer.

Fig. 33: Artwork © Rotimi Fani-Kayodé, *Milk Drinker*, 1983. Image courtesy Autograph, London, and *Revue Noire*.

Fig. 34: Artwork © Kapwani Kiwanga. Image courtesy the artist and MIT List Visual Arts Center. Photograph by Peter Harris Studio.

Fig. 35: Artwork © Kapwani Kiwanga. Image courtesy the artist and Galerie Tanja Wagner, Berlin. Photograph by Guadagnini e Sorvillo.

BETWEEN AN AESTHETIC HUNCH AND A HARD SCIENCE

Page 107: W. H. Auden, "Under Which Lyre: A Reactionary Tract for the Times," Phi Beta Kappa poem, Harvard University, 1946.

Page 108: W. H. Auden, "September 1, 1939," first published in *The New Republic*, October 18, 1939.

ON THE ETHICS OF ART AND ANTHROPOLOGY: A CONVERSATION

Page 115: *Top*: Image © President and Fellows of Harvard College. Courtesy Harvard Art Museums. Photograph by R. Leopoldina Torres.

Page 115: *Bottom*: Image courtesy the Peabody Museum of Archaeology and Ethnology, Harvard University, *Left*: PM2003.1.2223.396, *Right*: PM2003.1.2223.27.

Page 121: © Pitt Rivers Museum, University of Oxford.

Page 132: Photograph by AP Photo/Jim Mone.

Page 135: *Top & Bottom*: Image © President and Fellows of Harvard College. Courtesy Harvard Art Museums. *Bottom*: Photograph by Zak Jensen.

Page 136: Artwork © Wangechi Mutu. Image courtesy The Contemporary Austin. Photograph by Brian Fitzsimmons.

L'HÔTEL N'EST PAS L'EXPÉDITEUR

Page 141–142: Image courtesy The Contemporary Austin/Radius Books. Photograph by Brad Trone.

FARTHER AFIELD

Page 150–159: Artwork and text © Ed Atkins. Courtesy the artist. Image courtesy the artist and The Contemporary Austin/Radius Books. Photograph by Brad Trone.

Page 160–167: Image courtesy Nuotama Bodomo.

Page 168–175: Artwork © Theo Eshetu. Image courtesy the artist.

Page 176–183: Artwork © Cameron Jamie. Courtesy the artist and Gladstone Gallery, New York and Brussels. Image courtesy the artist and The Contemporary Austin/Radius Books. Photograph by Kyra Kennedy.

Page 184: © 2015, Duke University Press. All rights reserved. Reprinted by permission of the copyright holder. Image courtesy The Contemporary Austin/Radius Books. Photograph by Brad Trone.

Page 185: Public domain.

Page 186: © J. L. Bell. Image courtesy Kapwani Kiwanga and The Contemporary Austin/Radius Books. Photograph by Brad Trone.

Page 187, 188, 191, 192: Artwork © Kapwani Kiwanga. Courtesy the artist and Galerie Jérôme Poggi, Paris. Image courtesy the MIT List Visual Arts Center. Photograph by Peter Harris Studio.

Page 189, 193: Image courtesy Kapwani Kiwanga.

Page 190: Image courtesy the New York Public Library, Digital Collections.

Page 194–200: Artwork © Marie Lorenz. Image courtesy the artist and The Contemporary Austin/ Radius Books. Photograph by Kyra Kennedy.

Page 201: Image courtesy American Philosophical Society, Philadelphia.

Page 202–203: Photograph by Nathan Mabry.

Page 204–205: Image courtesy Nathan Mabry. Photograph by Marten Elder.

Page 206–207, 210: Artwork © Nathan Mabry. Image courtesy the artist. Photograph by Marten Elder.

Page 208–209: © CNAC/MNAM/Dist. RMN-Grand Palais / Art Resource, New York. AM2003-3. Photograph by Philippe Migeat.

Page 211: Image courtesy Nathan Mabry. Photograph by Robert Wedemeyer.

Page 213–219: Artwork © Ruben Ochoa. Image courtesy the artist and The Contemporary Austin/ Radius Books. Photograph by Kyra Kennedy.

Page 220–227: Text © Dario Robleto. Image courtesy the artist.

Page 228–235: Artwork © Shimabuku. Image courtesy the artist and Freedman Fitzpatrick, Los Angeles/Paris.

Page 233: *Top*: Artwork © Shimabuku. Image courtesy the artist; Freedman Fitzpatrick, Los Angeles/ Paris; and Air de Paris, Paris.

Page 236–243: Artwork and text © Julia Wachtel. Image courtesy the artist and The Contemporary Austin/Radius Books. Photograph by Brad Trone.

All efforts have been made to contact the rights holders of the images and texts represented here. Please contact The Contemporary Austin with any questions.

RADIUS BOOKS
227 E. Palace Avenue, Suite W, Santa Fe, New Mexico 87501
radiusbooks.org

THE CONTEMPORARY AUSTIN
Jones Center, 700 Congress Avenue, Austin, Texas 78701
Laguna Gloria, 3809 West 35th Street, Austin, Texas 78703
thecontemporaryaustin.org

Available through

D.A.P. / DISTRIBUTED ART PUBLISHERS
75 Broad Street, Suite 630, New York, New York 10004
artbook.com

ISBN: 978-1-942185-60-4

Library of Congress Cataloging-in-Publication Data available

EXECUTIVE DIRECTOR & CEO: Louis Grachos

CHIEF CURATOR & DIRECTOR OF CURATORIAL AFFAIRS: Heather Pesanti

PUBLICATION MANAGER & EDITOR: Julia V. Hendrickson

PUBLICATION EDITOR: Phyllis Goodale

PUBLICATION COORDINATOR: Chelsea Weathers

PUBLICATION ASSISTANT: Julie Le

COPY EDITORS: Erin Coupal, Chelsea Weathers

DESIGN: David Chickey, Montana Currie

TYPOGRAPHY: Adobe Caslon, and Proxima Nova

Printed by Editoriale Bortolazzi-Stei, Verona, Italy

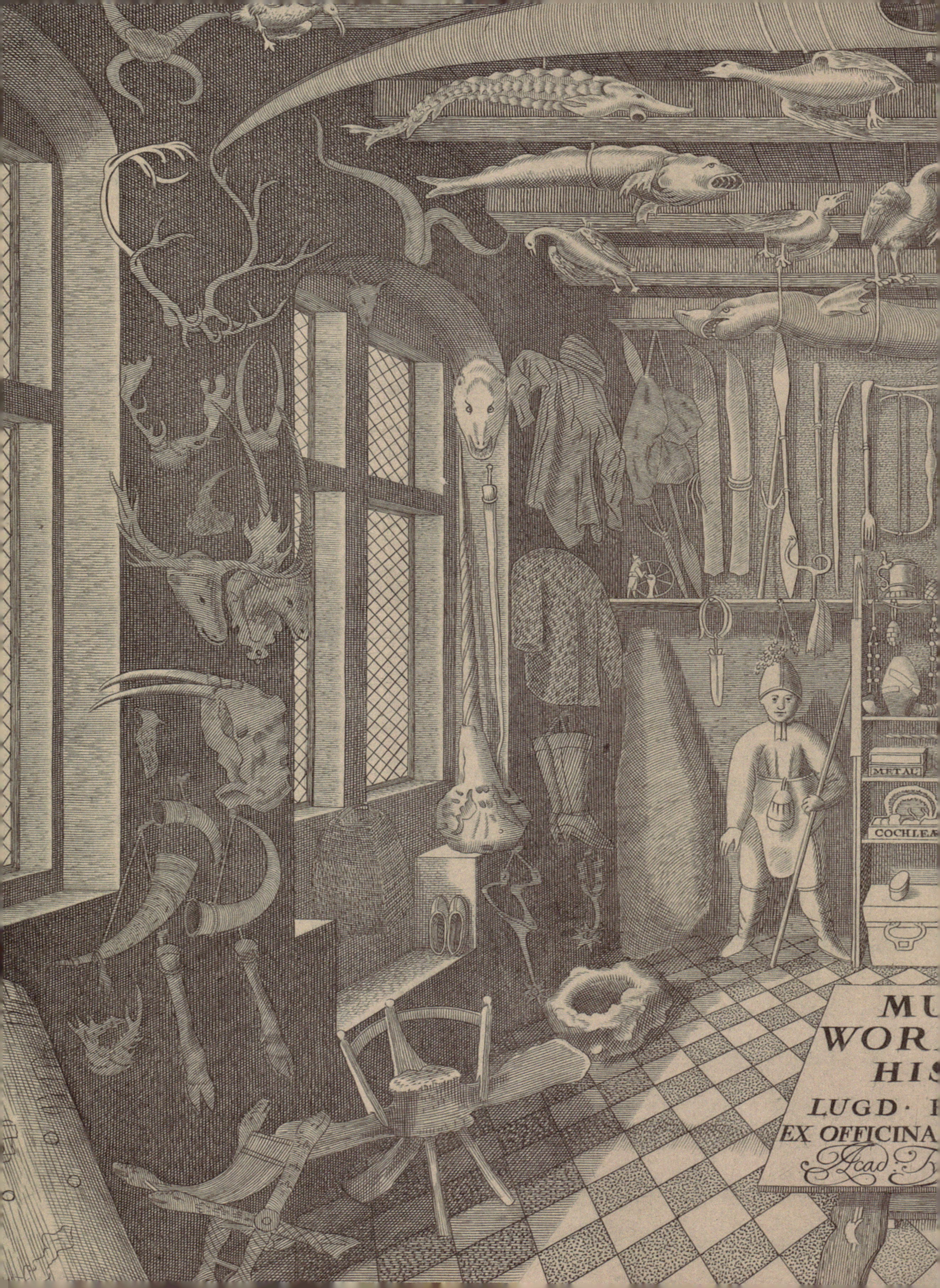
METAL
COCHLEA
MU
WOR
HIS
LUGD ·
EX OFFICINA